9-7
1ª 10.⁰⁰

Religion and Society in England 1790-1850

Religion and Society in England 1790-1850

W. R. Ward

Schocken Books · New York

Contents

Preface

The main objects of this book are set out in the Introduction, but it should be said here that some oddities of proportion (for example neither Blomfield nor the Ecclesiastical Commissioners receive their due) arise from the desire not to consume scarce resources of space with matters that have been well treated by other students. Indeed the further the preparation of the book proceeded, the more it assumed the character of what the archaeologists call a rescue operation. W. T. Whitley noted half a century ago how ill-stocked the British Museum was with Particular Baptist materials; in fact all the great English libraries are very establishmentarian in their holdings, and the great bulk of the printed materials used in this study have never been in any of them. It is a serious matter for historians therefore that collections of printed and MS material bearing upon the theme of this book have become inaccessible during its writing, and that much of the material which has been used is in varying degrees of jeopardy. Papers in private hands are always at risk, especially when they do not fall into any of the categories conventionally esteemed as valuable, and when their owners have no family tradition of preserving them. At the institutional level there are other hazards. Any reader of this book will be able to infer the reasons which led the relatively uninstitutionalised movements and denominations here described to set little store by such past as they possessed. Now that so many of them have become uncertain of their future, and are pinning their faith to institutional solutions in a time of great institutional break-up, the historical detritus they have transmitted is always likely to fall victim to the policies of the moment. The ecumenical politics of closing seminaries and horse-trading with ordinands are familiar enough; less familiar is the hazard to historical materials already in short supply which it has created. It is of course a characteristic commentary on the outcome of the story here related, that the principal guardians of its sources are the authorities of local government. Without the rich resources of Manchester Central Reference Library this book could not have been written, and my best thanks are due to many borough librarians in the North and Midlands for finding rare items and making them available to me; with my thanks I would couple the heartfelt plea that they do not permit the impending reorganisation of local government to render their collections inaccessible, and that they succumb no further to the blandishments of the commercial purveyors of (often quite unreadable) microfilm to destroy their stocks of local newspapers.

The obligations incurred in a work of this kind are legion. I am especially grateful to Dr J. C. Bowmer, the Methodist Church Archivist, for his continuous kindness and for the stimulus which his different training and sometimes differently held views have given; he is indeed a model of how to dam the tide of destruction with one man and a shoestring. The authorities of the Stockport and Bollington Sunday Schools and the Northern Baptist College kindly made invaluable loans from their archives; the Principals of Hartley Victoria College and the Manchester Unitarian College provided access to theirs, and kind hospitality. My Durham colleagues have born patiently with a Ranter in their midst, let him escape for two terms' leave at the final stage, and helped in many ways with the preparation of the text. The footnotes bear witness to some excellent work in the tracing and recovery of sources by a number of my pupils. (References to MSS. without shelf marks, newspapers without pagination, and pamphlets whose prolix titles suggest only too accurately the nature of their contents, create great economic problems, and it seemed best to secure the fullest possible documentation by presenting the references in groups at the end of the text. It is hoped that the inconveniences of this arrangement will not bear too hardly upon scholarly readers.) The Cambridge University Press kindly granted permission for me to use material which first appeared in a paper in *Studies in Church History*, Vol. 8. And, as is the way with historians, I owe much to the forbearance of my wife.

June 1972

DURHAM

Chief Mss. Collections
and Abbreviations

Bollington Sunday School, Cheshire. MS. Sunday School Minute Books.

Chester C[ounty] R[ecord] O[ffice]. MS. Episcopal visitations of Chester diocese 1789, 1804, 1811, 1821, 1825.

Chetham's Library, Manchester. MS. Minute Books of Manchester Sunday School Committee.

Devon C[ounty] R[ecord] O[ffice], Exeter. MS. Sidmouth correspondence.

Durham C[ounty] R[ecord] O[ffice] MS. Pease Papers.

Hartley Victoria College, Manchester. MS. Journals of Hugh Bourne
    MS. Memoranda Book of James Everett
    MS. Kilham Papers

Keble College, Oxford. MS. Correspondence of J. D. Dalgairns.

Lambeth Palace Library. MS. Visitation of Archbishop Manners-Sutton, 1806

Leeds Central Library. John Wray's (should be Thomas Wray's) MS. History of Methodism in Leeds, 11 vols.

Leeds City Archives. A large collection of archives of 19th century Leeds Methodism, individual items of which are referred to in the notes.

Manchester Central Library. MS. Visitation of Archdeacon Rushton, 1847.

Manchester Register Office. MS. Marriage registers 1837-50.

M[ethodist] C[hurch] A[rchives], 25-35, City Road, London, E.C.1. A huge collection of general correspondence of Methodist preachers, referred to by correspondents. There are also numerous collections of Presidential autographs referred to by title. There are also
    MS. Conference Journal, 1820-21
    MS. Conference Proceedings, 1828
    MS. Minutes of District Meetings
    MS. Correspondence of Thomas Allan
    MS. Bradburn Papers
    MS. Scrapbook of James Everett
    MS. Tyerman MSS. (3 vols)
    Thomas Wray's MS. History of Methodism in Leeds (2 vols).

P[ublic] R[ecord] O[ffice] MS. Baptismal Registers of Manchester dissenting congregations 1790-1832. (R.G.4)

MS. Chatham Papers

Sunday School Union, Robert Denholm House, Nutfield, Redhill, Surrey. MS. Minute Books of Sunday School Union Committee
MS. Minute Book of Kingsland, Newington, and adjacent villages Sunday School Society.
MS. Sunday School Union Common Place Book

Introduction

The generation overshadowed by the French Revolution was the most important generation in the modern history not only of English religion, but of most of the Christian world. For the Revolution altered for ever the terms on which religious establishments, the chief device on which the nations of the West had relied for christianising the people, must work. Of course for a generation or more the vitality of the churches had been undermined by the same forces which were everywhere sapping the Ancien Régime, the whole institutional complex of which the religious establishments were part. Every approach to this problem had its embarrassments. In France, Germany and Austria lay governments had shown a disposition to reorder their churches' affairs for them, a process the full hazards of which were realised only when the revolutionary assemblies in France embarked on a well-intentioned programme of bringing their national church up to date. Private action, the obvious alternative, raised difficulties of another kind; yet to those right through the Protestant world who pinned their faith to religious awakening, keeping alive the cycle of conviction of sin and assurance of salvation, there was no option but to use private channels of propaganda and devotion.

If this was true in Germany, it was still more true in England where the nub of the situation consisted in the weakness of public authority, the dispersion of power. The English state had been too weak to put down dissent, too weak to allow its clergy to play at politics in their Convocation, too weak to root the Anglican establishment in the American colonies, far too weak to overhaul a Church still largely medieval in its administrative forms, and incapable of generating policy. Here private societies must necessarily be the bearer of religious revival; more or less informal itinerancies must pick up those who fell through the old net of parochial pastoral oversight; Sunday schools must be organised for the religious and secular education of the young. In America public authority on the eastern seaboard was weak even by English standards, and on the frontier was almost non-existent. Here the experience of revival was quickly transformed into the technique of revivalism; the informal machinery imported from England for reconstituting religious society was driven much harder than it was ever driven by the English; and the organised battery of private benevolence which constituted the 'Errand of Mercy' must assume the burden of civilising and converting the populace as it moved West.

The atmosphere of crisis created by the French Revolution, and the wars to which it gave rise, drastically weakened the forces of discipline in society, and their resistance to the intellectual and religious solvents of the old order. In Germany enlightenment and the awakening alike reduced the confessional barrier between Roman Catholic and Protestant, between Lutheran and Reformed; the real work of the Church seemed to be passing to bodies like the *Deutsche Christentum Gesellschaft* and the missionary and Bible societies which succeeded it at Basel, embracing men of different religious traditions. To the awakened there seemed no impassable gulf between the Catholic and the Protestant doctrines of justification; it became possible for clergy and congregations to move from one confession to another. Yet in the end the greater concentration of authority told: Protestant establishments were able not merely to check the growth of neo-Pietism but to absorb it, as the English establishment could never either check or absorb English evangelicalism. Moreover in Germany the re-grouping of a minority Catholicism in defence of its rights evoked a powerful confessionalism which issues like Catholic Emancipation could never quite evoke in England.

The outpouring of undenominational religion at the end of the eighteenth century left a mark upon English popular faith which has never been effaced, but within a generation its institutional mechanism had been broken up by denominations pressing the clan spirit as a counterpoise to the divisive effects of social tension. The Church establishment had a particularly heavy weight to bear when the crisis of authority came. The weakness of the state compelled reliance upon networks of private influence, indeed the problem of public order was like the problem of inflation as seen by the government of Mr Heath—insoluble without restraint in the private sector. Not only was the Church the most obvious means by which the minds of men might be reached, nation-wide; but the abdication of many of the gentry and aristocracy from their old functions of social control in favour of a profit-able *laisser-faire,* had left local government in the hands of the clergy to a degree unknown before or since. Clergymen came to constitute a quarter of the entire nominal magistracy, had the effective management of the bench in huge areas, and (as Orator Hunt's father was wont bluntly to put it) acted ' the bashaw ' in the country villages.[1] Other religious communities thrived on the introversion of the Church in the 'nineties, but when their turn came to feel the pressure of social conflict, they reacted in a similar way, seeking to consolidate their in-group by anathemat-ising the out-groups.

In America warring sects had been welded by the experience of colonial revolt into an informal establishment. Here those who maintained the pastoral office in the Puritan tradition were as hostile to the army of undenominational societies which formed the ' benevolent system ' as English high-churchmen or Lutheran orthodox might have been, and in America as in England the fond hopes of a united Christendom which had been cherished early in the nineteenth century foundered in fierce denominational controversy. Yet the dynamism of American society, its very lack of political and social rigidities, the capacity of American religious bodies to act as vehicles for Americanism, gave the American informal establishment an absorptive power greater even than the formal establishments of Germany. Methodism and the benevolent system, episcopalianism, and eventually even Roman Catholicism were taken on board and made vehicles of American nationalism.

The English problem, therefore turned upon a unique social balance: the English Church faced the new forces of the age with neither the institutional power of the German *Landeskirchen* nor the dynamism of the American churches. Concurrent endow-ment was one of the great non-starters of the century; equally the supplanting of the formal establishment by an informal *Volks-kirche* was one of its unrealised dreams. England failed to secure either a formal or informal establishment of real effectiveness. Uniting in-groups by anathematising out-groups converted social

tension into the denominational warfare which formed the main
substance of the politics of the 'thirties and 'forties; it raised controversy to a deplorable level, and provoked a degree of physical
violence now difficult to conceive. Yet public order in England
continued to depend in a perilous degree upon the private
networks, and the social strains of the 'forties which on the
continent toppled the monarchies, in England divided the churches.
The Church of England (as a working establishment defeated
already) suffered secessions; the Church of Scotland experienced
the Disruption. The Old and New Methodist connexions were
broken and never recovered their expansiveness. The Baptists
endured great losses, and the Congregationalists found that they
had little beside their middle-class following left. Something of
what historians have christened the ' revolution in government'
was now unavoidable, and the churches were edged towards the
fringes of the national life. Only in Ireland did the churchmen
succeed in inhibiting the emergence of class politics.

It is the object of this book to trace and, as far as possible
within the limits of space and the intrinsic difficulties of account-
ing for movements of the spirit, to explain this process. Explanations are here at a premium, for the casual ways of the early part
of the period became quite opaque to historians writing from the
standpoint of the contests of the 'thirties and 'forties, and have
remained opaque to writers who have followed them. Percy Bunting was baffled by the fact that his strict Methodist grandparents
sent his father, the great Jabez, to not one but two successive
Unitarian ministers for his education in Manchester; he may not
have known that those pillars of conservative Wesleyanism, Joseph
Benson and Joseph Entwisle, also attended appreciatively on the
ministry of the Unitarian Dr Barnes in that town. Perhaps the
funniest religious biography of the whole nineteenth century is
William Jones' *Memoirs of Rowland Hill* (1834); it is not often
that a commissioned biographer begins by begging

not to be understood as palliating or being disposed to apologise
for Mr Hill's glaring inconsistency in trimming between the
conformists and nonconformists. This can only be resolved
into his total unacquaintedness with the nature, constitution, laws
and discipline of the church of Christ, as laid down in the New
Testament.

Nor at last did Rowland Hill's brother, Sir Richard, fare any better at the hands of his biographer, Sidney,

> . . . if he had lived in those days[1839], he would have seen the necessity of proving that charity, while it looks with tenderness upon imperfections that may be considered venial, cannot wink at flagrant inconsistencies. . . . Charity is guileless and patient, but not blind.

Dissenters could not reasonably expect to be loved if they went in for disestablishment. Yet pondering on the dissenting tradition from within, R. W. Dale made the opposite complaint, that the dissenters had forfeited a birthright of political activism for a mess of pietistic pottage.[2]

Evangelicalism became equally opaque. By the 1830s it was plain that the evangelicals were tenacious establishment men, despite the hammering they had received from the high-church. Yet in their *Life* of their father, Wilberforce's sons were embarrassed by his long affection for William Jay and his independent ministry at Bath, and played it down. There is equal embarrassment in Canon Smyth's defence that ' the fundamental divergence between Evangelicals and Methodists came over the problem of Church Order ', and his tortuous attempts to explain away Simeon's itinerating in Scotland and Henry Venn's regular appearances in the pulpit of the Surrey Chapel. The significance of Methodism was a matter of constant dispute within the flock and without. Already in 1795 Jones of Nayland had coined the slogan which obtained Canon Smyth's *imprimatur,* that Methodism was ' christian godliness without christian order ', and contemporary ' high ' Methodists can be found apologising for themselves in precisely these terms. But the complaint speedily came to be that there was far too much order in Methodism, and certainly preachers and flock were subject to an organised pastoral oversight which had no counterpart in the Church. Similarly, in the days when Methodists participated largely in Anglican rites they were ferociously denounced by high-churchmen for destroying the establishment; in the 'thirties when separation was virtually complete, they were fawned on for propping it up.[3]

From the standpoint of the denominational order as it existed in the 1830s, and in a ruinous way still exists, the religious history of the previous generation made very indifferent sense, its less formal ways became incomprehensible, discreditable, mere shilly-shallying. Yet the new denominationalism could no more destroy popular undenominational evangelicalism than it could understand it, and surrendered its own main function when the steam went out of English social tension after 1850. Its work in separating the churches from the characteristic religion and characteristic politics of a broad public now became extremely costly. The ecumenical end-product of this process, a single denomination with impeccable Catholic order and no popular appeal at all, is now in sight.

In elucidating this process a huge amount remains to be learned, and the account which follows is biased in a number of ways by the limitations of one writer's studies. In a period in which change and conflict are of major importance, factors promoting change and conflict, views capable of generating policy, receive more attention than factors of stability, which have been in any case too much the stock-in-trade of writers in the history and sociology of religion. An attempt is made on a sampling basis to see what was happening to religion at a grass-roots level in many parts of the country, but especially in the industrial North-west; it is some defence of this bias that Manchester was recognised by churchmen as well as others as the spearhead of the new industrial world, and had a disproportionate effect on opinion generally. This study has also been benefited and biased by generous access to the Methodist Church Archives; it is again some defence that Methodism grew further and faster than the other new religious movements, and that its constitutional arrangements made visible what was happening in a much wider area.

1 The Decline of the Old Order in England

One of the most intangible but ubiquitous pressures upon the eighteenth-century order was the increase in population. After a period of diminished progress, the population began to increase again with renewed vitality just before the middle of the century, and did not lose its impulse for a century and a half. Great swings in the rate of increase had always been a feature of demographic history, but unrelaxed pressure of this kind was a new challenge to churches, in common with other social institutions, and one which they were not equipped to meet.

At the lowest level the whole question of financing religious like other social services was transformed. In 1703 an income of £17,000 per annum, Queen Anne's Bounty, was returned to the Church to supplement poor livings. The Bounty Commissioners treated their annual income as capital, and broke it up into small lots to augment the endowments of poor parishes; they knew that, provided the situation remained stable, even their modest income would eventually overcome the age-old problem of clerical poverty. But it was quite impossible to provide any kind of endowed public service for a nation which grew endlessly. With the churches as with the schools, it was hard enough to provide the bricks and mortar; there was no question of adequately endowing the labour as well. The current income of an expanding public was the only source from which the demands of that public could be met. Voluntaryism might be unpalatable, but it was unavoidable, and unlike the schools, the Church never, after the Reform Act of 1832, benefited from the leverage of public authorities upon the current income of the nation.

Population growth also bade fair to modify church order. The Church of England like that of France had relied more heavily upon the parish for the christianisation of successive generations,

B

than upon anything else. In the new circumstances it was inevitable that increasing numbers should slip through the traditional network of pastoral oversight, and form a standing invitation to the zealots to go out into the highways and hedges, and compel the lost to come in. Itinerant religious propaganda had been by no means unknown in England before; now in face of a continuous problem, itinerancy itself became continuous, and the wanderings first of Anglican preachers, then of Methodists, Baptists and Independents entered the legend of the revival. By the 1790s the organised itinerancy of the Methodists was acknowledged as a working model for systematic imitation,[1] and though a connexional system and an itinerant ministry were as foreign to the traditions of the dissenters as they were to the Church, notable efforts were made to adapt to them. The French parochial system seems to have capitalised the results of the great seventeenth-century missions, but in the shadow of the Revolution, the English Church not only failed to capitalise those of the eighteenth century, but lost her own itinerancy in trying to suppress those of the Methodists and dissenters. The opportunity then let slip has never recurred.

Anglican spokesmen still hold that ' the outward form of the Church should declare visibly the continuity of its faith and life', a symbolic view common in the eighteenth century to dissenter and churchman alike. Symbolic methods of thought, however, are among the victims of the passage of time, and institutions, even religious institutions, are viewed in instrumental terms as devices for producing particular results; a managerial theology applying critiques derived from administrative theory is in being on both sides of the Atlantic.[2] The first crucial step in a process which has transformed the attitudes of believer and unbeliever alike was the adaptation of various dissenting systems to itinerancy, and the building of several new religious communities around it. For itinerancy was plainly a device to meet a difficulty, and as such it was only the first swallow of a hot summer. Missionary societies to raise funds, recruit and control personnel, and manage considerable businesses; political committees to defend rights and advance causes; societies to educate the people, and train and support clergy, spawned forth by the score. The Kingdom of God seemed delivered over to instrumental and associational principles, and disorderly organisations were created, quite impatient of symbolic understanding. Yet every machine retained its symbolic apologists, and the worst horrors were perpetrated by those who gave symbolic status to ecclesiastical arrangements which were no more than devices.

A Church which consisted in so large a measure of a confederation of country parishes could not fail to respond to the rapid changes which took place in the English countryside in the later eighteenth century. The distinguishing feature of English rural society was the degree to which it was already organised upon capitalist principles, and divided among landlords, tenant farmers and a labour-force working for wages. The commercial spirit operated powerfully here before the industrial revolution began, and was prominent in the Church as in lay society. Churchmen were improving their assets, screwing up their leases, or, like the parishes of Manchester, Bury and Rochdale, obtaining acts to let out the glebe in building lots for a term of ninety-nine years. Tithe was being extended to lands newly cultivated or hitherto exempt; old moduses or tithe compositions were being broken up to secure more favourable terms. By all these devices the incomes which the land yielded to the Church, as well as to lay entrepreneurs, greatly increased as the eighteenth century drew to a close.

In the great belt of open field country which stretched across the south Midlands into Lincolnshire and Yorkshire enclosure seemed to be the way to improvement and to the new agricultural markets.[3] In 1759 a spate of enclosure acts began, which swelled into a torrent whenever food prices were high or money cheap, and deeply concerned the Church. For no act could be promoted without the consent of the tithe holder, and many landlords wished to free their expected increase in output from the burden of tithe. The upshot was that tithe was in most cases commuted on terms favourable to the holder, and most commonly commuted for an allotment of land. The average glebe in the enclosure areas may well have been doubled or trebled by these means, and the agricultural improvers' tales of livings increasing in the same proportion overnight were not all exaggerated. In a generation many of the parsons rose to gentry status. Their new affluence often separated them from the people in the most literal sense; they abandoned the old mud-and-wattle parsonage in the village, and moved out, sometimes out of the parish, and began the building of those rural palaces which have been a millstone round the neck of their successors ever since. With genteel pretensions went fashionable amusements, and, of course, obligations to public service on the bench of magistrates.

To all this the lot of the labourers in an overpopulated countryside formed a wretched contrast. With them proletarianisation was succeeded by shorter labour contracts, less payment in kind, and pauperisation. High food prices during the war were followed by desperate efforts by the propertied classes to restrain the growth of poor relief, and cut the bread scales. Evangelicals noted that many Midland cottagers had been deprived of their cows by enclosure, and were now entirely dependent on paid labour;[4] and there was loss of amenity too. The same forces which were raising the clergy were depressing the labourers, and it was easy to regard them as clerically contrived, for the parsons were there to be seen promoting and executing enclosure schemes, restricting poor relief, and putting down rural crime.

The cost of ' adopting too much the manners of the fashionable world ' was admitted by the acuter clergy, and was the constant theme of popular reaction. In Methodism there was a strong vein of pietism, a conviction that the saints should walk together unspotted by the world; but when this was held to justify separate communion from the parish church, it was expressed overwhelmingly in terms of hostility to the fashionable habits of the clergy, and embodied the sense that a social chasm, recently created, made spiritual fellowship impossible. In 1793 it was maintained that

> the generality of ministers are such as God's word forbids us to join with. They neither live nor preach the gospel; they are for the most part such as live in pleasure and dissipation, in avarice and luxury, and in all the fashionable follies of the age.

Joseph Cownley could not ' look upon them as ministers of Christ or of the old Church of England whose fundamental doctrines they are continually exploding '. Or as Thomas Coke feebly explained to the Bishop of London,

> A very considerable portion of our society have imbibed a deep prejudice against receiving the Lord's Supper from the hands of immoral clergymen. The word immoral they consider in a very extensive sense, as including all those who frequent cardtables, balls, horse-racing, theatres and other places of fashion-

able amusement. I have found it in vain to urge them that the validity of the ordinance does not depend on the piety or even the morality of the minister: all my arguments have had no effect.

There was the same testimony from John Clare, the Northampton-shire labourer-poet a generation later.

Too high religion looks her flocks to watch,
Or stoop from pride to dwell in cots of thatch,
Scenes too important constant business brings
That lends no time to look on humbler things.

The good old times, when a poor clergy lived and prayed with their flock, went out when pauperism and enclosures came in:

These are the times that plainness must regret,
These are the times that labour feels as yet,
Ere mocked improvement's plan enclosed the moor,
And farmers built a workhouse for the poor.

These festering animosities opened the door to the Ranters by whom Clare himself was swept away for a time.[5]

The origins of the revival go back to the seventeenth century, and revival did not begin in the enclosure country. But the transformation of the revival into a mass movement, the Ranterism which succeeded it, the changing direction of its victories, owed much to the strains of the enclosure movement. Astonishing triumphs in rural areas where the parish system looked deepest rooted, and a tenacious understanding of Christian history in revival terms, were the monument to the peasant prophets and to popular hatred of the clergy. The Yorkshire and Lincolnshire revivalists had a legendary reputation in the old Wesleyanism,[6] while the Primitives became a denomination by their expansion down the Trent valley, and did brilliantly in the East Riding. By the time of the religious census of 1851, evangelical dissenters were here well ahead of the Church; they were leading also in Bedfordshire and Huntingdonshire, and were strong in the counties of Cambridge and Buckingham. Here the old dissent, the Independents and Baptists, had reaped one harvest, and the Primitives a second.

In all this there was nothing incongruous. Political reconstruction might answer to the lot of the *menu peuple* in towns, but religion was the one aspect of clerical control from which the labourers had any hope of escape. In revival the deprived could *en masse* exert a religious power superior to that of the official guardians of the faith, could cast their individual malaise upon the Saviour, and lay hold on new life. ' Plain, practical and awakening sermons,' it was found, ' which hold out human depravity and misery by the fall, and salvation by Christ, appear to be the most useful.' Rural Methodist converts who knew what misery was, and who came to regard the Church as the demon-possessed instrument of their degradation, were singing

What a mercy is this; what a heaven of bliss,
    How unspeakably happy am I,
Gathered into thy fold, with thy people enroll'd,
    With thy people to live and to die.

Of course the new forms of euphoric religion were as menacing to the faith and order of the old established dissent as to those of the Church, but that was a problem to be faced later.[7]

In the towns as in the countryside new developments which made their main impact long after the Revolution were rooted in the eighteenth century. It was everywhere noted that urban mobility and range of choice seriously undermined old denominational loyalties, while the old church order was modified by new ways of tackling new problems. Independents and Anglicans deplored the ' roving spirit ' which got into their town congregations; but in Manchester and Rochdale Unitarians, Roman Catholics and Baptists all attracted spectacular throngs quite distinct from their regular congregations to Sabbath evening lectures.[8] More important were the Sunday schools which were springing up in the 1780s even before Robert Raikes began his propaganda, and spread like wildfire afterwards. In the school histories one reads repeatedly how the founding fathers were moved by the evils which awaited children let loose in the streets on the Sabbath. Of course there had always been urchins up to mischief on the Day of Rest, but now there were so many more of them; not only the Day of Rest, but public order was in jeopardy. It was apparent, particularly to laymen, that the traditional institutions for the socialising of the young were quite unequal to the need;

and it was lay initiative which gave the Sunday school its primacy in the religious history of the period, for it was the only religious institution which the nineteenth-century public in the mass had any intention of using. The schools were the great triumph of municipal Christianity.

The Manchester Sunday schools were launched in 1784 by an address from the borough-reeve and constables, and placed under a committee on which churchmen, dissenters and Roman Catholics all served, operating on a system already in service at Leeds. The town was divided into districts, in each of which collectors raised funds for the committee; there were special sermons preached by all the clergy (including Roman Catholic), and also communion offertories which when distributed to poor communicants had been 'abused to improper purposes of drunkenness and disorder'. Preparing forms of worship for the schools, the committee printed the prayers in use at Leeds, together with two forms drawn up by their Anglican secretary, the Rev John Bennett, two more from Dr Barnes, the Unitarian minister at Cross Street, the Church catechism, and a selection of Watts' hymns. Committees of mixed denominational character superintended the schools in each district. This scheme succeeded beyond all precedent. Within a year ' a tribe of embryo-angels training for the skies' 2,300 strong had been enrolled, a score of towns and districts in the neighbourhood had adapted the Manchester plan to their own needs, and the town's committee was swamped with enquiries from all parts of the kingdom.[9]

The heart of the Sunday school movement, however, remained in the textile towns, where employment for children was so brisk that the Sabbath afforded their one opportunity for instruction. The weakness of the day-school tradition and the strength of the Sunday schools had a common origin. And the new ventures embodied a strong undenominational element. The greatest of them, the Stockport school, began on the Manchester pattern in 1784, with laymen, supported by their ministers, creating a Town's committee to establish and finance a school in each of six divisions of the town. Macclesfield followed the Stockport pattern closely when serious Sunday school work was begun in 1796. In neighbouring villages like Bollington and Higher Hurdsfield, the Sunday school was the first religious institution in the place, and began naturally upon the undenominational platform.

The result is particularly instructive at Bollington, a village where Methodists ran almost everything, including the school. But the school existed before the chapel was built in 1808, and finding the new chapel premises inadequate, erected buildings for the scholars upon an undenominational basis. Indeed much of the later signifi-cance of the school lay in its ability to shelter movements of protest against what became the Wesleyan establishment in the village. At Leek there was similar combined action. The politically notorious village Sunday school at Thornsett, Derbyshire, and the town's system introduced at Coventry in 1785, were also un-denominational. The famous school at Burslem was begun on Wesleyan initiative in 1787, but had a mixed management, aimed ' not to promote the religious principles of any particular sect, but, setting aside all party distinctions, to instruct youth in useful learning, and in the leading and uncontrovertible principles of Christianity ', and paid rent for its use of Wesleyan premises. The pioneer Sunday school work about Shrewsbury began from the Church catechism, but when it was gathered into the General Sunday School in 1810, the funds came from a general subscrip-tion and much of the teaching from the Methodists.[10]

North of Manchester, the Hillock School at Middleton Junc-tion, though mostly the work of Methodists, bore on its coping-stone the familiar legend, ' A school for all denominations '. At Rochdale, the children of the first Sunday School begun by James Hamilton, a Methodist tin-plate worker, were taken in turn to the parish church, St Mary's (Anglican) chapel, and to the chapels of the Unitarians, Wesleyans, and Baptists. The school was gov-erned by the teachers, who were subject to no test, though the President was the Methodist superintendent. At Colne, Bacup and Haslingden there was also combined action. In south-east Lan-cashire the convolutions of the story have baffled all the commenta-tors. But it seems that at Delph the earliest school was undenomina-tional. In Oldham the evangelical incumbents of St Peter's never lost touch entirely with the work of the schools, but the main initiative came from two families of hat manufacturers, the Cleggs and the Henshaws, who went their own way on un-denominational lines when there was opposition from the Church. Oldham, indeed, eventually boasted a National School at Cowhill so untypical that the trust included many Methodists, who estab-lished a school and public worship on the premises for communicant Anglicans and others, and the trust deed required the premises to be used on the Sabbath, for ' non-sectarian ' religious purposes. Bolton boasted some of the earliest schemes of Sabbath instruction, and here it was John Wesley who insisted on keeping the system open. Moreover the teachers ran the Ridgeway Gates School according to their own rules, with little respect to the jurisdiction of Conference.[11]

In Yorkshire too the undenominational system seems to have been common, perhaps the rule. Leeds, where the clergy had taken the lead, but most of the teaching was done by Methodists, had given the cue to Manchester. At Bingley the undenominational school was superintended by the curate, while at Rotherham the schools were supported from a common fund, and the dissenters all came to Church for the charity sermon. At Almondbury near Huddersfield, united effort was so successful that it led all parties to combine in erecting a National School. At Selby the Sunday ' subscription school ' was organised by common effort, and at York, though the town's system begun in 1786 seems to have been exclusively Anglican, the schools opened by the Wesleyans in 1791 were ' free to servants, apprentices, and children of every denomination '. In Sheffield the first Church schools failed and the field was left to the Wesleyans. The Wesleyan schools, however, were always restive before the preachers' authority, and when they needed new buildings they appealed to the whole town on the usual undenominational basis.[12]

The same pattern can be traced in various places in the South, and in 1803 the inevitable central society was established in London. The Sunday School Society was founded by William Fox, a Baptist deacon who united dissenters and churchmen in the good work. A few years later Quaker members of the Society launched the undenominational Sunday School Union, to promote the dissemination of new educational methods and materials, including its own catechism in verse, entitled *Milk for Babes*. In England undenominational adult schools never attained the power of those launched in Wales in 1811 by Thomas Charles of Bala, but societies to promote them were formed in the west and south, and they spread like wildfire from Scotland to Land's End. Sunday schools were soon linked closely with itinerant evangelism, and the inter-denominational Bath Sunday School Union was itself itinerant, despatching corps of teachers into surrounding villages to revive flagging Sunday schools or organise new ones, and, having trained new teachers, to move on and repeat the performance. Already the undenominational ' errand of mercy ', civilising and redeeming, which was to create such a stir in America, was in being in England, and to John Angell James, the future architect of the Evangelical Alliance, it bespoke the inmost counsel of God.[13]

> In the redemption of the world, there is first a union of counsel between the persons of the Trinity,—then a union of natures in the person of the Redeemer—then a union of the sinner to the Saviour,—and last of all there is a union of the redeemed with each other. Fellowship is the identifying law of Christ's kingdom.

The language thus evoked by simple Sunday school cooperation represented no more than a hardy theological cliché already subject to challenge. For the intellectual impact of the enlightenment had now been felt twice over. To those who responded favourably to them, the new ways bade fair to displace all the old shibboleths. The discomforts of subjecting the doctrine of the Trinity to the test of reason arithmetically conceived, had by 1790 led almost all the Presbyterians and General Baptists into Unitarianism, while, quantitatively speaking, the Church was probably a bigger vehicle of religious liberalism than them all. There were even Irish Roman Catholics who could extravagantly celebrate the disappearance of the issues separating Catholic and Protestant, ' the gloom of long reigning prejudice, scattering, as the clouds of night, at the approach of the rising sun '. There were some, like Joseph Priestley, in whom contempt for the past bred a hard and controversial spirit, but others sought a rationalist eirenicon and a rhetoric to match. William Hawkes, for whom the select Mosley-street Unitarian chapel was built in Manchester in 1789, had a

> mind . . . pure from the slightest taint of intolerance . . . his habitual and favourite subjects were those on which there is happily little difference of opinion among the wise and the good. . . . The tones of his voice happily accorded with the weight and value of the sentiments he expressed and contributed to render his ' strong reason and masculine sense ', still more interesting and impressive.[14]

The surprises which had been encountered in applying the canons of reason as currently understood to Christian belief, had of course persuaded some that the whole enterprise was a mistake, and as the dry bones of reformation theology came alive again under the power of the evangelical experience, old predestinarian doctrines were reborn and old controversies renewed. Was Arminian subscription honest subscription? Or was it the case, as Sir Richard Hill confidently averred after taking counsel with the superior of the English Benedictines in Paris, that ' Popery was about midway between Protestantism and Mr J. Wesley ' whose principles were ' too rotten for even a Papist to rest upon '.[15] And even within the Calvinist ranks, the further the reductionism of progressive intellectuals went, the higher the conservatives piled up their barricades, transforming high into hyper-Calvinism. When rationalism made inroads among the Presbyterians, the Independents stood out for orthodoxy; when the Independents yielded to new ways, the Baptists offered a refuge, and produced great stalwarts in Brine and Gill.

The famous free-for-alls which arose from this self-conscious return to the past have disguised the degree to which the evangelicals shared in the assumptions of the enlightenment, and constituted the second channel of its influence. For the one thing absolutely incredible to eighteenth-century evangelicals was the metaphysical approach to theology so characteristic of reformed theologians in the seventeenth century. With astonishing speed they came round to the view that the contest between the Arminians and the Calvinists was not merely unfortunate in its effects, but utterly mistaken in principle. For the evangelicals conceived that they were applying the inductive method in the field of religion, while the polemical backwoodsmen were sacrificing the truth to system. As one writer put it,

Calvinists and Arminians generally differ as widely in metaphysics as they do in theology. But Supreme Providence and free agency are so obviously taken for granted in both hypotheses, and the question about liberty and necessity is so evidently, *according to both,* in the very same situation in which it is likely to continue while the world standeth, that men must pay very little attention indeed to discriminating the proper provinces of speculation and faith, when, professing to learn revealed truth, they suffer themselves to be drawn into a metaphysical labyrinth. If the Arminian controversy shall ever be decided, it will be when, with respect to the abstruse doctrines of Scripture, theologians shall follow the same method which philosophers have learnt to do with respect to mysterious phenomena in nature; when they shall admit them as ultimate facts, and be willing to confess ignorance, rather than by attempting explanations to exhibit them in a light no less ridiculous than improper.

It was system, metaphysics, which seemed to account for the unhappy embarrassments of the past, especially in regard to reprobation, and, high and low, ' system' became the theological swearword of the hour. Long before Newman discovered that the Bible was not a textbook of school theology, Simeon was pronouncing that ' God has not revealed his truth in a system: the Bible has no system as such. Lay aside system and flee to the Bible. . . . Be Bible Christians and not system Christians.' Or as William Jay early inscribed in his study Bible,[16]

In reading this book let me guard against four things—
1. The contractedness of the Systematic.
2. The mysticism of the Allegoriser.
3. The dogmatism of the Bigot.
4. The presumption of the Rationalist.
Let me tremble at God's word, and let me in reading it keep three purposes in view:
1. To collect facts rather than form opinions.
2. To regulate practice rather than encourage speculation.
3. To aid devotion rather than dispute.

Early in the nineteenth century, the dissenting ministers of Manchester ' unanimously agreed that the best method for the spread of the Gospel was to preach in a way that the people could not discern whether they preached free will or free grace '. For when empiricism was the order of the day, there seemed little to choose between the two sides. As Sidney put it,

No persons . . . more freely invited sinners to Christ than the followers of Whitfield, or appeared to have a greater dread of entering on the question of reprobation as stated in the Institutes of Calvin. A real Arminian must also deny *total* depravity, but Wesley held, 'We are all born with a sinful *devilish* nature.' What could a Calvinist say more?

Since effectiveness was the great test of preaching, and both sides found the evangelical programme a weapon of unrivalled power, what should keep them apart? As we have seen with John Angell James, the evangelicals, like the rationalists, developed a manner to match the matter of the new mood. In 1791 the Yorkshire and Lancashire Particular Baptist Association advised that nothing was 'more injurious to the Christian interest than *Religious Bigotry*', and twenty years later Hampshire Baptist Association still held that churches went downhill when they paid more attention to speculative opinion than to personal religion. With Wesley gone, the Methodists dropped one red rag in the title of the connexional journal, the *Arminian Magazine*, and admitted that the old Calvinist system had 'been greatly improved during the last forty years'. The improvement was what was known as 'moderate Calvinism', 'practical Calvinism', Fullerism; insistence with the Bible that God had elected the faithful to life, and leaving the place of the rest in God's purposes in its biblical obscurity. Fullerism and empiricism greatly increased the pressure for open communion amongst the Baptists, for theological modernism and popular appeal seemed to go hand in hand. Yorkshire dissenters rejoiced that

> the separating walls of malevolent partition are thrown down—the vexatious quarrelling of envying and hating parties has ceased—and these communities now in some measure regard themselves as travellers, collected it may be in different bodies, but moving in the same road, guided by the same chart, following the same leader, and bound to the same hope.

Nowhere was the influence of enlightenment clearer than in the swelling rhetoric of the new spirit of union. To an old-style Independent it appeared that 'the human mind which had been debased by superstition and enslaved by priestcraft, had burst its fetters, and asserted its real dignity. . . . The bigotry of former times seems hastening to an extinction.' An evangelical, cross-bench between Methodism and the Church, beheld 'bigotry and persecution, ashamed of their distorted faces . . . retiring from the view of an enlightened population. Religion itself is now much better understood than formerly'. As late as 1822 a Wesleyan pundit could maintain that:[17]

> this, in good sense, is a liberal age, in which tens of thousands so blend orthodoxy with charity, that it is difficult to determine in which of the two they excel. Both the civil and religious world are now, and have been for almost a century, in a progressive state of melioration . . .

This cheerful conviction that the flesh and the spirit were alike breaking the dead hand of the past gained an extraordinary currency, though, as with itinerancy, urbanism and revival, it is important not to antedate its full impact on the evangelical world. The corrosives at work before the Revolution produced their most spectacular effects when intensified by the events which followed. In 1790 enlightenment was still most conspicuously the property of the old English Presbyterians, and led them into a conflict which was both the last of the old denominational order, and the prelude to those of the new.

2 The Crisis of the Old Order in England, 1790-1800

There was one point at which the steady erosion of the old religious distinctions was checked, and a new harshness injected into the situation. Under George III serious political issues revived, and with them many independent politicians, privileged corporations and professions which had long been in opposition, large municipalities, the University of Oxford, rank-and-file clergy, concluding that there were worse things in a wicked world than government, threw in their lot with the Court. In the 1790s these other interests were to constitute an establishment, battling for the survival of the old order. After the American war there were strident claims for parliamentary and fiscal reform, the freeing of provincial business interests, the suppression of the slave trade, and, once again, for the repeal of the Test and Corporation Acts. This last movement was made and broken by the dissenting élite, the Unitarians, who in many places supplied the leadership to all the new causes. To qualify for office by occasional conformity had lately become oppressive to the Unitarian conscience. There were now Unitarian churches with no Presbyterian ancestry, founded by men who had abandoned the Anglican priesthood for conscience's sake. And the running in the Unitarian world was increasingly made by hard men like Priestley who aspired to truth and social progress through free inquiry. Confident that the intellectual future was in their hands, and galled by the experience of slow denominational decline, they prepared a great blow at the institutional rigidities which must account for their practical disappointments. In all this they were seeking a displacement in the old system, not contriving a popular movement. Nowhere was this more clear than in Liverpool, one of the strongest Unitarian centres. Of their favourite causes, the suppression of the slave trade, the opening of the East India trade, and Catholic emancipation were directly contrary to the interests of working men in the port, while the repeal of the Test and Corporation Acts and municipal reform were at best indifferent. Unitarians were isolated, not merely by their religion and social status, but also by their politics.

The campaign for the repeal of the Test and Corporation Acts was managed by the London shop-window of the dissenting community, the Protestant Dissenting Deputies, whose great expertise lay in parliamentary lobbying. After a failure in 1787, they ran close to success on 8 May 1789, when a repeal motion went down in the Commons by only 124 votes to 104. This encouraging division proved to be the high-watermark of the campaign. The London committee proposed to develop the campaign by setting up regional boards of deputies, and provincial Unitarians, the very people most excited by the outbreak of the French Revolution, took the bit between their teeth, and began to demand a nationwide union of dissenters linked to London by a pyramid of elected councils. It was here that trouble began, for the effort to rouse a wider public brought out the clergy in force to pass their counter-resolutions, and gave a thorough fright to evangelical dissent.[1]

George Burder, the famous Independent minister of Coventry, went to the Midlands repeal meeting on 13 January 1790, but was frightened away by the ' degree of violence ' manifested by the Unitarians. What was afoot came out a few days later, when a convention of dissenters from the north-west assembled at Warrington, only to break up with the withdrawal of the Independents and Baptists. Not only were the Unitarians determined to monopolise the leadership of the agitation, but their chairman declared that

> there was ' the greatest necessity for *hypocrisy* in the business ', and that it would be ' neither wise nor prudent to tell fully what they had in view, or what steps they intended to take '!!!
> After which a Mr. T[oulmi]n, a neighbouring minister, rose up and said, ' *Their intentions were to remove the Liturgy from the Church and abolish Tithes.*'

This promise of genteel revolution not merely drove the Baptists and Independents to separate action, and gave the Manchester Church and King Club a new toast—' May the avowers of

" *Hypocrisy*" ever meet their just reward '—it embarrassed the London Deputies who always limited their brief to righting dissenters' grievances. Fox's repeal motion in 1790 was overwhelmed by 294 votes to 105, and although the machinery of agitation was kept in being, the liberal cause was routed. Hope of repeal disappeared for a generation, leaving a tradition that intemperate provincial agitation had been disaster. Certainly it evoked a conservative backlash of the most vicious kind.[2]

In Birmingham suspicion of the Unitarians' ulterior motives frightened off their friends and led to a merciless campaign of pulpit controversy. One Anglican incumbent virtually incited the destruction of meeting-houses, while on the other side, Joseph Priestley intrepidly boasted, ' with respect to the Church . . . I have long since drawn the sword and thrown away the scabbard, and am very easy about the consequences '. The consequences came in July 1791 in three days of unrestrained mob violence, when three meeting-houses were wrecked, Priestley's house with a great quantity of manuscripts and scientific apparatus burnt down, and the homes of numerous dissenters, reformers and members of the Lunar Society were threatened. It was a savage episode; no Methodist was hotter for Church and King than Joseph Benson, who was in Birmingham at the time, and the relief expressed in his diary when the troops arrived speaks volumes. Priestley viewed the riot as a contrivance of government to intimidate the reformers, and other Unitarians regarded it as ' a symptom of the general disorder which High Churchmen have inserted into every part of the kingdom, and into the vitals of government itself '. The limit of the central government's complicity seems to have been the preferment of the rector of St Philip's, Birmingham, to the see of Bristol, and recent inquiry has borne out the view quaintly expressed by Bogue and Bennett, the Independent historians, that ' the riots . . . [were] created, not by a legitimate English mob, but by persons superior to those who were the apparent actors in the disgraceful scenes '. Certainly the crucial damage seems to have been done by a disciplined corps with precise objectives and a safe-conduct from the magistrates; and a ' Birmingham Association for the Protection of Liberty and Property against Republicans and Levellers' smashed the dissenting interest as it became aggressive and vocal, and poisoned the whole political atmosphere of the country.[3]

c

In Manchester the failure of the repeal campaign was celebrated noisily every year by a new counter-revolutionary Church
and King Club, and on the King's birthday, 4 June 1792, the mob
came out in Birmingham style, tore up the trees in St Ann's Square,
and battered at the doors of the Unitarian meeting-houses ' with
violent cries of " Church and King "—" Down with the Rump "
—down with it! etc.' Repeatedly the mob took to the streets,
egged on by the clergy and unrestrained by the magistrates, the
shock-troops in a campaign by which the conservatives broke the
party of reform and deprived it of press and meeting-places. The
climax came in 1795 when the Unitarians declared in favour of
peace, and the clergy and Loyal Associations of Manchester and
Salford (who had been demanding arms) attacked them with an
address in which religious bigotry and class hostility are nicely
balanced :

> They who disregard their maker, and the duty they owe to him
> —revile the sacred writings—despise religious ordinances—
> contemn the adorable Redeemer of men—and scoff at revealed
> religion, have but very little claim to tenderness of conscience.
> To those hypocrites whose ears are *always shut* to the cry of
> distress, who oppress their servants, who exact with the
> GREATEST SEVERITY EXORBITANT RENTS FROM THEIR POOR
> TENANTS—who endeavour to compel the labouring poor to
> maintain the necessitous poor, and remove the burden from
> themselves, TO THEIR BOSOMS, the soft impulse of philanthropy
> is stranger. . . .

In the out-townships Unitarians' palings were hurled through their
windows with cries of ' Jacobins, Painites and Presbyterians ',
while Methodists hoped desperately that their reputation for
charity would make them ' the most safe of anybody '.[4]

It was a similar story in Liverpool. The houses of the Jacobins,
as the Liverpool Unitarians were known, were marked for individual destruction, should their campaign against the slave trade
succeed. They attacked the Corporation's methods of filling vacancies on the Council and in return were taken to the King's Bench
till their funds ran out, and mobbed in the streets. The Quaker
Rathbone and the Unitarian Roscoe attempted to rally what they
called their ' sansculottes ' at a town's meeting, but were shouted
down and jostled by an angry tory mob. This was virtually the

end of their existence as a party; the crisis left Rathbone a wreck, his hair turned white overnight. But still the collector of customs kept a careful check on the Jacobins' activities with a view to future prosecution.[5]

Elsewhere dissenters soon learned not to express sympathy with Priestley. At Yarmouth they had to arm to defend their houses. By January 1793, William Bull of Newport Pagnell was dreading persecution daily. At Warwick a dissenting Sunday school came under the hammer; at Bromsgrove the Baptist pastor, James Butterworth, was driven out. Timothy Kenrick, the radical Unitarian minister in Exeter, was in constant trouble with his congregation, who understood the risks to which his outspokenness exposed them. For the pressure undoubtedly worked— ' modern dissenters have shown a dereliction of principle'. Radical Unitarians and Baptists in South Wales might go on calling themselves ' sansculottes ', but even before the execution of Louis XVI and the deterioration of the situation in France, Independents, Baptists, Methodists, Unitarians, Roman Catholics were seeking security in protestations of loyalty to king and constitution. Pastors emigrated in despair, and substantial Unitarian laymen conformed to the Church or bought American estates as a retreat. As long as the contrivers of counter-revolution could count on support from below, the Toleration Act was a fragile thing. What could not be foreseen by either the old Church or the old dissent, was the astonishing speed with which that support collapsed.[6]

In the mid-nineties the old structure of authority in England was subjected to every trial short of revolution, a trial composed partly of a traditional subsistence crisis, and partly of a new ideological challenge. The English social pyramid, though steep in its scale of incomes, was very flat in terms of numbers above the base. Indeed Patrick Colquhoun, the acutest student of the problem of that day, reckoned that about one-eighth of the population, paupers, criminals and others ' presumed to live chiefly or wholly upon the labours of others ', were really below the base. Of the remainder, almost two-thirds were members of the labouring classes and servants at the base of the pyramid, and about one-fifth were members of the next rank above, lesser freeholders, shopkeepers, publicans and so forth.[7] In bad years high food prices oppressed the landless rural proletariat and town labourers alike, and killed the market for popular textiles so that industrial unemployment further savaged the incomes of the labouring classes. In these dark times great numbers of the two huge classes at the base of the social pyramid might be thrust into the morass beneath, magnifying the problem of public order out of all recognition. It was then that crime increased, and Bogue and Bennett's ' legitimate English mob' came out, often under respectable leadership, to pit its numbers against the movement of prices on a free market, forcibly auctioning food stocks at ' fair' prices. The law was harsh, and getting harsher, but criminal procedure was liberal; there were a few troops, but practically no police. Government must live by its wits, and whatever informal support it could get.

But in the traditional troubles there was little ideological challenge. Even the vicious assault on the Presbyterians portended little change in the system; it chiefly concerned members of the top sixth of the population on Colquhoun's scale, and not many of them. But the distress which culminated in the major food crisis of 1795 involved huge numbers, and was inflamed by two new factors, the artisan response to the stimulus of developments in France, and the real possibility that the rickety structure of authority in England might be pushed over by foreign invasion. The reaction in England came not to the outbreak of the French Revolution, but to the establishment of the Convention on manhood suffrage in August 1792, the determination of the French sansculottes to overthrow a monarchy which was sabotaging the war effort, and to end an assembly which could not handle the food crisis. The radical London Corresponding Society swept aside its staider predecessors and kept recruiting right through to 1795. In the debates in its provincial centres, the grafting of a radical political programme on to the older traditions of direct action began. A huge tide of loyalty set in on the other side. There were Loyalist Associations, the pious propaganda of Hannah More, the formidable setting of good examples by Wilberforce, the formation of Volunteer companies to oppose force to the new threats, and the inducements of liquor and uniforms to those of equality and reason.[8] And, not least, Habeas Corpus was suspended in 1794, which made it easier to use force and repeated arrests.

1795, a dreadful year over much of Europe, was a terrible

trial to both sides. There were innumerable food riots, and the government harried the overseers of the poor into reporting on the state of the harvest—in the next food crisis the clergy had to be the government's eye.[9] In October the king was mobbed, membership of the radical societies soared, and Church-and-King mobs disappeared for ever. But the countryside offered the best index of the gravity of the situation. In 1795 the Berkshire magistrates determined at Speenhamland to supplement labourers' wages from the poor rate up to a family subsistence level, and their example was widely followed elsewhere. When wage-earners had to be kept within the social pyramid by this device matters were serious indeed. But the radical movement failed to make a political issue out of hunger, and was in fact already beaten. The government strengthened its arm with Grenville's Two Acts, and by mid-summer 1796 food supplies had improved. The tide of emigration to America, usual at moments of despair, set in, and rural discontent took another course.

Subsequently the war became more of a national effort, but the next great crisis of 1797-8 arose from the coincidence of a financial blizzard occasioned by the war with rebellion in Ireland, and a threat of French invasion inflamed by naval mutinies at the Nore and Spithead. Again government turned the corner, and by the time the next bad years, 1800 and 1801, arrived, the government had put a legislative brake upon trade unions and newspapers, had broken up the Corresponding Society and other bodies with linked branches, were contemplating a wholesale reorganisation of police,[10] and a drastic limitation of the rights of religious toleration. English society being what it was, the crisis of authority occurred in religion as well as politics; crises of public order, 1793, 1795, 1797-8, 1800 were all crucial in the swelling tide of anti-establishment sentiment in popular religion. This pressure and the increasingly tough counter-pressure of the government and the Church, which finally endangered the Toleration Act, put all the churches in an equivocal position. Three samples of their impact on the denominational order may be examined: the transformation of the Methodism of John Wesley, urban opinion exemplified by the Sunday schools, and rural opinion exemplified in the outburst of itinerant preaching.

In Methodism the basic structural problems of the respective authority of preachers, trustees, and leaders, the ministerial status of the preachers, and the relations of the whole body with the Church of England were emerging before Wesley's death, and were all inextricably involved in the question whether the Methodist people should receive communion from their own preachers in their own chapels. Wesley's desire to remain within the fold of the Church was perfectly well known, but in the last dozen years of his life he often celebrated the Lord's Supper in large provincial chapels, and he gave preachers authority to celebrate in America and Scotland, i.e. outside the jurisdiction of the Church of England. As long as it was simply a question of the Methodists enjoying the fellowship of the ordinance together, the line might be held by modestly irregular devices of this kind. But mutual hostility between the Church and the Methodists would make it difficult to resist the demand of certain preachers for full ministerial status, and Wesley himself ordained three men to celebrate in England in 1789. Nevertheless what Thomas Coke described as ' a gradual imperceptible separation ' was made impossible by the events which followed Wesley's death.[11]

For although the demand for the sacraments was made in pietistic terms, and went down in the official history as ' not a political movement, not a sectarian clamour, but a spiritual and godly requirement ', everyone knew that separate communion meant separation from the establishment, and in this there was as much politics as religion. In the atmosphere created by the Church-and-King reaction of 1791 and 1792 it was reasonable to hold that separation would ruin Methodist prospects of usefulness, and fatally easy to use every device of hysterical unreason to reserve the drift while there was yet time. Reason and hysteria were equally operational to Thomas Coke. Were Methodists to become avowed dissenters, he held, the public would pass by their chapels

with the same unconcern with which they pass by the door of the Presbyterian Meeting-houses. But more than this, we should imbibe the political spirit of the Dissenters: nor should I be much surprized if in a few years some of our people, warmest in politics and coolest in religion, would toast (as I am informed a famous society did lately in the short hours of the night) *a bloody summer and a headless King*. Is not this . . . what Dr Priestley aims at? Nay, the Dr perhaps might even be more victorious still. When he had got us so very near him, he might take the Crown off the head of the Great Messiah by pouring into our ears and eyes all the poison of Socinianism.

By 1792 the partisans of separate communion found themselves against the wall throughout the North of England, victims within their own communion of a violent combination of property and authority like that which was hurled against the Presbyterians, ' the spirit of bigotted high-churchmen, which seems to infect *rich mongrel-methodists* through the land'. The Conference of 1791 had simply engaged to follow Wesley's plan, which in effect gave each preacher liberty to do as he wished, but the Conference of 1792, in the inflamed atmosphere produced by the Birmingham riots, reached a heated deadlock; the only escape short of secession was to put the matter to the lot. The decision of the lot was that the sacraments be not administered for a year, and the issue was postponed.[12]

The connexional year which began in September 1792 saw the whole situation transformed; the wave of artisan radicalism in the country had its counterpart in a clamour for separation among the ordinary members and adherents of the Methodist societies which no force within the connexion could control. The conservative counter-attack of the previous year was halted, the ' party of rich men ' isolated, and it was made clear to the preachers that they would have to face the political and financial risk of separation if they wished to keep their hold over the flock. From place after place in the North and West it was reported that ' the Lord's Supper must be tolerated next conference, or numbers of people will break from our Connection ', and they would find means of taking the chapels with them. Moreover not only did Tom Paine receive a modest welcome from Methodist sacramentarians, but the demand for services in church hours, even for the sacrament, was couched in terms more Painite than Biblical. Even in Wesley's lifetime Thomas Hanby had advocated giving the sacrament under the slogan ' Vox populi, vox Dei '; now there was a veritable chorus. Samuel Bradburn introduced services in church hours in Salford ' with some pointed observations (from the pulpit) on the *Rights of Man* '. Soon he was declaring ' Vox populi should be our motto ', and claiming ' *unbounded liberty,* founded upon the *Rights of Man* in all matters consistent with decorum and our main design to save souls '.[13]

Still more menacing was the attitude of these champions of the people to the power of property in the connexion, the trustees who maintained the chapels and serviced their debts, and who not surprisingly were the hottest supporters of the Church and the use of every instrument of social regulation to stem the anti-establishment torrent. Though they embodied one side of John Wesley's legacy, they received short shrift from preachers who saw the way things were going. Samuel Bradburn was always grinding his teeth against aristocracy:

> *The Leaders, not Trustees,* are the representatives of the people. I would sooner lose the whole premises belonging to the New-Chapel [Bristol], than submit to be governed by that tyrannical aristocratical faction. We must guard our own liberties, and our people's, or an aristocratical faction will rule us with a rod of iron.

Indeed, in his view, the issue between the Methodist people's assertion of independence and the trustees who supported the Church connexion was only the local aspect of the great divide which was opening in English life between the establishment and the rest. ' I am persuaded that the contest is only like Fox and Pit[t]. It is not who shall do the preachers most good, or who shall serve the people most, but who shall have the power to do their own will.' More political language about the eucharist is not easy to imagine.[14]

In the summer of 1793 Conference responded to the dramatic change in the country. The previous year the Church party had been dominant, now they crumbled. Two-thirds of the Conference voted that where members of a society were unanimous in their desire to receive the sacrament from their own preachers they might do so. As the Conference letter explained to the conservatives,

> it is *the people* . . . who have forced us into this further deviation from our union to the Church of England. Still we wish to be united to it as a Body at large. The few societies which [are unanimous for separate communion] need have but a small influence on the whole Connexion.

This was cold comfort. Preachers who had bowed to the will of the people had contravened the verdict of the lot in the previous year, and would have no greater respect for the verdict of Conference. If the Church connexion was to retain any substance, the trustees would have to fight for it as the partisans of established institutions were fighting everywhere. Neither side had any doubt as to the issue. Conference accused trustees and other supporters of the Church party of not being members of society, even of taking seats in dissenting chapels while pretending zeal for the establishment. The Church party could show in reply that when the Methodist reformers secured the ordinance which they claimed on grounds of Anglican laxity, they admitted ' all descriptions of people many of whom are not in the Methodist Society ', and that some of those who had shouted loudest for the Lord's Supper, ' after their demands had been acceded to, very seldom approached the sacred table '. Of course, what was at stake was not so much the sacrament, as separation.[15]

The battle was joined at Bristol, where the trustees of the Old Room, the first chapel Wesley had built, claimed control of the pulpit after his death under the trust deed. They excluded Henry Moore who had celebrated the sacrament at another chapel in their circuit, and were supported in their action by the other preachers, Benson, Rodda and Vasey. The official version of the story came to be that a national combination of trustees had chosen Bristol for a decisive effort to wrest power from the preachers; but it is not easy on this basis to explain the attitudes of Benson and his colleagues, none of whom were negligible men, nor the reappointment of Moore to Bristol after an absence of only two years instead of the eight required by Methodist professional ethics, still less the painful episode in which Benson, who in July 1794 had preached a ferocious Conference sermon against schism, was adjudged by a District Meeting in September to have withdrawn himself from the connexion; the chairman of the court was Samuel Bradburn, the most aggressive of the partisans of separate communion, who had been making trouble for Benson in Birmingham and Manchester for some years past. Certainly Bradburn and Moore had known before Conference that the course on which they were bent would lead to trouble, and were plausibly suspected of having brought on the clash; one of the Bristol preachers who supported Moore was candid enough : ' We have now set all Trustees at defiance and we will not sheathe the sword till we have put to flight all the Trustees through [ou]t the nation.' The methods which they used, at first with limited effect, to break the Old Room society were disreputable (and included cutting off alms to the poor supporters of the Old Room trustees), but in the long run they succeeded. For although Benson was supported by ' some scores ' of circuits, the strength of the sacramentarian position was that popular backing for ' Church' Methodism was being destroyed by the same complex of political and social forces as destroyed popular complaisance towards the establishment and made Church-and-King mobs impossible to raise. Moreover Benson (like his opponents) could only salvage one side of Wesley's heritage at the expense of another. And the political excitements of separation—' this act of shaking off the church and doing without its clergy '—struck a powerful chord in Wesleyan pietism. At Liverpool

the people were determined that they wd. wait [for communion] no longer. We were obliged whether we wd. or not [to] comply. The notice was only short yet we had I believe 600 people. We had a most extraordinary lovely happy meeting, such as I think I never saw before. I think I never saw so large a body of people so generally so deeply and for so long a time so much affected. Many were brought into liberty . . . There was no confusion at all. It was all solid. I felt so much of the divine presence that I thought I wd. most willingly die a martyr for the sacrament . . .

There is here the unmistakable sense of a burden rolled away.[16]

The worsening situation in the country helped to reunite the warring factions among the preachers. Six months was sufficient to show Benson and his friends that the tide was more than they could dam. At the same time Bradburn learned that the worse the prospects of public order, the greater the risk that the government might act against Methodism as against other forms of public assembly and propaganda; there was force in Benson's contention that Methodism could not be safe except as a movement unequivocally within the Church of England. Some at least of the hollow assurances of the sacramentarian party that they wished the body to remain in communion with the Church when they were obviously bent on separation, were intended for government consumption. But the loyal assurances given to Pitt in 1793 that they desired closer union with the Church had been patently unfulfilled, and at the end of 1795 the government came to demand pledges of Methodist loyalty under threat of penal legislation. Already Bradburn and Moore had perceived the drift of the times, and came to terms with Benson's party; after characteristic veering to and fro Coke joined them, and their preparatory agreements, circulated among trustees, ensured the harmonious adoption of the Plan of Pacification at the next Conference. The Plan forbade the sacrament to be administered in any chapel where there was no administration at present, except with the consent of a majority of the trustees, of the stewards and leaders, and of the Conference. Negative in form, the Plan provided a means by which the bulk of the Methodist community could move into practical dissent, and consummated the defeat of the struggles of the lay aristocracy of the connexion in the great urban centres of London, Bristol, Birmingham, Liverpool, Manchester, Leeds, Halifax and Newcastle, to bolster up the Church against the anti-establishment torrent of the rank and file.[17]

The Plan had also an administrative significance. Benson's defeat spelt defeat for one aspect of Wesley's heritage; it meant also the rejection of one of his possible successors, and illustrated the power vacuum created by his death, what Adam Clarke described as a ' total want of government '. Moreover hierarchy had suffered a check on the ministerial as well as the lay side. Nothing had so far replaced Wesley's continuous oversight over the whole connexion. In December 1793, the President, John Pawson, argued pragmatically that

> it will by no means answer our ends to dispute one with another, as to which is the most scriptural form of church government. We should consider our present circumstances and endeavour to agree on some method by which our people may have the ordinances of God, and at the same time be preserved from division. I care not a rush whether it be Episcopal or Presbyterian. I believe neither of them to be purely scriptural, but our preachers and people in general are prejudiced against the latter; consequently if the former will answer our end we ought to embrace it.

There was, moreover, reason to think that this was what Wesley had intended. In April 1794 Thomas Coke and seven other preachers met secretly at Lichfield (where there were supposed to be no Methodists) and prepared a scheme for the government of English Methodism by seven bishops, six of whom should be of their own number. The plan leaked out at once, and fell victim to an egalitarian reaction among the preachers. The result was that under the Plan of Pacification, Wesley's personal oversight was succeeded by the committee oversight of District Meetings which grew steadily in authority; his prejudice in favour of bishops was supplanted by what amounted to presbyterian ordination when men were admitted into full connexion; his desire to remain in the fold of the Church met with practical separation. Methodism had met the upheaval of the 1790s with radical reconstruction; among others, Alexander Kilham thought there might be more to come.[18]

Kilham was a brash young man of doctrinaire views and unconcealed dissenting opinions, who in 1792 had been censured by Conference for violent attack on the Church connexion as ' a specious trimming between God and the world '. Like so many artisans and small tradesmen of that day, his mind was cast in the social contract mould, and, whether in church or state, he saw authority rising from below. He was privy to Bradburn's conspiracies against Church Methodism through agents across the country, and seems to have accepted at its face value Bradburn's tub-thumping about the Rights of Man, and the people being the radix of all power in the connexion. But from the time of his reconciliation with Benson in 1795, Bradburn turned against radical politics, against Kilham in particular, and against religion of the people generally: ' their prayer meetings . . . are more like a pack of hounds in full cry than a company of Christians at the throne of grace! And the *tempers* of most of them are beneath the philosophy of a sincere heathen!' From that moment Kilham's hopes of securing Bradburn's leadership for a policy of Methodist reform were illusory.[19]

The mistake which made Kilham the first Methodist martyr to reform was more venial. The Plan of Pacification, concluded in an atmosphere of mob violence in Manchester, marked a great movement to the left under popular pressure. As distress deepened in the autumn and political radicalism was reborn, there was no telling how much further the movement might go. If the preachers had followed the flock into separation and a demand for the sacrament, might they not yield to a demand for lay rights? 1795

saw the end of Church-and-King mobs, and was the crucial year
in severing the Church from popular support. Could Methodism
remain unaffected? There was more reason in the view than
Kilham has been given credit for, and his autumn pamphlet,
ominously entitled *The progress of liberty among the people called
Methodists*, making the charges of financial and other irregularities
against the preachers which were always heard when hard times
brought home the cost of voluntaryism to the flock, seemed well
calculated to play on raw nerves.

Thomas Coke was now given by well-informed circles to understand that the government required a practical pledge of loyalty;
neither he nor Bradburn had any doubt that this involved the
expulsion of Kilham, who was showing up the ministry in the
worst possible light. The object was to be secured by pressing a
public declaration of loyalty which should expose Kilham as a
disaffected politician. Bradburn hammered at a preacher who
did not wish to sign :

> That the government have cause to be alarmed and have been
> so, I know beyond controversy. And if Alexr. Kilham and his
> abetters intend to pursue the path which they have done of
> late, active measures will be taken by the *higher powers*! . . .
> Your wish to be neuter so as to offend neither party, savours of
> want of principle, which in us would be shocking . . . [The
> connexional leadership was now united] and who is to stand
> against them? [K]ilham and company!!! Alas! they know
> not what they are about. Look at their influence and connexions!
> I mean to act as I have done, so far as I can; but never to give
> countenance to raw desperadoes, who proceed in a manner that
> tends to anarchy and ruin. As to the cries about the *poor*, the
> *war*, etc., a great deal of this is for want of information and
> attention. The distress of 9 in 10 of the poor *is entirely their
> own fault*, and unconnected with the war . . . and as to the
> war itself . . . I think it easy to prove that it has done more
> good than hurt to the nation.

To such comments on a famine of European dimensions was the
erstwhile champion of the Rights of Man reduced by the necessities of connexional politics. But Coke, who would do anything
for his missions, disgraced himself publicly. He hoped that this
display of loyalty would persuade Wilberforce to prevail ˈwith

the Arch. Bp. of Canterbury to ordain a Bror. Smith from New-foundland '. After all the Conference undertakings to put a stop to ordinations, this was asking for trouble, and the London preachers required Coke to keep his address secret until he had consulted twenty senior preachers in the country. Nothing daunted Coke appeared with his vellum in one of the London chapels the next Sunday morning, declaring ' The man who will not sign an address to the King is not a good man, and I will proclaim him on the housetop and through the nation '. Much provoked, the London preachers extracted a formal pledge that Coke would put the matter down till Conference, a pledge he had broken within a few days. The London comment was eminently justified that

> he will say anything and act contrary to what he has said to carry his point, and will set aside any number of preachers and treat them with contemp[t] to serve his purpose. This man going on year after year disquieting the connection with everything he thinks right and changeing (not like the Moon for that is regular) from one point and thing to another . . . should be stopt.

William Thompson, who had long-standing grievances against Coke's administrative ineptitude, exploded in wrath both at the attempt to ' call those Jacobins and rebels who do not sign the Dr's Address ', and at the admission, which would be implied by presenting a separate address, that Methodism was a separate body, not ' a society [gathered] out of the different sects and parties in the kingdom '.[20]

Nevertheless, though Coke did not get his address, Kilham's fate was sealed. He had shown himself unamenable to church discipline, he had turned the preachers against him by accusations of malpractice, and by the summer of 1796 the tide of popular discontent had ebbed; if peace with the government could be had at the price of jettisoning Kilham, that price was never likely to be lower than in 1796. A document affirming the justice of the transaction was prepared and, as Kilham bitterly recalled,

> the paper was taken to the communion table, and laid in the place where the memorials of the body and blood of Christ are laid . . . and Mr Bradburn, who had formerly professed

himself a friend to liberty and the rights of the people, stood by the communion table, like the governor of the inquisition, to see that none omitted signing.[21]

A desperate race for support followed in which Kilham was handicapped by the ebbing of social discontent in 1796, the rallying of national opinion before the threat of invasion, and the union of the preachers behind their grandees. For Kilham's enterprise showed, like later Wesleyan reform movements, that (whatever might be the case with revival) Wesleyan reform could not succeed without ministerial leadership. In the event he swept together irreconcilables of various kinds. A list of his agents, mostly in the North and Midlands, includes three merchants and a country banker; a schoolmaster, a farmer and a butter factor; three shoemakers, two hosiers, and two saddlers; a potter, a skinner, a cooper and a plumber. Conservatives reported that at Sheffield ' people are warm in Kilham's interest and most of them high republicans'; more to the point, their preachers, Bram- well and Henry Taylor, encouraged the belief that they would lead a secession, and, not for the last time, broke down in the crisis. The future also cast its shadow before, in that when separation came it included a Sunday school. In the turbulent colliery circuits there were familiar troubles. The Barnsley radicals were said to have gone over from Tom Paine to ' Methodistical politics ', and half the society was for Kilham; there was a sub- stantial backing on the Tyne and Wear, though some leading figures withdrew in the end. But Kilham won his chief victories personally. For several weeks at the beginning of 1797, he was kept at Ashton-under-Lyne by the last illness of his wife, and in the industrial area of north-east Cheshire, and adjacent parts of south-east Lancashire and the West Riding, it proved possible to take trustees, chapels and whole congregations out of Wesleyan- ism. Here the power of property and the trustee interest was bound to leave its mark, and the Wesleyan preachers were titillated over the generations by a continuous trickle of horror- stories from disillusioned New Connexion preachers seeking a return to the one true fold. And even at the beginning, when Robert Hall of Basford was drumming up the respectability of the New Connexion for the Conference of 1798, he had to con- fess that he might not be there himself:

Can you believe me when I inform you that I am at last brought to consent to carry a musket? A company is raising in our parish and also the same in most of the neighbouring parishes (to consist of persons of property, chiefly) for the defence of their houses and property *against a lawless rabble only*. I am so circumstanced that along with my partner and son I have enrolled myself in the company.

To this had a movement come whose chief hopes in 1795 had lain in Jacobinism and war-weariness. But when the Wesleyan Conference refused to yield representative government in 1797, Kilham's New Connexion had to lay hands on whatever resources it could. Its greatest resource, Kilham himself, perished from his labours in 1798.[22]

With conservative preachers struggling with reforming pressure in the circuits, the Conference of 1797 had to bid for support by concessions of its own. In the crisis the connexional leadership displayed conspicuous quality; they made substantial concessions to the local courts of the connexion, primarily of lay composition, the Quarterly Meeting and Leaders' Meeting, and combined them with long-overdue administrative improvements, and a revision of connexional law which cleared up many obscurities. Whether these changes arose from any consciously articulated doctrine of the ministry is doubtful, though without them ' many of the Preachers wd. have left our Connexion ' to head the Kilhamites. A generation later it was held that the Plan of Pacification and the Regulations of 1797 preserved both the connexional principle and the authority of the Pastoral Office unabridged, and simply provided procedural safeguards against their abuse. But an authoritative assessment of 1810 was pessimistic.

For fear of a larger division, the conference agreed to make considerable sacrifices, the preachers resigning considerable portions of power, respecting temporal matters, division of circuits, receiving and excluding members, the appointment and removal of leaders, stewards and local preachers. It is doubtful whether the concessions made were not something larger than will be for the general good, and more than scripture and reason will justify.

The corner was turned. Only five per cent of the membership

was lost to Kilham, and that loss was immediately repaired by great revivals. But the jettisoning of Kilham did nothing to improve relations with a government now seriously concerned about the fate of the Establishment, and under pressure to put down the English itinerancy. There was no assurance that the central authority in Methodism, so repeatedly weakened since Wesley's death, could cope with the new forces of spontaneous revival or social conflict among the people. Of the great men who had travelled with Wesley, Thompson and Mather had run their course; Benson was pledged to a policy of union with the Church now rejected by both sides; Coke had shown himself a man of no judgment; Bradburn had unmistakably revealed his defects of character. 'It has too frequently happened among us', Pawson complained about him, 'that our very great men have not always been the most devoted to God.'[23] What was clear was that the social crisis of the 1790s had irreparably damaged the informal relations which had subsisted between Methodists and the Church, and, in the regulations of 1797, had created the criterion distinguishing official from schismatic, Jacobinical, Kilhamite, Methodism; it was much less easy now to maintain that the true heritage of John Wesley was a tradition of inspired innovation. A new and more contentious denominational order was being forced into existence.

The year 1795 was crucial not only for Methodism, but for the Establishment in the towns. It saw the last Church-and-King mob in one of the Manchester out-townships, the loss of which painfully exposed the weakness of the Church. Before 1796 was out the Anglican clergy were nagging at their fellow citizens for boycotting them *en masse*—' at least *two-thirds* of the inhabitants . . . suffer each succeeding Sabbath to pass over their heads like any other day ', and middle-class attendances were also declining. The clergy, encouraged by the bishop, put on special lectures, but to no effect. In 1802 they resorted to united action by the borough-reeves, constables, special constables, the commander of the barracks, and Church and Chapel-wardens ' to enforce a more general observance of [the] sacred day by vigorous efforts of the police ', but it was still no use; nor were prosecutions of shop-keepers and ale-house keepers who opened on Sundays. At the episcopal visitation of 1804 the clergy of the Manchester collegiate church who had been able to dispose of mob violence

D

a decade before, were frankly querulous: ' Conventicles are open for all that have leisure and curiosity . . . Yet amidst those papists and Calvinists and Methodists, common foes, I hope it may be said " Fear not, Little Flock " to our Established Church.'[24]

The most startling evidence of the swing in popular opinion, however, was provided, not by the conventicles, but by the Sunday Schools, which now found their fate linked with the itinerancies in the countryside. There were places like Chester and Coventry where the Anglican clergy prevented combined Sunday school effort from ever getting off the ground, but in the North-west the system was a model, and it had been clearly appreciated that there must be no sheep-stealing. Unhappily just this result seemed to follow from the social crisis of the mid-nineties; as a broad public turned its back on the Establishment, the children of the lower classes poured into the non-Anglican and especially the Wesleyan schools, and exposed the Wesleyans to those charges of denominational imperialism which had always been the Achilles heel of the movement. This development was even less the result of policy among the Wesleyans than the clamour for separate communion; the schools were a growing embarrassment to them, but the damage was done. In 1795, one of the Anglican pillars of the Manchester schools, the Rev Cornelius Bayley, old friend of Wesley as he was, produced a Sunday school catechism enforcing a very high doctrine of the church, Sunday school charity sermons in dissenting chapels ceased, and dissenting schools began to be opened outside the town's system; most sinister of all, in 1799 and 1800 when Pitt's government was known to be preparing legislation against both itinerant preaching and Sunday schools, Bayley and C. P. Myddleton, incumbent of St Mary's, withdrew financial support from the town's committee, and launched a campaign to break it up.[25]

It was the same story in Stockport. The Town's Committee functioned satisfactorily for nearly a decade, but then, much as in Manchester, the school associated with the Wesleyan chapel in Hillgate outstripped all others in size, almost doubling in numbers between October 1793 and 1795, and increasing by half again in the next twelve months. The Town's Committee was unwilling to allow the Hillgate school more than one-sixth of the funds collected for the six schools in the town, the managers had to raise funds by sermons in the Methodist chapel, and the school became in fact a Methodist school. Again, this was no act of policy; the Wesleyan trustees never corporately did anything for the Sunday school, their promises speedily became inadequate for the throngs of children, and the school committee were burdened with immense expense in renting cottages and other unsuitable accommodation for the 2,000 children they had on their books by 1800 (in 1793 there had been 500).[26] The Wesleyans had again become the beneficiaries of the tide of anti-Establishment sentiment.

It was social tension also which underlay the vehemence of the clerical counter-attack upon many of the south Lancashire and north Cheshire schools at the end of the 'nineties, and it is noteworthy that evangelical clergymen, looking to the state to save the day for the Church, turned their back on cooperation with dissenters and led the clamour against the political hazard of the schools. The charges poured in. There were Sunday school conductors who had gone Paineite ' about the year 1793 when almost every person became a politician '; the Rights of Man had prepared them for the Age of Reason, and infidelity was the reason why the children had stopped coming to Church in the mid-nineties. Sabbath-writing, the mainstay of so many schools, was ' seldom admitted, except where there is a slight mixture of infidel characters among the managers ', and though the Manchester schools taught no writing they were as bad, for they met in church hours. Some schools were ' Seminaries of Faction ' with teachers who had taken the oaths of United Englishmen. These accusations were generalised by the *Anti-Jacobin* into the allegation that Sunday schools were ' in many instances . . . channels for the diffusion of bad principles religious and political . . . [and] viewed with a favourable eye by the Jacobins themselves ', and reached their climax in the celebrated charge of Samuel Horsley, Bishop of Rochester, in 1800, designed as a signal for legislation by the government, with the claim that the expansion of non-Anglican Sunday schools and conventicles since 1795 was the work of Jacobins whose overtly political activities had been suppressed by the Two Acts.[27] The expected bill never got into Parliament, but after the crisis the Sunday school movement was never the same again.

The Manchester Town's committee, financially embarrassed by the contumacy of Bayley and Myddelton, negotiated desperately for their return, but finally had to admit defeat. The Anglican clergy took a proportion of the joint property, and established a new committee under their sole control. Their first weapon in salvaging their remnant was inevitably excommunication; their second advertisement. Children absconding to the schools of the opposite party were not to be readmitted, nor were children of the same family to be allowed to attend schools of a different establishment. They then laid plans for the first of the famous Manchester Whit Walks, which took place in 1801 and have continued to be one of the less desirable aspects of the town's religious life ever since. Moreover Sabbath writing-classes, which were known to be a great draw and against which the old Town's Committee had always set its face, were offered by both sides for a time after the disruption. Once the Anglicans were gone, the movement could not function in the old way, and though appeals to the general public continued, financial considerations were bound to strengthen the ties between the schools and particular congregations. The Wesleyans were now so much the dominant party amongst the remnant that they virtually annexed the system, in due course laying hands for denominational purposes on school property to which they had very little claim. Here the process of disentangling Wesleyanism from dissent took longer than the more familiar process of its separation from the Church, but was as decisive, and as politically important, in the end. For the new Anglican, Wesleyan and Sunday School Union systems (embracing the evangelical dissenters) could find no room for two parties influential in the Town's Committee, the Unitarians and Roman Catholics.[28]

In Stockport the same combination of forces produced a somewhat different result. By the end of the century, the Hillgate school had enrolled more than twice as many scholars as the rest of the town's committee put together, and was in some difficulty with its recurrent expenses. One of the moving spirits, Matthew Mayer, a Wesleyan of apostolic labours, embodied the quintessence of undenominational evangelicalism and much business acumen. Mayer realised that it would be much easier to raise a large capital endowment for a specially designed building, than to keep up annual subscriptions to pay the rent of cottage premises. So it came about that the astonishing building which still stands on the brow of the hill in Stockport was erected in

1805, by means of an appeal to the whole town on an undenominational basis, the school claiming in substance to have superseded the decayed relics of the Town's Committee system. The undenominational principle now had an endowed and institutional form, full parity with ' public hospitals and other large charities '. Within a generation the Stockport school had become the largest in the world, educating no fewer than 6,000 children; its surplus of home-produced teachers was launching one Sunday school after another, a process which vividly illuminates the mechanics of the evangelical revival as a whole; and the school's fascinating role as an educational publisher and pioneer became a subject in itself—it was the Sunday school which established the first technical education in the town, and at one stage supported its own chemistry laboratories. In Stockport the denominations failed to dismember the Sunday school; as we shall see, they countered by trying to turn it into a denomination on its own.[29]

In and about Manchester the crisis for the schools coincided, or was contrived to coincide, with a great push for political action in 1800. Elsewhere it was drawn out across the next decade. At Rochdale the children were cold-shouldered at church, but the catechism class was ordered to attend as late as 1807. However, there is no later record of church attendance, and by that date the church was running its own Sunday school which did not collapse till the 'twenties. In Yorkshire, the liturgy and the National Society were often the crux. At Leeds the Methodists in the schools were accustomed to use extempore prayer at the opening and closing of the school sessions, but in 1895 a general meeting of subscribers strictly confined the schools to such portions of the liturgy as the clergy should select. This was a challenge the Methodists were strong enough to resist. By 1806 they had enrolled 2,000 of the children in new premises (Benjamin and Michael Thomas Sadler were superintendents), and annexed the undenominational platform. The new body was known simply as the ' New Sunday School ' and was supported not only by dissenters, but by sympathetic members of the Establishment. At Bingley the erection of a National School under clerical control was the immediate preface to the break-up of Sunday school cooperation. At Almondbury combined Sunday school effort led to the erection of a National School, but then the clergymen forbade the Methodists the usual practices of singing and prayer.

This arbitrary prohibition as might be expected, resulted in disaffection, strife, and ultimately division. Many of the teachers indignant at the insult offered to the hardworking Methodists protested against the injustice. But the protest was unheeded. And as they would not submit to be wholly ignored in the conduct of a school in which they had toiled so patiently and assiduously, they resolved themselves into a committee for the purpose of establishing a purely Methodist school. The children and their parents sympathised to such a degree with the injured party, that, immediately after the division, so few as twelve scholars have been seen marched down from the old National school to the church on the Lord's Day.[30]

The animosities here preserved faithfully portray the movement of opinion away from the Establishment which threatened to empty the church schools in Manchester, and actually emptied them in Stockport and Rochdale; faithfully portrayed too is the futility of insistence upon church order. Precision, so dear to nineteenth-century churchmen, did not enable the Church to hold on to its own, it dislodged it from expanding enterprises.

Bishop Horsley in his charge of 1800 linked together town and country, Sunday schools and itinerant preaching, in one grand charge of Jacobin conspiracy. Driven out of politics since 1795 by the Sedition and Treason Acts, radicalism had taken another course, and hence ' sedition and atheism are the real objects of these institutions rather than religion '. To this night-marish account of the recent religious upheaval, Robert Hall the Baptist replied that the great movement of village preaching arose as a by-product of foreign missions.[31] Both these explanations sought to link the village-preaching with the English response to the French Revolution, and each had seized a portion of the truth.

The Revolution had occasioned the collapse of French power overseas, and in so doing seemed suddenly to have breached the dikes which had contained missionary enterprise for so long; it seemed also to have brought about the downfall of the Papacy in Europe, and with it a shaking of apocalyptic significance. Neither the need nor the opportunity had ever been so great, nor had the response. It was now that the great flowering of undenominational theology took place; the divisions of the past were not merely impossible in the light of modern thought, they were intolerable in view of the opportunities created by the tottering of Anti-Christ. In 1793 the Baptists launched the first formal modern missionary society, and their example stimulated the Independents with a good deal of support from Methodists, Anglicans and others to launch the London Missionary Society in 1795. As men cheerfully shouldered the great missionary burden, denominational divisions seemed to crumble, and in an astonishing degree, national divisions too. Most of the local missionary societies now organised in Scotland became auxiliaries of the London Society, while from Rotterdam and Basel, Zurich and East Friesland, Sweden and Germany, came letters of sympathy, liberal contributions and manpower. The way was open for the amazing career of a man like Steinkopf, stumping England and the continent, linking the English evangelicals with his vast circle abroad in the common causes of the Missionary Society, the Religious Tract Society, the Bible Society. These bodies were a model for the men of the *Erweckungsbewegung* in Germany, itself entering an unconfessional phase; in England they were reinforced by the British and Foreign Schools Society, a battery of undenominational organisations for Ireland, an undenominational press and pulpit exchanges of unheard-of liberality. Methodists in the country often furthered their cause by the use of Baptist premises. There was general euphoria at the end of bigotry and the triumph of Catholic Christianity. William Jay might well think that Our Lord's prayer that his followers might be one had been fulfilled: ' it was not a oneness of opinion, or a ritual oneness: but a oneness of principle and affection, and dependence, and pursuit and co-operation. For this *has* taken place among the real followers of the Lamb, and among them only.'[32]

In the short run the missionary enterprise had a far more powerful impact at home than in the mission field, and it intensified the solvents at work on the old denominational order. Congregations could not fail to perceive that there was a mission field on their doorstep as well as overseas, and, with friends of other denominations, to send out preaching parties into the villages. The enthusiasm generated by missions overseas germinated in soil which had been well prepared. Methodist preachers had long been aware that ' where there is little trade, there is seldom much increase in religion, the people . . . [being] in a state of great bondage to their wealthy landlords '. By the mid-nineties in several counties this bondage had succumbed to the spread of industry and the contagious independence of the sansculottes. A Baptist evangelist reported optimistically in 1796 that many of the Cornish, ' being either miners or fishermen, are more in a state of independence, and less subject to the influence of superiors, who may be hostile to itinerant preaching, than those counties which depend wholly upon agriculture.' The Methodists had proved what could be done with miners. An Anglican incumbent noted that the knitters, stockingers and weavers of the Midlands were free of old forms of dependence, and subject to new ones not organised on a parochial basis:

> The several inhabitants of a parish are rarely united now, as in former times, by a common attachment, as well as dependence upon some one family . . . by which the proper influence of the clergy has been backed and supported . . . The dissolution of parochial union is still more complete where manufactures are established . . . labouring manufacturers . . . often work for a master tradesman in a town at some distance. They have, therefore, little or no connection with their immediate neighbours; and as they frequently reside where they have no settlement, they have not even that species of dependence upon them which is founded on the expectation of parochial relief.

But it was not merely that society permitted new kinds of independence; as dissenters noted, there were politically inspired inducements to take advantage of them.

> The other effect of the French Revolution on the minds of vast multitudes of the people of England is the elimination or extinction of bigotry to a sect . . . The partialities and prejudices especially of the inferior classes have dwindled almost to nothing. It is now a more common idea among them, that it is reasonable everyone should judge for himself in matters of religion. Where no prohibition is issued by the nobleman or squire, they now go more readily to hear a minister of a different denomination from their own . . .

and if they approve of the preacher and his doctrine, they feel less reluctance to become dissenters or Methodists.[33]

The alarming feature of the mid-nineties, however, was the way the tide turned in huge tracts of deep rural England, touched only by industries directly linked with agriculture, and liberally supplied with ecclesiastical plant and manpower. Though owing something to the French example, the evangelical torrent here was discontinuous with urban Jacobinism, and gained its main impetus from the subsistence crisis of 1795. The town of Hull, indeed, entered its course as the evangelical dynamo *par excellence* in 1794; a Methodist cause which had been completely stagnant for twenty-two years suddenly doubled in numbers and set alight the adjacent countryside of the East Riding and Holderness. Lincolnshire did not boast a Hull, but, like the East Riding, was full of the animosities generated by the commercialisation of agriculture so profitable to the Church. In 1799 the Bishop appointed a commission of clergy to discover what had gone wrong in a hundred parishes. It reported that ordinary congregations numbered less than one-third of the people (as low a figure as in Manchester), a proportion of whom were Methodists : communicants were about one-sixth of the adult population. The trouble lay partly in the gradual secularisation of rural society, the business and entertainments which went on on the Lord's Day, and with which the old dissent coped no more vigorously than the Church. The great menace was the new wave of itinerant preaching referred to generally as Methodism, and particularly that turbulent class who were to become known as Ranters, who specialised in cottage prayer meetings and seemed

> to have no point of union, except a determination to calumniate the clergy and revile Establishments. . . . Some of them have pretended to exorcism. . . . They have frequently denounced the reprobation not only of particular persons, and families, but of whole villages; and publicly execrated the churches, as being nothing but a heap of stones.[34]

Clearly the sentiment to which the Primitive Methodists appealed so successfully in Lincolnshire was festering before the Primitive connexion was born; and clearly a religious establishment which appeared to the labourers to be subject to demon possession was in a poor way.

In the south Midlands the old dissent was still alive and responding theologically and in other ways to the new currents. There was a long history here of close relations among the old dissenters, and much grass-roots cooperation among men of the new evangelical ways within and without the Establishment. Indeed just as in the northern Sunday schools the undenominational principle seemed to be taking shape at one growing point of the church order, so in the south Midlands it seemed to be taking shape in the other, the itinerancy. Particularly at Olney and Newport Pagnell in Buckinghamshire a little group of Independents had pulled together with the Anglican evangelical, John Newton, and had created a dissenting academy under William Bull, the Independent minister of the latter town. It was among their friends in the next county of Bedford that the big developments began, and it was Bull who became President of the Bedfordshire Union of Christians in 1797. This circle had taken advantage of the interest aroused by the formation of the London Missionary Society, to organise village preaching. ' Sometimes a Churchman, and Independent and a Baptist, join in the same visit; for it is our happiness in this object, as in that of the Heathen Missions, to lay aside party differences, and to unite in heart and practice for the sake of doing essential good.'[35]

It was soon clear that the early efforts lacked system, there was no planned itinerancy on the Methodist pattern, and it was known that a gospel ministry had not made even occasional contact with more than one village in three in the county. But why should there not be a united and itinerant ministry in Bedfordshire? Late in 1797 the Bedfordshire Union of Christians was formed to create just this. Supported principally by Baptists and Independents, but also by Anglicans, Moravians and Methodists, the Union quickly established an itinerant ministry for 100 towns and villages, and gathered cross-bench Union congregations which still exist in Bedfordshire, practising open communion, and subscribing to both the Baptist and the London Missionary Societies, and pushing the work beyond the county into Huntingdonshire. The Bedfordshire Union, moreover, evoked an immediate response in Warwickshire, where a similar union was established under the influence of Sir Egerton Leigh. Soon afterwards Sir Egerton was ordained to an itinerant ministry, and the dark corners of the county were treated to the prophesyings of a baronet, one regarded in the evangelical literature as 'a signal monument of sovereign grace', though an admittedly dull man.[36]

How nearly the new schemes met the mood or the need of the moment was demonstrated by the speed with which they spread, or were begun on local initiative quite independently of the Bedford plan. Cambridgeshire indeed had created an association to support an itinerancy in February 1795, and the collapse of old loyalties in the following months convinced the preachers that the fields were white already to harvest. In 1797 and 1798 they went forth in hosts to reap. County associations for promoting itinerant evangelism, mostly on an undenominational basis, were set up in Hampshire, Dorset, Wiltshire and the West of England; in Surrey, West Kent, East Kent and Greenwich; while in Berkshire similar work was undertaken by an undenominational Evangelical Society at Reading which quickly gathered four new congregations. There was soon an undenominational association in Worcestershire and Herefordshire, Westmorland early caught the flame, and in 1798 an undenominational Northern Evangelical Society was set up to carry the gospel into the villages of Durham, Northumberland, Cumberland, and Westmorland. In Hull four congregations of Independents, Baptists and Lady Huntingdon's Connexion established an itinerancy in Holderness, gathered a congregation at Hedon, where every Wesleyan attempt had been defeated with violence, and built a meeting-house 'open to ministers of evangelical sentiments of all denominations'.[37]

The undenominational itinerancies in short seem to have been established over most of the country except in Suffolk and Essex where the Baptists and Congregationalists acted independently, and except where the Methodist itinerancy was in process of sweeping the board on its own; in the Methodist areas itinerancies were established on a denominational basis, outside them there was some Methodist support for the rest; and there was least harmony in south Lancashire, an area to become notorious not merely for the politics of class conflict, but for conflict within and between denominations. The itinerancies were speedily reinforced from two sides. The Bedfordshire Union, determined to employ untrained and lay agents, immediately exposed the famine of short model sermons which they might read or copy. George Burder, the celebrated Independent minister of Coventry, met this need with several series of *Village Sermons* which sold like hot cakes, and were supplemented with *Village hymns* and *Village tracts*. No less welcome ammunition came from fund-raising societies in London, both denominational and undenominational.[38]

It was mortifying for the Establishment that after urban Jacobinism had been suppressed an unprecedented tide of itinerant preaching and revival should roll across their rural strongholds. The County Associations incurred the suspicion which fell upon combinations of all kinds, but still worse was the dark shadow of Ranterism which lay behind them. Progressive evangelical dissenters, not to say Wilberforce, bristled at the sight of ' raw ignorant lads going out in preaching parties every Sunday ', but the new and frightening thing was that it was not the preaching which did the damage, but the prayer meetings. So experienced a practitioner as Hugh Bourne, the Primitive Methodist, held that ' too much preaching was appointed, which . . . operated injuriously, preventing the people's gifts from being sufficiently exercised in prayer meetings '.[39] Prayer-meetings for conversions, and for developing the fluency of potential exhorters and local preachers; prayer meetings which excited violent emotion and went on all night, were something new, and differed from the rigidity of the old Wesleyan class meeting as sharply as they did from the liturgy of the Church. Yet they were crucial to the Methodist revival in the West Riding in February and March 1794; they were successfully adapted for promoting revival in towns like Manchester and Leeds; and they transformed the old dissenting prayer meeting from ' a select company of Christians, who excluded others ' to a congregational gathering open to all.[40]

In the country where the supply of preaching was less in both quantity and professional quality than in the towns, the cottage prayer-meeting had to bear the main weight, and even where it was not built up into a great climax as Bourne and Clowes built it up with their ' praying labourers ' on Mow Cop, it had one specially ominous feature. The asset of the lower orders lay in their numbers; these were being welded into a social coherence with some independence of the official management of the parish. It was the secular solidarity of the village community against the upper classes which the prayer-leaders exploited to gain entry to the cottages, and it was the moral pressure of numbers in the prayer-meeting itself which broke down resistance and incorporated one small group after another into the circle of the praying faithful. The prayer-meeting gained its evangelical reputation as the power-house of the Church by virtue of the initiative of quite humble people taking advantage of, and themselves intensifying, a sense of social alienation. The Lincolnshire clergy's report, though defective in terminology, saw clearly enough the menace ' of those more private assemblies, which are generally known by the name of classed [*sic*] meetings, and at which those persons preside who do not take upon themselves the name of Teachers or Preachers.'[41] The meetings which were fully public to the village labourers were ' more private ' to the clergy; their worlds had moved apart.

The Church must act quickly, but the atmosphere of crisis that was built up did not make it easier to find a substitute for Church-and-King mobs. As wiser heads recognised, the problem was a social crisis exploited, but not created, by the evangelicals, and if secularisation, the abuse of the Sabbath, were the trouble, there were plenty of laws to appeal to, and no bench of magistrates was under greater clerical influence than that of Lincolnshire. It was hardly possible to stop people praying in each other's houses, but the flood of itinerant preaching, a thing never contemplated by the Toleration Act, was more vulnerable. The preachers of the Bedfordshire Union might ' particularly pray for the King, for Magistrates and the minister of the parish '; the Methodists might put on displays of loyalty; but they were plainly severing the natural links between the upper and the lower orders at a time when everything else seemed to be conspiring in the same direction, and the organised invasion of other people's parishes was giving openings to Ranterism which might defy any system of control.[42]

At all events a great howl was put up against the hazards of itinerancy, beginning in Wiltshire and Hampshire, going on to the south Midlands, and fetching up with the Lincolnshire inquiry, pressure in the *Anti-Jacobin*, and Bishop Horsley's charge, a howl designed to replace the broken weapon of brute force with legal authority to act. With the axe about to fall on dissenting itinerancies, itinerancy by Anglican evangelicals not unnaturally ceased, though hardly from the simple-minded attachment to church order attributed to them by Canon Smyth; episcopal pressure made it impossible for those not deeply pledged to minister in unconsecrated premises to do so. So irregular a man as Sir Richard

Hill took fright at the 'mischief, discord, disputings, vain jangling and confusion' arising from preaching on a less than regular basis, and refused to assist a Sunday school without 'the fullest proof that the teachers were perfectly well affected to our establishment in Church and State'.[43]

Throughout 1799 and over the following winter, Pitt's old tutor, Pretyman-Tomline, the Bishop of Lincoln, was pressing the government to take legislative action, and early in 1800 Michael Angelo Taylor, MP for Durham, was known to be preparing a bill to restrict itinerancy by giving magistrates a discretion to withhold licences to dissenting preachers. The whole fate of the Sunday schools and itinerant preachers was by now in the balance, and it is still not entirely clear why neither of the bills came into the House. Three factors seem to have operated. The Bishop of Lincoln plied the government with his clergy's report, but the reaction of the Grenville family was thoroughly Josephinist; in their view what was needed was a reinvigoration of the parish system, and the removal of the financial and other obstacles which at present prevented the bishops' enforcing clerical residence. Certainly if punitive measures against the itinerants were to wait on the ending of clerical absenteeism, a long struggle was in prospect. At the same time, Wilberforce, fearing that the measure might interfere with the private gatherings of the evangelicals, was keeping up a counter-pressure on Pitt, and Michael Angelo Taylor, subject to threats from his dissenting constituents and blandishments from his election agent, John Ward, the leading Methodist in Durham, dropped his bill. Moreover the crisis for the itinerants coincided exactly with that of the Act of Union with Ireland, and it was no doubt difficult for Pitt to ask simultaneously for Catholic emancipation and restricted toleration for dissent. No doubt Anti-Christ contributed to the salvation of Vital Christianity, and so did the Archbishop of Canterbury, who wanted the augmentation of livings but resisted the enforcement of residence.[44]

Though the Toleration Act had been preserved by a whisker, the writing had been on the wall for the itinerants, 'provoked' it was reported,

1 By the general aspect of the times menacing thrones and altars. 2 By the manner in wh. too many dissenters and a

few Meths. have entered into the politics of the world. 3 The union in missions and village preaching wh. has lately spread much among dissenters, and wh. in a few years will certainly strengthen them very much. Distrusting their politics the government fears their religion. 4 The Meths. who have been considered a handful of well-meaning enthusiasts, begin now to draw the attention of government as a numerous and increasing body. Lastly, they fear if some check is not given a few years will carry us back to the days of Cromwell.[45]

Moreover Church reform had gone the same way as the government's projected reform of the police, and most of the fiscal reforms pressed by the Select Committee on Finance which reported in 1799; the Church had reached its turning point and failed to turn. Even more decisively than in the Sunday school world, the Church in the name of order had forfeited its foothold in the new ways without seriously inhibiting any of its competitors. Moreover the great dream of united effort, though not ended, had suffered irreparable damage. The Church had tried to strike down the dissenters, and had revived a high and exclusive doctrine of episcopacy; dissenters must now act in self-defence. The Wesleyan Conference created a committee to ' guard [their] religious privileges in these perilous times ', and the London dissenting ministers did likewise, with devastating effect when Sidmouth moved against itinerancy in 1811. Conflict was forcing new denominational organisation into being. Moreover another twist had been given to the screw of evangelical pietism, and an old equivocation underlined. R. W. Dale later charged the evangelicals of this period with being insufficiently political; part of their defence must be that they were threatened with the loss of their basic rights of prayer and preaching. With those potent weapons, they proceeded to the ruin of the Church as a national establishment, with all the political consequences that entailed. And, as we shall see, the preservation of the Toleration Act enabled the same weapons to be used for the spiritual, theological and administrative reconstruction of dissent.

3 The Defeat of Establishment in Church and Dissent

The failure of Pitt's government to put a brake on the Church's rivals was a foretaste of things to come; in the next generation high churchmen felt repeatedly betrayed by the politicians in whom they put their trust, until the whole Establishment seemed likely to go down in the crisis of Reform. How rapidly the situation deteriorated, the first dozen years of the century were to show. Wholesale abstention from the public worship of the Establishment became a matter of general comment. Methodism and dissent were booming, and the bishop of Chester admitted privately that

> the established religion cannot exist much longer in the country; and I think the line from Manchester through Yorkshire to Richmond, the extremity of my diocese, will convince anyone of this truth who shall pass it on horseback. I wish that Dissenters may not now be the majority in that tract.

Nor was there any mistaking the political consequences, for ' every addition [separatism] makes to the number of its supporters, alters the proportion existing in the country between the monarchical and democratic spirit '.[1]

Establishment was bereft of any policy except the restriction of itinerant preaching. Already in 1802, one of the hottest Methodist sacramentarians was wondering if separation from the Church could be put into reverse as the price of saving itinerancy. The incumbent of Lenham, Kent, pressed upon the Primate in 1806 that

> novelty and itinerancy are the grand buttress by which . . . [Methodism] is supported. They should be taken away and the *shepherds of Methodism* confined to one *fold*. Their flocks

would soon be surfeited with the *dry husks* and *washy garbage* with which they are fed, and return to the fold which is *nutritiatary* and *imperishable*. . . .

With this in view Anglican apologists continued to declaim against enthusiasm and the conspiratorial hazards of the County Associations, and to whip up exaggerated loyalism—even the prophecies in *Old Moore's Almanack* were supposed to have been rigged by disloyal Methodists. By 1809 success seemed within their grasp, and the Huddersfield clergy were ' rejoicing . . . that Methodist preachers will soon be silenced and that Methodism will be intirely overthrown '.[2]

The new saviour of the clergy was to be the earl of Sidmouth, who had been pushed into action by the Bishop of Gloucester. He was now collecting information about the utter inadequacy of many of the itinerant preachers with a view to legislation and dividing the forces of dissent. Thomas Belsham, one of the aggressive younger Unitarian leaders, agreed that ' for an ignorant booby who can neither read nor write, to demand to qualify as a dissenting minister, and for such a man to assume the office of a Christian teacher is an insult upon common sense and common decency '. But the Methodists were the crux. Their whole system was built on itinerancy, and two of their most important leaders, Thomas Coke and Adam Clarke, proved susceptible to Sidmouth's persuasion. Excitable and unstable, Coke cherished fond hopes of episcopal ordination for his brethren. In 1801, when things were past their worst, he kept writing to the Home Secretary warning him of disaffection among the working classes; posing to government as an expert on the popular pulse and to the preachers as an habitué of the great, Coke seems to have deceived no one but his biographer, and was an obvious candidate for Sidmouth's blandishments. Adam Clarke was of altogether finer stuff, but was betrayed by the very simplicity of character which endeared him to many humble Methodists. Moreover, he had to justify himself against the vicious hostility of many of the preachers. For Adam Clarke was the polymath of the connexion; his scholarship exposed him to the jealousy of ministers with intellectual pretensions, and made it hard for him to travel with his brethren. To complete his valuable eight-volume scripture commentary it was desirable that he should be settled within reach

E

of the London libraries; in 1808 he became editor of Rymer's
Foedera under the Record Commission, and for a time was
Librarian of the Surrey Institution. If the rule of itinerancy was
breached for Adam Clarke, could it be maintained against lesser
mortals? Even responsible men believed that secular scholarship
put him in serious spiritual hazard—' floods of literary applause
rush upon him in all directions. The great and noble commend,
perhaps flatter him.' Clarke's own letters make it sadly clear that
the good man was susceptible to flattery, the more so because
of a vein of pessimism. Convinced that the inveterate enemy of
Methodism was the Bishop of Lincoln, Clarke was only too ready
to believe that his work for the Record Commission gave him
access to the political interest of the Speaker, and that even Sidmouth was defending the true interests of Methodism against
subversion by the bishops. At all events Sidmouth cajoled Coke
and Clarke into giving full support to his bill in advance and
advocating it before the Wesleyan Committee of Privileges.[3]

Sidmouth seemed wise in his choice of moment as well as
of the men. Since 1809 when he first took up the question, the
Midland counties had been sliding into loom-breaking and Luddism, and, when he introduced his bill in May 1811, troops had
been drafted in and the disturbances seemed to be approaching
their peak. Moreover the troubled areas were drawing Primitive
Methodist missions into broader pasture than the Potteries could
ever provide. Deference was collapsing all round. The bill provided toleration for ministers of separate dissenting congregations, for regular itinerants of the Methodist kind who should
be certified to Quarter Sessions by householders as ' of sober life
and conversation, and of sufficient ability to preach or teach and
officiate.' But for the ranters, the ' raw lads ', even perhaps for the
respectable element among the Wesleyan lay preachers, there was
to be no toleration at all. Yet Sidmouth had miscalculated. The
dissenters had alerted their machinery in the country more than
a year before. The old organisations, the Protestant Dissenting
Deputies, and the Ministers of the three dissenting denominations,
brought in protests by the shoal, while John Wilks got up a
mixed movement of evangelical dissenters and Methodists, which
as the Protestant Society became his permanent star vehicle.[4]

Still more striking was the revolt of the Wesleyans, who immediately sent a deputation headed by Thomas Thompson, a

Methodist MP, to press Sidmouth to withdraw his bill. The main-spring of this reaction was a London solicitor who acted regularly for the connexion, Thomas Allan, a man forgotten by history, ill-paid and often worse-used by the little knot of London minis-sters who provided most of what central administration Methodism then had, yet revealed by his papers to have been perhaps the most valuable servant of the connexion in that day. A scholar by instinct, Thomas Allan left a theological library to Conference which bore comparison with those of Dr Williams and Sion Col-lege; yet as a local preacher ' he would only officiate in the work-houses and small chapels, delighting mostly to address Gospel truth to the poor, the aged, the infirm, the friendless and the afflicted '. At the 1810 Conference Allan presented to Jabez Bunt-ing, the rising star of the connexion, a memorandum calling for major reorganisation in four important departments of Methodist life, the financing and administration of the missions, the selec-ting and training of preachers, the spiritual instruction of Metho-dist children, and ' 4th . . . the situation of the Methodists with the Legislature '. This programme constituted Bunting's life work, and in it Allan called the connexion urgently to anticipate Sidmouth's charges, and organise to meet them in advance.[5]

Allan was professionally aware that pillars of the Establishment were seeking not merely to change the law, but in a real and desperate sense to take it into their own hands. In Gibraltar, the West Indies and Jersey, efforts were being made to deprive Metho-dists of rights they had long supposed they had, and in England their lay and itinerant preachers came increasingly under the scrutiny of the magistrates. Even before Sidmouth moved his bill, magistrates who had been understood to have no power to refuse a licence duly requested by a dissenting preacher, began to do so, and in 1811 there was even a prosecution under the Con-venticle Act for holding a prayer meeting in a private house. But when the crisis broke, Allan was in touch with the dissenters and the parliamentary opposition, was ready to interview Spencer Perceval to get the bill withdrawn, and if he failed, to get up an elaborate agitation in the country.[6]

Bunting also did his share, displaying none of the toryism or denominational narrowness in which he was to glory in his prime. He set Richard Watson, who at this stage in his career had

forsaken Wesleyanism for the New Connexion, to write a celebrated letter to the *Manchester Exchange Herald* addressed 'To the
Protestant Dissenters of Manchester and its Vicinity', and himself put ferocious resolutions through his District Meeting declaring the bill 'erroneous in principle, unconstitutional in its spirit
. . . no modification of it can reconcile us to its adoption'.[7] In
any case provincial Methodists shared the suspicion of compromising men in London which characterised every extra-parliamentary
movement in the nineteenth century. John Ward, a Durham
Methodist solicitor, independently enrolled the sceptical Lord
Holland to lead the cause, beat up six votes in the Commons, and
demanded wrecking tactics if the worst should happen.

> I will in that case collect all our class leaders, local preachers
> & prayer leaders throughout our country (an 'exceeding great
> army') & we will go in a body to our Sessions (I John Ward
> the younger at their head) & take the oaths at once. Thus instead
> of *hundreds* there will be *thousands* of dissenting preachers in
> the Kingdom. So much for the policy of intolerant laws! &
> the wisdom of aristocratic statesmen!

John Ward's Durham militants coveted 'the honour of being the
Confessors, if not the *Martyrs* of the Truth', nor were they
alone. One eminent preacher, Charles Atmore, topped off a new
edition of Samuel Chandler's *History of Persecution* with the
sufferings of Wesley and Lord Sidmouth's bill; another, Richard
Reece, improved Foxe's *Martyrs* with menaces of his own.
Christianity was

> naturally and necessarily subversive of injustice existing any-
> where. Christianity is not subversive of trade, or learning, or
> government, but of the injustice which mankind incorporate
> with them; yet it may impoverish a merchant, or subvert the
> throne of a monarch.[8]

Under pressure like this Coke collapsed, and drafted a petition
against the bill in his own hand, while Adam Clarke sought to
make his peace with Sidmouth privately, and discovered conscientious objections to declaring himself a dissenting minister, though
he must have been perfectly aware that the Toleration Act had
never protected any but dissenting ministers. Having failed to get
Sidmouth to withdraw his bill, the Committee of Privileges

whipped up 30,000 signatures against it in record time, many more petitions being cut short by the failure of the bill in Parliament.[9]

The next blow to Sidmouth was opposition from within the Church and government itself, opposition which illustrated again the great fragmentation of power in England. Wilberforce entered the fray once more, insisting upon security for Anglicans to ' meet together for devotional exercises without declaring themselves dissenters '. This seemed to Sidmouth's high-church biographers to smell of very indifferent churchmanship indeed, though Sidmouth's own papers reveal the high-church hysteria which Wilberforce was up against. In Plymouth Dock, it was complained, only one of the Anglican daughter chapels was orthodox. ' The Rector of the Parish is . . . *totally deaf,* so as not to hear the report of a cannon, though he might feel the shock,' and employed an evangelical curate who was hand in glove with the dissenters.

> . . . the only compleat mode of giving them a curb, at the same time checking desertion from the Church of England by its unworthy ministers is to convoke a Synod of Bishops (by Majesty as Head of the Church), and deprive those turbulent malevolent spirits of their stalking horse, viz. the 39 articles, by diligently examining them, and expunging all such parts as appear to have danger, and which so highly gratify those selectors of Bible sentences. When the obnoxious parts are removed by regal authority, let all Bishops and clergy under them, swear to the performance of the *new* Articles, or . . . relinquish all clerical benefice . . .[10]

This was conservative revolution indeed. Moreover, the government had both social and parliamentary inducements to withdraw from the brink. Methodism and Ranterism had doubtless contributed to the unsettled state of society, but with Luddism going full blast, official Methodism was a force of social order, and it was absurd to provoke it to attitudes of martyrdom. Equally, the government had just survived the first rocky days of the Regency, and Liverpool was bent on reconstituting the party of Mr Pitt, and frustrating the Whigs, on a largely Protestant basis. By this line the forces of dissent were shrewdly divided; henceforth they contended against their disabilities under rival liberal and

Protestant banners. ' Lord Liverpool ', it was reported, ' is allowed to have put the extinguisher on the business ', and the second reading of Sidmouth's bill was negatived without discussion. The second threat to the Toleration Act had ended in public disaster. Dissenters and Methodists were cock-a-hoop, though the wiser of them recognised that the immediate result was simply to shift the field of battle.[11]

For preachers everywhere found themselves prevented from taking the oaths under the Toleration Act at Quarter Sessions. Thomas Allan summarized the situation thus:

1. Appleby. Westmorland. Qur. Sessions.
   a. Magistrates would not administer the oaths unless application were made thro counsel. (This is an expense and contrary to the Act.)
   b. They refused to administer the oaths because the Preacher was not the only person who preached to the congregation at *Brough*.
   c. Witnesses of the appointment to preach were also refused, but written appointment required.

   The above magistrates were chiefly clergymen, 5 out of 8, a clergyman in the chair. The lay magistrates would have administered the oaths.

2. Beverley. Yorkshire. Qur. Sessions.

   Preacher refused because he had not a *separate* congregan. A thing never mentioned in the Toleration Act.

3. Ipswich Quarter Sessions.

   Preachers refused because they had not separate congregations.

4. Hereford Quarter Sessions.

   Oaths refused without certificate from a separate congregation. (Clergyman on the bench very energetic in the refusal.)

5. Leicester Quarter Sessions.

   Preachers refused the first day because they had not Certificates. Went home 12 miles & came next morning & presented Certificates from congregations by 10 o'clock—were kept till 12 o'clock and then told it was too late. They remonstrated that their certificates were delivered two hours, they were then told that they could not take the oaths, not having separate congregations. Were later told they might apply to King's Bench. (Many of the magistrates were clergymen.)

6. Lincoln Qur. Sessions.
Preachers refused the oaths because they preached to more congregations than one. The magistrates said they might apply to the Court of K. Bench.

7. Malton (Yorkshire) Qur. Sessions.
Preachers refused oaths because they had not separate congregations. (The magistrates who were clergymen were the only persons who interfered).

8. Manchester.
Preachers refused oaths on two grounds.
1. Because they preached to more than one congregation.
2. Because more than one preacher officiated to the same congregation at different times.

9. Spilsby (Lincolnshire) Qur. Sessions.
Preacher refused because he was not confined to one congregation.

10. Stafford Qur. Sessions.
Preachers refused because not confined to one congreg. &c. . . . Were told they might apply to Court of K. Bench.

11. Oakham (Rutland) Qur. Sessions.
Preacher refused because he preached to more than one congregation. The Magistrates said the law was *now altered.* The preacher was told if he brought a certificate of his preacher to only one congregation and no other person preached there, he would have a certificate, but if he preached otherwise, *he would be taken up as a vagabond.*

12. Aylesbury (Bucks) Qur. Sessions.
Preachers refused because only 8 persons signed their testimonial, and because the Meeting House was not particularly described in the petition, altho' a copy of its register was produced.

13. Kirton (Lincolnshire) Qur. Sessions.
Preachers refused the oaths because they had not exclusive congregations. Lament that clergymen are thus prejudiced.[12]

The clergy had grounds for that stiff distrust of the parliamentary supremacy which characterised them increasingly over the next generation, and were clearly determined to make a fight of it while their power lasted on the county bench. In all sorts of ways the law was being stretched and twisted, and but for the huge sums raised by John Wilks' Protestant Society for litigation, itinerant preaching would have been killed in some places. The Wesleyan Committee of Privileges, which liked to pose as a pillar of the *status quo*, complained bitterly that 'their religious practices [were incessantly] traduced and vilified, and they themselves represented as *vermin fit only to be destroyed*', that the legislature was being pressed to put down evangelical religion as 'inimical to public security and morals',[13] that there was a growing disposition to enforce the Conventicle Act; and they did not know what to do.

Thomas Allan, who was throughout in touch with the dissenters, now saved the day by a direct approach to Spencer Perceval, a Prime Minister of evangelical sympathies, who had opposed Sidmouth's bill the previous year. In a skilfully conducted interview, Allan played not only the Protestant line, but also what is commonly regarded as the Halévy line, that 'among colliers, miners and mechanics, Methodism had been the grand instrument of preserving subordination'. To this approach Perceval responded kindly, promising legislation to meet the case, and Allan submitted a draft bill of his own. Two days later, Perceval was dead, shot by a madman;[14] but the coalition, which had been built up around him, had no intention of letting his successor, Liverpool, off the hook. Allan bargained hard with him, personally lobbied all the leading members of both houses, and finally got the government to push through his own Toleration Bill. The Conference of 1812 uttered a heartfelt thanksgiving and warned the flock against 'dissimulation of evil-disposed men', such as the northern Luddites.[15] The following year, William Smith, the leader of the Protestant Dissenting Deputies, obtained an act which legalised the holding of Unitarian views, and enabled English Presbyterians to fly their true colours. Neither of these acts was trouble-free[16], but they enabled the new religious and social forces of the age to work themselves out. They emphasised that though the state would still help the Church, it would not save the day for it. Before Peterloo the English Church was finished as a working establishment in the traditional European sense, but no one yet noticed that the social forces which had led to this result had also taken the heart out of the old-established dissent.

For the English Presbyterians and the Quakers had a similar experience to the Church, a long period of slow decline succeeded by sudden crisis, and reacted in a similar way. The Presbyterians and Quakers had each been somewhat ' undenominational ' communities, the one looking first to a more comprehensive Establishment, and then to the application of enlightened reason to religion, the other supporting a plea for the liberty of the Spirit by a strict Society discipline. It was entirely in keeping that the one sought to halt apparently inexorable decline by throwing up new barriers of doctrine, the other by intensifying discipline.

For fifteen years after 1809 the Unitarians were continuously engaged in painful reappraisal of their unmistakable decay, without being able to distinguish the short from the long-term factors, or the cumulative consequences of decline from its immediately operative causes. It did not help to hark back to the perennial weakness of Independent organisation, nor to sermons so learned that they were thought to be preached in Latin, nor even to the hazards awaiting the social climbers.

> Our grandmothers, who enveloped their persons in stuffs and woollens, were proof against a degree of cold and moisture which would be certain death to the half-clad females of the present generation . . . [and] where the females are prevented from attending public worship, we seldom observe much regularity in the other parts of the family.[17]

In all the tightly knit congregations of dissent there was a considerable risk of separations arising from personal animosity, but cantankerous Presbyterians, unlike Independents or Baptists, did not form new communities of the same denomination when they seceded. Old Presbyterian families had evidently lost their grip on their principles, no doubt because ministers had for so long disguised their progress into heterodoxy by preaching on practical and uncontroversial topics; congregations knew that they were not Presbyterian in polity or doctrine, and no more. Leading men like Lant Carpenter at Bristol began to recommend ' a total separation from trinitarian worship, and . . . societies in which no ambiguous phraseology shall be admitted, but *strict caution* be observed that the prayers, hymns, and every part of the worship shall be *strictly* unitarian', including of course the use of the new Unitarian version of the New Testament.[18]

So public a proclamation of the party line had to wait on William Smith's Toleration Act of 1813, but there was evidence that openly and aggressively Unitarian congregations were doing well, and were immune to secession.

A new race has arisen, which has discarded, in a great measure, the indifference of the people on whose ruins they have stood. These have principles well defined, properly valued, and of confessed importance . . . they have . . . arrived at definite conclusions and distinct views . . . around which those may assemble who daily leave the labyrinth of old opinions.

In various towns the Unitarians had ' the genteelest meeting in the place', and attracted new men on the make in business, often immigrants with no old-Presbyterian roots, who imparted new vigour to the decaying cause. They called ministers who had come into the denomination precisely because it was Unitarian, and whose preaching had a new polemical edge. There were the ex-Anglicans, Lindsey, Jebb and Disney; ex-Independents like Priestley, Belsham, Wellbeloved and W. J. Fox; ex-Baptists like Joshua Toulmin, Robert Robinson, William Vidler, Robert Aspland, and Richard Wright; ex-Methodists like Joseph Cooke. Men of this kind were happy by the latter years of the Napoleonic wars to proclaim that Presbyterianism was not merely decayed, but dead; they partially reconstructed the denomination, creating machinery for political defence and home missions; they propagated their faith in some completely new places, and secured some following amongst working-men; they had an eagerness for controversy which upset staid congregations like Renshaw Street, Liverpool, where doctrinal brawling smacked too much of the evangelical fanaticism they abhorred. ' Show yourselves decidedly to be of a party ', was their motto.[19]

That Unitarianism had any future at all owed much to the zeal and toughness of the new men, yet their diagnosis of the old-Presbyterian problem was superficial, and their prescription was repudiated in the next generation. James Martineau, Hamilton Thom, and J. J. Tayler looked on the polemical narrowness of their predecessors much as Newman and his friends regarded the Protestant high-churchmen; they found them ' dry '. Too much doctrine and too little faith, too much knowledge and too little mystery, seemed to them the mark of the recent past, and ' renouncing a dogmatic theology, [they] look[ed] for salvation in the *spirit* of Christ himself, wrought into the believing soul ', and craved that ' the grand poetry of the Bible should be brought home to their feelings, and rendered additionally impressive by the blended recommendation of solemn music and holy song '. They were also deeply disturbed by the class character of English church attendance, and from the mid-thirties energetically pressed the Domestic Mission policies which originated with Joseph Tuckermann in Boston, Mass. The truth was that the Unitarians were hit more cruelly than the Church by the social tension which succeeded the Revolution; only partially successful as an antidote, the 'rage for purely doctrinal preaching' was, by the 'thirties, everywhere in retreat before a ' more-earnest and affectionate preaching of the life-giving spirit of the gospel to the conscience and the heart ', which had once seemed the hallmark of evangelicalism.[20]

Early in the eighteenth century Presbyterian congregations had embraced a fair cross-section of society from the titled downwards, and although families of rank deserted the dissenting cause as the political system settled down, it could be remarked as late as 1818 that ' the poor no longer crowd the aisles as formerly, and even the pews seem swept by a whirlwind ', as if this was a matter of relatively recent history. But the Church-and-King mobs drove the timorous among the affluent into the arms of the Church; and when radicalism infected the town artisans, and revival swept the countryside, the poor had more exciting options than crowding Presbyterian aisles. The Unitarian élite did not spare their poorer brethren, and had a vivid sense of being on the social escalator.

Among a people of this character and condition, taste and refinement, which were diffused with rapidity within this period, found ardent cultivators. It was the same in the established church. Both sects outran the multitude, and were in a great measure abandoned by them, who were too much distanced to continue the race. The establishment was not so much deserted as these dissenters. Its splendour created an attachment not easily sacrificed. Its ministers shackled by settled creeds had not departed so far as their presbyterian brethren from the gross corruptions of the rude community.

By the end of the war, many of the industrial centres of the West where Unitarians had been strong were in decay, ' the lower ranks of life' had ceased to worship in the London Presbyterian congregations, and though there was still a fringe in the North, they were not heard of after the early 'twenties. Even where locally the Unitarians were the ' government' as they were at the end of the eighteenth century in Nottingham Corporation, their liberal politics could not undo the effects of their social conservatism. The challenge to Unitarianism at both ends of the social spectrum in this generation was piquantly illuminated in the next. James Martineau believed that there were two ways of reaching the poor, either through their senses (a way open to Catholics but not to Unitarians) or their affections. The Liverpool Domestic Mission should provide a man of talent to live with the poor, help them to discover their neglected abilities, become respectable citizens, develop tastes which would lead to a spontaneous demand for a church. Christian love, in short, should put the poor on the same escalator as the rich. The prosperous, alas! were as difficult to keep to this programme as the poor; in the 'thirties, as in the 'nineties, good times played on their hopes and bad upon their fears. As J. J. Tayler saw it in the Chartist upheaval of 1839:

> The Church acts upon the scattered and disunited ranks of the Unitarian body, with a more absorbing influence than on any other class of Dissenters, because a large proportion of its members are brought by their birth and connexions within the attraction of that magic circle of fashion and rank, whose fascination the aristocratical constitution of English society renders almost resistless . . . Even over minds of a nobler order the Church at the present crisis exercises no feeble sway . . . as the only effective bulwark against the encroachment of domestic barbarism.[21]

The new horizontal stratification of English society had deprived the Unitarians first of their popular following, and then of their social function.

It was much the same story with the Society of Friends, whose special rights under the Toleration and Marriage Acts, and informal exemption from church rates in places like Manchester, constituted them the most privileged dissenting establishment of all. Fellow-dissenters regarded Quakers as greedy, and noted how the new commercial opportunities seduced some of them from their old testimony against suing at law; but they tolerantly admitted that 'the system of most other sects allows a wider range of concupiscence. . . . A Quaker, therefore, who loves money something more than these followers of divers lusts and pleasures, may not be inferior to them in virtue or principle'. Nevertheless the general threat to property took the heart out of maintaining 'the peculiarities' against other religious bodies. Statistics of Quaker decline are scanty, but tell their own tale. In 1785 the Wiltshire Monthly Meeting comprised 11 meetings, in 1800, 7; in 1827, 3; in 1828, 2. Between 1800 and 1850 the Quakers lost about a third of their national strength; how much more they lost in the 'nineties is not known. The Society's one hope of survival in a world being sharply divided on other lines seemed to be to separate itself as far as possible by screwing up its peculiar observances. Yet the exercise of discipline not merely reduced the numbers, it showed that the Society was not keeping its distance from the world. In the Warwickshire North Monthly Meeting admissions exceeded disownments in every decade before that of 1780-90, but from then onwards the haemorrhage increased apace, and from 1800 to 1850 there were 45 admissions and 170 disownments. The key indicator of absorption in the world lay in disownments for marrying out of the Society; for 119 marriages in Warwickshire North in the second half of the eighteenth century there were 37 disownments for marrying out; for the next half century the figures were 155 and 84. From 1800 to 1852 Darlington meeting produced only 87 admissions against 104 disownments, and between 1800 and 1819 made only three admissions. In Darlington, as in a number of other meetings, disownments for marrying out were about equal to disownments from all other causes put together. And of course the discipline effectively deterred any infusion of new leadership from the outside such as reinvigorated the Unitarians.[22]

Yet there were Friends, as there were Unitarians, who perceived the springs of new life in a kind of naturalised evangelicalism, and under the leadership of J. J. Gurney an evangelical Quakerism grew up in the 'twenties. The whole issue was sharpened by the Hicksite disruption among the American Quakers in 1827, and 'that desolating heresy which has lately swept thousands after thousands . . . into the gulf of Hicksism and Deism '. The English Yearly Meeting of 1829 replied to the Hicksites with a formal profession of faith in the inspiration of scripture, but the domestic circumstances of the Society invited the question whether free-lance Quaker mysticism could ever square with an authoritative witness to revelation in scripture as understood by evangelicals. The challenge was bluntly put by Isaac Crewdson, a minister of the Manchester meeting, and a man much concerned to promote piety among young men.

> Between mysticism and the religion of Christ there is this essential difference—the former is chiefly a religion of *feelings,* the latter is a religion of *faith,* for it is founded on the *testimony of the Spirit of God* transmitted to us in Holy Scripture. . . . Setting up the light within as ' the primary rule of faith and practice ', we believe, lay at the very root of Hicksism; and the depreciation of the scriptures, (or as it was artfully termed, SETTING THEM IN THEIR RIGHT PLACE) followed as the baneful and inevitable consequence of this unscriptural doctrine.

The Crewdson family and many of their sympathisers could not stand their ground against the vehement reaction this pamphlet evoked. The Crewdsons sought baptism at the fashionable Mosley-street Independent Chapel, and established an Evangelical Friends Meeting House to maintain fellowship while they each pondered their future. Before long the chapel was sold to the Baptists, the Crewdsons themselves approaching the undenominational Union Chapel, Oxford Road, for the privilege of occasional communion without membership. The undenominational tradition might provide a home for the Crewdsons, but the Friends, having drawn the line against the Hicksites on the one side and the evangelicals on the other, were narrower and more denominational than ever. The Quaker *enfants terribles* of the next generation, men like John Bright (who was deeply hurt by the disownment of his sister Priscilla for marrying out) and John Stephenson Rowntree, were to call fiercely for liberalisation. Easier discipline helped the Society to regain some lost ground, but as long as the forces which had separated prosperous Friends from their old popular following dammed the free movement of the Spirit within the Society, there could be no fundamental change of fortune.

Instead . . . of deciding all questions in these meetings by the ordinary mode of voting . . . they have adopted the singular one of deciding by weight, that is, by the dicta of the weighty Friends, who for the most part are men of weighty purses too . . . Thus is the government of the society thrown into the hands of an oligarchy of the most dangerous kind.[23]

The decline of the Quakers was to be even sharper and less capable of remedy than that of the Unitarians.

It was now a question whether religious revival, which had profited so handsomely from the crisis of the 'nineties which had proved ruinous to the old religious establishments, was a sufficient antidote to a recurrence of social tension.

4 The New Dissent and its Problems 1800-1820

The Independent and the Baptist denominations caught the tide which the Presbyterians and the Quakers missed, but they did so at the expense of internal struggles and the loss of characteristic old traditions. In 1814, the *Methodist Magazine,* having condemned the Socinians out of hand, proceeded to distinguish clearly between the new and the old among the dissenters.

1. Those who have little but the form of godliness.
2. Those who have both the form and the power of it.
1. Among those who are nearly sunk into a form, without the power of godliness, there is a great degeneracy respecting family religion . . . a vast crowd of old dissenters who have some light into the doctrines of the gospel, are living totally without family worship. . . . Their ministers often dwell on the most important truths of Christianity, with much clearness. But if they can drink, and sport, and trifle with their ungodly hours, we cannot look for better fruit.
[2] But all are not lost. . . . The holy flame is burning, may we trust it is increasing in strength and clearness. . . . Holy Presbyterians, Independents, Baptists (one in Christ), unite to teach, to warn all they can. . . . Watched over by zealous and affectionate pastors, they are instructed in relative duties with great minuteness. They are regular in reading the scriptures, and in family prayer; their sabbaths are sacredly appropriated to public, family and closet devotion.[1]

It could hardly be more squarely put that, to the new movements of opinion, the ways of the old dissent were as unpalatable as those of the old Establishment, and must, in present circumstances, lead to paralysis. For the old Independency was in decline as obviously as the old Presbyterianism.[2]

The more clear it became that the mission of the day was not
so much to gather the saints out of a corrupt church as to convert sinners out of the world, the harder it was to maintain the
full independence of congregations or denominations. The utility
of undenominational associations like those which spawned forth
for village preaching in the late 'nineties, and multiplied for
every purpose in the new century, was not to be gainsaid, and
they revived a corporate existence among dissenters. Yet to those
for whom congregational independency had a symbolic status,
or who dreaded the risks involved in liberalising the old Calvinism, there was no doubt that the pass was being sold. Rowland
Hill, an apostle of the new ways, thought that Independency
had ' a natural tendency to create a contracted spirit ', and regretted
that Whitefield ' did not frame a liberal and open connexion ';
the modern Independents were ' very different in several points
of view from the *stricter* Independents of an earlier date '. The
conservative Walter Wilson agreed entirely, and abhorred not
merely the new pietism, but the whole evangelical syndrome.

> Within the last twenty years, a spurious candour has sprung
> up, to which principle has been sacrificed. . . . The great
> mass of modern dissenters have thrown all their weight in the
> hands of nondescript persons, who are more remarkable for
> their religious zeal, than for its judicious application; and
> who direct their energies to the execution of schemes as wild
> in their nature as they are unproductive. By giving way so
> much to that laxity of principle and indiscriminate zeal which
> distinguish the Methodists, dissenters have lost that peculiarity
> of character for which their forefathers were so eminent. . . .
> The true spirit of nonconformity has been dead by at least
> one generation; and its present representatives, I believe, con-
> sider it a happy omen for their age of liberality. . . . Dis-
> senters of former days have been greatly blamed for not possess-
> ing what is called a ' missionary spirit '. . . . It is true they
> did not beat up a crusade in the religious world for the wild
> purpose of proselyting the savage Hottentot, or the untutored
> islander, but they conducted plans of instruction for the rising
> generation of their countrymen which turned to infinitely better
> account. . . .

Yet even Wilson could not return to the past, and urged congrega-

F

tionalists to keep a foothold of authority for the old upper crust, by adopting a Presbyterian system.

> Notwithstanding the faults that are discernible in the Church of England, and the just exceptions that are taken to diocesan episcopacy, yet the *respectable part of the community* will sooner submit to them than to mob government. It is a notorious fact that our congregations exhibit a dearth of society to well-educated persons, that has a strong tendency to drive them from their communion. . . .[3]

Here, in a denomination being transformed by rural revival, was a refusal to hold communion with the lower orders, the obverse of that so vehemently expressed by Methodist artisans in the mid-'nineties.

It was in fact the evangelicals who developed an institutional superstructure for the Independents; County Unions were revived or developed from village preaching associations,[4] and the London Missionary Society acted as a sort of denominational union, until efforts to form a Congregational Union succeeded in 1831. The Union did not at first amount to much, and in the counties the Independents were hard put to to support a church-based and an itinerant ministry as well;[5] but conservatives could not mistake the religious implications of the changes, and waxed violent that

> any class or order of men in the kingdom should *dare* to erect themselves into a society for . . . exterminating doctrines which in *their* judgments are unsound, and introducing—by means of agents or emissaries—a certain system of religious belief, which they arrogantly pronounce to be the only true faith . . . when its casuists, in a far greater part, are block-heads, tainted with the mania of preaching without a single requisite that should fit them for that high and important distinction . . . a bloated race of lay priests . . . can we see this and not ask ourselves, are these untaught mechanics to be our dictators?[6]

For the 'untaught mechanics', though awakened by the evangelical doctrine of the person and the work of Christ, had never learned the old notion of the union of the pure church of the saints with Christ himself, and were constrained by the times to reverse the role of the Church in the work of salvation. In the seventeenth century it had been possible to assume that God would see to conversion while the Church saw to sanctification, that what an imperfect but basically Christian society needed was the politics of reformation. Now it was apparent that the Kingdom of God could not be realised without the conversion of sinners, the great work of the Church; sanctification must be left to chance or the Holy Spirit, and politics must come a very bad third. The progressive evangelical press attacked the high and hyper-Calvinist doctrines of grace, and pushed ' the external interests of religion, Sunday schools, missions, societies under every name '; and it had to admit that the new activism came close to being a religion of works.[7]

Here indeed was the rub. Not for the last time, new liberal ways swept all before them amongst the congregationalists, but among the Baptists there was a sterner fight, and the issue between Fullerism (or moderate Calvinism) and hyper-Calvinism symbolised the clash of a complex of attitudes, the hyper-Calvinists rejecting not merely the doctrines of the moderate Calvinists, but also ministerial training, associational life, foreign missions, and at first, Sunday schools. So far as the new order in the church was concerned, they were classic non-joiners, and when the new order got on top they were apt to secede and form very Strict and Particular congregations.[8] Occasionally the breach went the other way. William Gadsby, who became the leader of the conservatives and a rallying-point for the Gospel Standard Churches, was called to a deeply divided congregation in Manchester in 1805; having failed to get him out, the progressives withdrew, built the York Street Chapel against him, and immediately joined the Yorkshire and Lancashire Association. The Association's empiricism was poison to the hypers, for it did not consider ' our associations as originating in any divine appointment . . . nor so particularly sanctioned by Scripture example as to be necessary to the existence of churches ', but as growing out of ' a principle common to mankind ', the mutual advantage of co-operation.[9] Certainly the great wave of evangelism divided the Baptists in a new way, and there is some reason to think that (in contrast with the Congregationalists) the conservative position formed a last-ditch defence of the poorest in the denomination, a proclamation of their acceptance before God, irrespective of all worldly considerations whatever. Certainly the hyper preachers were reputed to be ' men of the lowest class, destitute of education and generally inclined to rigidness and severity ', and there was a curious kinship between Gadsby and the distressed Manchester hand-loom weavers. His pithy comment on Psalm cxxvii 4-5 ('As arrows are in the hand of a mighty man; so are the children of the youth. Happy is the man that hath his quiver full of them . . .') was that ' there were no hand-loom weavers in those days '.[10]

In dissent as in the Establishment, the question how the Church should adapt to a rapidly changing situation led to a great controversy about baptism. To dissenters of empirical mind and an instrumental view of the Church, it was obvious that combined action and open communion would pay rich dividends, and that the issues traditionally separating those who practised infant baptism from those who baptised believers only were matters of secondary importance on which good men might properly differ, but ought not to refuse each other communion. William Steadman, the great Baptist apostle of the North, even played down the institution of believer's baptism, since without conversion there could be no confession of faith, and all might share in the harvest of souls. Moreover in bumper years, when that harvest seemed limited only by the number of reapers, what could be the practical significance of doctrines of a limited atonement?[11] Yet to the hypers, it was all in all that the Church should not merely be, but be seen to be, an elect remnant; to admit persons who had not received believer's baptism might be convenient, but it was betrayal; there was no alternative to the exaltation of strict communion and the doctrines of grace.

The Establishment must also face the question of coping with a fluid situation. Richard Mant, later an Irish bishop, held that in baptism rightly administered, supernatural grace, regeneration, were conferred upon all, and that no other regeneration was possible in this world. Mant, like the old high-church party generally, was calling in effect for the use of every institutional means of social control, and by implication for a compulsory mass baptism which the Church did not practise. His conservatism, like that of the hypers, implied new departures. To Mant, as to the hypers, the evangelicals were a menace—on their banners ' regeneration is, as it were, inscribed as a watchword—regeneration not in the fruit of Christ's holy ordinance of baptism, but the effect of their declamation '. By this stage it was no use for

Anglican evangelicals to plead for open communion—even the Bible Society was under fire for circulating a scripture text un-encumbered by comment approved by Church authority. But John Scott, the evangelical incumbent of Hull, like the dissenting moderate Calvinists, emphasised the unpleasant moral conse-quences of the view that no unbaptised person could be saved; if the sponsors' promises of repentance and faith made on behalf of the candidate for baptism on the charitable supposition that they would be fulfilled in due course, were not in fact fulfilled, the divine promises of spiritual blessing conditional upon them were null and void. Without the baptism of the Holy Ghost, without spiritual regeneration in the evangelical sense, the baptised could never be a member of the spiritual church of Christ.[12] This implied that the Church could find security only in a spiritual vitality empirically recognisable in the ordinary members. Non-conformist partisans of open communion declared of the hypers that ' we know not a more characteristic symptom of this mental disease, than its employment of means totally inapplicable to their intention '; Scott might have said as much of Mant.

The strains which afflicted all the new movements were most manifest among the Methodists. They were the newest among the large religious communities, and their domestic conflicts could be confused neither by ancient precedent, nor by the assumption that their polity was a datum of the biblical revelation. Their progress was the fastest and most general, and they were now established in communities of very different kinds from Land's End to Shetland. Above all their connexional organisation forced local disputes up to the centre, and central policies down to the fringes. Issues which in the Independent denominations produced obscure local secessions, led in Methodism to contests connexion-wide. The constitutional arrangements of the 'nineties were tested on four fronts successively, by revivalism, by social radicalism, by the Sunday schools, and by the post-war fall in prices which made every social adjustment more painful. These problems were not peculiar to Methodism, simply more obvious in it.

It was on the edge of the Potteries, in a countryside diversified by industrial employment, that the Primitive Methodist Connex-ion, in which Ranterism was in a measure institutionalised, was launched in 1811. In 1800, Hugh Bourne, a small timber con-tractor and schoolmaster, established himself as a practitioner of revival amongst the colliers at Harriseahead. Already in 1802 they were apprised of the first spectacular camp-meetings which had been held in America the previous year, and with an unerring sense of theatre were bent on trying their hand at the same thing on Mow Cop.[13] When, after a final impulse from an American professional revivalist, Lorenzo Dow, the event took place in 1807, the Wesleyan Conference declared against camp-meetings in England, ' even supposing such meetings to be allowable in America ', and the following year Bourne was excluded from membership. Later on a small number of other Methodist officials who had associated with the Mow Cop men, such as William Clowes and James Steele, were also expelled, and they provided the leadership of what always had been an independent revival, scrupulously declining to poach members from the old flock. Thus, escaping the obsessions against ministerial authority which were the bane of the Methodist reformers, the Primitives gave connexional shape to revival, poured down the Trent valley into the kingdom of General Ludd, and beyond it, into their happiest hunting-grounds in the deep countryside of Lincolnshire and the East Riding.

Why did Conference act as it did? The Mow Cop meeting had no political significance; 1807 was a year of low social tension; and in any case it was the regular itinerancy which excited political animosity at that moment. The truth is that Ranterism challenged Wesleyanism hard where it teetered between form and formalism, and had been a considerable embarrassment both in the country and in the great Northern towns. Wesleyans had a firmly articulated schema of the Christian life, beginning with conviction of sin and finding liberty and working up to entire sanctification, which had its own imaginative appeal. It enabled the believer to judge his progress experimentally, and guided the class-leaders through the official system of spiritual inquisition. Everyone under-stood its merits, but no official person would yet admit its limita-tions, or the fact that it already showed signs of becoming a bore. There was the same formalism about Wesleyan preaching. At the bottom were the exhorters. The exhortation consisted of reproving sin, pleading with the sinner to flee from the wrath to come, describing the speaker's own experience in these matters, and testifying to his present joy. The framework of the exhorta-tion appears to have been rigid, held together by these topics, the main scope for individuality lying in the personal testimony. The distinction between exhorters and preachers, whether itinerant or local, lay in ' taking a text '. This was a public declaration that the speaker had ceased to ' exhort ', and also that he accepted a new restraint, that of dealing with the specific doctrines brought out by his ' texts '. John Phillips of Osset wrote: ' The doctrines I preach are, the fall of man, repentance towards God, faith in our Lord Jesus Christ, and the holiness without which no man can see the Lord '. In 1802, Joseph Entwisle emphasised that ' the Head of the Church has put great honor upon a few *leading truths* by wch. Methodist sermons are characterised; and a man need never lose sight of them for the sake of variety '.[14] The undertaking to preach ' our doctrines ' still required regularly of Methodist itinerants, began with this technical sense, and applied to all those who had completed their apprenticeship as exhorters.

This system of instruction and control had little hope of containing a society as dynamic as that which was developing in the North, where men readily joined religious societies and as readily passed on. In 1814 the contrast with Bristol struck John Barber forcibly.

> The people here seem rather of a dull heavy cast: and in the country in particular are ignorant, and stupid in a high degree, and seem to have very little religion. But if there are not as many flowing into the Societies as in the North, there are not so many leaving.[15]

Moreover, the current breakthrough was being made less by exhorting, preaching or class-leading than by cottage prayer-meetings led by unofficial persons. It was characteristic that William Clowes, the great Primitive, was an unusually impressive man in prayer, not least in silent prayer. Even in his Wesleyan days he spared his class the official inquisition, and humanely encouraged their initiative in religious exercises of which they were capable.

> The class rapidly increased, until the house became so full, that there was hardly room to kneel. In leading my classes I used to get from six to ten to pray a minute or two each, and thus to get the whole up into the faith; then I found it a very easy matter to lead thirty or forty members in an hour and

a quarter for I found that leading did not consist so much in talking to the members, as in getting into the faith, and bringing down the cloud of God's glory, that the people might be truly blessed in their souls as well as instructed in divine things.

Of course (as he ingenuously reports) souls were converted in every room in the house, even in the larder. Bourne too, though always more anxious, fussy, and finally more gimmicky than Clowes, had the same gift of prayer and vividness of visual imagery.[16]

Moreover a far-reaching process not only of political, but of spiritual, education was going on among working-men. Half the interest of the journals of Bourne and Clowes lies in the light they cast upon the progress of humble men for whom adherence to the Establishment was out of the question and official Wesleyanism offered no way forward. One day Bourne was struck down at one of those country corners where the saints so often wrestled with God or with Satan:

> Coming home at the praying place in Mr Heath's field, I felt as if I was held by an irresistible power, and I sank down into nothing before it, and everything that I did was contrary to God. I felt it die away—I gave myself up to God. Immediately came ' the spirit of burning ', and I was made 'a habitation through the Spirit '. I wondered at myself; I could scarcely believe what the Spirit witnessed.

Bourne was learning fast. But it was not all immediacy, for the men from the Potteries were in touch not only with American revivalists, but with James Crawfoot and the Magic Methodists of Delamere Forest who specialised in visions; with Peter Philips, a chair-maker of Warrington, who led the Quaker Methodists of that place into contact with the spirituality of the Society of Friends; with James Sigston a schoolmaster notorious in the annals of Leeds Methodism. The bizarre visions of the pious women in their circle, establishing the celestial pecking-order of the prophets and seers of Cheshire and north Staffordshire, reveal a lively awareness of a range of spiritual possibilities far beyond the Wesleyan discipline.[17]

Then there was exorcism, a service in brisk demand amongst ordinary folk, to whom the times seemed inordinately out of joint. There were spectacular cases in Wesleyanism, like James Everett's watchnight service at Oldham Street, Manchester in 1816, which was packed beyond capacity owing to the popular belief that Satan was to be visibly cast out in their midst, or the sofa-raising Lancashire boggart of Middleton that was cast out by a Wesleyan local preacher.[18] Though accused by Wesleyans of being in witchcraft, the Ranters practised exorcism energetically and without a blush. As a young man Clowes could defeat though not destroy the notorious Kidsgrove bogget, and in 1810 Bourne relates how they were grappling together with a spirit world almost Methodistically organised.

> I visited Clowes. He has been terribly troubled by the woman we saw at Ramser. I believe she will prove to be a witch. These are the head labourers under Satan, like as the fathers are head labourers under Jesus Christ. So we are fully engaged in the battle. These, I believe, cannot hurt Christ's little ones till the[y] have first combated the fathers. It appears that they have been engaged against James Crawfoot ever since he had a terrible time praying with and for a woman who was in witchcraft. For the witches throughout all the world all meet and have connection with the power devil. . . . Well the Lord is strong and we shall soon, I believe, have to cope with the chief powers of Hell . . . I am certain the Lord will give us the victory.[19]

Right through the Protestant world revival was mainly a rural phenomenon, but the brakes rarely came off more suddenly than they did for rural immigrants to the great northern towns in the first two decades of the nineteenth century. Sudden release from old social pressures, and the personal disorientation to which this often led, exposed them to religious excitement of a very high voltage, aptly known as 'wildfire'. This kind of Ranterism led to a series of clashes with the Wesleyan preachers, and was sharpened by social antagonism. The uninstitutional movements of God's grace, so dear to the revivalists, evoked a powerful echo in men who were at the losing end of institutions, and chilled the marrow of those with a stake in institutional stability. There were always men of substance who dabbled in revivalism, but everyone knew that men's leanings, one way or the other, were deeply influenced by their social standing. Already there was little love lost between the revivalists and the knot of wealthy intermarried Woods, Marsdens and Burtons with whom Bunting, the architect of early Victorian Methodism, allied himself, and who maintained a cross-bench position between Methodism and the Church, with brothers in the ministry of each.[20]

With the turn of the century the revivalists began to claim the same rights of private edification amongst Wesleyans as the latter had claimed in the Church. Separate places of worship began to go up, and secessions began in Preston, Stockport and Macclesfield.[21] The reactions of the Wesleyan preachers are vividly illustrated in the surviving correspondence about the Macclesfield men, who published their rules as Christian Revivalists in 1803. The superintendent minister, Joseph Entwisle, was a wise and kindly man whose ' simple and unaffected devotion ' was acknowledged far outside the connexion. He took a generally hopeful view of the circuit and ascribed its admittedly flat state partly to factory work which kept people much too late to attend weeknight meetings, and partly to the fact that the secession of the revivalists had evoked rather too much conservative backlash among ' the leading friends '. But the junior preacher, Jabez Bunting, already regarded in the third year of his ministry as a preaching and organising prodigy, saw the whole matter in black-and-white terms.

> The people in this town are tired of parties and divisions:
> & in general equally of the rant & extravagancies of what is
> called Revivalism. . . . Divisions *from* the church, though
> awful, are perhaps after all less to be dreaded than divisions
> *in* the church. . . . Revivalism as of late professed & practised
> was <likely if>not checked, to have gradually ruined genuine
> Methodism. <I a>m glad, however, that they have been the
> first to draw the sword. But as they have drawn it, I earnestly
> wish that our preachers would take the opportunity of returning
> fully to the spirit & discipline of ancient Methodism, & with
> that resolve to stand or fall. The temporary loss of numbers
> would probably be more than recompensed by the increase
> of real scriptural piety, the restoration of good order, & the
> establishment of brotherly love.[22]

Bunting's doctrinaire conviction that he was possessed of the Wesleyan tradition in some sense in which his elders who had

travelled with the great man were not, was ominous for the
future of Methodism, and for a generation the older men were
generally more liberal than Bunting's young hard-liners. His
immediate anxiety, however, was that the Macclesfield revivalists
were in touch with their brethren in Leeds, Manchester and
elsewhere.

William Bramwell, a Methodist preacher with aspirations to
be a revivalist, had served in Leeds in 1801, and had linked up
with James Sigston, a schoolmaster. In 1803 Sigston and 300
members were convicted of breaking the rules in support of
Bramwell, seceded, and set up as the 'Kirkgate Screamers'.
Bramwell's successor was a believer in discipline who was ' convinced that the whirligig work carried on by a certain class of
beings is an awful burlesque on real religion', and Bramwell
himself resigned on the eve of the Conference of 1803, making
haste to Manchester to lead the Band Room, and the Christian
Revivalists into separation.[23] The Band Room, where, incongruously, the young Bunting had preached his trial sermon, was an
establishment maintained by Broadhurst, a prosperous draper,
and founder of the celebrated textile firm, a home for revivalism,
neither fully in nor fully out of the Methodist community. Broadhurst was now prepared to separate, but the flock would not
move; immense pressure was put upon Bramwell, and to the
disgust of the young preachers, Conference received him back into
the fold.[24]

The Methodist preachers, admitting privately that 'we only
wished their annihilation as a party, which we consider as an
excrescence on Methodism that greatly injured the body' prepared
for the worst, requiring Broadhurst to restrict admission (as the rules
of bands required) to members of Society, and resolving upon

3. Keeping the Leaders of the Party in their proper place in
the Leaders Meeting.
4. Making none a new Leader who were known to go that
band and . . . *To promote our own Body Bands at the
same hour as much as possible* which would be the most
effectual way of bringing them to nothing, without injuring
the Society.

This was not a promising basis for reconciliation, and in 1806
the conjunction of two events, a serious recession, and the station-

ing of Jabez Bunting in Manchester, brought about a rupture. It was in bad times, when the popular appeal of Methodism flagged, that the revivalists found the formalism of the upper crust most irksome, and were most tempted to go it alone. There were fresh disputes about admission to the Band Room, and Bunting was not a man to lose the opportunity. He produced a fierce pamphlet insisting on ' the due administration of ecclesiastical discipline ', and described Christian testimony before an unselect company as giving that which is holy unto the dogs. If the general public were not excluded from Band Meetings, from what meetings could they be kept out?[25] Bunting's zeal for exclusion was remembered against him, and also his pamphlet, the writing of which was held to be unconstitutional. Another group of revivalists took their leave, and the exercise of discipline hastened rather than delayed the threat of union amongst revivalists which had emerged at Macclesfield in 1803.

It was not the fissiparousness of revivalism, but its capacity for union, and its threat to the forms of Wesleyan spirituality and instruction which moved Conference against camp-meetings. In 1805 the first conference of Independent Methodists was held in Manchester, uniting the revivalists not merely of the Band Room, but of Oldham, Warrington, Stockport and Macclesfield as well. The Primitive Methodist connexion was another unpremeditated union of revivalists, who had begun and remained in close touch with the Independent Methodists, but who obtained great expansiveness by a degree of connexionalism and a paid, though poorly paid, ministry, which picked up much of that rural Ranterism which had been spreading since the mid-'nineties. They profited also from that more general, unspiky, undenominational evangelicalism propagated at the same time. Baptist chapels, Independent, New Connexion, even Wesleyan chapels were opened to them, and Union chapels (the very cataloguing of which has not yet begun) admitted them to their cycle.[26] Though on a small scale, these coalitions created the impression, later more actively canvassed in America than in England, that revivalism rather than denominationalism was the fundamental antidote to the tensions of church and society.

That this was not quite true was one of the lessons of the last great wave of urban revival which the preachers had to face. In 1816 Methodism seemed again on the flood-tide, especially in the towns of the north-west, of Derbyshire, and about Leeds.[27] But before long it was reported from York that while 400 new members ' of the lowest order ' had been added, the pews were unlet as the chapel respectability were driven away to the Independents.[28] Social tension had already passed the point at which it could be sublimated in religious revival, and, as events slid towards Peterloo, even Bunting's much-prized unity of the Church was put at hazard. After Peterloo the ' wildfire ' never returned. The Tent Methodists, a body of revivalists, who established themselves in Ancoats, in down-town Manchester, in 1821, soon proved dismally unsuccessful; failure led to quarrels among the organisers, and drove them back into various forms of institutional religion. Their chapel was sold to the Church of England, but remained unprosperous as ever. Ancoats remained where it was.[29]

Cornwall, however, was a different story. Here the modest liberty of tinner and fisherman, the cohesiveness of village life, the indifference of the Cornish to the politics of parliament or class, made spontaneous revival possible right into the 'thirties, while the unpopularity of the Cornish Church (and especially of Bishop Philpotts)[30] left no obvious alternative to Methodism for the more substantial classes. Revival broke out at Redruth in 1814 in a staggering meeting which would not break up for nine successive days and nights. We read that

> hundreds were crying for mercy at once. Some remained in
> great distress of soul for one hour, some for 2, some 6, some
> 9, 12 and some for 15 hours before the Lord spoke peace to
> their souls—then they wd. rise, extend their arms, & proclaim
> the wonderful works of God, with such energy, that bystanders
> wd. be struck in a moment, & fall to the ground & roar for
> the disquietude of their souls.[31]

Two thousand, of all social classes, were converted in ten days. Events of this kind continued till 1819, and broke out again in the 'thirties.

The Cornish revival was far too explosive for the Methodist machine. The official system of collecting weekly class-monies which worked properly hardly anywhere, was here almost inoperative. Circuits made shift according to their lights, and poverty led them to keep down their ministerial staff to the lowest practicable level.[32] The Cornish local preachers never quite amassed the power of those of the Isle of Man, who established themselves as an unofficial Manx Conference,[33] but they seem to have gathered huge classes during the revival and kept them under permanent oversight as class-leaders. The double hold of converting power and pastoral leadership gave them an ascendancy which did not bend easily to the preachers' pressure. The hazards were aggravated by poverty, for it was no sacrifice to a Cornish artisan to grasp professional status by taking a class of a hundred into separation, and living humbly as a preacher on their offerings.[34] But poverty also protected Cornwall from much in English Methodism, and in the 'thirties Bunting's stream-lined schemes for levies per head of members in districts seemed impossible even to ministers hottest for standard connexional practices.

Fed by reports from Cornish preachers of irregular ways, and even by demands that the President or Secretary of Conference should annually attend the Cornish District Meeting to keep things in order, Bunting took the view that the Cornish were ' the *mob of Methodism*, they have always been rude and re-fractory '.[35] Yet this judgment was to miss the main point of a splendid series of preachers' reports. George Russell, who had been unbearably irked in 1810 by the Derbyshire Ranters, whose religion, he declared, bore ' a near resemblance to the religion of old Nick ', took a cool and not unfavourable view of the revival at Helston in 1814.

Notwithstanding some disorder and extravagance wh. appeared during the height of the work, there were none of that *Ranterism* and *false fire* wh. have followed the revivals in Yorkshire, Nottinghamshire, Lancashire, Derbyshire, etc. This is a characteristic of the Cornish revival wh. in my opinion speaks loudly in its favour. I know not of an individual who is disposed to speak of a preacher as a ' Dead Stick ', ' a dead soul etc.' . . . [Though the Cornish Methodists are less friendly and less attached to the preachers than others] tho' our labour is so great as to justify one in calling it drudgery; tho' not a few of the Cornish Meths. are filling their heads with foolish notions about Conference corruptions—the great danger of settling chapels on the Meth. plan. etc., & tho with all their religion they cannot think of paying so much for heaven as

Meths. do generally; yet our having to preach to full congregations, our having large & numerous societies, our covering the
county from sea to sea, are circumstances which operate powerfully agt. the disagreeables I have noticed.[36]

The Cornish people in short were making Methodism a popular
establishment, a *Volkskirche*, without parallel in any comparable
area in England. Cornish society was free and disorderly, and so
was Cornish Methodism. But if it could not yet be overtaken
by *episkope* as officially understood, it had the strength arising
from popular community observance, and hence a freedom from
the quirks to which English revivalists were subject. Too much
has been made of the excitements aroused by Dr Warren in 1835
and Wesleyan Reform in 1849. What finally undid Cornish
Methodism was not liberty, but the decline of the tin industry
and the erosion of Cornish separateness by more powerful forces
from across the Tamar. Of these Buntingism and its Methodist
rivals were only the foretaste.

The Wesleyan preachers' feud with the revivalists was soon
overshadowed by the second great challenge, that of convulsive
social discontent, which threatened to overwhelm them both. In the
great social division of the 'nineties the Methodists had been mostly
on one side, and the preachers had gone with them against the propertied trustees. Now as the preachers wept for the great
Methodist Burton family who brought up the cannon to defend
their print works at Rhodes, and mowed down the Luddite hands
to whom they were said to be so kind; as the Luddites of Greet-
land tried surreptitiously to bury comrades from the gallows in
the Methodist graveyard; as suspicion arose that the chapel loft
at Holmfirth was used as a depot for stolen property, it was clear
not only that Methodists stood on both sides of the social conflict, but that the forces within the connexion were differently
aligned.[37] There was no doubt now on which side the connexional
leadership would come down. Publicly and privately to ministers
of the crown, the case had been argued against Sidmouth's bill
that Methodists were a force of loyalty; now that Methodism
had its reprieve, the bill must be paid.[38] There were ecclesiastical
as well as political inducements for the conservative stance of the
old connexion preachers; it brought back magnates from the New
Connexion, frightened, it was reported, by ' the connivance of

some of their preachers and other official persons at the Luddite system and practices'. Even the Old Chapel at Huddersfield which the Kilhamites had carried off in 1797 was believed to be ripe for the picking.[39] The rise of Luddism indeed posed the question, so often to be posed in the new generation, whether forms of middle- and working-class cooperation could be sustained, whether Methodism could contain social discontent within its own ranks.

In 1812 Bunting was stationed at Halifax, in the heart of the West Riding troubles. So firm was he with the Luddites that for months on end he could not go out at night alone. Late in January 1813, 17 Luddites were hung at York, six of them sons of Methodists, and Bunting commented privately:

> However solicitous to make the best of this, it is after all an *awful* fact—and it confirms me in my fixed opinion that the progress of Methodism in the West Riding of Yorkshire has been more swift than solid; more extensive than deep; more in the increase of numbers than in the diffusion of that kind of piety, which shines as brightly and operates as visibly *at home* as in the prayer meeting and the crowded love feast. I read of no people, professing serious religion, who have not as a body far outstripped us in that branch of practical godliness, which consists in the moral management & discipline of children.

The Methodist tub, in short, could no longer contain the torrent of anti-establishment sentiment: what was needed was less revival and more denominational drill, and in particular, Bunting's current nostrums, the control of Sunday schools and catechising of children.[40]

Bunting's exaggerated and unempirical respect for ecclesiastical indoctrination could hardly be better illustrated, but preachers without his inclination for drawing ecclesiological consequences would not yield to him as a pillar of social order. In 1809 great things were reported from the Durham coalfield—'whole families of several individuals unite themselves at once to our societies. This is truly conversion *per stirpes* & not merely *per capita*'. But in 1810, a trade union called the Brotherhood was formed, and Daniel Isaac, then a preacher in the Shields circuit, conspired with the preachers of Sunderland and Newcastle to suppress this dangerous conspiracy. We visited all the collieries where we had Societies; instructed our members and hearers respecting the evil of the Brotherhood both in a religious and civil point of view, and exhorted those who had taken the oath to abjure it, and the others to keep clear of it. Many immediately abjured, and disowned the fraternity; and the secret charm which had held them together was dissolved. . . . The sons of violence knew that I was their principal enemy and often vowed revenge [but with the aid of a good stick and a good pair of heels, Isaac evaded all attacks] . . . Mr. Bunting travelled two years in the Halifax Circuit during the period that General Ludd triumphed in the neighbourhood. I believe he bore a public testimony against this bold conspirator and made himself rather unpopular for so doing. But what did he effect? Gen. Ludd was not frightened away with his fine speeches, but maintained his ground in spite of the philippics of the mighty Demosthenes. To be sure I did not so much in the way of oratory, but I had the merit of *combining* and giving an impulse to the energies of my brethren, which succeeded in anhiliating [*sic*] the Brotherhood. . . . I believe the members of the Brotherhood were as numerous as the Luddites; but who would not rather encounter an army of enervated weavers than a handful of sturdy colliers?

The Pastoral Office as a device for social control could be shrewdly assessed by ministerial spite.[41]

The post-war crisis, however, was very much worse. A dramatic fall in prices made every social adjustment more painful, and financial and political difficulties led the preachers to give a new precision to Wesleyan pietism, urging members to give the Society their undivided loyalty, and keep out of social enterprises which are commonly supposed to have been the fruit of Methodist experience in democracy. Of course the oaths and political attitudes of such societies could be a nuisance. In 1811 the Birmingham District Meeting resolved to expel members who joined sick clubs under the name of Druids. Just before Peterloo a Methodist Benefit Society at Bury St Edmunds petitioned the King to dismiss his ministers, and in consequence were forbidden the use of Methodist premises and the Methodist name. But Bunting's comprehensive denunciation of the Burnley Oddfellows sought to

G

dissociate the matter altogether from the conduct of the clubs.

> If these clubs have any *political* object or business, then as
> *secret,* they are, I believe, unlawful, & certainly very dangerous.
> If on the other hand they are merely *convivial,* which I suppose
> to be the case, still it is *highly* improper & unscriptural, that re-
> ligious persons should join themselves with carnal & careless
> persons in such associations . . . To frequent public-houses, with-
> out any call of business, necessity or duty, and voluntarily to
> choose for ourselves the company of the unawakened & ungodly,
> are practices which cannot be adopted without grieving the Holy
> Spirit and endangering our peace and purity. . . . [Unless they
> can produce] weighty reasons which justify their venturing into
> temptation, you are authorised to put in force against them the
> Law of Christ & the Discipline of the Church. . . . .[42]

Combination amongst the saints could appear still more menacing.
In 1819 the Manchester superintendent discouraged a fund raised
by his local preachers to relieve those of their number in distress,
' local preachers [being] so apt to loose their places on the plan '.
The Manchester local preachers were indeed comparing the
Methodist constitution unfavourably with the unreformed constitution of the land, and talking of combining to defend their
rights. ' I hear that some of the local preachers are quite mutin-
ous ', wrote Bunting, ' They must have a firm Superintendent.'[43]
At Peterloo they had John Stephens, a former Cornish tin-
miner, and a man of ' morbid disposition ' but of stern action
when roused. His junior preacher, the famous Thomas Jackson,
was required to patrol the streets at night, keeping order, supported, as he recalled, by ' a noble band of men ', the flower of the
Manchester Methodist plutocracy. Stephens painfully enforced
discipline in the Leaders Meeting, in his first year removing 400
from the membership roll, and admonished them to go ' either
to the New Connexion or the devil '. He followed up the Peterloo
clash by a sermon on Mark xiv 7, ' For ye have the poor with
you always ', explaining to the poor the advantages of this state
of affairs; and proclaimed his intention to ' blow the sacred trum-
pet to call Jehovah's hosts to battle, and manfully unfurl the
banners of his country, his Sovereign and his God '.[44] At the time
of the Pentridge rising in 1817, the Committee of Privileges had
stood out fervently for loyalty, and great efforts had been made to

show that Isaac Ludlam, who was executed for his part in it, was not only not a Methodist local preacher (as reported), but had never held office, and had been expelled from the Society for bankruptcy eighteen months before.[45] Stephens was now genteely but firmly supported by another address of the Committee of Privileges, drafted by Thomas Allan.[46]

On the other side the radical *Manchester Observer* mercilessly flayed the Wesleyans and their discipline, and reported cases like that of the Rochdale class leader, who came under investigation by the preachers for committing the sins not only of taking radical replies to Stephens's sermon into his class, but also of hearing the New Connexion preacher with profit.

Mr. C[hettle] : I have been further informed that a friend of yours said there was occasion for reform among the Methodist Preachers, but I have not heard that you said so; however, in fact, you hold the same opinion, for a Reformer, of course, wants a reform both in Church and State.

Mr. L[essey] : We ought to be thankful for the privileges we enjoy under the present system of government, as a body of people.

C[lass] L[eader] : We enjoy no other privileges under the present system of government, except an empty pantry, an empty pocket, an empty belly, a bare leg and a bare foot; those are the privileges that I enjoy. As you wish to bend my mind against my principles, I desire you will appoint some other person in my stead, as class leader, for I cannot conscientiously agree with you on the present state of the country.

All over the North as desperate superintendents sought to cut the canker from the body, rumours mounted ever wilder about the confidential relations of the Methodist leadership with the government. Jacobins at Bolton claimed that Stephens had ' received a cheque for £10,000 for services done to Government, signed *Sidmouth* '. Yorkshire radicals alleged that the connexion had ' lent the Government half a million of money to buy cannon to shoot them with '. At Marple they made it a million.[47] The truth was more prosaic, but perhaps more discreditable; the upper crust, lay and ministerial, were using the full Halévy doctrine that Methodism was saving society from revolution, to press the government for legislation making camp-meetings illegal, while securing the indoor gatherings of the Wesleyans.[68]

Of course in the smaller textile towns where there were few men of substance for the preachers to call on, they could be desperately isolated. J. B. Holroyd, the preacher at Haslingden in Rossendale, reported that two-thirds of the population in his circuit were radicals, and there being no magistrate or chief constable, they were manufacturing pikes and drilling nightly. Five ' marked kingsmen ' were to be assassinated on the day of the revolution, including the Anglican incumbent and himself.

> One evening a few weeks since just as I came out of my own door to go into the chapel, the procession was just drawing up in front of the house. I did not judge it prudent to go through the crowd but stood inside the garden gate; they gave three of the most horrid groans I ever heard, and with each groan a young man brandished a pike within a yard of my breast, accompanied with such dreadful oaths, enough to make one's blood run chill. . . . It is with grief I say that our society is not free from the contagion. Some have left us this quarter. . . . They do not think it right to give anything towards the support of those who encourage and pray for a number of tyrants. . . . The above are not the sentiments of our leading friends in Haslingden, quite the reverse, but they can render the preachers no efficient support in opposing the general impetus. . . . [The previous Sunday he had been attacked by a group of officeholders about Castlereagh's Six Acts] when they told me in plain terms that [the] Methodist preachers were as bad as the Church ministers in supporting Government, but it was asked, Will Lord Castlereagh support you??[49]

So far as camp-meetings went, the answer, fortunately, was that he would not.

Holroyd here set out the basic pattern of the Methodist crises of next generation; the great social division in the flock, with the poor and the radical on the one side, and the preacher in alliance with ' the leading friends ' on the other, with calumny on one side opposed by church discipline on the other. The itinerant ministry which only yesterday had been a device for retrieving the lost from the highways and hedges and compelling them to come in, was now being used as a social regulator in a way ruinous to the self-respect which had been one of the Methodism's greatest

gifts to many of her humble sons. It was only too evidently pos-
sible to be right with God and wrong with the Methodist preacher.
On their side the preachers did not need Bunting to tell them that
Methodism hated democracy as it hated sin; recession and democ-
racy killed their evangelistic appeal, and set the flock by the ears.
It was so now at Marple:

> With regard to the prosperity of the work of God in those
> parts, our present prospects are far from flattering. <Cob>bit,
> Hunt and politics, with many are everything, and the cursed
> spirit of infidelity, and opposition to Government leads them
> from God, and everything that is sacred and good. There are
> persons in this vil<l>age who are labouring with all their
> might, to <sh>ut up Methodism in its pecuniary resources, by
> instilling into the minds of all our members . . . the propriety
> of withholding their regular subscriptions from us, in order to
> starve out these men who take part with their tyrants and
> oppressers. . . . This cursed doctrine is very pleasing to the
> carnal mind, and aided by the present state of trade, they are
> too successful in these their diabolic efforts.[50]

The temptation, of course, was to lose patience, and accept the
invitation of the Committee of Privileges to administer discipline.

It was also arguable that being gentle with the flock produced
no better results. The Congregational minister at Leigh in south
Lancashire was genuinely sympathetic with the sufferings of his
weavers, but

> thought it my duty without dictating their political creed to
> exhort them to patience and to peace; to remember that they
> were professed followers of a king whose kingdom was not of
> this world etc. I thought I had done it charmingly, and that I
> had offended nobody; because I allowed that each had a right
> to choose his own political principles, only that, as Christians,
> they ought ever to maintain a Christian spirit: My hopes were
> disappointed. White hats were instantly worn as flags of
> defiance. One deacon threatened to resign, and it appears has
> resigned his office. Some of the hearers, and one member, have
> left the chapel, others who have not left are as cross and crooked
> as they can be.[51]

Neither the New Connexion, nor the sects which championed the radical cause, could capitalise the opportunity. A generation later the Chartists were to find that they had a hard core of leaders and organisers; a considerable and potentially stable body of the second rank who were prepared to play supporting parts and who enjoyed the fellowship of the movement; and a vast mass who were swept in and out of the movement in response to the trade cycle, and whom it was impossible to organise for long. In effect Bunting and his coadjutors were acknowledging that this was already true of Wesleyanism, and were welding the first two into a denomination at the cost, perhaps on a certain level of realism, the small cost, of writing off the third, that great mass which had poured into the Sunday schools and chapels since the mid-'nineties.

For there was no lack of quite explicit *realpolitik* amongst the Methodist preachers.[52] One of their characteristics in the age of Bunting was an uncanny capacity to anticipate the manoeuvres of the big battalions, a shrewdness which in the 'forties proved intolerably irksome to men of strait principles. And already pastoral coarseness set in. In February 1821, John Stephens was monarch of all he surveyed, assured that the trade cycle would raise Manchester Methodism to more than its former glories:

> The objects we have kept in view are, 1st. to give the sound part of the society a decided ascendency. 2. So to put down the opposition, as to disable them from doing mischief. 3. To cure those of them that are worth saving. 4. To take the rest one by one, and crush them when they notoriously commit themselves. . . . They are completely at our mercy. . . . They are down and we intend to keep them down. That they are not annihilated is rather from want of will than power. . . . Methodism stands high among the respectable people.[53]

There was, of course, a limit to what could be accomplished by these means. Richard Reece got his way in Leeds as Stephens did in Manchester, and the bill fell due in a great clamour for local rights in 1827.[54] In some Lancashire towns like Bolton, and on Tyneside, there were immediate and serious losses, and an Independent Methodism emerged, which reacted against the authority of the Pastoral Office by adopting an unpaid and therefore unseparated ministry. Immediately after Peterloo, a huge meeting was held on the Town Moor at Newcastle, one of the speakers at which was Wm H. Stephenson, a young schoolmaster at Burton Colliery,

and local preacher at North Shields. Robert Pilter, the superintendent at North Shields, reported that this gave 'very great
offence to most of the Travelling Preachers & respectable fds.
in this neighbourhood & to none more than myself, and I have
been advised at all events to *put him off the plan*'. Stephenson,
however, would not be dislodged without a trial, and told Pilter
he 'had better let it quietly pass as ¾ of our people are Radical
Reformers'. Pilter then appealed to the President, Jonathan
Crowther, whether he should try to get Stephenson expelled, and
was advised quite clearly to be as conciliatory as he could.

> We should . . . as far as possible avoid exasperating or harden-
> ing any description of men against us, & especially on grounds
> merely political. . . . I do not see why we should *volunteer* our
> services in support of the government, more than any other body
> of people, whether dissenters or Churchmen. I do not fear any
> of these expelling or punishing their people, on account of their
> politics . . . If you expel such men the Kilhamites & Ranters will
> greedily gather them up. In politics I think our present duty
> is neutrality. . . .

Stephenson was nevertheless tried, and though he was acquitted,
means were found of dislodging him, and the colliery dismissed
him from his school. Class-conscious recrimination began in the
press, and within a year fourteen Independent Methodist chapels
had sprung up in the vicinity 'whose preachers, like the primitive
teachers of Christianity, claim[ed] no pecuniary reward for their
labours'.[55] Trouble continued in the North as long as the excitement which built up around Queen Caroline lasted, and Bunting
put down an attempt of the young Stamford Methodists to address
the queen direct.[56]

 'It will pain you to hear', wrote Adam Clarke, in 1821, '. . .
that this year, through what is called Radicalism, we have lost
between 5 and 6000 members . . . such a blow as we never had
since we were a people.'[57] What the preachers could not foresee
was that Peterloo had for ever severed official Methodism from
urban revivalism. No doubt Manchester would in time have
exhibited the metropolitan secularism which made London the
graveyard of religious enthusiasm; but what actually happened was
that the great floodtide of 1816 and 1817 was suddenly terminated
and never returned. As happened more broadly with the Wesleyan

reform secessions of the 'fifties, the connexional machine could repair the membership losses, but could never evoke old expansiveness. The years 1819-20 were the moment of truth for the Wesleyans, as the years 1792-3 had been for the Church; Wesleyanism was never going to be a popular urban religion.

Peterloo also raised in an acute form the problem of control in the Sunday schools. The Church had been the first to challenge the undenominational principle when it seemed to be getting out of hand; the Wesleyans were not far behind. One of the undenominational schools which went over to the Kilhamites was that at Nottingham; for a few years Wesleyans continued to teach in it, but in 1803 a Wesleyan school was built in competition which soon outstripped the original body.[58] But the real clash came in Stockport. No sooner had that school got into its new buildings in 1805, than they began to look for preachers for their charity sermon. The Rector of Stockport was sympathetic, but would not preach in unconsecrated premises. The School Committee then turned to Bradburn, Benson, Bunting and other Wesleyan stars who had the greatest drawing-power in Stockport, and could not understand why they all declined their invitations; they finally discovered that Conference was imposing economic sanctions. Conference's terms were that no preachers should be heard in the school but Anglican and Methodist, and not more than one of the former to three of the latter. This impertinent blockade was no more successful than the Warrenite attempt to cut off supplies to Conference a generation later, but it excluded Methodist preachers from the school for many years. The next step was to organise rival schools, and to attempt to turn the undenominational system into a denomination on its own.[59] It was a similar story in Macclesfield. Undenominational effort went on successfully for a time, under the leadership of a Methodist, John Whitaker, but the usual tensions grew up. Anglicans and Methodists tried to put down Sabbath teaching of writing and arithmetic, while Whitaker (like that other old-style Methodist, Mathew Mayer at Stockport) defended them as part of the undenominational tradition. The crisis came with the planning of the Big School, which was opened in 1812 at a cost of £5,639. The Anglicans were in a strong position as they had in prospect the National School which they opened in 1813 and could use as a Sunday school. They withdrew and so did the Wesleyans; Adam Clarke who was to have preached the

opening sermon also withdrew, and John Whitaker left the
Methodists. The school nevertheless thrived, and, like the Stockport school, even obtained royal patronage.[60]

The Stockport affray, carefully concealed as it was, taught the
connexional leadership that Sunday schools even when managed
by Methodists, might, like radicalism, be a channel for diverting
social movement out of the orbit of the denomination. Conference
thereupon required that the travelling preachers should be members of the committees of Methodist schools, and that the superintendent should preside. As the Macclesfield case showed, this
regulation could not operate where the schools, though run by
Methodists, were not Methodist schools. But the intention was
clear enough and it might be implemented where, as in Manchester
an undenominational system was gradually falling into Methodist
hands. The schools here could not fail to feel the impact of popular agitation. Immediately after Peterloo, the Anglican committee
yielded to the pressure of subscribers, and resolved to exclude all
children who appeared in drab hats or other political emblems.[61]
The Wesleyans followed suit, the Manchester Quarterly Meeting
resolving to exclude teachers wearing any political badge, and
also any children who had been turned out of their schools for
political reasons.[62] The next to act were the Roman Catholics,
again, it was said, under pressure from wealthy subscribers, and
the witch-hunt began to spread to surrounding towns and villages.[63] The Stockport school had also had its troubles since the
hard times of 1817, and now 26 young rebels refused to attend
church on their rota. Alleging that they were organised ' by some
of those persons now suffering in gaol the punishment of their
crimes ', the school committee expelled them with the utmost
ignominy, and presented an address of fervent loyalty to the
magistrates.[64]

In all this there was nothing surprising, but it was significant
that the Manchester Quarterly Meeting was asserting an authority
over undenominational schools to which it had no right at all,
and that under this pressure the radicals made an effort to capture
the undenominational tradition for themselves. In the Sunday
schools as elsewhere, social tension was driving denominationalism
forward, and denominationalism was reproducing its image in its
enemies. James Scholefield, one of the schismatic Swedenborgians
who in Manchester bore the name of Bible Christians, now organ-

ised a Union (or undenominational) Sunday school in connexion with Christ Church, Hulme. Scholefield replied to John Stephens' sermon on behalf of the radicals, and in 1823 opened his own chapel in Every-street, Ancoats (later part of the University Settlement), and from it he dispensed radical politics (he was a friend of Cobden, and active in the Chartist Convention), vegetarian recipes, ' Scholefield's Cholera Mixture ', and an undertaking service for those it failed to cure. The Union school he left behind in Hulme lasted at least fifty years, and claimed to be the first scientific institution for the working classes in the country; but the tory press did its best to destroy it at birth owing to the ' almost universal connection between radicalism and infidelity '. In fact the school practised the familiar mixture of undenominational instruction, and gleefully claimed that ' hundreds of poor children who would have been deprived by the liberty of the Wesleyans of the means of attaining useful knowledge, have been rescued from ignorance, and are now training up in habits of virtue and *temperance*'—a damaging shaft indeed. And in best civil-war style, when the two Union schools at Oldham arranged themselves a sermon by a friendly curate in an Anglican chapel, the boys of the Anglican schools were turned out by the teachers to break up their procession and pursue them with yells of ' Shoddy Reformers '.[65]

The Methodist Conference had better look to its guns, and it resumed the unfinished work of legislation to which it had been provoked by the Stockport school. In 1819 it enacted that ' a Sunday school is strictly and entirely a *religious* institution', i.e. it must not teach writing, as the radicals and most of the undenominationalists (not to mention the working class at large) wished. During the soul-searching at the 1820 Conference, Richard Watson urged that ' the best way to acquire influence [in Sunday Schools] is to be in everything & for everything—catechisms should be introduced for catechetical teaching in public by the Preachers', and it was required that ' as many of the children as can possibly be accommodated with room, ought invariably to attend our [i.e. not Anglican or other] public worship *at least once every Lord's Day*'. The 1823 Conference forbade Sabbath writing and required catechetical instruction. Finally the 1826 Conference appointed a committee in which Bunting was the moving spirit, to embody all the lessons they had lately learned in the northern

Sunday schools in a ' general outline of rules and recommendations '. These were to be binding on all new schools established in
the connexion, and Conference ' hoped that those schools, already
existing, which claim a relation to Methodism, and are supported
in part by collections made in our chapels will be induced, as
speedily as possible, to adopt the same leading principles, and to
work by the same general rules '.[66] This amounted to an invitation
to the preachers to use the power of the purse to get control of
the undenominational schools, a squally course indeed; but first,
the preachers must face the direct consequences of the economic
blizzards of the peace.

The alliance of the preachers with the men of substance in the
connexion was clinched by the post-war fall in prices, which
executed cruel judgment on the Methodist euphoria of the previous
decade. Normally sober men had then believed that the new
faith was about to subdue the world, and the hundreds of young
preachers were called out, on whose shoulders Bunting climbed to
power. In those years the connexion came to resemble a modern
cut-price motor-car insurance company tempted or deluded by a
large cash flow into prodigal disregard of its future liabilities, and
falling into morally venial but financially ruinous mistakes of a
basically actuarial kind. The Methodist system of paying preachers
not a stipend, but allowances for travelling and the maintenance
of a house and family, created an open-ended liability. The problem of ministerial allowances was taking shape before the end of
the war, but the collapse of prices afterwards made the burden,
and especially the continual increase of preachers' families, seem
intolerable. Joseph Entwisle, not an anxious or querulous man,
spoke for scores of his brethren : '. . . unless we adopt a system of
economy *we shall certainly sink the vessel* . . . Our families
increase upon an average 30 in a yr.—and everyone expects House
&c. Servant &c.—the same as those who have travelled 30 years.'
Anxious statisticians throughout the connexion were betting on
the fertility of the manse, and astonishing proposals were made to
dismiss preachers with large families, or station them according
to the ability of circuits to pay.[67] In 1819, the year of Peterloo, the
candle seemed consumed at both ends. The intake of new preachers
had to be restricted, and the Legalised Fund, a kind of group-
insurance scheme by which the preachers provided for their
widows, and for the retirement of aged and disabled brethren, a

fund which should have been bursting at the seams with the subscriptions of recent young recruits, lacked the cash to meet its
obligations.[68]

Everyone knew that the principal cause for the multiplication of
preachers was the multiplication of chapels, and hence of pews to
let and mortgages to be serviced, for whatever the aspirations of
conference to be the living Wesley, it was not behaving as Wesley
had behaved. In his lifetime, related William Myles,

> there were never more than one third of the preachers married
> . . . And he would not let a chapel be built unless two thirds
> of the money was subscribed before a stone was laid, and it
> stated whether it would call for an additional preacher. Now
> near three fourths of the preachers [a body which had trebled
> in number since Wesley's death] are married, and chapels are
> built or purchased without, in some cases, one fifth of the money
> subscribed, and immediately a travelling preacher called out.[69]

How the agricultural industry agonised to service high war-time
debts from low peace-time prices is well known; but no industry
was more heavily mortgaged than Methodism. What had been a
running sore became suddenly a disease of fatal proportions. In
1817 a small connexional Chapel Committee including a lay
element was established to examine, and, if necessary, veto, every
proposal for chapel-building or purchase. The following year
' itinerant mendicant preachings in behalf of our chapels ', which
had removed far too many preachers from their pastoral charge,
were put down in favour of an annual subscription and public
collection to a General Chapel Fund. The Chapel Committee was
hardly a long-run substitute for the living Wesley, while in the
short run the Chapel Fund could not reduce the size of the obligations to be met, and added one more to what had come to seem an
overwhelming number of special collections. When, after Peterloo,
the collections themselves began to fall off, it was hard to know
what to do. ' One says Radicals are the cause, another the Ranters;
another bad trade; another want of silver; another rainy weather,
and many the late regulations of Conference. . . .' Bunting himself,
in the last years of the war, had fastened on the connnexion what
was now a most inconvenient burden by putting overseas missions
on a sound financial footing; and his elation of 1815 had now an
ominous ring: 'The poorer classes have now learned by experi-

ence the privilege of giving. They know the consequence &
efficiency conferred on them by their number. . . .'[70]

There seems no evidence to suggest that the preachers were able
to analyse the economic roots of their difficulties; what vexed them
was the loss of an impetus which they had fondly ascribed to sound
doctrine and polity. Jonathan Crowther wrote in 1817:

> About five or six years ago our machine seemed to possess such
> incalculable force, that almost all things seemed to be possible
> to us, yea, even in temporal things. . . . We are now arrived
> at a new crisis of our affairs. The connexion is in danger of
> being overset by its own weight.

In 1818 Charles Atmore feared 'the *zenith* of Methodism' was
past, and could not imagine how they could get through Conference without driving ' the people mad with our collections '. There
were independent reports of great losses to the Primitives in the
villages owing to constitutional dissatisfaction and ' the wish for
a cheaper religion '.[71] These despondent confessions of inability
to trim the ends to the means were the counterpart to radical
allegations that the preachers were subsidising the government.

It was a matter of remark, moreover, that itinerancy in the old
sense was rapidly coming to an end. A market in urban religion
had been discovered which could be commercially tapped. The
right kind of chapel in the right site could attract a congregation
of gratifying number and affluence. But as the preachers made no
bones privately, the brethren were only too willing to be anchored
by connubial bliss and by the financial and pastoral obligations of
the new causes to the neglect of their rural ministry.

> The present plan of the preachers living in great towns [opined
> William Myles in 1819], such as Hull, York, Sheffield and
> Leeds; and only just preachg. in the country is the real cause
> of the increase of the Ranters. The Pastoral duty is neglected;
> and you cannot get some of the brethren to think they are
> accountable to God or his people, as they are not Superintend-
> ents . . . yet facts prove we do no good in a town where we have
> not a married preacher or two settled—

and here the financial stake was largest. The old hands in the
ministry were quite bitter. ' Paul taught the people publicly and

from house to house ', wrote one. ' We have very little of domestic teaching.'[72]

This was a cut indeed. For if the rise of Methodism on the macroscale had been an aspect of the rise of the provinces against the centre, on the microscale it had often been an aspect of the rise of the fringes of the parish against the nuclear village, the parish church, and the central apparatus of service and control. For one remote parish in Montgomeryshire, it has been shown how the revival forwarded this process by shifting the centre of worship from the parish church to the hearths of outlying farm kitchens, and that even when domestic prayer and prophecy were institutionalised, the chapel buildings were scattered at remote intersections of routes avoiding the village, a monument to the centrifugal forces which underlay them.[73] What was true of Llanfihangel was true of English parishes too, and the steady decay of the old style of itinerancy which involved journeys from home sometimes of weeks on end, sleeping, praying and preaching with the people in their homes and rural meeting places, involved subtle changes thoroughly unpalatable to many who remembered what Methodism was originally like. No doubt this distaste did play into the hands of the Primitives, who harvested a second crop from the Wesleyan mission fields and in some parts of the country maintained an old-style itinerancy into the present century.

There were two symbols of the new era which bore directly on the financial crisis. The first was the steady disappearance of the circuit horse. For circuit stewards had it calculated that ' the expenses attending a horse support a single Preacher ', who might be of more service to the central chapels, but who, unlike the horse, would ere long establish a claim to additional allowances for wife, house and children, coals, candles and servant. If when the horse was exchanged for an unmarried preacher, the country societies could be disposed of to a new circuit, the local financial advantage could be maximised.[74] This ruinous process, the creation of financially unsound country circuits, was the second symbol of the decline of itinerancy. It was a general abuse, particularly notorious in the old Methodist urban centres of London, Bristol and the North-east, and it aggravated the burdens created by Thomas Coke's domestic missions, which gave rise to forty circuits hardly any of which were capable of spiritual or financial independence.[75] Then there were the Scottish circuits which in

1817 mustered only about 85 members per preacher, and were a classic case of mismanagement of every kind, local and central.[76]

Methodist connexionalism being what it was, these mistakes at the fringes had immediate repercussions at the centre, and the preachers in Conference found themselves struggling to pay what was due to them as individuals in the circuits. The theory of Methodist finance was that each Society contributed to the support of the preachers stationed in the circuit, while the chapel supported the trust.[77] Thus pew rents serviced or reduced the chapel debts, while the Society, through its class monies or otherwise, met the preachers' allowances. If the pew rents failed to meet the expenses of the trust, and especially the interest upon debt, then the trust also must be supported by the Society. Circuits which could not meet their obligations (the chief of which were the preachers' allowances) returned a deficiency to the District Meeting; and District Meetings which could not meet their deficiency returned it to Conference. Conference in turn must meet the accumulated deficiency from the proceeds of the Yearly Collection, a fund apparently first opened for the temporary sustenance of Coke's home missions, but soon used as a milch-cow by all the insolvent Districts in the connexion.[78] If Conference could not meet the deficiencies, preachers whose circuits had defaulted on their allowances did not receive them at all. Unscrupulous circuits discovering that they were not absolutely committed to their financial undertakings would bid for preachers by offering ample allowances they intended to return as deficiencies for someone else to pay; unscrupulous preachers connived at circuits which cooked the books, and avoided returning deficiencies by contracting illicit debts for their successors to discover and pay.[79] The straw at which everyone clutched was the Book Room, the publishing concern which had a monopoly of the Methodist hymn book, a nominal monopoly of the literary output of the preachers, and dealt extensively in pious ephemera which went out in boxes to every circuit in the kingdom. No other publisher had as many salesmen as the Methodist travelling-preachers. The expected goldmine was, however, a persistent disappointment. In 1804 Robert Lomas, who had served in the family business in Manchester before entering the ministry, was appointed to the Book Room to set its affairs to rights. After his reorganisation, Lomas recommended that the business be turned over to a lay professional, and produced a suitable candidate willing to serve for a modest salary. Conference, however, wanted the Book Room as an office of dignity for a preacher (as it has done ever since), and never drew the potential dividend.[80]

There was thus little to offset the effects of the savage deflation which destroyed the connexion's financial control, and acutely raised the question of what the proper remuneration of a preacher was. Certainly the preachers compared their lot with that of their Anglican and dissenting brethren and steadily raised their financial and pastoral pretensions.[81] By the end of the war there had been some increases, and the ministers' complaint was not that wartime price-increases had eaten up their allowances (indeed according to Dr Elliott's calculations, the money income of the Leeds preachers increased about $2\frac{1}{2}$ times, 1798-1824, and their real income about $3\frac{1}{2}$), but that they could not fulfil their social expectations.

> A preacher (and especially in the present state of Methodism in this country) fills a respectable station in society; and he and his family are necessitated and expected to appear becoming in that station; but for this, his income, in general, will not afford him the means . . . Provision, it is true, is made for the *sons* of the preachers who are received into the publick institutions of the Society, at Kingswood and Woodhouse Grove . . . But what provision is made for the education of their *daughters*? [8 guineas a year for 6 years]. . . . will seriously thinking persons deem this sum adequate to such an education as the daughter of a Methodist Preacher should receive to enable her to preserve that rank in society in which she was born? . . . without education a person is fit only for the drudgery of life, and must necessarily fill a place in the lower ranks of society.[82]

This is not a radical caricature, it is the *Methodist Magazine* in 1815. Yet the key to the situation lay less in the preachers' private aspirations than in the Conference view that the interests of the work of God and the professional interests of the ministry were in this crisis inseparable; neither could survive without the money of those who had it to give, without sacrifice on their own part, or without an absolute determination to enforce discipline on themselves and their people. In 1818 the preachers could see no way of clearing a deficit of £5000 except by bearing it themselves, relinquishing claims to unpaid allowances for half the sum, and taking up the unsold publishing stock of the Book Room for the rest.[83] In 1818 and 1819 they cut back recruiting; in 1820 they elected without a single negative the first President who had not travelled with John Wesley, and the youngest ever, Thomas Coke excepted. But he was Jabez Bunting, the toughest and most iron-willed of their number.

It was now too that the preachers laid claim to the full dignity of the Pastoral Office which Wesley and some of his immediate successors had been so anxious to deny them,[84] and the emphasis was subtly transferred from feeding and guiding to the teaching and ruling which from an early date characterised Bunting's view of the office.[85] In 1818 Conference tacitly defied the Conference rule of 1793, adding the title of Rev to the names of all the preachers on the Missionary Committee (Adam Clarke won a laugh at the 1821 Conference by saying he applied the title in the Latin root sense ' to those whom he thought deserved it in the ministry ');[86] in 1819 ex-President Jonathan Edmondson announced his intention of writing ' a Treatise on the Pastoral Office adapted to our circumstances as itinerants '; in 1820 Bunting created an uproar in Conference by proposing from the Presidential chair that the young preachers be received by imposition of hands.[87] On this point Bunting could not yet carry his brethren with him, but he gathered up the Conference conversation in the Liverpool Minutes which set forth so compelling a picture of the new ideal Methodist minister, resolute in pastoral oversight and yet earnest in evangelism, that Conference required them to be read annually at District, and later, circuit meetings, and by candidates for the ministry.

A generation later during the disastrous Reform secessions, the 1851 Conference declared itself bound

> by the principles set forth in the New Testament and by the sacred trust transmitted to it by Mr Wesley and his coadjutors, to maintain the PASTORAL OFFICE in unimpaired integrity; and consequently, bound to uphold the SPIRITUAL AUTHORITY which is appropriate to that office. . . .

The syllogism of which the deposit of Wesley was the premise has been upheld by the latest and best student of the question, Dr J. C. Bowmer.

> A Doctrine [of the Pastoral Office] which was inherent in the

H

system as devised by Wesley was only formulated as circumstances forced it upon the preachers. This is not to say that there was anything artificial about the doctrine or that it was devised to defend an otherwise intolerable situation. Had it never been challenged it would have continued as an accepted but more or less undefined tradition, but, being challenged, precise formulation was necessary.

Having made this claim Dr Bowmer admits that he can find no evidence of its development between the death of Wesley and the Leeds crisis of 1828. The view taken here (also taken by the Conference historian and apologist George Smith) is that what took place was not so much the definition of a deposit from John Wesley as of the new pastoral functions which the preachers were performing as they moved from an old-style itinerancy to the sham church-based itinerancy they have maintained ever since.[88]

The Peterloo crisis which is recognised to have critically transformed the situation of the Church establishment,[89] could hardly fail to have a shattering effect on the much more fragile machine of Methodism; the only way through seemed to lie in a great assertion of pastoral power. How ' intolerable' the situation had become is indeed suggested by the later challenges to which Dr Bowmer refers. As the storm broke in 1817, the connexion was known to be precariously dependent on four Districts which paid their way, produced a surplus on their Yearly Collection, and gave up the whole of their profits on the book trade to assist other Districts. The four pillars of financial salvation were Liverpool, Manchester, Leeds and Halifax.[90] It was an unfortunate accident that these were the areas where the class war was hottest; but no accident that the radicals recognised a change in preachers contending not for order but survival, for resources that disorderly Cornwall could never produce; no accident that Bunting, John Stephens, Richard Reece and the other toughs of the connexion, migrated among the town circuits which were at the core of those Districts; no accident that in every one of those circuits there took place between 1825 and 1835 at least one of those great constitutional conflicts in which the high Wesleyan doctrine of the ministry was hammered out. These conflicts constitute the next chapter in Methodist history; but it is necessary first to inquire how reform failed to save the Establishment from serious trouble.

5 The Insufficiency of Reform
1820-1835

The hub of the social history of English religion in this period comes at the half-way point, the social and political upheaval of 1819-21 which began with Peterloo. Down to that time it seemed possible that popular evangelicalism might sweep the board as it did in Wales, or as popular Catholicism did in Ireland. Many of the more durable religious communities of the modern world took up a stance of revolt or resistance to authority in this very period, but unlike the Catholic churches of Belgium, the Rhineland, Poland, or even Ireland, the evangelicals never won the backing of whole communities at every social level, and the intensification of class hostility created very difficult circumstances for them. What was implied at Peterloo could be seen manifestly worked out in the recession of 1837-42. By the same token it was no longer possible for Establishment to work in its old way upon the mind and sentiment of a great part of the nation. Adaptation to new circumstances was clearly needed, and reform began. The tragedy was that before reform had done its work, the English situation became so inflamed by the intense religious struggles of Ireland and Scotland that progress was halted, and the whole religious establishment put in danger. For the next generation the story is more difficult to expound, and requires a viewpoint moving constantly from the fringes of Great Britain to the centre, from the metropolis to the provinces, from the parliamentary battles to the local agitations which continually acted on each other. The next two chapters seek to show how the Establishment and the greatest of the evangelical voluntary churches were affected by renewed social tension, and how the fires were stoked which blazed cruelly in the Church conflicts of the 'thirties and 'forties.

In 1800 the Grenville family had felt unable to restrict the Toleration Act without overhauling the parochial organisation of the Church. This hornets' nest was disturbed by some smart lawyers who discovered an opening for profit in the sixteenth-century acts requiring clerical residence, which provided for enforcement by informers under a monetary penalty. This was oppressive upon conscientious London rectors who might live hard by their church, and still be non-resident in the parish, and it carried portentous implications for the whole Church. Half the 11,000 livings had non-resident incumbents; most commonly because the incumbents were pluralists and resident upon another benefice; often because there was no suitable parsonage house, or none at all. Some clergy did not reside because they were ill; some because they were royal preachers, chaplains to the nobility, cathedral officers or university dignitaries; some were absent without any leave at all. Parliament gained immediate relief by suspending the act requiring residence in 1801, but repeated attempts to regulate the question afresh broke down on the difficulty of securing justice not only for incumbents, but for non-beneficed clergy, for patrons, parishioners and other interested parties. Underlying the problem was the fact that the revenues of the Church, immense as they were, were not equal to the expectations founded upon them. In the Church, as in English society generally, great wealth and poverty existed side by side. If the sees of Canterbury and Durham enjoyed a princely £19,000 p.a., there were 4,000 livings below the £150 p.a. which established itself as the clerical breadline, including about 1,000 below £50 p.a. Even the Bishop of Llandaff could hardly be expected to reside in London during sessions of Parliament and work a see which had no bishop's house, on an income of £900 p.a. Pluralities, in short, became the abuse they undoubtedly were because they were in the first place a necessity.

The simplest solution to clerical poverty might have been to equalise clergy stipends, but to this there were three fatal objections. According to Morgan Cove, a contemporary commentator, if all the revenues of the Church, including those of the bishops, were pooled, the dividend would have been only £167 per head—hardly the Promised Land for parish clergy. Moreover as Sir William Scott put it,

As the revenues are at present distributed, the clergy, as a profession, find an easy and independent access to every gradation of society. . . . Alter the mode of distribution, and you run the risk of producing a body of clergy resembling only the lower orders of society . . . and it is well if they are not infected by a popular fondness for some other species of a gross, factious and a fanatical religion.

Clerical equality meant Presbyterianism, subversion to a hierarchical society, in the nineteenth as in the sevententh century. Still more compelling was the fact that advowsons, the right to present to benefices, were a freely marketable commodity, mostly in lay hands, whose value would be totally upset by the equalisation of stipends. This expropriation and redistribution of lay property was entirely out of the question.[1]

The law severely restricted the right of the clergy to add to their stipends by outside work, though it had never prevented their doing so illegally. Wade cites one of the notoriously poor Welsh clergy, who taught the village children five nights a week, operated a ferry service across the river, and shaved for a penny every Saturday night.[2] Wilberforce spoke in the house of a curate turned weaver. Education was sanctified by long tradition as consistent with the clerical character, and so too was agriculture, the principal outside activity of the clergy. Many incumbents had been in the past worker-priests, farming their own glebe, and giving the Church such time as was left over. Some were still in this position, though it seems impossible to discover how many. Some were tenant-farmers of other men's property, and here the Henrician law was impossible to administer. A parson might legally farm to support his family, and might sell surplus produce, but he might not farm for profit on the open market. In a money economy this distinction could not be sustained. Sir William Scott, the parliamentary spokesman for the clergy, had, however, no prepossessions about a separated ministry. To him

the parish priest is, by the very constitution of his office, in some degree an agriculturist; he is, *ex officio*, in part a farmer . . . [farming provided food for his family, employment for his flock] and many motives of pleasing attachment to the place, which furnishes the healthy and amusing occupation of his vacant hours.

This view of the clerical vocation was hardly apostolic, but did not lack relevance to a church overwhelmingly given to service in country parishes. The clergy's rights were accordingly gradually extended; the Residence Act of 1817 permitted them to farm up to 80 acres as tenants, and later they were enabled to enter business partnerships, especially those dealing in fire and life assurance. Yet by 1831 these measures had made little difference to the problem of non-residence, and could not raise the remuneration of the profession as a whole.[3]

Clerical stipends nevertheless received a real impetus from the wartime boom in agricultural profits and from government policy. In 1809 Spencer Perceval, the evangelical Chancellor, made the first of eleven annual parliamentary grants of £100,000 for the augmentation of poor livings, which were particularly valuable to the poorest clergy when the agricultural bubble burst at the end of the war, and the staple revenues declined again. But calculations made for Derbyshire show that the bulk of the gains made from agricultural improvement and high prices were retained, rectories having risen from an average of £141 in 1772 to £459 in 1842, and vicarages from £54 to £195. And over the country as a whole, the average net value of stipends had been raised to £286 by 1835 when living was cheaper than at the beginning of the century.[4]

If it was difficult to root parsons in their parishes, it was still harder to prise loose the dead hand of the past on the parochial structure, vital though this was to the reputation of the Establishment. The most rapidly developing part of the country was in the northern province, but this province counted only 6 bishoprics against 20 in the South: Norfolk contained 731 parishes and Suffolk 510, but there were only 70 in Lancashire and 193 in the West Riding of Yorkshire. Nor could things improve while it required an act of parliament to create every new parish. Not that Anglican provision was necessarily confined to the parish church. In the parish of Manchester, an extreme case of the unwieldy northern parish, the population increased from 125,911 in 1801 to 515,581 in 1851, and the number of Anglican churches from 23 to 56. Certainly the factors which caused a steady process of church-building there to dry up almost completely between 1794 and 1820 had nothing to do with the legal difficulties of creating parishes. But there was a considerable Anglican feeling that non-parochial chapels drained the life out of the parish, and, outside London, they existed in large numbers only in the sees of Lich-

field, Chester and York. Unquestionably the existence of concurrent pastoral oversight led to abuse and inconvenience. Under
Hardwicke's Marriage Act (1753) marriages might only be solem-
nised in the parish church, and the Manchester district clergy,
unable to marry their people, felt their flock could never compre-
hend what their status was. Moreover, the townsfolk flocked to
the parish church in unmanageable numbers. The publication of
the banns was ' equivalent in point of time to the reading of a
chapter of the Bible,'

> marriages are very often celebrated on the Sundays, and there
> is an accumulation of people in the neighbourhood of the
> church for those marriages. The registration of marriages goes
> on during Divine service—the issuing of certificates goes on
> during Divine service. The same with regard to baptisms; there
> as an accumulation of numbers, who resort to the old parish
> church; there are meetings in the neighbouring public
> houses, sponsors assembling there; in short scenes, I do
> not say of gross scandal, but of indecorum . . . which . . .
> operates very injuriously to the interest of the Church at
> Manchester.

There was unfortunately more than indecorum in the hasty
conduct of marriages; it was known that no inquiries would be
instituted, and couples for miles around who wished to marry in
defiance of the law, or of family disapproval, flocked to the Manchester parish church.[5]

In 1816 it was computed that in parishes where the population
exceeded 2,000 and there was Anglican accommodation for less
than half, there was a population of 5,265,079 and church accommodation for not much more than a million. In 80 such parishes in
London there was no provision for eight-ninths of a population
exceeding 930,000. In five parishes in Aston, Deritend and Birmingham, church accommodation for 24,000 sufficed for a population of 185,000; in Leeds the church found room for 3,400 of a
population of 67,000. In detail these figures are suspect, but there
was no disputing the general impression they conveyed. Moreover
everyone knew that not only in non-parochial chapels, but also in
parish churches where parishioners were supposed to have a common law right to accommodation in the nave, they were excluded
from much of the accommodation by the pew system. Churches

were filled higgledy-piggledy with boxes of all sizes, shapes, and amenities, which eventually excited quite immoderate high-church animosity, and undoubtedly made a mockery of the Anglican claim to be the poor man's church. Of course, nonconformists were also heavily dependent on pew rents, but they did not levy church rates on the public they excluded: and church rates proved to be the Achilles heel of the church-building programme.[6]

Towards the end of the Napoleonic Wars, the cause of church-building was energetically taken up by the Hackney Phalanx, an influential circle of high-church clergy and laity, an intermarried group of Sikeses, Stevenses, Daubenys and Watsons, who had already been instrumental in founding the National Schools Society in 1811, had obtained a foothold in the SPCK, and had managed two important relief funds at the end of the war. Their pressure and severe social tension moved the government to action; in 1818 a Church Building Commission on which the Hackney Phalanx was strongly represented was established by statute, with a million of public funds to spend. In 1824 a windfall repayment of a wartime loan to Austria which had been written off produced another half-million, and, as state funds were used to prime the pump of private generosity, a considerable programme of church-building was begun, which over fifteen years cost six million pounds. This extension was long overdue, but at various levels it was a disappointment. It gave public testimony to the state's support of the Church, but this rang hollow at a time when the Cabinet was treating Catholic Emancipation as an open question. The churches themselves were often too large and expensive to answer. Some never gathered a reasonable congregation; some (like St Matthew's, Campfield, in Manchester)[7] were hamstrung by unrealistic scales of pew-rents fixed by the Church Building Commissioners; the indifferent success of too many proved a telling argument for leaving the provision of religious amenities to the play of market forces. Worst of all, Anglicans as well as nonconformists displayed an unexpected animosity towards the indefinite extension of church rates, to pay for amenities chiefly enjoyed by pewholders.

Manchester showed what a labyrinth church extension could become. Learning that it was to be favoured with three or four new churches, one of the largest vestry meetings ever held in the town resolved in 1820 to sanction no vote for the purchase of sites, the churches being unnecessary. The Church Building Commissioners finding their sites notwithstanding, and the churchwardens frustrating a Unitarian attempt to call a parish protest meeting, Richard Potter (the ' Radical Dick ' of later fame, who became a tremendous figure in Unitarian, liberal and warehousing circles), took a private census at the town churches. He concluded that Manchester Anglicans were already grossly overprovided for.

> In the year 1816 . . . a great outcry was raised in this town . . . that the existing churches were not sufficient for the accommodation of the inhabitants, who became irreligious, seditious and immoral, only because they had not the benefit of attending the service of the church as by law established,

and St George's had been purchased as a mainly free church. On ten separate census occasions, 1820-22, it was never more than a third full, and generally much less. There was plenty of room in the other churches too, and if Potter's figures, which no one seriously attempted to discredit, may be believed, Anglican church attendance in the centre of Manchester in the aftermath of Peterloo was below what it has often been in recent years, denuded of churches though the town centre now is.[8]

The second line of attack was to show that while the Church was entailing expensive luxuries upon the ley-payers, serious obligations were being neglected. The spire of St Mary's, the *Guardian* believed, was about to fall down, and the chapter would not repair till the Bishop intervened.[9] ' Close-fistedness ' at St. Mary's, a notorious tithe-suit prosecuted by the chapter against the parishioners, were followed by an opinion obtained from Dr Lushington, condemning the pew-rents long taken by the chaplains from the north and south galleries of the collegiate church. Even the collegiate church clock, in which the parish had a vital interest, was neglected. Nevertheless the communion plate for the parliamentary churches was executed in silver (not pewter) without the ley-payers' consent, and there were rumours of painted windows and even a bell. It was not difficult to rouse the vestry and get up a petition against the parliamentary grant for church-building in 1824.[10]

In 1827 and 1828 there was a concerted attack on the rates for the new churches in the West Riding, and the Manchester ley-payers were exhorted to follow the example of those at Leeds. The tory *Manchester Courier*, always a mouthpiece of the chapter, felt it time to expose

> the conduct of a small but clamourous [Unitarian] faction, whose object is to throw every obstacle they can invent in the way of the fulfilment of the legislature's benevolent design, to supply the want of the church accommodation. It would seem . . . that this spirit is not confined to the towns of Manchester and Leeds, but is generally diffusing itself through the country. . . . It could never be a question, when once it was found that the aid of Parliament was necessary, whether the projected places of worship should belong to the establishment. The inseparable connection which exists between Church and State, pointed out the only course which the Legislature of Great Britain could adopt. . . . [It is not religious principle but political animosity against the church establishment which underlies the clamour.] Those who have been the observers of the system pursued by a certain set of politicians, of whom the *Morning Chronicle* is the daily organ, and Mr. Hume the parliamentary orator, cannot have failed to observe the persevering hostility with which they pursue the clergy, the universities, Church property, and Church privileges.[11]

This leader illustrated the whole problem; the traditional political theory; the efforts of the Unitarian élite to provide material for the parliamentary radicals; and the implicit admission that the reason why wealthy Unitarians had resumed their old radicalism was that in present political circumstances, the support of the legislature for the old forms of establishment could no longer be presumed. And in fact dissenters and Catholics were relieved of their major disabilities in the next two years.

Of the old and great social interests with which the Church was supposed to be intimately connected, none was older or greater than that of agriculture, and none more bitterly vocal. For in 1814 corn prices broke, and in 1820 broke again more decisively, imperilling an industry whose capital structure was geared to high wartime prices. A violent agitation secured a Corn Law in 1815, but the law could not nullify the effects of a general European glut. Low prices drove the farmers to a furious clamour against the overheads on the industry, and especially taxes and tithe. The only way to reduce taxes was to cut public spending and the interest on the national debt; placemen and the monied interest became a great bogy to the farmers. And the tithe issue caused the Church to be cruelly harrowed by its old agricultural supporters. Local meetings of clergy to defend their interests were sorely abused, and by 1822 radical pamphleteers could see no hope of salvation except by a capital levy, beginning with Church property.[12]

As a regressive impost, tithe fell cruelly upon diminished agricultural incomes, and it was no longer one of the inevitable hazards. Over a great tract of country the tithe system had been dismantled piecemeal by the enclosure legislation, and in 1799 Pitt had considered allowing landowners to redeem it; in return the clergy were to be paid from the funds, with the prospect of cost-of-living bonuses.[13] The bishops defeated this attempt to transform the clergy openly into state pensioners, but clearly tithe was no longer taken for granted in England, much less in Ireland, where events were moving inexorably towards the catastrophe of the great famine. Tithe-levying was also a source of anxiety. Unless there was deadlock between parson and farmer, tithe was now infrequently taken in kind, except in the North-west and South-east. In Cumberland, Westmorland, Lancashire between Ribble and Mersey, and in Cheshire, at least some of the produce was tithed in kind, though even here the custom was steadily dying out. The real home of tithes in kind seems to have been in Hampshire, and parts of Sussex, Middlesex, Surrey and Kent. Most parsons cut out the cost of collection and settled for a cash composition at less than the value of the tithe, and many leased their tithes to landlord or farmer for a period of years. Leases of this kind had been advantageous to improving farmers during the booming war years, but the boot was on the other foot when prices tumbled thereafter. Cases were quoted where the tithe became as large as the rent. Of course, parsons, like landlords, often met the farmers in their distress, accepting less than their legal due to keep the farms tenanted; but in a difficult market, tithe, the reward of a co-parcenary owner of the land who risked no capital in the industry, began to appear intolerable. The Irish Tithe Composition Act of 1823 indicated what might come; in 1828 an unsuccessful Tithe Commutation Bill was promoted, and early in 1830 the Primate himself introduced a bill.

The tithe question showed how the bases of the political and

social influence of the Church were disintegrating quite independently of any forward move by the Church itself. It implied
that Parliament might not uphold the union of Church and State
in the terms in which churchmen understood it, and made public
opinion, which was indispensible in church reform, very treacher-
ous to use. Public opinion offered an invaluable lever to raise the
performance of clergy and patrons, but might, if the truth were
bluntly told, turn to an all-out attack upon the Establishment. It
was, for example, easy to argue that the Church held her property
by a title as sacred as that of any layman; but it became apparent
that church property was annexed to the fulfilment of certain
purposes, rather like trust property. Unfortunately no one knew
what the purposes of cathedrals, with their tangle of literally
sinecure offices, were; and although everyone understood the
purpose of clerical residence, no one knew how to secure its general
enforcement. If Irish Catholics demanded emancipation, it was
possible to beat the tub of the union of Church and State; yet
high-church clergy especially came to distrust Parliament, and
to appreciate the risks as well as advantages of establishment. This
revulsion of feeling stiffened a sense of clerical independence and
separateness, which was the Anglican counterpart of the growth
of the doctrine of the Pastoral Office amongst the Wesleyans. But
high views of the clerical office did not go down well with laymen,
and the incessant onslaughts by which high-churchmen drove
evangelicals towards liberal alliances were downright hazardous.
In fact while the storm gathered, church reform reached an im-
passe, and in 1828-9 the leaders of the unreformed state purchased
its survival at the expense of the unreformed Church.

The repeal of the legal disabilities of Protestant dissenters in
1828 was the first and more surprising blow to the old constitution. After the war the lead had been taken by Unitarians of
the new polemical cast who considered the disabilities of the Test
Acts by no means annulled by the annual Indemnity Acts, and
looked to repeal to break-up a log-jam of other grievances, the
most bitter of which was being bound to Trinitarian marriage
ceremonies. Men of this frame of mind displayed the same trucu-
lence which was envenoming the church-rate battles.[14] They had
no intention of being

    cringing, abject suppliants, begging for a boon, intriguing and

negotiating with ministers and jacks in office for their permission to smuggle a small quantity of toleration through the
Houses of Parliament . . . Above all, let there be no cant about
the clergy and the Establishment. We believe the latter to be
an unscriptural institution.

There were, however, two difficulties with this stiff line. Experienced politicians like William Smith, the chairman of the
Protestant Dissenting Deputies, argued (rightly as it transpired)
that the best hope lay in intriguing with the jacks-in-office at
some favourable juncture of parliamentary events. And, secondly,
the dissenting claims were in principle much like those of the
Catholics, who could exert much greater leverage; but by 1827 the
Baptist Ivimey reported that the majority of evangelical dissenters
were strongly opposed to any further concessions to Catholics.
The Unitarians had no reluctance to link repeal with emancipation,
but, of course, could not guarantee that if the Catholics succeeded
first they would lend a hand to the dissenters.[15]

The death first of Liverpool and then of Canning, and the evident disintegration of the tory party, enabled dissenters of all
shades to agree on agitation, and to win unusual parliamentary
support. Whigs and even Canningites could now support repeal as
a first step to emancipation, and Russell could advise dissenters to
unite their ranks by keeping clear of any formal junction with
the Catholics. Tories might hope that repeal would stiffen the
residual Protestantism of the Protestant constitution; even in
Oxford it was reported that ' the sentiments of the university in
regard C. & T. Acts may be considered as none at all '. A division
in favour of repeal went against the government by 40 votes.[16]
The first stage in the disintegration of the old tory and court party
had dealt one blow to the Anglican ascendancy; the next stage was
to deal another. For one result of the ministerial changes made
by Wellington was the by-election in County Clare which O'Connell carried triumphantly, and used to force emancipation.

Rural Ireland, moving rapidly towards social collapse, was the
scene of a passionate Catholic revival, and an equally passionate
evangelical revival which established a dominance in the Protestant churches. Dublin Castle could neither mend the economy nor
govern the country, and the Act of Union had in any case turned
Ireland into a domestic English problem at the very time when

massive Irish immigration, particularly to the North-west and to London, was transplanting that problem to English soil. On two fronts, therefore, that of high constitutional policy, and that of the local struggle for employment, housing and health, the fears and animosities engendered by Ireland sharpened and confused English denominational tensions. It is instructive to take one sample of what was happening on each of these fronts.

It has been argued that whether evangelical dissenters were sympathetic or hostile to Catholic claims depended on whether their roots were in London-based or in provincial agitations. The case of Methodism suggests a different view and reveals not only an important example of the English response to the Irish situation, but a means by which Protestant opinions were disseminated from the centre outwards. No English evangelical body was more closely involved with the Irish than the Methodists. Irish Methodism was vigorous and expanding, and if it was now even harder to get English preachers to accept appointments in Ireland than in Scotland, Irish celebrities were prominent here; William Myles, the elder stateman who travelled with Wesley, was a great bugbear of the young Bunting; Adam Clarke, the connexional polymath; Gideon Ouseley, the eccentric Gaelic preacher and evangelist, who would appear at intervals, preserved from the daily punch-up only by ' bones of iron & strength of brass ', bringing revival to Leeds, itinerating at large, begging in Liverpool for the work at home.[17] Nor could the English preachers turn their back upon Ireland. After the war, as English Methodism was torn apart by social conflict, the Irish came to blows on the sacrament question. As in England in the 1790s, the majority determined to receive the sacrament from their own preachers, while in 1818 the minority separated and set up as Primitive Methodists, ' primitive ' in this case implying that they continued to receive the sacraments within the Establishment. The English preachers could hardly discourage the Irish majority from doing what they themselves claimed to have done under providential leading, however oddly their advice consorted with their claim to be ' the grand instrument of preserving subordination . . . both in England & *Ireland* '; the Irish Primitives insisted that sacramentarianism was associated with armed rebellion.[18] Still worse, separation wrecked the finances of the Irish connexion at a time when circumstances were critical in England; by 1822 the English Conference was driven to a full-scale investigation of the Irish Conference's affairs.[19]

But Ireland was more than a millstone about the neck of the English connexion. There was a tradition inherited from Wesley himself that the Irish people suffered from invincible religious ignorance, were ' yet without the knowledge of God ', and that the origins of the Gospel revival in Ireland had been with the Methodists. The Catholic revival made no difference to this story; in 1848 it was still claimed that

> in the great struggle between Popery and Protestantism—the enemies & the friends of Scriptural & spiritual religion—Ireland is not unlikely to be the battle-field—and in proportion to the prominence and danger of the position which Irish Wesleyan Methodism seems destined to occupy in the conflict is the honour bestowed upon all those connected with the cause.[20]

But all Irish evangelicals knew that they must offer hope as well as hate, and were indeed buoyed up by a vivid sense of opportunity to be grasped. Gideon Ouseley's analysis of Irish attitudes in 1812 may stand for the rest.

> I distinguish them into 4 classes & and their clergy—The first and 2d. ranks. Shire men of property (of these I think we have not very many in the Kingdom) and their mercantile and farming men—these are more enlightened, and in general care little about their peculiar tenets, they either know them little or if they do, scarce believe them at all, and are mostly inclined to Deism, these are the most tolerant & best minded; I am satisfied they hate the persecution & intolerance of the Clergy & bigots—but then, they oppose it not, they dont wish to interfere with their clergy, so they stand neuter as to anything said or done against Protestants, but they stickle hard for their rights as they call them, and I think only for the custom, family pride and that childish unwillingness all men feel to change their religion, they wd become protestants.
>
> The 3d. class, those a little above the rabble, who can read etc., these are generally the worst, the most bigoted, these read defences of their religion, swarms of which, filled with bitterness & misrepresentations of the protestants & their doctrine [are] very carefully spread among them, and dare not read any protestant book, except by stealth, thus their minds are

soured & prepared for mischief—but if they were rightly instructed they wd. be amicable beings.

The 4th. the peasantry, who are by far the most numerous, are tho' illiterate, a smart, keen, intelligent [race] & when not exasperated & inflamed by their clergy & by such as they deem to know what is fit to be done, they are generous, kind, good-natured people and rather inclined to be pious, & to respect religion more than any of the other orders, if not perverted & corrupted which alas is easily done. Many & many a time have I seen these poor sheep, at my first coming among them, before they were warned by *their teachers*, flock around me with countenances full of affection & good-will, & stand sobbing & not infrequently falling down on their knees & weep aloud in the open street or field; but when it was found out by these woful men, they were cursed, put under penance, counselled, threatened or beaten etc.—so the next time they would avoid me or come to persecute. These poor creatures & the 3d. class are the clergy's principal tools & fools, & when raised to it, which I say is too easily done, are capable of any wickedness, & specially if they hope not to be detected. As to the R.C. Clergy themselves . . . they are semper idem, always the same, ever at enmity with & opposed to everything . . . but there [*sic*] own supersition . . . they are uniformly intolerant & could they but have their will would be as bad as those in the darkness of Spain and Portugal etc. They can never bear competitors in religion. . . . They want an entire monopoly. . . . I would be happy at their full emancipation (for I love to do them good) but we dread the consequences.[21]

Here the hope of detaching portions of the highest and lowest orders of society from Catholic obedience combined explicitly with the fear that competition on anything like equal terms would be wrecked by emancipation.

This point told, for the two chief lay advisers to the Committee of Privileges in London, Joseph Butterworth and Thomas Allan, were Protestant constitutionists of a surprisingly Eldonian kind. Allan, indeed, was not only a king-pin of the Protestant Union, but much involved in the legal arrangements of Lord Eldon's estate. Butterworth was active in the Hibernian Society, and energetically collected horror-stories about Catholic Ireland from

Ouseley and elsewhere, when emancipation became a serious issue in 1812 and 1813.[22] Butterworth and Allan were a fascinating and conservative pair who resented the growth of the Pastoral Office among the preachers from the opposite angle to the radicals; both smarted from the occasional arrogance of preachers in the Committee of Privileges;[23] both wished the itinerants would accept the same status as the local preachers. Allan feared that even the Irish Primitives had not been favourable enough to the Irish Church.[24] To men of this kind the lurid material which Irish Methodists supplied against Catholic Emancipation was as gold. A meeting of the Committee of Privileges late in 1812 was characteristic of many to come.

> Mr. Butterworth . . . obtained a wonderful mass of information from Ireland, relative to the conduct and views of the Catholics. It appears that they hold the very worst sentiment which their forefathers did three hundred years ago : that if they had the power they wou'd not leave [one] Protestant alive in the Kingdom. At the same time it is believed that if Government does not comply with their request [for emancipation] there will be another rebellion. We believe this will be the less evil of the two. . . . But if we were to come forward in a public manner, it is highly probable that most or all our friends in *Ireland wou'd soon be murdered.*

In 1814 massacre was expected again; in 1823 Adam Clarke had a dreadful journey in his native isle, and related that ' the Papists were insultingly bold, & if strong measures are not resorted to by government, I have no doubt that a general massacre of the Protestants is at the door '.[25]

The correspondence which thus poured into the centre and was duly disseminated to the fringes of Methodism explains clearly enough why, when the Catholic crisis came to a head in 1829, there were Methodists everywhere hot against the Catholic claims,[26] and why there was only one member of the Committee of Privileges who sympathised with emancipation. Eldon and the Protestant party were anxious to bring the Methodists out, yet the Committee was overruled by the determined minority of one, and the Church left to its fate in its hour of trial. For the one man was the President, Jabez Bunting, who believed in emancipation, who knew that it would in any case be carried, and who argued that the connexion ought not to interfere as a body in a matter in which its interests were not directly involved; moreover in the bitter aftermath of the Leeds secession (to be discussed in the next chapter) he held that he should avoid any political act on which his enemies could seize.[27] The well-worn allegation that any public move by the English Methodists would lead to the Irish brethren being murdered in their beds now recoiled disastrously upon the Protestant constitutionists.

At the local level the emancipation question was no less inflammatory and unpredictable in its outcome. Even on Merseyside, where an important Orange interest was created, there was no simple awakening of Protestant confessionalism. Before 1800, as we have seen, the Manchester Catholics had participated in the town's system of Sunday schools. Their priest, Fr Rowland Broomhead, laboured apostolically throughout the area, and was forward in every good work. Much loved, he was more of a public figure than any Manchester Catholic priest has been since, and was rewarded by liberal Protestant support for his last great effort, the building of St Augustine's, Granby Row, a church which later delighted Pugin; and when he died in 1820, there was ' such a funeral [as] Manchester never before witnessed '.[28] Broomhead's successor, the Rev. Joseph Curr, was a broomhead of quite a different character. Almost at once the worst features of Irish confessional strife were transferred to Manchester. Mr Coombs, Independent minister at Chapel Street, Salford, censured Popery in a sermon, and ' the consequence was two Papists came to his chapel, beat his door-keeper, and commanded him to tell Mr Coombs that if ever he presumed again to speak against their holy faith, his life should answer for it '. Curr himself had no more wisdom in 1821 than to begin a public attack on the Bible Society as a device to seduce Catholics from their faith.[29] This foolhardy assault let loose a vicious pamphlet warfare on both sides, allegations of forced conversions, and organised pulpit polemics.[30] It also revealed how interlocked the English and Irish situations could become.

The evangelicals, obsessed with the idea that Rome and the high-church were ganging up against them, regarded the attack as a broad hint to the Bishop to put down the Bible Society, and brought up the big guns of the Hibernian Society, with the doctrine that the woes of Ireland all stemmed from ignorance and priesthood. The editor of the *Catholic Vindicator* robustly replied that the trouble with both Ireland and England was tyranny, tyranny supported by the apologists of Bible and Hibernian Societies, and called on his compatriots to nurse the memory of the Peterloo massacre and not be misled ' by the illusory and frothy language of interested bigots '.[31] With James Scholefield, the radical Swedenborgian, supporting the Catholics because the Bible Society drew off pennies which might otherwise return Orator Hunt to Parliament, one of the great nineteenth-century spectres had been raised—the union of Irish and English discontent—and the lie was given to the claim that Bible Societies were the great antidote to social tension.[32]

In 1825 Manchester was treated to another twist to the plot, a foreshadowing of the temporary alliance of dissent with popular radicalism which blossomed spectacularly in 1830. On 22 April a private meeting prepared an anti-Catholic petition to the Lords. The old Pitt Club in the town now hardly dare raise its head, and the entire initiative was taken by a little knot of evangelicals and Wesleyans. The Independent and Baptist ministers, however, refused to put petitions to their congregations, and a counterblast was organised by the Unitarians with Congregationalist, Baptist, liberal evangelical and Quaker support. At their public meeting, however, the honours were taken in a speech from the floor by Jonathan Hodgins, a cotton spinner in a fustian jacket. In his view the differences of Protestant and Catholic had no significance to the working-man.[33] Before emancipation there was no prospect of the hair-raising skirmishes of the 'forties when bands of Chartist Irish would try to break up Anti-Corn Law meetings, and be resisted by a strong-arm corps of O'Connellite Irish arranged by Cobden; but the denominational situation in the 'twenties bore this resemblance to it, that though in detail the Irish impact was unpredictable, it was certain to exacerbate whatever contests were in progress. A crisis across the water and perpetual suffering and violence at home, were the highly flavoured Irish ingredients in the struggles of class and denomination.

Catholic emancipation was nevertheless a cruel blow. It had for so long been held that the British constitution derived its characteristic excellence from the struggle against Catholic aggression under James II and his successors; it was so shocking that the surrender should be led by the parliamentary representative of the Church,

Sir Robert Peel, MP for the University of Oxford, that a bitter sense of betrayal flared up. Peel lost his seat in a battle which drew together Keble, Newman and other younger fellows of Oriel College in warfare against the Provost and other senior men who supported the traditional Canningite and liberal-tory line of their house. Not merely the Tractarian personal alliances, but the Tractarian frame of mind was born, for it was quite clear that the Church and its privileges could no longer be defended on the grounds of the ' Church-and-State men '. Yet the Protestant Constitution party had one more shot to fire. They concluded that if the unreformed political system could produce such a result it was time to change it. In the elections of 1830, Eldon had his Northumberland tenants voting for Lord Grey, and on 25 November, a meeting of the Ultras decided to support Brougham's motion on reform. That night Peel was beaten, and Grey assembled a reform government which included four Canningites, four friends of Liverpool, and the ultra-tory Duke of Richmond.

The Ultras were to repent their rashness, for the reform crisis exhibited some at least of the classic symptoms of revolution. Political disintegration took place against a background of middle-class disaffection, and an upheaval in which rural and urban discontent combined. There was cholera, a harbinger of revolution and perhaps a sign of the Second Coming. In the autumn of 1830 the City was vexed by an outflow of gold, and provincial business men concluded that they could no longer protect their interests without parliamentary representation. The industrial working class also moved for its rights either under middle-class leadership, in the Political Unions, or independently, as in the Ten Hours agitation. Class cooperation and class division alike brought reform nearer. The political unions helped to secure a great reforming majority at the election of 1831, and with the *Manchester Guardian* calling for reform as a means of putting down venal voters from below, the government had every inducement to regain middle-class allegiance to the constitution by concession. In whatever respects the Reform Bill failed, in this it just succeeded; and in so doing it increased the influence of industrial boroughs where the political strength of dissent was concentrated.

The first crisis came, however, in the countryside. A large area containing the southern and eastern counties from Norfolk to

Dorset had suffered low prices for corn and very low wage-rates. Only around London did the labour force benefit from any urban or industrial competition for its services; demobilisation increased the surplus labour on the land, while industrial concentration eroded the possibilities of supplementary employment. Farm labourers spun out the market for their labour by calamitously reducing their productivity; employers replied by shortening labour contracts, and reducing the scales of poor relief. Since the end of the war there had been a serious increase in rural crime which let up only in the good years of the trade cycle. Any further turn of the screw would produce open resistance, as it had in the mid-'nineties, and (in the eastern counties) in 1816 and 1822. The bad year, 1829, turned the screw; the government bought off civil war in Ireland by Catholic emancipation, but it had no concession for rural England. By the following autumn things were desperate, and trouble which had broken out in Kent in mid-summer spread rapidly through the southern counties, and as far north as Norfolk. Demands for higher wages were backed up by rick-burning and machine-breaking. The scale of the disturbances (which eventually brought 2,000 prisoners into the courts) was serious; but still more menacing was the connivance of the normal props to public order, the rural middle class, the farmers. Farmers convinced the labourers that without reductions in tithe they could not increase wages; indeed in East Kent they ignored an appeal to enrol in the yeomanry, and resolved ' that at the present alarming crisis, it is the duty of the landowners and clergy, by a liberal abatement of rent and tithes, to assist the farmers '. At Benenden Heath near by, the arguments for cheap government were applied to the Church. A meeting resolved that ' the well-paid labours of those eminent men, who, attracted by the splendid revenues of the Church . . . have so simplified the clerical duties as to make them practicable by persons of ordinary abilities and acquirements.'[34] had made it possible to run the church by men modestly paid by voluntary effort.

With the farmers in this frame of mind, it is not surprising that the labourers, though sparing of violence against persons, did turn against clergy and lay impropriators, nor that in East Anglia where there was a tradition of resistance, Captain Swing circulated notices saying, ' Oh ye church of England Parsins, who strain at a knot and swaller a cammell, woe, woe, woe be into you, ye shall one day have you reward '. As clergy by the score reduced their claims for tithe, *The Times* denounced terrorism against the cloth inspired by the farmers; and for the Church, with the political order crumbling and the props of its rural authority breaking under direct pressure, the situation looked as black as possible. Savage repression finally put the labourers down, but the farmers gained their point, and the church authorities virtually gave up the tithe system. When tithe was finally commuted for corn-rent in 1836, the Church got a very much worse bargain than in the days of enclosure bills. The corn-rent was computed as the average of the last seven years' yield, and where (as in the great majority of cases) there had been a cash composition, the composition rather than the tithe was taken as the basis of assessment. Nor could anyone foresee how costly to the Church a rent-charge varying with the price of corn would prove, when prices tumbled again in the 'seventies.

The tithe issue, however, cost more than money. In the South-east, where the conflict was severe, dissent made little progress, notwithstanding reports that the farmers were opening conventicles to spite the parson, and that dissenting or Methodist preachers often spoke for the labourers. The farmers were in no mood to add the expenses of voluntaryism to those of tithe, and the labourers had endured enough. By the time of the Religious Census of 1851 organised religion was in a poor way over most of the southern counties (Dorset excepted). Only in Norfolk which lay full in the track of the Primitive Methodist advance from Lincolnshire and Nottinghamshire were there substantial gains for evangelical dissent. Victorian commentators were bound to be impressed by the virtues of free trade in religion, when in rural areas where dissent was strong, total church attendances were almost everywhere higher than in the South where the Church had preserved an apparent ascendancy; in the extreme cases, well over half the population of Huntingdonshire or Bedfordshire, virtually every man woman and child, who according to Horace Mann's calculation was free to attend,[35] was in church or chapel, compared with barely a third in Kent and Sussex. But the truth may be that the sting had been taken from the tithe issue in the enclosure areas, before the agricultural depression began.

The immediate consequences of the reform agitation hardly permitted reflections of this kind. In October 1831, the Lords rejected the Reform Bill by 41 votes, Archbishop Howley and twenty of the bishops being in the majority. ' Englishmen—remember it was the bishops and the bishops only whose vote decided the fate of the Reform Bill ', declared a radical placard, and a rabbling of bishops began which was ominously reminiscent of events in France. For quite suddenly, alliances against the Church mushroomed on a large scale, which for a decade had been presaged by local contests. There had been, for example, a curious case at Ashton-under-Lyne in the summer of 1821. Samuel Waller, a respectable cotton-spinner and Ranter, was prosecuted for causing an obstruction by open-air preaching in the streets; on refusing to enter into sureties not to offend again, was sentenced to three months' imprisonment. The chairman of Quarter Sessions said religion had nothing to do with the case, it was a simple matter of nuisance. It was just this which the public could not believe. For Waller's open-air meetings obstructed the entrance to the parish church. If this looked like aggression, it could be replied that all the land in Ashton belonged to Lord Stamford and the glebe; the former's leases protected him from nuisances on the property including ' the trades of a butcher, slaughter-man, tallow-chandler, soap-maker, soap-boiler, fell-monger, and dyer's, and also chapels, meeting-houses and places of public religious worship ', while the rector, a notorious non-resident, related to the earl, and installed by his patronage, obtained an act enabling him to grant leases of 999 years, and forbidding the tenants to allow the building of chapels and meeting-houses or any rooms to be used for public worship without the rector's consent. Add to this that the case had been instituted by the churchwardens, that the Ranters were roughly handled by the deputy constable, who was a lapsed Methodist, that the chairman of Quarter Sessions was the Rev. W. R. Hay, lately presented to the fat vicarage of Rochdale for his services in ordering the charge of the Yeomanry at Peterloo, that Waller was given security by John Potter, one of the political leaders of Manchester Unitarianism, and Thomas Harbottle, a radical Independent, that George Hadfield, perhaps the bitterest disestablisher the congregationalists ever produced, was his solicitor, that the case was taken up nationally by John Wilks and the Protestant Society, and it is clear that all the elements of the clash with the Church which took place in the reform crisis were present.[36]

Between 1830 and 1832 this clash was generalised on a huge scale, and as the press teemed with attacks on the Church, it was easy for dissenters of a relatively moderate cast to be swept into a cry for disestablishment, a thing which had never before seemed practical politics. The sheer arrogance of Unitarians, for example, was startling.

> Beseiged as the Church of England is on all sides, her defenders would do well to capitulate, whilst honourable terms may be had, and not to wait from indolence or obstinacy or false pride until the Establishment is stormed by popular indignation which is fast gathering around the dilapidated edifice.[37]

With the dissenting élite taking this tone, there was reason for Thomas Arnold's famous aphorism that 'the Church, as it now stands, no human power can save'. The extraordinary contrast between the ambitions of dissenters in 1832 and their timorous inability to ask with one voice for the repeal of the Test and Corporation Acts as recently as 1826, is explicable only in terms of the sudden changes in the political atmosphere in which the period abounded, rather than in terms of changes in dissent itself. Nevertheless, important changes there had been, and pre-eminent among them, a further increase in numbers, and an equally significant increase in public knowledge of dissenting expansion. Peel had ordered a return in 1829 of the number of Anglican and non-Anglican places of worship with ' the number of the sect '. The only portion to be published was a highly in-accurate return for Lancashire,[38] but it was followed, especially in the Manchester area, by incessant inquiries by the Manchester Statistical Society, by laborious clergymen, by opponents of establishment or supporters of church rates. None of the studies succeeded in delineating that perplexing phenomenon, the English religious community, but they leave a general impression that by the mid-'thirties most of the developments recorded in the Religious Census of 1851 had taken place, that (except where monopoly had done its worst, as at Ashton, and almost half the heads of families made no religious profession) the constituency of the churches embraced most of the population; and in Manchester was divided into three roughly equal sections, Anglican, dissenting and Roman Catholic; these together mustered about a fifth of the population in their Sunday morning congregations with the Roman Catholics the best (though not good) communicants, the dissenters (including Methodists) having the best Sunday school following, and the Anglicans distinguished by the very small proportion of their active congregations which communicated.[39]

The statistics and the often wild polemic which was constructed from them, made at least two things unmistakably clear: that the Establishment did not provide pastoral oversight for the nation, and that the religious situation was characterised no longer by toleration but by pluralism. Even Lord Fitzbooby in *Coningsby* knew now that ' the Wesleyans are really a very respectable body ', though he had ' never heard of them much till lately '. At the lowest this meant (as the Anti-Corn Law League appreciated) that dissent offered a more promising vehicle than ever before to agitators with any kind of grievance against the privileged order, and the new status promised by the Reform Act was followed by a great leap forward in the dissenters' numbers. 1833 and 1834 were two of the best years the English Methodists ever had. The North Western Particular Baptist Association multiplied its membership two and a half times between 1833 and 1844, the dramatic increases going to large urban churches, with able pastors and middle-class members with the resources for building, Sunday school organisation and lay-preaching. This new strength they began to put into political action, not least against the Establishment.[40]

Dissenters, indeed, surprised themselves with their new militancy. The Unitarians, as we have seen, developed a stiff objection against being required, under Hardwicke's Marriage Act, to marry in the parish church. Evidence was produced from Blackstone and other sources that the common law had always regarded marriage as a civil contract, and held it good if the celebration fulfilled the requirements of a contract; indeed, Hardwicke's Act itself, which did not extend to the marriages of Quakers and Jews, would have made it impossible for those parties to be legally wed, but for the common law provision. There had been cases between the Toleration Act and Hardwicke's Act in which the courts had recognised the validity of marriages concluded in dissenting meetings. Why then had the old-Presbyterians not protested at the time of Hardwicke's Act and obtained the same concession as the Quakers? Perhaps their preference for conformity was due to the fact that, while the ecclesiastical courts could not declare a dissenting marriage invalid, they could be sufficient of a nuisance to make conformity worth while.[41] The sign of the times was that Unitarians no longer thought conformity worth while. Protests in church and a political campaign began which must end grievously for the Establishment, either in the concession that portions of the Prayer Book service be omitted at the parties' request, or in the creation of wholly new machinery for celebrating dissenting or civil marriages.

Moreover a good portion of the evangelical world which had been ambivalent towards political action for so long, now seemed converted. When the Reform Bill passed its second reading by 302 votes to 301 the editor of the *Baptist Magazine* perceived the ' finger of God ' and noted that the House of Brunswick had attained the throne by the same margin. Methodists felt that the ' Reform Bill affords an opportunity for pious people to express themselves ', while the Clapham Sect rejoiced that the bill would enfranchise ' the great bulk of the middle classes of society, among whom, rather than among the very high or very low, lies most of the piety and good sense and right feeling '. Of course they had an axe to grind; outmanoeuvred by Canning on the slavery question, they concluded that there would be no abolition without parliamentary reform. It was never certain how far this unpolitical politics would lead. In 1831 when canvassing for Macaulay and Sadler was proceeding in Leeds, Richard Watson, the Methodist luminary, came out powerfully in favour of Macaulay.

> On the great question of slave emancipation we cannot for a moment hesitate to give the influence we may have with the people connected with us. Sadler, to say nothing of the ambition which has made him court the high-church and despise us, has never opened his mouth in parliament against slavery. . . . I would not vote for a radical candidate even for the sake of his vote against slavery; for God will not send deliverance by such means; but all differences of opinion within the constitutional range I would lose sight of, and would most honestly support a measure which is so intimately connected with the prosperity of missions, negro fellow-Christians, and fellow Methodists.

Watson's rather blustering attempt to align the moral and the denominational interest collapsed as soon as his views were published, and Sadler visited him; he begged to be rescued from the charge of ' gratuitously attacking Sadler '.[42] If this was a poor start to twenty years of Methodist effort to exercise influence through the electorate, the Clapham Sect would certainly stick to their guns, and might well add their weight to all the forces seeking changes in the present Church establishment.

The Congregationalists were also on the move, especially in the North and North-west. Ministers and laymen had learned the techniques of platform oratory and organisation in floating Bible and missionary societies: they created a denominational press, and in 1831 launched a denominational organisation in the Congregational Union.[43] This body was to extend the work of the County Unions in organising itinerant preaching, but, more important, was

> to shew to our own people, and especially to the rising portion of the community that they are not connected merely with an isolated church . . . but united in the closest bonds with hundreds of churches . . . [and] to carry into fuller effect the great principles of civil religious liberty which we cherish as our birthright and consider essential to the spread of true religion at home and abroad.

The Congregational Union proved a disappointment, but its political hopes and its reference to the ' rising portion of our community' indicate the real problem in Congregationalism in this period. For in 1800 northern Congregationalism had been a village religion, a religion of working-men; by 1830 it was the religion of an urban aristocracy, and was already losing what hold it had upon the town labourers;[44] moreover the urban aristocracy was calling the political tune. In the North-west at least, there is reason to think that this transformation owed much to Scottish influence.

Scots immigrants penetrated the North long before there was distinct religious provision for them. They speedily discovered that English Presbyterianism bore little resemblance to the kirk; indeed in Northumberland where they were most numerous, title deeds in Presbyterian chapels were drawn to tie the pastorate to the Westminster Confession. Elsewhere some Scots leaked off to the English Establishment; many were entirely lost to religious observance (in Manchester in 1837 only one-third of the Scots

families were pew-holders in any place of worship, and few
even of them attended with any regularity);[45] but many also found
a home amongst the evangelical Calvinists gathered in the
Independent churches. Here they found not only the Westminster
Confession, but very frequently also ministers who were Scots,
English-born sons of Scots parents, or Englishmen with some
Scottish education. The Scots influx into Lancashire Independency
set constitutional problems,[46] but it put Congregationalists on the
road to commercial success along which the Scots travelled further
and faster than any of the other Christian immigrants. The
baptismal registers of the Manchester Independents in the first
generation of the nineteenth century when they became important
in the town, contain so many Scots names as to suggest that their
migration created the opportunity which was capitalised by the
Congregational ministers like Thomas Kennedy (a minister of
the Church of Scotland), R. S. McAll, Robert Halley (both sons
of Scots parents) and, most important of all, the entirely English
William Roby. It was probably the Scots, moreover, who changed
the tone of voice of the northern Independents. The doctrinaire
stridency of Congregational politics in the 'thirties was altogether
alien from the ' catholic Christianity ' of the previous generation.
Scottish ecclesiastical controversy was generally incomprehensible
to the English, for its principal preoccupations were neither faith
nor order, but establishment and other matters, pursued with a
pertinacity in inverse proportion to their general importance. By
1830 this frame of mind had infected English Independents like
George Hadfield, the Manchester solicitor, who was English
enough, but whose narrow bitterness inflamed the contests between
Church and dissent, savaged the endowments of the Unitarians,
the establishment of dissent, and drove a great wedge between
the Independents and the average run of Wesleyans.

The Scots, moreover, not only sharpened English denominational conflicts, but, like the Irish, transferred their own to
English soil. Of this process, one example of unique importance
must suffice. In 1801 a number of Manchester Scots seeking
' a regular supply of sermon ', called Robert Jack, one of the
infant prodigies of the Associate ministry, who gathered an
important, prosperous and peaceful congregation.[47] As he aged,
they looked out for an assistant to help, and ultimately succeed
him, and in 1827 acquired a firebrand in William McKerrow,

the son of a radical and voluntaryist artisan from Kilmarnock. In 1830 when circumstances were becoming critical for the English Church, one of McKerrow's brother ministers, Andrew Marshall of Kirkintilloch, launched a great controversy against the church establishment in Scotland. This dispute, as we shall see, engaged many of the most famous names in Scotland, and was fanned by Voluntary Church Associations with their own press in the larger towns.

Despite the clamour, there was not much organisation of this kind in England, and this was McKerrow's despair. Throughout 1834 he fought the establishment question in the press with Hugh Stowell, the formidable leader of the evangelical and Orange interest in Salford, and he was prominent in the agitation the Manchester dissenters put on that spring. His speech set the keynote to his career:

> I stand before you as a Scottish dissenter, and take the liberty of representing on this occasion my brethren of the north. They are dissenters from a purer and a better church than that which is established in this land. They complain not of mitred, and titled, and over-paid bishops; nor of sinecures, pluralities and tithes. They are not subjected to that degradation con- nected with marriages, births, burials and universities, to which you have so long submitted. They cannot petition therefore, for the removal of those things known by the name of ' Dis- senters' Grievances '. They occupy the high ground of com- plete religious freedom. They are . . . demanding a separation of the church from the state. Will you join them in the struggle —will you assist them in the conflict? (Loud cries of ' We will, we will '.) . . . You have only to will it and you are free.[48]

If McKerrow sought to foment the English conflict to the point where it could be of value to the Scots—and it was now that Scots propaganda began to circulate widely south of the border, and Voluntary Church Societies began to form in English towns —he gave yeoman service to every radical cause in return. He was active in the Anti-Corn Law League and the Peace Society, in the agitations against the Factory Education Bill and the May- nooth grant, and was one of the original proprietors of the advanced *Manchester Examiner*. The Lancashire Public School

Association was founded in his vestry and principally by members of his congregation. He was among the founders of the United Kingdom Alliance, and a key-figure in establishing Presbyterianism proper as an English denomination. If in his early years he needed a spur, it was provided by the Kirk, which followed up his appointment in England by an organised attempt to compete for the loyalty of the Manchester Scots,[49] an attempt which ensured that in a few years they too would suffer the agony of the Disruption. McKerrow, however, was only the most distinguished of a vitriolic brood. When one finds George Legge, Independent minister of Gallowtree Gate, Leicester, at a church-rate meeting of 1839, attacking the ' white-livered, pigeon-hearted addle-headed, power-worshipping, rank-admiring, money-loving, knee-cringing, mealy-mouthed, lick-spittle dissenters ' of London, and hounding the Establishment as a system which

> is the masterpiece of hell—(Loud cheers)—which is pervaded by the spirit of anti-Christ, which while arrogating to itself the exclusive possession of Christianity has left the greater part of the land a worse than heathen darkness (Hear, hear)— the fountain of all infidel principles . . .[50]

one hardly needs telling that Legge was a Scot summoning English dissenters to the assistance of the Scots voluntaryists.

The first session of the reformed Parliament was a disappointment to the dissenters, whose claims, not for the last time, took second place to the clamours of the Irish. This frustration gave the cue for the provincial doctrinaires, and especially Hadfield, who attracted attention by demanding the expulsion of the bishops from the Lords. Hadfield's critics saw this as the attempt of a wild man to wrest control of nonconformist leadership, or as an unconvincing effort to bid up their price to the government by blackmail.[51] He was nevertheless able to get up a widely representative platform for a huge meeting in Manchester in March 1834, which continued for eleven hours on two evenings, condemning establishment in all its forms, setting up a committee to watch the whole question of dissenters' claims, and beholding McKerrow reaching real stardom for the first time. On the participants this meeting made so deep an impression that they came genuinely to believe that it was their gathering which had goaded Tractarianism into existence.[52] Yet the meeting did not carry even local nonconformity unanimously with it. Dr McAll, minister of Mosley Street Congregational chapel, who had an unrivalled reputation for spiritual and intellectual power, withdrew from his public functions to concentrate upon 'the improvement of ministerial character . . . the cultivation and increase of religious zeal amongst our congregations'. He and Raffles of Liverpool gathered 55 ministers who

> alternately wept together in the bitterness of soul over the iniquities of our holy things, and mourned over the desolation of Zion . . . and under the force of emotions none could control, no relief could be obtained, but in repeated, importunate and protracted prayer to God.[53]

After this evidence of pent-up anxiety, it is not surprising that when McAll was summoned to reply to Dr Chalmers' celebrated lectures on church establishments in 1838, his health failed and he died. Equally hard was the case of J. J. Tayler, minister of Mosley Street Unitarian congregation, who, at the great meeting, seconded the motion that all establishments were an infringement of rights of conscience. Immediately he was smitten in conscience for what he had done, and as one of the pioneers of 'romantic' and unpolitical Unitarianism, he was particularly open to the argument that he had allowed 'no consideration for the historical relations of the country'. His health collapsed, he publicly disavowed his action, and went off to study in Germany for a year to regain his peace of mind.[54]

The various committees of 'lick-spittle' dissenters in London had meanwhile worked out a minimum programme, aimed at rectifying what might be fairly described as dissenters' grievances. So conservative a sheet as the *Manchester Guardian* summarised it thus:

> An abolition of all exactions from dissenters for the support of the Church.
> An admission to all the national seminaries of education without subjection to any religious test.
> The right of marriage without the Church service, their own ministers officiating.
> The right of burial in parochial burial grounds, their own ministers officiating.

A general registration of births.

All these claims are upon the face of them so well founded, that even though the ministers should not be prepared to concede the whole in the coming session of parliament, we cannot conceive that they will hesitate to acknowledge their reasonableness, and to pledge themselves to an early compliance with them.

The intentions of the government were, however, as ambiguous as a programme which demanded access to parochial burial grounds without contributing to their upkeep. They were certainly casting about for palliatives which might head the dissenters off disestablishment, and were encouraged by conservative Unitarians and others.[55] But the government's extreme niggardliness, maddeningly exemplified in their approach to dissenting marriages, only inflamed the contest between the whigs and the radicals in provincial dissent, drove it down to London and up to the government itself.[56] But in the spring of 1834 the issue began to swing decisively to the whigs, for the government began to founder on the Irish Church question, and its viability became even more doubtful than its credibility. The Unitarian *Christian Reformer*, rabid a year previous, now rebuked the dissenters for lack of realism.

Of one thing we are sure, that intemperate language and violent proceedings are hurtful, if not destructive to their own interests. If on matters of *time* and d*egree*, they quarrel with a friendly government, they may soon have to fight a battle of great *principles* with a government decidedly inimical.[57]

Indeed, before the year was out, Peel and the tories were back in office, and the Church was safe. By this date too the Methodists, still a thrusting and aggressive body, were publicly supporting the Church in politics; but, like the Church, they had had an uneasy time during the reform crisis.

6 The Inner Tensions of Methodism 1825-35

The disestablishment politicians could not fail to seek evidence of Methodist support, but, at the time of the great Manchester meeting of 1834, it was not clear whether that support would be forthcoming, or whether the Reform era would not plunge Methodism like the Church into an internal and external crisis. The structural weaknesses in the Methodist community were exposed, particularly at the points where it made contact with a broad general public. This public, which the Church met in baptism, Methodism met in the Sunday schools, and its old informal relations with the schools became as uneasy as the Anglicans' attempts to fit their inherited doctrine and discipline of baptism to new circumstances.

Neither in practice nor in principle were the schools easy for Methodism to assimilate. In times of financial difficulty the cost of the schools was bound to be suspect, and there were always Trustees who resented the loss of pew rents occasioned by the attendance of Sunday scholars who required free accommodation at public worship, and 'who perfume ye house of God with a school effluvia'. When Bunting launched his drive for the control of the Manchester Sunday schools in 1826, he admitted that many of the chapel trustees concerned were opposed to him. The children were such a nuisance on church premises that 'nothing . . . short of absolute necessity can justify the practice of teaching a school . . . in any place of public worship'. At Darlington, for example, 'females had frequently to sit on forms on which ink had been poured, perhaps not always by mere accident'.[1] And at a deeper level, there was a tension between the Methodist ideals of an evangelistic mission and of a pietistic society set apart from the world in pursuit of sanctification. The old dissenters tended to say that Methodist membership was far too

K

easy to obtain; Methodists on the other hand worried occasionally that such a tiny proportion of the Methodist community (let alone the Methodist constituency) entered the Society, and worried at regular intervals that children of members could not be got to meet in class. As one leading minister put it in 1836,

> . . . few, comparatively speaking, of the children of the Methodists have joined the Society, many are well-wishers, but they have not fully and decidedly given ' their own selves to the Lord and unto us by the will of God '.[2]

Already there were proposals to grant them less exacting forms of membership, even membership by birthright.

Nowhere was the contrast between the walled garden of the saints and the broader mission more obvious than in Sunday schools. Here, related more or less closely to the Societies, was a popular religious institution with an unselective entry, which was open to gusts of popular radicalism, whose government generally involved a social contract in which the chief rights went to teachers and subscribers, and which embodied a community ideal of undenominational religion, general education, social service and entertainment, which appeared the more demeaning to the preachers the more their consciousness of peculiar status developed. The schools, moreover, raised the dilemma about Society membership. At Bolton in 1820, almost one-third of the membership was made up by scholars from the school, but the schools were usually indifferent recruiting grounds for the Society, a disappointment it was all too easy to attribute to the schools' failure to measure up to a full denominational standard. As a Salford preacher confessed in 1824,

> I have thought it my duty to tell some of the most zealous advocates for Sunday School Unions, that it is my opinion . . . they are doing more *evil* than *good*. The children are trained up without any regard to God's public worship; and reverence for the sanctity of the Sabbath, or any respect for the ministers of the Gospel. . . . Ask nineteen out of every twenty of the boys and girls you find running around in the streets of a Sunday evening in this populous town, whether they did not belong to some Sunday School, and they would answer, ' Yes ', and perhaps the major part of

them to the 'Union Schools'!! Is not this a serious evil?

And as denominational competition sharpened, it could always be argued that if Methodists did not secure full control of their schools, some other church would.[3]

The breach between Conference and the Stockport Sunday school in the years 1807-9 seems to have been carried through entirely on the issue of the control of the school pulpit, and when in 1826 Bunting moved under the new Conference minutes for control of the schools for all denominations in Manchester, he skilfully put the issue first again—' there was no *security*, either by *creed*, or in the *deeds* of those schools that pure Christianity should be perpetuated in them '.[4] From the beginning, however, attention tended to focus upon one ethical issue which seemed to denominationalists to explain why the schools recruited so in differently to the Church, the teaching of writing on the Sabbath.

Sunday writing lessons seem not at first to have stood for any very significant differences of opinion. The Stockport school always had them, the Manchester schools did not, except during the brief period of competition when the Anglicans withdrew. William Hey, who opposed Sabbath writing in Methodism, supported undenominational Lancastrian education, as long as it respected the sanctity of the Sabbath. In 1788 the connexion magazine spoke warmly of John Wesley's favourite school at Bolton : ' The children are enormously improved in their manners, morals and learning, and their natural rusticity is worn off. Many can now read their Bible well and write a tolerable hand.' But a decade later, both in Scotland and England, evangelicals, within the establishment and without, began to conclude against the practice, and in the first decade of the nineteenth century it came to symbolise the difference between the men of undenominational instincts and those for whom salvation lay in the new denominationalism.[5] There was a logic in this, for the strong public demand for Sabbath writing was bound to impress men of pragmatic outlook, yet to others of deductive predispositions it might well appear the archetype of those carnal instincts which must bend to the data of revelation. Anglican evangelicals turned against Sabbath writing in principle when they were trying to salvage the Church in the late 'nineties; in Methodism the transition can be conveniently dated by the conjuncture of the views of William Hey and Jabez Bunting at the time of the issue with the Stockport Sunday school.

William Hey, a prominent Leeds surgeon, had been converted under John Wesley, and although he had left the Methodists in 1781 because he felt they were endangering the Church connexion, he kept up his Methodist links. In 1807 he presented an elaborate paper on Sunday school management to that very Liverpool Conference which gave the first rebuff to the managers of the Stockport school, a paper which argued *a priori* that

1. The appointment of a Sabbath which was instituted before the fall of our first parents was an act of the greatest kindness to mankind on the part of the Almighty: and experience has abundantly proved its intimate connection with the state of religion in general. . . .
2. The whole of that day should be employed in exercises of religion . . . except where the necessities of our nature, or a charitable attention to the wants of others call for our assistance.

In this religious instruction was certainly comprised, but not the teaching of writing, for

1. it does not in any degree promote the salvation of the hearer . . .
2. it is a mere worldly accomplishment, since [unlike reading] it does not prepare a man for knowing the will of God . . .
3. If it be said, that it may enable a person to do good, the same may be said of other kinds of learning and of many manual employments . . .

Hey held also that Sabbath lessons were ' injurious to the minds of the teachers ', but the crux was that if the Sabbath was as he defined it, the argument was foreclosed.[6] Hey's paper made an impression upon Jabez Bunting, who despite preaching successfully on behalf of the undenominational Sunday School Union in 1805, was ripe for doctrine of this kind. From the beginning of his ministry, he had been preoccupied with the problem of church order, and was acutely conscious of the questions raised by Sunday school administration. From the time of Hey's paper he was screwing up his courage to put down Sabbath writing, it was ' a masterly speech ' from him which consummated the breach with the Stockport school in 1809, and he was behind the first Conference legislation for ministerial control of the connexional Sunday schools.[7]

Older ministers of empirical outlook still recommended caution. Entwisle agreed that

> the most excellent plan is to teach reading only on the Sunday & writing &c. on other evenings. But in our *very best & most methodistical & useful schools writing has been taught.* No schools have been better conducted, or more useful in a religious view than those in Bolton. Yet I am informed that they have always taught writing, and that an attempt to lay [it] aside would be ruinous.

Moreover, the apparently impregnable argument *a priori* from a supralapsarian Sabbath tottered perilously when Lancaster developed a method of teaching children to read (which all agreed was lawful on the Sabbath) by means of spelling and writing on slates. In 1810 Sion Chapel Sunday School achieved great success with the new methods, and the question whether any breach of the Lord's Day was involved went right up to the general meeting of the Sunday School Union in London; after a warm discussion the sanctity of the Sabbath was saved by a single vote (females not voting). Despite this near squeak, the sabbatarians found new arguments hard to come by, and apart from a general feeling that the limited Sunday school time available was best devoted to religious instruction, could only advance

> another objection from a political consideration, that of placing the poor above their condition in life, as well as putting into their hands a power which may be employed to the injury of society—the art of forgery.[8]

The pro-writers were less disposed to enter arguments of general principle, though in 1837, Joseph Barker, then in his New Connexion phase, presented the case in swinging style, beginning from the premise that as teaching children to write who could not be reached except on the Sabbath was a work of mercy, it could not possibly be unlawful. The pro-writers made short shrift of the subordinate props to the sabbatarian case. There would never be enough church accommodation for all the children to attend every week. Nor did secular subjects diminish the time available for religious instruction, for the writing class was the incentive to attendance in the crucial adolescent years, and led countless young people in the textile areas to put down the roots of a lifetime's devotion to their school as a religious, social and educational institution. Nor could the schools afford to do without it, especially in towns, when middle-class teachers moved into the suburbs. The greatest Anglican school in the country, Bennett Street in Manchester, was put in real difficulties by this urban migration, for the elder scholars were not literate enough even to fill up the roll; Stockport, of course, always had a surplus of homebred teachers.[9] Moreover, as Barker bluntly said, the educational theory of the sabbatarian party was unbelievably crude: requiring children to spend the Sabbath in continuous religious exercises was ' likely to drive them away from God ', and was less profitable than singing and prayer, reading, writing and religious instruction in roughly equal proportions. The Methodist legislation of the 'twenties put a veto upon Sabbath writing, but if the price of conformity was the loss of the schools, preachers had every inducement to tread softly, and in many places the writing classes continued as long as there was a demand for them.[10] Nevertheless there were preachers who sought to implement the official line, and the constitutional adjustments between the schools and the new high-powered ministry were made perennially more difficult by the unpalatable change of policy they so often involved. To these adjustments we must now turn.

Consolidating Sunday school legislation in 1826, Conference invited the preachers to ' induce ' the undenominational schools to come into the Methodist system. Jabez Bunting, opportunely stationed in the Manchester South circuit, at once moved in a circuit meeting, pressing the need for soundness in the faith, and though ' frequently interrupted—was very impassioned and argumentative—insisted on going on ' for three hours. He claimed that ' they were all hoaxing the public, by pretending to be for children of all denominations, when they were secretly & in their hearts working for Methodism & Methodists in their personal & individual creed '. The friends of the schools were in no doubt about the labours of Methodists in them, nor the recruitment of classes that went on, but pleaded the terms of their trust deeds, the fact that the schools had been built by general subscription, and that as recently as 1816 the schools committee had publicly declared they were ' not confined within the limits of a sect '. But financial pressure told, and in 1830, ' to secure the cooperation of the *Wesleyan Methodist Preachers* ', the Schools' annual meeting passed the remarkable resolution that

> this Institution (in conformity with what is required in its Trust Deeds) shall be entitled that of ' The Sunday Schools for children of all denominations '; and it shall be carried on *in connexion with the Wesleyan Methodist Society,* whose religious doctrines shall be *exclusively* inculcated in its schools.

The Superintendent minister should chair the meetings; the preachers should be members of the Committee; almost all the officers and committee should be members of the Society; the Wesleyan catechism should be regularly and exclusively used. The schools submitted completely in return for guarantees of financial stability which proved illusory; the bill to the connexion fell in later.[11]

The new regulations also bore on the situation at Leeds, for although the New Schools there had been taken over by the Wesleyans in 1816, there was considerable official anxiety as to what might happen if the spirit of democracy in the teachers' meeting were to infect the leaders' or local preachers' meetings of the Leeds circuit. Some of the teachers

> were known among their companions by the names of the principal members of the opposition in the House of Commons. one was called Lord John Russell; another was known as Mr. Hume; a third, as Mr. Grey Bennett. As these and other persons were active in fomenting discord, and promoting unmethodistic proceedings, a rupture, sooner or later, was imminent. It was supposed that it would take place in the Leeds Sunday schools, where most of the mischief had been engendered . . .[12]

although in fact it took place in 1827 over the celebrated organ in the Leeds Brunswick chapel, and both issues were envenomed by a neglected matter, the 1826 division of the Leeds circuit.

The division of the Manchester circuit after much acrimony in 1824 and again in 1827, and of the Leeds and Liverpool circuits in 1826, though a not unexpected consequence of a long period of prosperity and growth, was very hazardous. The division of circuit assets and liabilities proved contentious, but less irksome than the recognition which the new arrangements made of the importance of the new chapels wealthy Methodists had built for themselves in their migration towards the suburbs. In each case circuit division foreboded trouble in decayed town-centre chapels. As long as the whole Methodist congregation worshipped in one or two of the old chapels, it coped with its social strains; once social division was translated into geographical separation, it was a different story, and the Pastoral Office, however magnified, proved an ineffective substitute in the town centres for the old influence of substantial laymen now in the suburbs. The Liverpool case put the Leeds men on their guard, while the Leeds revolt fed back upon Liverpool.

The 1824 Conference expressed a wish for the division of the Liverpool circuit, but when the Superintendent got to work he met trouble arising from a peculiarity which Liverpool shared with Leeds and some other large town circuits, that there was a single Leaders' Meeting, not for each Society, but for the whole circuit. The leaders assembling in the Quarterly Meeting were therefore used to acting as a body and had no mean pretensions.

> The Leaders meeting sometimes act as a parli[a]ment, make Rules, have a secretary beside the Stewards, who writes down what they call their measures and orders. Sometimes as a Court of Justice; and when they wish to use harsh language towards the Preacher, as a Court of Inquisition. . . .

The Superintendent's patience finally gave out, and he expelled McClintock, an aged leader with a sharp tongue, and an undoubted troublemaker, David Rowland. Such a stir was produced that the next Conference had to send down a Presidential Commission (which of course included Jabez Bunting). The Commission found that McClintock had been illegally expelled, and restored him; but they insisted on the division of the Liverpool circuit before the next Conference, and required the immediate break-up of the circuit Leaders' Meeting as ' *indispensable* to the proper execution of Methodist discipline ', it being ' absolutely impossible, while there is but one such meeting in so numerous a Society, that the Superintendent and his colleagues should sufficiently perform their duties in that meeting as Christian Pastors.' The Commission required the Stationing Committee to provide the circuit with a completely new ministerial staff, gave the incoming Superintendent his instructions, and promised to reconvene if he found ' any unexpected difficulties in the immediate division of the Leaders' Meetings.'[13]

John Riles, the new Superintendent, knowing ' what sort of stuff the Lancashire materials were composed of, when religious politicks were blended with radical feelings ', did not sleep for more than five minutes at a time for weeks before his crucial meeting. But he ' was fully apprised of all their manoeuv[r]ing and low cunning ', and of their simple-minded assurance that the division of the Leaders' Meeting could not take place without their consent. On the day, he spun out the routine business, and

> then rose and requested the attention of the meeting to what I was about to announce, viz. ' I stand here as the accredited Pastor of the Liverpool Methodist Society, by the appointment of the Conference, and as such, I divide the Friday evening's Leaders Meeting held at Mount Pleasant Chapel Vestry into six divissions [*sic*]. . . . As soon as I had concluded the sentance, [*sic*], a man from the other side of the room vociferated with apparent bad feeling, ' What did we come here for, if we have no voice in the business?' To which I replied, ' *To hear what I have to say, and do what I bid you, as your Pastor* '. I then gave out a verse and concluded with a prayer, and the meeting was dismissed by a few minutes after nine o'C . . . I need not say that all the real friends of Methodism rejoiced, and the ungovernable were taken so much by surprise that for the moment they were confounded. When they had recovered themselves, which they did not do, till they got in groups in the street; the first thing they could articulate was, ' It is the most arbitrary, tyrannical step we ever knew or heard of ' . . . though there are a few rough spirits at Leeds St., we hope ere long, either to kill or cure . . . We have gained an important point, by having driven the factious from their *talking Fort*, . . .

Riles reported that ' all our principal friends express their satisfaction at the change which has taken place ', and prepared to install them in the key administrative posts.[14] But victory must be paid for; some statement of the doctrine which underpinned so naked an exercise of the Pastoral Office must soon be made; the Leeds men had been warned what circuit division implied, and four months of personal strain determined Riles to resign his ministry next Conference.

The Leeds situation was still more complicated, for circuit division affected not only the Leaders' Meeting but two other originally
independent institutions, the prayer meetings and the Sunday
school. The cottage prayer-meetings had been a feature of Leeds
Methodism for over a generation; Bunting now hoped they would
be brought ' under complete discipline, & reduce[d] . . . to their
proper level '. The Sunday school was a bitter bone of contention :
the Leaders of the new Leeds West Circuit fought for months for
the control of the branches within its boundaries, while the Leeds
East leaders fought to maintain the unity of the school, well knowing the reorganisation that might follow. The same parties who
contended for the unity of the school, fought also to maintain
the unity of the Leaders' Meeting, and claimed that they had been
promised that the united Local Preachers' Meeting should remain
after circuit division. Matthew Johnson, Yewdall and other Methodist radicals prominent in these affrays, were also notorious in the
Leeds vestry, at the head of the new assault on church rates. There
were stiff-necked laymen on the conservative side too, and specially
W. Gilyard Scarth, one of Bunting's intimates. Hence when the
gunpowder was unexpectedly ignited by the Brunswick organ
question, neither the connexional management nor the Leeds
radicals were as interested in the organ, as in extraneous issues on
which they were already at loggerheads.[15]

The Brunswick chapel for which the organ was required was
new, fashionable, and reputed the largest in the connexion; and it
exposed uncertainties in connexional law which, it is quite clear,
divided the preachers at the time, as they have divided historians
ever since. In brief, an organ might not be introduced without
Conference consent, after investigation and approval by a District
Meeting. In this instance the trustees, as vested with the property,
applied for the organ, while the local preachers, who were held
to have no constitutional standing, stirred up the Leaders, repre-
senting the spiritual interest in the Society, to oppose the application. The District Meeting reported against the organ, but on
appeal to Conference, and on giving written assurance that ' the
granting of our petition will occasion no unpleasant consequences
in the Society ', the trustees gained what they wanted. At once an
uncontrollable agitation began. Whatever the niceties of the law, it
is clear that the organ case was frivolously pressed. Before the
Brunswick chapel was opened in 1825, there had been sharp

opposition to the idea of the organ, and the issue had been dropped until it was overshadowed by the division of the circuit. For reasons that are hard to imagine, the Superintendent did not summon trustees from outside the new circuit, ' because they were members of another circuit & had no right to interfere.' Indeed the whole trustee application was an extreme and impermissible assertion of local rights, for they held that the wishes of nine-tenths of their pewholders (who certainly had no constitutional standing) ought to override the views of Leaders not attached to the congregation, and of preachers from other circuits at the District Meeting, whose ' interference . . . [they considered] an intrusion on our brotherly and christian liberty to which *we ought not to submit* '. Of the 15 trustees who met, eight were for the organ, six against and one neutral. It was to meet the wishes of this slender majority that Conference disregarded an adverse majority in the Leaders' Meeting of more than 20 to one, and set aside the advice of the District Meeting. The only conclusion open to the radicals was that the organ question, like the reconstruction of the circuit and Sunday school, was to be a demonstration of who was master in the Methodist household.[16]

Matthew Johnson proceeded to hold illegal secret meetings of local preachers, and persuaded about 50 of them in both Leeds circuits to refuse their preaching appointments. Thomas Galland, preacher in the East Circuit, replied with illegal anonymous pamphleteering, and an attempt to secure a Leaders' Meeting guaranteed to expel offenders, by offering to take back Leaders who would assent to a document affirming the principles of Wesleyan Methodism. Gilyard Scarth, Treasurer to the Brunswick trustees, impeached Matthew Johnson at a Quarterly Meeting and called on the Superintendent, Edmund Grindrod, to do his duty. Johnson's suspension confirmed the solidarity of the local preachers, who held that as they shared in Johnson's guilt, they should share in his punishment. The anxiety which had almost finished Riles in Liverpool, now overwhelmed Edmund Grindrod, and when his doctor advised that if he did not obtain relief he would die in six weeks, a presidential commission descended upon Leeds. The commission was headed by the President, that old war-horse John Stephens, who was ' in excellent spirits and says he hopes we shall so dispose of the Leeds business as to read a useful and lasting lesson to the whole Connexion ', and accompanied by Bunt-

ing as President's adviser. The legality of Bunting's presence has
always been disputed, but is hardly worth debating; he was a more
intelligent and moderate man than Stephens, and the real abuse
was that he was already deeply involved, as the man who moved
Conference to permit the organ.[17]

Bunting privately assessed the case as he had assessed Peterloo
and Luddism before that.

> The organ is the *mere pretext* among the *heads* of the schism;
> & would, I believe, be cheerfully abandoned, if there were any
> ground whatever to believe that such a concession would cure
> the evil. . . . There was a *radical* faction there whose meetings
> had assumed all the fearful characters of a *Methodistical Lud-
> dism* (*secret vows or bonds* &c included) and of whom it was
> indispensable to the permanent peace of the Society that it
> should be forthwith purged. . . . We at one time had no hope
> but in dissolving the Society, & beginning again, because though
> the great mass of the Society, & nearly all our more respectable
> friends were right, the *poor Leaders, & younger Leaders &
> Local preachers* were largely infected with the spirit against the
> first principles of our existing church government. . . . The great
> mass of disaffection is among persons who worship at the *Old
> Chapel. Nine-tenths* of the Brunswick congregation & Society
> are on one side.[18]

Class separation when translated into geographical separation was
too much for Wesleyan fellowship. ' Bella, bella, horrida bella '
continued after the commission departed, with desperate battles for
the keys of the Sunday schools; but in the end the Sunday school
committee and the Leaders' Meeting were broken up, and the
prayer leaders' meeting ' settled on a right footing *in all points* '.
Bunting was nervous about Conference, but had no need to worry;
in its hour of trial Conference prefaced its heart-searching by
electing him President on a minority vote.[19]

The losses were severe. A secession connexion, the Leeds Protestant Methodists, claimed to have taken from the parent societies
28 local preachers, 7 exhorters, 56 leaders and 900 members—
but the immediate cost to the Leeds circuit was 1,040 members,
2,000 hearers, and almost as many Sunday scholars. James Sigston,
the old firebrand, took advice from all quarters on the proper
constitution of the Christian church (from the Congregationalist

Thomas Raffles among others), and, paradoxically, what had begun as a radical revolt against an extreme assertion of local rights by the Leeds rich, ended with a constitution so heavily weighted in favour of the lay and local elements as to be condemned by other Methodist malcontents as Independency. Nevertheless the Leeds constitution set the pattern for later Methodist reformers, and in the mid-'thirties the Leeds men threw in their lot with the Warrenites.[20]

The Leeds conflict became public property as the Liverpool transaction had not. The *Leeds Mercury* gave it extensive coverage, the Leeds propagandists were abroad in the country, and the publication of the proceedings of the Special District Meeting provided an appropriate text for a clash between Superintendents and Quarterly Meetings round the country. There is no space here to follow these reverberations, nor even the well-contrived revolt in the London South circuit which almost carried off a chapel, and which produced a 40-page *Address* for private distribution amongst members of the 1828 Conference, demanding constitutional clarification.[21] Events in Sheffield and Liverpool illuminated so much of the past and future of Methodism, however, as to demand comment.

In Sheffield the sources of unease went back deep into the history of the Sunday schools. We have seen that the Sheffield Methodists, despite the loss of a school to the Kilhamites in 1797, developed their work with great success through the undenominational framework. The first challenge came from Jabez Bunting and his friend Edward Hare, who were stationed there together in 1808. They abolished Sabbath writing, with the consequence that the elder boys and girls left the schools, the schools themselves began to break away, and the Leaders' Meeting in July 1809 was told that support for ' opposition schools ' would be incompatible with Society membership. A traditional Union Sunday School was established in Spring Street, and James Montgomery, an adherent (though not a society member), came out strongly in the *Sheffield Iris* in favour of Sunday writing.[22] Bunting then left the Sheffield circuit, and the superintendent William Myles made peace with the schools to the accompaniment of vicious back-biting from Hare and Bunting. Sabbath writing was restored, the opposition schools given up, and Conference took a risk in the cause of reconciliation; as Myles' successor in 1810,

they appointed William Bramwell, who had behaved so equivocally in Sheffield at the time of Kilham's expulsion. Bramwell and
the school committee appealed to the town for a big school on the
Stockport pattern at Red Hill, in which their 2,300 children could
be united. The events which followed were in quite the old style.
A Sunday School Union embracing all the denominations in the
town was formed, and if in the first year the Unitarians dropped
out for doctrinal reasons, and the Anglicans, because they could
not control the liturgical practices of the schools, the first anniversary of the Union was a Pentecostal outpouring which established
the event in the round of great Sheffield occasions for generations,
and gave a great impulse to the Bible, missionary and charitable
societies sustained by the same parties. Moreover, the agents of
the Sheffield Union scoured the whole countryside, establishing
schools for their ' wild population '. A decade later nearly 9,000
children were in their care.[23]

When the Sheffield circuit felt the impact of the Leeds crisis,
this recent history was *à propos*. On the last occasion Sheffield had
defeated the man and the policies now dominant in the connexion,
and had turned its victory to splendid account; moreover, behind
the Sheffield contests over the Leeds organ there was pressure from
the preachers to go back on the Sunday school agreements of 1809
to 1812. The Sheffield Quarterly Meeting of January 1828, petitioned Conference.

> to have the introduction of organs into our chapels, as well
> as all material alterations in the mode & form of Divine Wor-
> ship subject to the same regulations as are in force with respect
> to the Administration of the Lord's Supper . . . because it is a
> much less thing to grant the Leaders a veto concerning an
> organ than concerning the Lord's Supper. . . .

The refusal of Conference to yield, and the arrival of propagandists from Leeds and Barnsley raised the tempers of the radicals, while ' some of your Gents who take the Toryish side of
the question ' were tempted to protest against the South London
Address. The radicals arrived in force at the October Quarterly
Meeting determined to revolt if they were roughly handled. The
superintendent however resolved ' to allow of a free conversation &
to hear all that the dissatisfied party have to say, & fearlessly
and good temperedly to meet their objections '. His reward was a

set of resolutions differing little from those of the previous year, a point of consequence, as the Conference to which they would go was to meet in that very circuit. The radical ferment continued to work in Sheffield, but separation, when it came, was a minor affair, not the great break-up which the Leeds men hoped would make their fortunes. And the next chapter in the Sunday school saga went the preachers' way.[24]

Liverpool also responded to the calls of South London and Leeds. The Liverpool North radicals came to their Quarterly Meeting in January 1829, with seven resolutions, one of which condemned the Leeds Special District Meeting out of hand, and asserted that the entire lawful government of a circuit ' is vested in the Leaders; Local Preachers; a Quarterly Meeting with the Superintendent at their head '; any outside interference was illegal and mischievous. ' You will perceive ', commented John Scott, the tough-minded superintendent, ' that the rogues go further than the Southwark leaders and make out Methodism in the circuits *to be* a parish vestry government—this the Southwarkers only *want to make it*.' He declared this resolution to be *ultra vires*, but ultimately had to go to Conference with a remonstrance against the Leeds proceedings from a special circuit meeting of office holders. There were similar transactions in the Liverpool South circuit, and the rumblings went on, though without coming to a head and without preventing some prosperous years in the early 'thirties.[25] The Liverpool skirmishes were inconclusive until 1835, but they had a two-fold importance. They drew Jabez Bunting out of London for the last time, complete with an assistant to help him recover from a broken bone, to Liverpool North. And they led also to John Beecham's publishing *An essay on the constitution of Wesleyan Methodism*[26] for the enlightenment of the radicals of Liverpool South. This, and other tracts which appeared at the same time, broke a literary silence on the doctrine of the ministry which had continued since Wesley's death, and sought to base the modern practice upon Scripture and the heritage of John Wesley himself.

Beecham's method was predominantly *a priori*. ' There are a few principles common to all governments whatever; and one of these is, that every body politic must have a head.' This was the legislature, and Beecham had no difficulty in showing that Conference had always been the legislature of Methodism, and its *Minutes* the legislation. The radical appeal from Conference policy

to circuit rights was asking the intrinsically impossible. ' It recog-
nises no legislative assembly to make such laws as circumstances
occasionally require—no supreme authority extending over and
controlling the whole.' It regarded the Superintendent ' not as
the representative of Conference acting by its authority, but as the
organ and servant ' of the Quarterly Meeting. This Hobbesian view
of what the Methodist constitution must in the nature of things
be, claimed no more than ' that power which every branch of the
Church of Christ possesses, to frame such regulations for the management of its affairs, as do in its judgment accord with the fundamental laws of Him who is the supreme Legislator of His church
on earth.'

The right of District Meetings, including Special District Meetings of the Leeds type, to intervene locally, was not merely a per-
petuation of John Wesley's personal superintendence of the whole
connexion, it was part of the nature of things. Not only were the
radicals kicking against what must be, they were condemned at the
bar of history. The Kilhamite radicals of the 'nineties had parted
company with official Methodism because of the composition of
Conference, not its omnicompetence. Lay representation in Conference met their complaint; and the hopes of the New Connexion
of picking up schismatic Methodist reformers in the next twenty
years all foundered ostensibly on their insistence upon the sovereignty of a reformed Conference. Between Kilham and Sigston
et hoc omne genus stood Jabez Bunting and the reality of active
central administration; nothing would now satisfy the radicals but
some dismemberment of that central authority.[27]

It was not, however, enough for Beecham's purpose to argue
that Conference was the locus of that sovereignty inherent in all
corporate bodies; not nearly enough if he wished to use the Kilhamite Conference as a stick with which to beat the radicals.
Again the argument was mainly a priori. The Pastoral Office was
a datum of scripture, and the strength of Methodism lay in its
proper recognition of the Pastoral Office. The whole office was
filled in the first instance by Christ himself, and it was perpetuated
in the Church by his ministers. The pastor's business was to feed
the flock, but also to teach, rule and exercise discipline over it,
and the apostolic injunctions to the pastorate not to lord it over
God's heritage, were really a testimony to the fulness of their
lawful power. The next step was the most difficult, for Beecham

had to safeguard against attacks from opposite sides. It might be held, as Wesley had held, that Methodist itinerants were not pastors in the full sense of ordained ministers; or it might be held that as the burden of pastoral oversight in Methodism was divided among an army of local preachers, class leaders and so forth, they were entitled to a share in the exercise of government and discipline. Beecham cut this knot boldly by arguing that a pastor must be not merely personally qualified and called by God to his office, he must be wholly separated to it. Valuable as local preachers and class leaders might be, they failed at this hurdle. The principle of separation appeared also to create a much needed link with Wesley. The Conference Minutes of 1768 had quoted the injunction to ministers of I Tim. iv to give themselves wholly to reading, exhortation and teaching, and asked whether the preachers could do less than the Ordinal required of the clergy, especially as they received their allowance to enable them to travel. Wesley's authority, however boldly introduced, showed how precarious Beecham's deductions had become. His argument that Conference had sovereign power assumed that the Methodist connexion was now a separate church, with full powers, not a ginger group within the Church provoking the official pastorate to jealousy. In any case the requirements of the Ordinal had never been understood to preclude what amounted to a part-time ministry, and in Beecham's generation the law was widening the opportunities of secular employment open to the clergy. It could of course be empirically established that an itinerant ministry could not proceed except on the basis of separation, but empirically-based arguments would not carry the implications Beecham needed.[28]

If Beecham's premises were granted, all the rest followed. The preachers in Conference exercised the plenitude of pastoral power, and the rights of other parties conferred, for example, in the legislation of 1795 and 1797, could not be more than procedural safeguards granted to prevent the abuse of a power which, in principle, the pastorate could not share or surrender. How far Methodism was now from its old empiricism could hardly be more manifest. ' Whatever subordinate agencies may be employed, the ministry of the Gospel is the leading and principal instrumentality for originating, conserving, and extending the church of Christ on earth ', claimed Beecham,[29] his eyes closed firmly to the fact that the immediate embarrassment in the schools and revivals arose precisely because the ministry had not been the principal agency in them. Nor could his syllogisms establish whether the ministry was strong enough to sustain the role it had chosen in the social conflict of the day. This question was raised again by the Reform Bill excitements. As one of the Hull preachers reflected in 1835,

> every intelligent Methodist who has observed the operation of political power in this country during the last few years must be aware, that the Reform Bill, a measure most unnecessarily & injuriously extensive, both in what it destroyed & in what it created, has produced, or if not produced, has greatly aggravated & influenced, such a lust of power in a considerable number of our people, that it is becoming very difficult indeed, in some places, to exercise that pastoral authority, with which I believe the New Test[ament] has invested the minister of Christ, & which is indispensable to order & good government. The Leaders Meetings, for instance, have in my judgment, greatly too much power, particularly where they have been allowed to remain, as here, altogether. The Leaders Meeting of this town consists of above 100 persons, the much greater part of whom came together, not to show their class-books, that the preachers may become acquainted with the state of their respective classes, & visit the sick & absentees whose cases may seem to require it, & give them such advice as their office as leaders often needs, but to *vote* in determining how this & the other shall be done—the government of the Society, & its affairs really being much more in the Leaders Meeting, than in the Superintendant [*sic*] . . . as to lay delegates in the Conf[eren]ce, or what some now call a house of Commons to meet in the same town, & at the same time, with the Lords, such a proposition, I hope would not be entertained for a moment. . . .[30]

Beecham's doctrine had more than domestic implications; it assumed that Methodism was in the full sense a church, and hence distinct from the Establishment. What the relations between the two were to be was a matter of much obscurity in the 'twenties. Adam Clarke was pro- and anti-church by turns.[31]

The intentions of other leading men were very dark indeed. Local congregations knew that they thrived upon a generalised kind of anti-church sentiment, without becoming ideologically committed against liturgy, episcopacy or establishment. Rank-and-file preachers were much moved by local circumstances; hostile when education policy favoured the Church, when the clergy would not recognise Methodist baptisms, when there was competition for the flock, they responded quickly to a little flattery or kindness.[32] In the mid-'twenties there were persistent rumours of a substantial move towards the Church. At the Conference of 1823, a majority of seven was reported against an attempt to bind societies to the Liturgy and introduce episcopal ordination. Moreover ' this attempt to approach towards the Church of England, though defeated will be renewed. Should this conclusion be correct, it is easy to foresee that the Wesleians will divide into the two branches of Churchmen and dissenters '. Certainly James Dixon, returning to Conference that year after some years' absence, was surprised to find that questions from the Ordinal were being put to men about to be taken into full Connexion. Three years later, London and provincial papers carried the story that 'amongst many other changes which are to take place in our connexion we are to have three bishops, viz. Messrs. Bunting, Newton & Watson '. During the Leeds conflict, Bunting actually received an offer of preferment in the Church.[33] Yet, at the very same time, there was an attempt to assert the Anglican reference of Methodism, which was lay-inspired, treasonable, and really in those traditions of Wesleyan reform which took a more characteristic shape at Leeds.

Irish Primitive Methodism offered a working model of a Methodism which was anti-preacher and pro-Church, and the Methodism of Beverley in the East Riding, where Mark Robinson attempted to revive Church Methodism in 1825, had reminded William Myles of Irish Primitive Methodism as early as 1819. In Dublin Arthur Keene, the Methodist man of influence, had rigidly opposed the sacrament in chapel, until there was a separation; in Beverley ' the principal friends ' would not have a resident preacher in the town. As so often elsewhere, the division of the Hull circuit was the preface to trouble. Claiming the support of 1,000 members, Robinson put round a circular in the tones of the Bristol trustees of '94 :

It has long appeared to me, & several respectable friends who are members of our Society, that there is a rapid dissent effecting in the country from the Established Church by the Methodists who seem determined to set up a rival Church, as is intimated by morning service, administering the sacrament, burying the dead, erecting organs, employing vergers with their uniforms and wands. We think also that there is a growing love of power in the preachers, which is shown in the enactments of Conference, which will tend to increase the power of the travelling preachers, & to lessen that of the local preachers.

He claimed to have Anglican support, and would get a preacher from the Irish Primitives if Conference did not yield. With ministerial authority of every kind in the East Riding being shaken by aggressive Ranterism, there was not the least prospect of success for this antique programme. Before the summer was out, Robinson had been dislodged, had divided the Beverley Society, and produced an embarrassing class-ticket, bearing the title ' Church Methodist Society, Established by the Rev. Jno. Wesley, 1739 ', and the quotation, ' " If some quit the Church, others will adhere to it; and then there will be dissenting Methodists and Church Methodists "—J. Wesley '.[34]

Creating embarrassment was Robinson's *forte*. Four Beverley trustees published a pamphlet, complaining bitterly that those who in the 'nineties had opposed communion in chapel, had no idea that in a generation they would be liable to expulsion, and including the documents of the anti-sacramentarian trustees in the East Riding of 1794, some of whom were still alive and now on the other side. Robinson canvassed the local magistrates and clergy, winning the support of Archdeacon Wrangham of Hunmanby, the father-in-law of Robert Wilberforce, corresponded with the Poet Laureate, was said to have an introduction to one of the Archbishops, and obtained ' interviews in London & the neighbourhood with the *Home Secretary,* Mr. Peel and other great men '.[35] Robinson failed to snowball a revolt, and early in 1828 the Church Methodist chapel was closed, the last preacher offering himself to the old connexion; moreover the support which he received at Easingwold and Wisbech was of the standard radical kind,[36] and when the Leeds conflict was at its height Mark Robinson was in the fray, posing to the radicals as a victim of preachers' tyranny, and haranguing the Leeds clergy for an hour in the vestry of the old church. In 1835 during the Warrenite crisis in Manchester he appeared again; but his attempts to create a Methodist tory radicalism failed as completely as tory radicalism failed generally in the next decade.[37]

Robinson's escapade drew from Jabez Bunting an explicit formulation of the Methodist order and orders, based on the assumption that ' Christ has instituted a distinct order of men in his Church, to be its *Pastors* and executive rulers as well as its teachers '.

> What can Mr. R. mean in his pamphlet by ' the attempt to introduce Episcopal ordination into the Conference '? If this apply to anything at all modern it is one of the many dreams into which he has been led by his zeal to degrade the Conference and to draw some of the uninformed clergy into a ridiculous & inconsistent sanction of his schismatic & democratical system. We already have among us, & had before Mr. R. was born, what is substantially a good & valid *presbyterian* ordination of our ministers, which every preacher receives when admitted into full connexion. And some of our wisest & oldest men, both preachers & laymen, have thought, that the ordination, good as to its *essentials*, would become still more exactly scriptural in its *mode* & *circumstantials*, by adding to our present edifying ceremonial the ancient & expressive custom of the ' laying on of the hands of the Presbytery ' (not of the *episcopacy*, to which in Mr. R.'s sense of the term we neither do make, nor wish to make any pretension) on the part of such ministers as the Body may from time to time appoint. . . . This would not be *episcopal* ordination. It would only be presbyterian ordination still, though *with* imposition, instead of our present presbyterian ordination without that imposition of hands.

In two respects this carefully spelled-out statement looked forward a decade. It was addressed to Humphrey Sandwith, a Bridlington surgeon, who had been brought up with Mark Robinson at Beverley, and now bore the burden of controversy on Bunting's behalf. In 1836 he was summoned to London as editor of the *Watchman* in which Bunting and his allies warred against radicalism and offered political support for the Establishment. It then transpired that some of the hottest defenders of the Church regarded Wesleyans as disqualified for this supporting role by their explicit affirmation of Presbyterian orders.[38] Then, secondly, the preacher appointed to retrieve the situation at Beverley in 1825, was that wealthiest and most whiggish of Methodists, Thomas Galland. He called for the appointment of two young assistants, William Bunting, the son of Jabez, and Joseph Rayner Stephens, the son of John Stephens of Peterloo and Leeds fame, ' a truly valuable young man, and likely to prove both as regards depth of piety, superior abilities and assiduity in their cultivation, a very efficient servant of the Connexion '.[39] Nine years later when Jabez Bunting was championing the Establishment, Thomas Galland was disputing the principle of it with William, and Joseph Rayner Stephens was in dire trouble as secretary to a disestablishment society.

John Stephens had fathered a family of sons of sparkling talents but eccentric character, and two of them were now to drive him to despair, Joseph Rayner who had returned from a curious mission in Stockholm, and John the younger, who turned Joseph's fortunes into profitable copy for the sensational journal he had devoted to Wesleyan reform, the *Christian Advocate*. In 1832 Joseph Rayner Stephens was stationed in Ashton-under-Lyne, and what evidence there is about his early days suggests that, on constitutional questions, he was a martinet like his father, stiffly asserting the authority of his superintendent, and declining to preach for the restive Ridgway Gates Sunday School at Bolton. Ashton, however, left its mark, and so perhaps did a friendship with Charles Hindley, a radical millowner in the town. In the New Year 1833, at a dinner for Hindley, Stephens ' in a most eloquent speech ' proposed the toast to Freedom; in March 1834 Stephens was secretary to the Ashton Church Separation Society, and at the Manchester disestablishment meeting, Hindley claimed that he had been pushed into public action by a body of Ashton Wesleyans who insisted that their name be attached to a memorial. Bunting exploded with wrath. ' Jos. Stephens's Ashton doings fill me with indignation. It is plain he wants us to exclude him. The thing cannot be tolerated.'[40] Both Bunting and Stephens were in for unpleasant surprises.

Stephens found that Methodist laymen could push in more directions than one; a group, whose names have never been divulged, delated him to the Chairman of the District, Robert Newton, who informed Stephens that he was charged before a District Meeting with having implicated the Methodist ministry by attacking the Establishment Church, and accepting the secretaryship of a society alien from Methodism. A week before the trial on 29 April 1834, further, more specific charges were laid. The essence of Stephens' case was that he had liberty to act as he did until Conference had pronounced on the issue of disestablishment, and he came prepared to argue the point with the aid of adverse comments from John Wesley upon the union of Church and State under Constantine. To this the Chairman retorted sharply ' We are not here to pronounce on the abstract question of Church and State, but to express a judgment on Mr. Stephens's public acts as a Wesleyan Methodist minister.' The rest of the case was reported by John Bowers, an unsympathetic member of the District Meeting:

> At this point he kept ' at bay ' for a considerable time, resolutely refusing to say one word until it was proved that his conduct had been ' alien ' from Methodism. . . . [Resolutions condemning his public conduct, the facts of which were not in dispute, were unanimously carried, and he was required to give up his political activities] He declined ' to give any pledge with those resolutions '. This was not said in a tone of contumacy or defiance, but with deep & (undeniably) unaffected emotion. He wept profusely. He was expostulated with most tenderly; a *time was allowed him* (until the close of the meeting) to deliberate on his final decision. His conduct to those who knew him most familiarly has been perfectly inexplicable. He was disposed at the opening of the case to quibble & trifle. From this he was quickly beaten off, & did not again attempt it. He was prepared with a long and elaborate defence: & I can scarcely conjecture his motive in persisting to withhold every part of it.[41]

Of course, if the premise of the case was that to advocate disestablishment was unprofessional conduct, Stephens could have no defence.

The Radicals of Ashton and the neighbourhood drew the obvious conclusion and did not wait for Conference. Throughout the area meetings were got up in favour of Stephens which led to expulsions, and there was excitement as far away as Halifax and Birmingham.[42] The climax in Conference was ' a glorious

speech ' by Bunting, a strange blend of sense and nonsense, which
came a little oddly from the man who had bound the connexion's
hands while the Protestant constitution tottered in 1829 :

> Our question is not whether at the beginning it was best to
> unite Church and State, nor whether, if the house had to be
> constituted now, it should be just as it is; our point is : Must
> Wesleyan Methodist ministers arm themselves with pickaxes,
> and pull down the house in which our father was born and in
> which he thought he died. . . . Remember when we gave
> our people the sacrament in our own chapels, we publicly
> guarded against its being taken as a sign of separation. For the
> Conference to join the agitation against Church and State would
> require a new constitution; and *we have no right to alter the
> constitution without calling* a Convention. But what should we
> gain by so doing?

Bunting showed his statesmanship less in these arguments than
in his determination, despite suffering continuous personal abuse
in the *Christian Advocate*, to limit the use of force to the minimum
which would achieve the end; events had confirmed his initial
assumption that Stephens wished to be excluded. Bunting proposed simply to suspend Stephens until he promised to stick to
his pastoral work. ' Let us *talk ourselves nearer together*', he
concluded, a plea especially powerful to preachers with sons in
the ministry. In the event J. R. Stephens resigned from the connexion, but no other preacher went with him.[43]

A price had nevertheless to be paid. Thomas Galland declared
in Conference that the resolutions of the District Meeting against
Stephens had been drawn up before the case was fully heard, and
put two points that told increasingly with the years :

> There are two kinds of neutrality [in the disestablishment
> controversy] :   (1) a total abstention from the subject, or
> (2) fair play by allowing advocacy on both sides. Mr. Bunting
> admitted that the Manchester resolutions *lean towards* the
> Church. Yet the Church does not recognise our orders.

What could be more absurd than a special relationship acknowledged by one party only? Then there were losses in the North.
Wesleyanism in Stalybridge was almost wiped out; at Ashton it
had recovered from the hammerblows of Alexander Kilham, but

could not recover a second time from the loss of Stephens's following. At Royton, the Wesleyan Chapel was shut up for years, there were substantial losses to Stephens at Bolton and Oldham (including, almost inevitably, a large Sunday school) and other Stephensite congregations were gathered at Dukinfield and Halifax. In the best traditions of Wesleyan *realpolitik*, Gregory commented that if the disestablishment agitation had not been put down,

> a vast secession would have been the inevitable result, a secession led by ministers such as Bunting, Newton, Entwisle, Anderson and Hannah. These would have been followed by our choicest laymen; the most respected, generous, cultivated families in Methodism. There would not have been a single thousand pounds subscribed to the Centenary Fund [in 1839].

Certainly this doctrine came home to roost in the little connexion Stephens gathered. In the New Year of 1836, with the suddenness of his conversion to disestablishment, a suddenness disguised by the use of misdated correspondence by his biographer Holyoake, Stephens took up the Factory Movement and tory radicalism, and began to preach a terrible retribution for proletarian misery. He soared to national fame, but within a few months he had lost five of his seven preaching places. There were limits to what even the Methodist radicals of North-east Cheshire would stand. ' Had he served the God of Israel instead of the calves of Jeroboam, he would not have been so soon forsaken ', commented his father. Perhaps the God of Israel was after all the God of the big battalions.[44]

Stephens was quickly overshadowed by a much larger upheaval which gathered round Samuel Warren, and drew not only upon anti-Anglican sentiment, but on various sources of Methodist malaise, disquiet at the pastoral pretensions and social alliances of the preachers, uneasiness at Methodist loss of impetus. The English Primitives with few resources had grown from nothing to 50,000 members in eighteen years—the Wesleyans could not match this. Even the Cornish Wesleyans, despite the backsliding which notoriously followed their revivals, were multiplying half as fast again as the connexion at large : yet revivalism and Cornwall in particular were under an official cloud. Others produced depressing calculations of the number of members increase per travelling preacher per decade, which showed a figure for the 'thirties of well under half that for the late eighteenth century, the most rapid decline in productivity, thus measured, coming in the 'twenties. To the revivalists this signified that the connexion had not set its heart on the one thing needful. Others pointed to the declining morale of the connexion; there were expulsions every year, ' and yet the Preachers and their intolerant coadjutors would have us believe that the Leaders and people are *always wrong*'. Those who fretted against pastoral power and the new centralisation, became more doctrinaire in their defence of local rights; those impressed by the need for discipline urged improved professional training for the preachers.[45]

Suggestions for the better preparation of the preachers were a hardy annual, and in the 'twenties important changes in the Methodist pulpit became apparent, which stemmed partly from platform pleading for the Missionary society and other causes, partly from the rising literary tastes of the Methodist people, and partly from the pressure of Richard Watson and Jabez Bunting. In 1829 the first advice on probationer's reading was to brush up

> the various topics of *eloquence* viz. Cicero On Oratory, *Quintilian* On Eloquence, Dr. *Geo. Gregory*'s work on Literature, Taste & Composition, Dr. *Blair*'s Lectures on the Belles Lettres, Dr. *Geo Campbell*'s Philosophy of Rhetoric, an incomparable book! *Lord Kame[s]*'s Elements of Criticism, Dr. *Priestley*'s Lectures on Oratory, *Dr. Ward*'s Lectures on Oratory, Mr. *Irving*'s Elements of English Composition, *Walker*'s Rhetorical Grammar, *Mason*'s Letter on Elocution, *Job Orton*'s Letters to a Dissenting Minister, *Baxter*'s Reformed Pastor & *Fenelon*'s Dialogue on Eloquence.

And in 1831, Bunting chaired a Conference committee which ' recommended the principal objects should be to teach the young candidates *Methodistical divinity and discipline; the creation and cultivation of a taste* for classical knowledge, and at least an elementary acquaintance with it '. Given the fact that the Missionary Society wanted a proper college in which to prepare its candidates for overseas service, it was clear that a seminary would be started as soon as funds and support could be produced. The Irish Conference (who of all parties might be supposed least likely to benefit from a college-trained ministry) was induced to give financial backing, and in 1834 a committee seemed all prepared to recommend Conference to purchase a property in Hoxton which was being sought by other bidders as a lunatic asylum.[46]

In May 1834 opposition came unexpectedly from one of the members of the committee, Samuel Warren, superintendent of the Manchester Oldham Street circuit, and joint author with John Stephens of a standard manual of Methodist law. He complained of the fact that a committee appointed to secure a property was nominating its members to the staff, and, worst of all, making Bunting President, a place which many believed (as Robert Newton did not fail to inform Conference) Warren coveted for himself. The reasons for Warren's conversion are unlikely ever to be known, but on the eve of it he was in secret conclave with James Everett and James Bromley, two of the biggest troublemakers in the connexion; and Edmund Grindrod's allegation that he ' put himself into the hands of men, many of whom care not a straw for him, any farther than he may secure their party purpose ', was almost certainly well founded.[47]

The causes and course of Warren's agitation are less important than the fissures it revealed in the Methodist edifice. Rolling together the discontents of late years, he claimed that the college scheme was designed to promote the power of ' *a Dominant Episcopal Faction* '.

> From hence the Connexion must prepare itself to receive a Liturgical Service, a splendid Ritual, an illegitimate Episcopal Ordination, a cassocked race of ecclesiastics, and whatever else may render this new, this improved edition of Methodism, imposing and magnificent in the eyes of the world.

Organs were now small beer indeed. Warren brought forward his October Quarterly Meeting, secured thundering testimonies of support, refused to stand trial before a District Meeting, and was suspended. ' So this affair is ended ', reported Percy Bunting; in fact it began, with almost revolutionary violence.[48] Four days after Warren's suspension, a missionary meeting at the Bridgwater Street chapel in Salford was broken up by Warrenites led by a local preacher, Captain Barlow, and another strand was woven into the conflict, when Edmund Grindrod, the Superintendent, was attacked on the platform for refusing to open Salford Methodist pulpits to Aitken, the popular Manx evangelist. The missionary meeting was eventually held at a later date, with police scattered through the chapel and galleries. A meeting for the trial of Captain Barlow fell into such disorder that no verdict could be arrived at in the presence of the accused.[49] The following Sunday morning, Robert Newton, who had replaced the suspended Warren as Superintendent in Manchester, preached (under police escort) in Oldham Street chapel, but was hissed and then abandoned by his congregation; at Oldham Road in the evening his service was broken up, and, as he left the chapel escorted by a party of friends and police officers, he was pursued down the Oldham Road by a hooting rabble, and had to take refuge in the Oldham Street vestry. A month later he was kept out of the pulpit and Warren preached to a crowded congregation. Warren's attempt to get the courts to overturn his legal exclusion from the pulpit was predestined to failure, but the damage was done. The Oldham Road chapel was ' desolation ' from that time on.[50]

The worst feature was the way the agitation spread. The assistant editor of the radical *Manchester Times* was a supporter of the Warrenites, and improved every occasion; the market-men from Rochdale and Stockport took their own horror-stories into Yorkshire; the Warrenites launched a ' Grand Central Association ' to carry the cause of reform round the connexion. John Beecham and the London preachers in close touch with Bunting, produced batches of counter-propaganda, including formal statements of the doctrine of the Pastoral Office by Cubitt and Vevers, sent them out with the monthly Book Room parcels, and charged them up surreptitiously to Book Room funds. Warren began to hold Leaders' meetings in Tib Street Sunday School in Manchester and divert the class monies to his Association; as tempers rose, financial pressure was applied to Warren personally, which may help to explain his dependence on a group of substantial men who saw him out of Wesleyanism, and eventually out of his own Wesleyan Methodist Association. Mrs Bealey, a wealthy Methodist of Radcliffe, called in a loan she had made to Warren's son, on account of his father's activities; the crucial solicitor's letter was written by Bunting's son, Percy.[51]

At the Conference of 1835 Warren and his immediate friends were expelled, the rest of the preachers acting together with great unanimity, and even Bromley and Everett deserted him at the

last. Conference was beseiged by delegates of the reforming association, but the President had beaten up an impressive body of
wealthy laymen, especially from Manchester, to give backing to
the preachers on the other side. The rich undertook to make it
clear that the Warrenites could inflict no financial damage on
the connexion; Bunting undertook to make ' *minor alterations in*
administration (not affecting our fundamental position)' to suit
them. Among the chief of these were that the public funds of
the connexion were to be managed by committees of preachers and
laymen (the latter of course not elected but selected by the
former). The alliance between the lay aristocracy of the connexion
and the Conference leadership which had been operative from
the time of the Luddites was publicly sealed. The verdict of the
Conference historian was that the changes were ' too late, . . .
too limited fully to answer their intended purpose, and [so]
surrounded with protective clauses as to be generally inoperative '.
But in extenuation of Bunting's conservatism, and of his enemies'
wildness, it must be observed that he was subject to a backlash
from preachers in the country, convinced that nothing short of
an unmixed assertion of the Pastoral Office could stem the tide
of radicalism.

> *The government of the Societies*, is already too *liberal* . . .
> persons are placed in the very important office of a Leader
> without any trial at all, which I very much lament, the more
> especially as a large portion of them are poor men . . . I may
> . . . remind you that the Scriptural & Methodistical right of
> the Superintendent to *apportion* as well as deliver a sentence,
> needs to be more explicitly stated than it is in the minutes of
> 1795-7. . . .[52]

While there were preachers who thought to save the day by
plugging the gaps in the legislation of the 'nineties, Bunting had
little room to manoeuvre, and the reformers no hope at all.

The core of the Warrenite movement, permanently organised in
1835 as the Wesleyan Methodist Association, consisted in the
conjunction of two different situations, in Liverpool and Manchester on the one hand, and in Rochdale on the other.[53] The
Manchester Warrenites began with a proud boast of having
emptied all the town chapels, and packed their own Tabernacle,
a temporary wooden structure, to excess. ' No aristocratic neglect

or priestly intolerance can roll back the ark of freedom, or arrest the course of a people ardently aspiring for religious liberty.'[54] Indeed they reduced the Manchester Wesleyan membership by 2,600, and recruited 2,800 members themselves, but like the Leeds Protestants, they rapidly entered a process of continuous decline. The original high hopes were based on a double delusion. The general public was always profoundly bored by Methodist bickerings about ministry, and public indifference proved more effective than priestly intolerance in rolling back the ark of freedom. As in Leeds in 1827, the reformers' great gains were in declining inner-belt chapels where the Pastoral Office, lacking the support of substantial laymen now in the suburbs, could not keep order. What the reformers abused as ' aristocratic neglect ' was the condition of their success; but a decaying bag of assets was a poor basis for a progressive institution.

The greatest triumph of the Manchester Warrenites has passed unrecognised—it came in a Sunday school revolt against the new denominational control. In the Chancery Lane, Angel Meadow, London Road and Tib Street schools, the old connexion secured the property and equipment, but lost most of the teachers and children to the Warrenites. Four teachers and 29 children remained to the Chancery Lane school, while the rest of the staff and 800 children gathered in a local dye-house. When a hymn was given out, there were scenes of indescribable emotion; ' sighs and tears, mingled with the voice of praise and thanksgiving, were heard from all parts of the room. After a moment's pause all knelt down. Solemn prayer was offered to the throne of the heavenly grace, and God was specially present.' Eight years later this school returned, but there was no return by those who left the London Road School (which lost 800 of its 1,100 scholars); out of the school they founded grew the United Methodist Church in Hyde Road. So many teachers were expelled by the Wesleyans that the Warrenites had little choice to put on a drive in the annual meeting of the old schools ' for children of all denominations ' to overturn the agreements made with the Wesleyans in 1830. This failed, but below the level of church membership the Warrenite haul was a rich one.[55]

Events in Liverpool closely resembled those in Manchester, though the total damage was less, and the Sunday schools never occupied a place in Liverpool life like that in Manchester. The

Liverpool radicals produced an immense volume of propaganda including a newspaper, the *Circular*, which ran from 1830 to 1833, and Warren and the Theological Institution clearly had little to do with their revolt. Liverpool Methodism had never simmered down after the division of the circuit. In 1831 Bunting was growling that

> We have, chiefly at Leeds St., a bad radical faction, ever on the alert to seize any occasion of annoying us. I have already had two rencontres with them. One was caused by their attempt to have a public exhibition of Sunday school children, & a Tea-Meetg. of teachers *on Good Friday*, to the disparagement and neglect of our Sacramental Service & evening preaching on that day. . . .

And he was particularly irked by David Rowland. Liverpool radicals displayed a quite extraordinary degree of hostility to the lay grandees of local Methodism; the rich of Brunswick chapel would have no local preachers in their pulpit, and the organ cases (Bunting had forcefully assisted the introduction of an organ into Liverpool Brunswick in 1811) were regarded as the liturgical symptom of the preachers' courting the rich. It was the class bias of the preachers which was held to have put them against the popular evangelism of Robert Aitken, and the independence of Sunday schools. The Liverpool radicals were also distinguished by a sharp anti-Anglicanism, and a peculiar personal instability. David Rowland, James Picton, Henry Pooly (the only worldly success among them), Thomas Bew (a plasterer whose obituary recorded that he ' could always discover some unpleasant clanking in the machinery, and was ready with some advice to remedy it ') moved not only from job to job, but from religious allegiance to religious allegiance, not one remaining loyal to the principles he had championed in 1834. Young, republican, theologically liberal, they were fractious in temper and insecure in social position. Jestingly describing themselves as ' disaffected proletarians ' they had no practical sympathy with workers' movements.[56] It may be that Liverpool was so dominated by foreign issues, the Welsh dissenters looking to contests in the Principality, the Scots to issues north of the Border, and the Orangemen successfully presenting the Church as a bulwark against the Irish horde, that locally the politics of Methodist reform were insufficiently serious politics to attract men of real calibre.

Liverpool illustrated vividly the interplay of social circumstances and ministerial politics. The circuit division had united in the North circuit the wealthiest and the poorest of the major Liverpool societies, in Brunswick and Leeds Street, and the revolt produced real shipwreck in the latter. In the South Circuit the parallel was with Pitt Street, already on the slide, and depressed by secession to the condition described by the superintendent in 1850:

> Pitt St. chapel . . . has been for some time back the weak point of our circuit. The population around it has become to a great extent Irish, & of course Popish; and the neighbourhood has become proverbially poor, squalid, noisy and every way uninviting. These changes have led to the diminution of our congregation, & to the removal of our more respectable friends,

which, as usual, exposed the Pastoral Office to a sharper challenge than it could counter. Yet there were important differences between the circuits, which seem to relate directly to ministerial policy. Throughout, the North Circuit had the more aggressive staff. John Scott and Jabez Bunting were the most formidable of superintendents, and when the crisis came in 1834, Samuel Jackson expelled David Rowland without recourse to a Leaders' Meeting, well knowing that he might not carry the Leaders with him. He confessed in private, ' I hope now to get rid of the entire squad, and begin afresh. . . . What a mercy that there is an absolute government in heaven, that there the spirit of liberty is unknown '. Certainly the cold war which had existed in Liverpool North for some years was now open and hot.[57] In the South Circuit social circumstances were similar, but successive superintendents used a much looser rein. Robert Newton was heavily committed to fundraising for missions; William Henshaw had some sympathy for the radicals, and was regarded by Bunting as soft. In the crisis the Superintendent was George Marsden, one of the older generation, abused by hard-liners in the North Circuit as ' extremely slow, & . . . trying to save thereby the members '.[58] Yet the softer policy paid; membership losses in the South were lower, and more important, had been entirely recouped by 1838. The hammerblows in the North Circuit had hardened attitudes on both sides unbridgeably.

In Liverpool there had never been undenominational Sunday schools, and there could be no conflict over the recent Sunday school legislation. Nevertheless the Liverpool Warrenites made their chief constructive effort in gathering substantial schools on slender resources; already in 1837 they educated over 1,100 scholars, and over the next decade the strength of their schools increased as steadily as that of their congregations declined. Their views on church government apart, the Warrenites, like the Wesleyan Reformers later, were identifiable in the spectrum of Methodist opinion, by being much more wholeheartedly dedicated to Sunday schools, liberal politics and teetotalism than the connexion as a whole. Nor in Liverpool was there any denying the harsh justice of a Conference party propaganda sheet ' that, in the main, when compared with the connexion at large . . . [the radicals] are not the most experienced or elderly, or intelligent, or spiritual. Nor, are they, by any means, the most respectable and wealthy '.[59]

Fortunately for the Warrenites, Rochdale was an entirely different case. As we shall see later on, the Church in Rochdale was the centre of a conservative network which the liberals were determined to smash, and which might distort the development of the town through its glebe leases. For all these reasons Rochdale dissent was unusually radical, and played a uniquely important part in the church rates and disestablishment agitations; and in Rochdale dissent, Methodism was unusually significant. In the mid-twenties there were no evangelical clergy anywhere in a huge parish, and relatively little evangelical dissent. Methodism seized the lead, doubled its membership in the next decade, and covered the parish thickly with chapels, cottage meetings and preaching rooms. Prosperity bred self-confidence; in 1829 the Rochdale Quarterly Meeting was rebuked by Conference for sending up a memorial supporting the Stewards and Leaders of Leeds, but kept gunning till 1832, insisting that Conference was misinterpreting the rules of 1795 and 1797. Immediately afterwards, J. R. Stephens' case ' caused considerable excitement in Rochdale ', and threats of financial blockade. The preachers just kept control.[60]

When Warren moved into open revolt, the Rochdale men moved too, even offering to pay for a special meeting of the Legal

M

Hundred 'to allay the present unhappy agitation of the Connexion', and produced an address on the causes of discontent which the Superintendent refused to put to the vote at Quarterly Meeting. It read thus:

1. the unconstitutional interference of the Special District Meeting in the Leeds affair;
2. the introduction of a Test, relative to the Doctrine of the Eternal Sonship, and the consequent expulsion of a faithful minister;*
3. Conference's erroneous views on the Union of Church and State question, the retirement of ministers from the connexion because of this and the grieved minds of thousands of our members;
4. the establishment of the Theological Institution against the wishes of the people;
5. the trial of Dr. Warren;
6. the assumption by the preachers of a power to prevent free discussions in Quarterly Meetings, by refusing to put to the vote resolutions moved and seconded by accredited members of such meetings; or threatening to vacate the chair, and thereby dissolving the meeting;
7. the expulsion of pious members in opposition to a majority of the Leaders' Meeting;
8. the alteration in rules, particularly that one which expressly says 'No leader or steward can be put out of his place, but by a majority of leaders, or a Quarterly Meeting';
9. the disrespectful manner in which Conference has treated memorials from various circuits;
10. the omission of the Plan of Pacification from the Conference journals;
11. the exclusive management of many connexional funds by the preachers;
12. but the greatest cause, and that out of which those and all others flow, is the total exclusion of the laity from all the legislative, and from all or nearly all executive power.

Here the accumulated friction of a decade was used to detonate the explosive in the tail.

* Bunting, Richard Watson and their friends maintained that Adam Clarke held unsound views on this doctrine, and it had been an issue of some friction among the preachers.

The Conference of 1835 rejected any negotiations with the Warrenites, and the following September, the Superintendent declared that unless the officers and members of the Rochdale Society submitted to certain tests, ' he would hold no communion with them '. The Union Street trustees, nevertheless, went ahead with a public meeting on Wesleyan reform, and Jabez Bunting's solicitor son, Thomas Percival, helped the Superintendent to secure an injunction, forbidding any assembly on connexional premises unless conducted by a minister. ' The Rochdale Chapel case is in train for being satisfactorily settled,' remarked Bunting, ' & those fine premises rescued from the Warrenites.' In fact Rochdale suffered one of the worst blows ever to befall a Methodist circuit. In the country causes, even more than in the town, the Warrenites made huge gains; in a year the circuit membership fell from 1,900 to 700, while the Rochdale Association boasted a membership of 1,700. The heaviest losses were amongst office-holders—the bulk of the trustees and local preachers went out. The disaster was completed by a conflict over a second property, the Sunday school. There had been no attempt in Rochdale to enforce the new Conference regulations on the schools, but, as soon as the Union Street trustees resigned, the new trust acted at once. The teachers refused to accept the rules, and claimed that their rights were safeguarded by an agreement of 1822 under which the school committee had built the premises. This contract never having been stamped was void in law, and the Superintendent locked the teachers out. The teachers nevertheless took the flock, and a year later they moved, a thousand strong, into the new Baillie Street Sunday school. It was entirely consistent with the attitudes of the Baillie Street congregation that part of the premises were made available to a British school, the first purpose-built institution for higher education in Rochdale, and in 1872 the first Board school in the town. ' Most of those who go to the Association chapel are Radicals ', said one of the first Trustees, ' there are hardly any Tories amongst us.'[61]

The Baillie Street chapel and school cost £6,200, two-fifths of which were raised by the sale of £1 shares. Shares could be purchased for five shillings down, and monthly instalments of 2s. 6d. (much more than the threepence weekly asked by the Rochdale Pioneers for their shares a decade later). The large shareholders were men of substance, George Ashworth, a woollen

manufacturer, James Hoyle, a corn miller, on whose premises
the Warrenite rebels first found refuge, John Howard, wool-
stapler, ' a sturdy crotchety man ', Robert Handley, a tailor, and
John Petrie, one of the founders of the engineering industry in
Rochdale, who chaired the Baillie Street building committee, and,
as treasurer, stood financial bail for the whole Wesleyan Association from 1836 to 1854. The wealth and energy of these men
gave Baillie Street a unique importance in Rochdale public life,
and delivered over to it the leadership of free Methodism. They
were men of the kind Bunting took into partnership to save the
cause of authority in the old connexion, and eventually they sought
to limit democracy in their own Association. Two forces had set
them at loggerheads, the narrowness of Bunting's political vision
and the ethos of Rochdale. Based on the rich men of Manchester,
Bunting's caucus had no place even for the rich of Rochdale.
But it was also true that the contest of the new Rochdale with
the old bred a degree of hostility to the Church, and traditions of
direct action, which did not consort with the national policies
Bunting pursued (on the whole successfully) in the 'thirties.

Two further studies may complete this examination of the
challenge to authority in Methodism, an obituary of Dr Warren,
and a tour of the Sunday schools. It was a serious question whether
the new Methodist reformers would now link up with each other
or with the reformers of the last generation, the Methodist New
Connexion. Though wooed by Warren and Thomas Allin of the
New Connexion, the Stephensites were not prepared to stay in the
old connexion to help the one, nor to embrace the comfortable
Kilhamite bourgeoisie of north-east Cheshire to please the other;[62]
they were not the offspring of revival, and did not fit the Primitive Methodist groove; they had come out in support of an ill-
used preacher, and could hardly go to the Independent Methodists
who had dispensed with a professional ministry. Stephens' conversion to Tory Radicalism only confirmed that they would continue as a small local connexion. The New Connexion, however,
made a really determined attempt both to widen the breach in
the old connexion made by the Warrenites and to secure their
alliance. Throughout the winter of 1836-7 negotiations continued,
the crux being whether the Warrenites would be satisfied by the
New Connexion nostrum of an omnicompetent Conference, half lay
in composition. The negotiating parties reached joyful agreement,

but the occupational risk of professional ecumenists is to be repudiated by their constituents. On this occasion the W.M.A.
diplomats were torpedoed by the Rochdale Quarterly Meeting,
who were no doubt already aware that they were going to have
to carry the new Association whose battles they had fought. They
refused to accept ' the control of any Conference (however
constituted) assuming a higher authority than that of the Annual
Assembly of the Wesleyan Association '. This body simply
admitted and stationed preachers, recommended rules to Societies
for their adoption, and represented a complete reaction against
Buntingism.[63]

This triumph of circuit rights had immediately to be paid for
in two quite different ways. The Warrenites had won an outlying
victory at Dudley, where, after the Leeds proceedings, the officials
had become ' nearly all disaffected ', where the superintendent was
ill-supported by his colleagues, and where, when the clash came,
' the Sunday schools were scattered or broken up '. When negotiations with the New Connexion began to falter, the Dudley men
exercised circuit rights in their own way, and joined the New
Connexion. A great outburst of evangelism followed which chilled
the hearts of the old connexion preachers, and made Dudley and
Stourbridge (which had been divided in the Wesleyan circuit
reorganisations of the late 'twenties) two of the bright lights of
the Methodist New Connexion.[64] A more unexpected rebel against
lay power and circuit rights was Dr Warren. After the Conference
of 1837 it became known that Warren was in effect finished with
the Wesleyan Methodist Association. Relations between him and
the Wesleyan leadership were far too bitter for him ever to go
back, and eventually it came out that he was seeking ordination
from the Bishop of Chester, on the grounds that the constitution
of the Association was too democratic. All Souls, Every Street,
in Ancoats was built for him, the subscribers including some who
had left Wesleyanism with him. This curious aspect of the special
relationship between Methodism and the Church never ceased
to provoke the ribaldry of the Methodist preachers, and to the end
of Warren's days they mocked a man who had gone from the
front rank of the Methodist ministry to the thankless drudgery
of a slum parish. Even his church was insignificant, and, withal,
empty. ' It was indeed a case of " All Souls ", but few bodies.'[65]

Warren had not made the Warrenite revolt, and his defection

did not end it. In particular the Sunday schools were restive, and the sad scenes in Manchester were reproduced elsewhere. At Moston, north of the town, the congregation itself met in the Sunday school, a clause in the lease of which reserved it for the use of preachers appointed by Conference at 6 pm every Sunday. The whole school and congregation came out for the Warrenites, and had the chagrin to see a preacher arriving weekly to take possession of an empty building, while they were without accommodation. At Bury the attempt to enforce the Conference rules drove both teachers and children to the Warrenites.[66] No Methodist Sunday school stood higher in prestige than Bolton, yet their revolt preceded that of the Warrenites. The rules at Bolton were agreed among the teachers a generation before Conference turned to the subject, and the Conference rules were 'treated with neglect'. The school itself was left behind by the preachers in the Old Chapel, as they developed the work in the new Bolton chapels. After the Peterloo troubles, pressure was put on for the children to be brought to service at Bridge Street, but not till 1833 was full connexional discipline introduced. After disputes in the school so severe as to deter Joseph Rayner Stephens from coming to preach, there was a separation, and a sizeable body of teachers, scholars and 200 members, known as the Refugees, sought shelter in mills and elsewhere until the Hanover-street school was built for them. This school was never connected with Warren's movement, but joined the next group of Methodist reformers of the 'fifties, and via the Wesleyan Reform Association, came ultimately into the United Methodist Free Church.[67]

The Burslem Sunday School, as we have seen, had a patchwork origin, but by 1816 the teachers could justly claim that 'there is no school in the country, and few in the kingdom that can compare with it', and, with its branches at Longport and Norton, it numbered nearly 1,700 scholars and 200 teachers. Its trust was mixed denominationally, and they rented the old chapel from the Wesleyans. The Sunday school, however, partook of the character of the Burslem circuit, a 'hotbed of Kilhamitism, Ranterism, & every other ism that is subversive [of] all rule and order', and in 1834 discovered an ingenious method of blocking a proposal in the chapel, to move morning worship back from 9 to 10.30 am, by appealing to the Plan of Pacification of 1795: this forbade service in church hours except when supported by a majority of

Trustees and Leaders. The school was supported by the Leaders, and its interest was that the elder scholars who attended service received a ticket entitling them to a Sabbath writing lesson. The superintendent, however, rejoiced that the appointment of a new trust enabled him substantially to get his way, and change the name of the school to ' the Burslem Wesleyan Methodist School ' on the eve of ' the Warrenite foolery and wickedness '. Alas, when, in 1836, the attempt was made to stop instruction in writing, most of the teachers and children refused to yield, and showed their strength in the community by securing the erection of a new undenominational school, which quickly gathered 1,450 scholars. Many local preachers, class leaders and members left at the same time, and formed a church which joined the Wesleyan Methodist Association in 1849.[68]

In the Midlands and North the contest had a varying issue. In Sheffield the bitter feelings of the past were revived by a circuit division, contrived by Samuel Jackson in 1831. He then set about ending the independence of the great schools. He first united two of them, one of which, on Sheffield Moor, was quite new, into a ' Sheffield Wesleyan Sunday School Union ', and did his best to get Bunting up to Sheffield to advocate the Wesleyan principles of school management, which the new union was to embody. ' If we can succeed in this enterprise ', he confided, ' it is probable that in a few years the Sunday school jealousy will die away and Sunday writing perish with it '. No new schools in the Union were to have Sabbath writing; the old schools were ' not to be interfered with, but the subject shall be open for free and friendly discussion at their meetings '. With this carefully prepared bait, Jackson pressed the Red Hill, Bridgehouses and Park schools to join his scheme and although ' these schools held off for a time, not seeing their way clear to leave the Sheffield Sunday School Union, with which they had been so long and so harmoniously connected, their prejudices and scruples were overcome [in 1832] '. Though the New Connexion propagandists did their best to exploit ruffled feelings that remained, connexional policy seems here to have recorded a success.[69]

In Newcastle it was a different and memorable story. The *Newcastle Standard* reported on 26 November 1836 that

the Carpenters' Tower and Boys' Jubilee Schools in this town,

which contain about 500 scholars and 70 teachers, have been
virtually expelled from the New Road Wesleyan Methodist
Society by the establishment of a new School under the Conference rules simply in consequence of a large majority of the
teachers (about 70 to 20) having attempted to resist the efforts
of the minority in the Committee of management to compel
them to leave the Newcastle Sunday School Union with which
they have been connected for 20 years, and to join the Wesleyan
Sunday School which has lately been established by a few respectable friends who are favourable to ' Methodism as it is '. . . .

The rump of the schools adopted new rules which put the sole
management in the preachers. The official version was that, finding the school uncontrollable the preacher had determined to start
a new school on Methodist principles, with the ' sound ' teachers,
and children newly gathered. Certainly he pulled no punches in
detailing his grievances. The leaders, he claimed, were ' distinguished for their hostility to Methodism '. One had been a dele-
gate to the Warrenite Grand Central Association; two were mixed
up with the *Christian Advocate*; a fourth ' after repeated failures
in business, united himself to the Kilhamites, and imbibed all
their prejudices '.[70] The piquant feature of this lament at the
oppression of the Pastoral Office by Tyneside radicalism, was that
the writer and prime mover in the business was none other than
James Everett, the quondam abettor of Samuel Warren, who in
the next decade proved the most poisonous enemy of ' Methodism
as it is ' that the connexion ever produced.

In Blackburn the response to Dr Warren was such that ' the
school was almost entirely broken up, the plan lost 20 preachers,
and the congregation, which was previously large and respectable,
was reduced for a while to a mere skeleton '. At Heptonstall also
the attempt to put down Sabbath writing drove part of the congregation to the Association.[71] The final case was that of Chester,
which resembled that at Sheffield, but turned out less happily for
the preachers. The Chester schools, as we have seen, began on an
undenominational basis independently of the chapels, and had
been developed partly by public subscription and partly by the
generosity of George Lowe, a local goldsmith, and his family.
Their rules embodied the main principles for which Conference
stood, but the teachers saw no reason to accept a government on the

lines of the new regulations, most of the members of which would come from outside the school. Nevertheless the Chester preachers laboured to introduce the new model ' with much more zeal than discretion ', and a crisis began when the superintendent, William Jackson, returned from Conference in 1829.

He gave the interpretation of *law* to the *recommendations* of Conference and urged as a justification of what he *intended to do,* and afterwards of what he *had done,* the severe rebukes he had received from his assembled brethren, for not having brought the refractory teachers into subjection the previous year. . . .

Towards the close of the last year, 1829, Mr. Jackson *insisted* upon a *new committee* for the government of the schools, and he *appointed* one . . . He was apprized of the injury that would follow, by several of the judicious leaders; but this was met with the assurance that he had the concurrence of Mr. Robert Newton, Mr. Jabez Bunting, Mr. Watson, and several others of the influential preachers, in his purpose. . . . The teachers of the schools, however, being bound by no Methodistical law, refused to acknowledge the authority of Mr. Jackson's new formed committee, and never condescended to amalgamate themselves with any of their proceedings. . . . [An opening came when a number of young men rehearsed for the Sunday school anniversary on the evening of Christmas Day] our worthy Superintendent designated their meeting . . . as a gross violation of morality, and what was still more serious, an infraction of Methodist law . . . [Preaching was then withdrawn from the Handbridge school, and financial support from two of the three schools, John Street and Handbridge. A remodelling of the John Street trust produced support for official policy, and it was determined to get rid of Mr. Lowe] At this memorable assembly, it was determined . . . that the old superintendents of the school should be *expelled,* and that new ones, formed according to Mr. Jackson's own heart, should be appointed. This meeting was held on the Friday evening, and on the next night a little *before midnight,* locksmiths were in operation, the locks taken off, new ones put in, and on the Sabbath morning, the Rev. Mr. Jackson, the new treasurer . . . and two or three fresh superintendents, long before school hours, had taken possession of the school . . . [nevertheless] the children rejected their new visitors, and with one voice declared their attachment to the men who for years had taught them the way of truth.

Subsequently the doors were bricked up, the windows barricaded, and the premises guarded by bludgeon men.[72] Once again Wesleyan discipline had settled for the property and given up the flock. There were limits to the power of the Pastoral Office to remodel the undenominational tradition in its own image; what it could do was to break up an institutional mechanism, and in the process, permanently damage the Wesleyan constituency.

7 The Dénouement I: The Attack upon the Church and its Failure

The period with which nineteenth-century church history has conventionally begun forms the conclusion of this study, not so much because its molehills of inspiration have been inflated into mountains of hagiology, as because the essential elements of its experience had already been distilled in the reform crisis. And when the steam went out of English social tension, as it rapidly did after 1850, the surviving doctrinaires of the heroic age looked curiously dated. If one party is often described as 'post-Tractarian', others might fairly be called 'post-Orange', 'post-prophetical', 'post-Buntingite' or, among the Independents, 'post-Calvinist'. At one level, revivalists and teetotallers had by 1850 almost reached the limits of what could be done by bringing on the crisis of individual decision; at another, the education policies in which churchmen and voluntaryists had put their trust had by the early 'fifties failed to answer, and in Manchester the warring parties had already approached the compromise which the state would take up in 1870. The liberal party in the Church in 1850 had the ear of government and the self-confidence of a rising force, but if it could not yet be foreseen that they would not capture the universities for their Christian viewpoint, nor carry through their perennially promised reconstruction of the faith, they had clearly found no successor to Thomas Arnold. There were no longer giants in the land, and no room for heroic solutions. In the 'seventies and 'eighties sects and parties might clash noisily, but secession was no longer the accepted consequence of defeat. Everyone understood in his heart that less was at stake.

The warfare of denomination and party reached its greatest intensity under pressure of the social conflict of the 'thirties and 'forties. This period had three distinctive characteristics. The weakness and dispersion of authority in England which had frustrated the efforts of the Church to beat down its challengers while there was yet time, now proved equally fatal to the efforts of dissenters to mobilise their strength in the country for a final assault upon the Establishment. Moreover the denominational spirit showed itself unable to contain the continued movement of opinion away from the religious establishments of the *ancien régime;* unable to prevent the development of a sense of working-class unity in which non-participation in church life was the norm; strikingly unable to contain the lesser disagreements within the churches themselves. The final three chapters discuss the related topics of the failure of the assault upon the Church, the limitations of Church policy and schism. The first two of these subjects, particularly, require a number of local inquiries to show how the politicians of Church and dissent sought to compel parliamentary action, or compensate for the lack of it, and how new pastoral problems were created for the Church by increased pressure upon its endowments.

Church rates had been forced into an issue by church extension, but the question remained one of status rather than cash. The rate was the local evidence of Anglican ascendency; to defeat it offered dissenters the possibility of securing disestablishment by parishes when they had failed to secure it by a single bold stroke. It was characteristic that dissenters in Manchester and Oldham who furiously contested the compulsory rate, contributed liberally when it became voluntary, while the high-churchmen of Bury became contumacious at the new-style voluntaryism and refused to pay.[1] This odd consummation was preceded by virulent warfare, the strategy and tactics of which may be illustrated by the campaigns in Manchester and Rochdale.

In Manchester the church rate issue was taken up by the radicals in 1831 as a counterblast to clerical resistance to the Reform Bill, and in the following year there were, as in other towns, great scenes at the vestry for allowing a church rate. A crowd ' for the most part of the lower orders, none of whom could have established a right to vote, or of persons who have at the most contributed a few pence in the course of the year ', stood ' upon the seats and backs of the pews, sent forth shouts and hisses, [and] . . . soon drove away the greater part of the respectable spectators, filled with disgust and indignation . . . or with melancholy forbodings. . . .' The churchwardens were in a weak position with their accounts, for they had incurred expenses of doubtful legality, and admitted that their rate ought to have produced far more than it did (Quakers and many others enjoying a practical exemption); but it was over the new rate that the real battle threatened, and peace was finally preserved only because neither side was fully organised to fight.[2]

In 1833 the battle began at the Easter vestry which chose the churchwardens and sidesmen. Archibald Prentice, Scots radical and proprietor of the *Manchester Times,* and a party of labour radicals, including James Scholefield, the Bible Christian pastor, and Elijah Dixon, a veteran of Peterloo and now a Baptist, who had celebrated his conversion by total immersion in the Rochdale canal, set out to secure their own list in order to control the poor-rate management; the church rate was implicated because it was not practicable to separate its collection from that of the poor rate. The defence of authority now developed upon the pillars of conservative evangelicalism, Benjamin Braidley, the borough-reeve, and head of the biggest Anglican Sunday school in the town, and James Wood, tory and Methodist, Churchwarden and lifelong friend of Jabez Bunting. Nevertheless they could not control the vestry, and could only get their way by appealing to a poll under Sturges Bourne's Act, in which the plural votes of heavily rated ley-payers told.[3]

Six weeks later at the vestry called to lay the church rate, the middle-class radicals cut a much better figure, being determined both to have a disestablishment demonstration, and to keep up the pressure on the government for the abolition of church rates by law. The churchwardens reduced their demand from 3d. to $\frac{1}{2}$d., but were met with an amendment for a six-months adjournment moved by George Hadfield, the Congregationalist solicitor, and Thomas Potter, the celebrated Unitarian warehouseman. The effect of this amendment was to refuse a rate, for the cost of collection separate from the poor rate would consume the whole yield. Hadfield made a violent and irrelevant attack upon the Church. ' He held its doctrines, every one of them, its discipline, its establishment, its connexion with the state, as erroneous and unjust . . . and no . . . infidelity in his opinion, existed so great as the polluting streams of political power. . . .' But James Wood and Samuel Fletcher, an evangelical Congregationalist, supported the rate, and the *Manchester Guardian* also deplored the effort to put pressure on the government out of doors. Here was the cleft in Manchester liberalism which was deepened by the animosities generated by the Anti-Corn Law League and its successor bodies, and ultimately cost the liberals the representation of the town. The radicals were again infuriated by what they held to be an illegal appeal to a poll under Sturges Bourne's Act, and this time they resolved not not to be disgraced by the result. The bellman was out, beating up their voters, and in a desperate finish, the supporters of the amendment triumphed by a majority of one in a poll exceeding 7,000, respectable dissenters, according to the *Guardian,* voting on the other side.[4]

James Wood, the Methodist, now sank to the ultimate infamy in radical eyes by calling for a scrutiny. In Manchester there was always a case for scrutiny because of the complications created by tenants who compounded with their landlords for their rates, and of rate-payers who were not fully paid up. After two months' toil the scrutineers apologised for the error of the vestry chairman, the Rev. C. D. Wray, one of the fellows of the Collegiate Church, in allowing compounding landlords to vote on the gross assessment of their property; but by striking out 273 votes for the motion and 403 for the amendment, they made it possible for the rate to continue. The radical press nevertheless was cock-a-hoop that ' the example set by Manchester in its opposition to Church rates . . . is spreading throughout the kingdom ', and would force the Government to act; it also guessed rightly that there would be no attempt to take the recalcitrant to court. The later Braintree cases were simplicity itself compared with the litigation which might have arisen from this Manchester rate.[5]

On the next occasion the rising temper of the Church defence made a major battle unavoidable, and both sides prepared for the fray. The clergy of the collegiate church responded to the schemes of church defence being organised by William Palmer in Oxford, prepared to form an association of ' friends of the Church ', and were treated to an entirely misconceived defence of church rates, on the analogy of chief rents, by C. D. Wray. Wray was nevertheless right enough in holding that the principle of establishment was at stake. In March 1834 the dissenters had their great disestablishment meeting described in chapter V, and both sides were marshalled. The battle was not joined till the late summer, as the churchwardens waited to see whether Althorpe's church rate bill passed, and by that time the United Committee of Dissenters had established an organisation in every part of the vast parish. Again a half-penny rate was asked, and in a turbulent vestry meeting, Hadfield and Potter again moved an amendment condemning the rate on the score of its injustice, and the fact that the arrears of 30,000 ley-payers would keep the church going till church rates were abolished nationally. Yet Hadfield belied his own logic by a wild appeal to revolution—' the repeal of that law would never be carried in the House of Lords till that awful collision took place which he should deprecate as a calamity '— and must have known that there was no reserve of untapped revenue. In Manchester township alone, the poor rate on 15,000 assessments was paid by landlords, who were not liable to the church rate; another 5,000 occupiers enjoyed partial or complete exemption from the poor rate, and this, like parish relief, conferred legal exemption from church rate; and in the out-townships, it was much the same.[6]

The fireworks at the vestry were as nothing compared with the poll, which almost to the end promised victory to the forces of law and order. The Church Protection Society had placarded the town and circularised congregations; they brought in their voters by coach with great effect. Again the radicals had no option but to make a vast and expensive effort at the end. The bellman was now reinforced by a band which marched in the out-voters by squads, and by fleets of coaches. Still more sinister, there was widespread distribution of voting tickets to unqualified voters, especially by the overseers of Salford, and there was continuous violence around the polling, designed to discourage the respectable possessor of plural votes. On the last day this huge effort converted a deficit of 739 into a victory of 7,019 to 5,897, to the accompaniment of ' a wild tumult of joy ' and threats to repeat the scene in every large town until the government effected ' the complete extinction of this ecclesiastical impost, which . . . the dissenters, and indeed the mass of the people in populous districts will no longer bear '. In Manchester it was the latter group who were being used for leverage against Church and government. There was a scrutiny to come which took nearly twelve weeks. Continuously obstructed by the Salford overseers, the scrutineers finally disqualified 800 Salford voters against the rate, and 1,665 all told.

As only 186 votes for the rate were rejected, the rate was laid by 5,712 to 5,354.[7]

When Chancellor Raikes came to swear in the Manchester churchwardens in May 1835, he charged them to enforce the church rate, ' the separation of the church from the state . . . [being] the separation of the state from God '; but they knew they were being asked more than they could perform. Prentice and Hadfield put on a public meeting the night before the vestry, and another noisy scene in church. The churchwardens, however, now accepted defeat and did not proceed to a poll. Whether from desire to preserve the peace, or fear of expensive litigation, the church rate in Manchester continued on a voluntary basis, was paid mostly by dissenters, and gave very little further trouble.[8] Yet in one sense the result of all the sound and fury was curiously inconclusive. The tory press always claimed that the majority of legal votes had always been for the rate and that, had they polled in 1835, ' the result would have been another triumph for the Church '. Partly for this reason the Manchester church-rate battles did not have the snowball effect their organisers intended. Where the issue produced a political confrontation, as at Shaw, the rate survived.

> The utmost excitement prevailed . . .; and it is stated by the opponents of the rate, that several of the millowners of tory' politics, and one principal firm whose views are of the tory-radical school, exercised such an influence over their hands in favour of the rate, as to oblige them almost forcibly to vote for the rate, contrary to their conscientious feelings. About 600 of the ratepayers were unable to vote as they had not paid their rates, in consequence, in a great measure, of their distressed condition, and many declined voting either way owing to the various influences at work.

Even in Manchester popular hostility was directed more at Sturges Bourne's Act than at the rate, and where an operative Orange interest could be got up as in Liverpool, Warrington, or Wigan, the rates had extraordinary staying-power. There was a small flurry of cases in the disturbed years of 1848 and 1849, but one gains the impression that from the time recession set in 1837 public attention was directed to other things; the way to progress seemed to be by individual refusal to pay (which in Rossendale eventually endangered the rate itself),[9] or by the pertinacious litigation by which Samuel Courtauld, the celebrated crêpe manufacturer of Braintree, seriously weakened the practical authority of the Church to levy rates. In urban areas church extension helped to make rates abnormal; the wardens of the new churches often lacked the power or the will to try a new rate, while the carving-out of new parishes or ecclesiastical districts from the old often made it seem no longer worth while to continue with rates which had been continuously levied. By the early 'fifties a majority of prospective rate-payers were for various reasons no longer paying, though the proportion of parishes in which a rate was refused was very small, and Parliament had little inducement to press on with the abolition of the rates.[10]

In Rochdale, however, the parish church was the centre of a conservative network which was assaulted by the radicals even more violently than the Wesleyan establishment: here the church rates issue focused a clash of forces which had important consequences far beyond the parish.[11] As early as 1826 the Rochdale vestry had cited the retiring churchwardens before the Consistory Court at Chester, and appointed a professional auditor to attend at every celebration ' to ascertain the real quantity of bread and wine necessarily used . . . and that no white wine be purchased as it is not used for sacramental purposes '.[12] Foolishly the Rochdale wardens increased their expenditure by half in 1829 and 1830, by unauthorised increases in salaries to bell-ringers and singers, with the result that the vestry in 1831 reduced by half the 4d. rate for which they asked. In February 1832 the wardens called another vestry on the grounds that after the payment of salaries— to which the last parish meeting had strongly objected—there was no money left for the repairs of the church. W. W. Barton, the pioneer of the Methodist New Connexion in Rochdale, who had moved the previous reduction in the rate, arrived at the door a quarter of an hour early, only to find that the wardens had put the clock forward, constituted a meeting with a few friends and granted a penny rate. Of course, at the next vestry in June 1832 there were fresh attacks on the salaries, and provision for repairs to the parish church was reduced.

In 1833 the ratepayers ' became conscious of their strength for the first time '. The parish elected nine churchwardens, the tenth being nominated by the vicar. Barton now carried two nominees

N

of his own, in a poll of 2,766; at the next meeting the church-wardens' accounts were rejected, and the rate reduced to one penny in a poll of 3,400. (In a parliamentary election never more than 700 voted.) By 1834 the rates issue had become inflamed nation-ally, and Rochdale was being primed with arguments as to what expenditure was legal, and what was not, by George Hadfield, the Manchester solicitor. Barton moved that the vestry be adjourned twelve months, i.e. that the rate be refused, worsted the wardens in the vestry, and carried the poll by a majority of 147, in spite of the most strenuous efforts of the church party ' who in some instances paid the rates due from individuals in order to qualify them to vote for the rate'. The wardens pro-ceeded to levy a 2½d. rate on their own authority, and resistance began in the parish. Bailiffs removed the dining table of John Petrie, iron-founder and pillar of the Wesleyan Methodist Associ-ation, and his daughter vividly recalled how ' for a week or two we picnic'd in the front kitchen—we youngsters glorying in the notion of persecution for truth's sake, but enjoying the whole thing immensely'. More important, the opposition secured their martyr, whose sad fate did yeoman service to John Bright and their other propagandists. The bailiffs made a claim of 4d. upon James Brierley, a poor dying weaver of Spotland. ' They seized a looking-glass, but this would not cover the costs, and their ruthless hands then seized his family Bible and sold it for an illegal rate'. The church party (as we shall see) had in the end to manufacture a rival sob-story, but they never equalled the original. Barton, Petrie and others were summoned before the magistrates for refusing to pay, but they contested the legality of the rate, on the grounds that only eight of the ten wardens had concurred in the proceedings. On this plea the case went to the Consistory Court at Chester, and thence to the Archbishop's Court at York; but the churchwardens' proceedings all ran into the sands, and their suits for non-payment of rates were dismissed with costs.[13]

If this was a depressing result for the wardens, Barton had had the salutary experience of being prosecuted by the two wardens he had carried in 1834, along with the rest. The radical press began to call for wardens who were really staunch against the rate, and, in May 1835, the military were called in to protect Rochdale church during an election in which a ' reform ' list of wardens triumphed over a tory list by 1,972 to 1,498, reform in this instance implying the exclusion of every item from the accounts except necessary repairs to the church. Rochdale was now blessed with two wardens, James Leach and Henry Kelsall, who were still subject to legal proceedings taken by their predecessors, but they gradually got the rate down to ½d. and kept things quiet for a couple of years.[14]

In 1839, however, the situation began to come to a head. Much of the rate granted the previous year had not been collected, and this was ground for refusing a new rate. The wardens nevertheless determined to call another parish meeting and try again. The radicals placarded the town, inciting the leypayers to remember ' who robbed the dying man of his Bible ', and an hour before the meeting had 1,000 supporters waiting in incessant rain in the churchyard. ' There was a tremendous rush into the body of the church ', the rate was overwhelmingly rejected, and a poll called for which led to ' an unexampled conflict '. The voters poured in all week, nearly 2,500 polling on the last day. The police kept order around the church, but as the end of polling approached, it was obvious that not all the voters would get in. The vicar, therefore, without notice, but according to his own account with the consent of both sides, extended the polling for two hours, and carried the vote by 2,897 votes to 2,886. The radicals, John Bright prominent among them, lashed themselves into a fury at what they held to be a desperate and illegal throw by the vicar, knowing his party to be in arrear, and knowing that anti-rate voters would go home at the expected close of polling. ' It was determined . . . not to pay the rate, and litigate it if necessary. . . . Three groans were given for old Peterloo.'[15]

' Old Peterloo ', the vicar, W. R. Hay, who had ordered the charge of the yeomanry on that occasion, and had never been allowed to forget it, was to campaign no more. In December 1839 he died, but his successor, J. E. N. Molesworth, was a still tougher, more resourceful, and more combative character. Molesworth's appointment brought the Rochdale conflict to a head in a peculiarly significant way. That Molesworth could not fight singlemindedly as part of the old tory caucus in the town showed how the problem of church defence was changing; his defeat was a compelling demonstration that church defence as conceived by high-churchmen of his generation had no future. The very incarnation of the church militant, Molesworth fell out not only with ley-payers, glebe-holders and the Rochdale Commissioners, but also with the bishop, the Ecclesiastical Commissioners and the congregation. And although Molesworth always denied whig allegations that he had been ' selected by the tories as the favourite reward for political services ' his most spectacular row, the church-rate contest of 1840, was highly political.[16]

At the end of March 1840, Abraham Brierly, the vicar's warden, with the support of only one other warden, raised the temperature by numerous prosecutions for unpaid rates, even for sums as small as $2\frac{1}{2}$d., and when the election of churchwardens came on, the church was packed to suffocation, ' almost the whole of the leading tory party were present; and the vicar was attended by the curates of the parish church, and the incumbents of Whitworth, Little-borough, Milnrow, St Mary's, St James's and St Clements '. The vicar again nominated Brierly as his warden; then the tories pro-posed John Lord as warden of Castleton, and the radicals proposed Thomas Livesey, a Chartist. According to the radicals the show of hands was five or ten to one in Livesey's favour, but the vicar de-clared Lord elected. Immediately pandemonium broke loose, and the dispute went on for over an hour, the vicar holding his ground. On each of the other vacancies the tories moved a name, and the radicals an amendment; but now, on a similar show of hands, the vicar declared the radical elected, and the tories demanded a poll. A highly-organised election, in which the *Guardian* attacked the vicar's party as tories, and the *Courier* denounced their opponents as Chartists, had a curiously inconclusive result. The Rochdale bells tolled for victory of the tory list by 3,002 votes to 1,187; but then the London papers arrived with the decision of the Queen's Bench in the Braintree case. The all-out tory effort had assumed that if the wardens were unanimous (as in 1834 they were not) they could levy a rate on their own authority should the parish refuse; Lord Denman now held that they could not.[17]

When the vestry to levy the rate came round, the vicar ' greatly to the astonishment of the many parties present, declared the show of hands to be in favour of the rate '; but there was no arguing with a hectic five-days poll. The rate was refused by 4,047 to 3,981; the parish clock was stopped, the bells silenced and the dispensary closed. Only a desperate move could now save the day, and a private meeting of the parish clergy and rate-payers resolved to gamble upon another poll. This evidence that the

Church was taking the initiative at the local as well as the national level guaranteed that no holds would be barred. When the clergy appeared at the vestry,

> hissing shouting and groaning greeted them. . . . Mr. James Fielden, brother to the honourable member for Oldham, took his station in the pulpit . . . amidst the cheers of the multitude; the same did Mr. John Bright and Mr. Barton . . . [Owing to the number who could not get in, the meeting was adjourned to the Church yard. Bright proposed that no rate be granted and] lashed the clergy most unsparingly for the present church-rate agitation, and the meeting appeared highly delighted with the castigation . . . [Bright added that] at the poll which took place a few days since, he heard the son of a clergyman declare, in the open meeting, when widow Brierley, the wife of the poor man, who had his bible taken for an illegal church rate of 4d. when on his deathbed, came up to vote against the rate, that Brierley ought to have had his bed taken from under him too.

In a parish of 50,000 inhabitants only the ultimate effort could bring out more voters than before. This time the radicals took the initiative with

> the appearance in a body, of almost seven hundred of the operatives of Messrs. Fielden of Todmorden, who were regularly dragooned, and walked through the streets with a band of music at their head. At this time the utmost excitement prevailed, but the presence of about 300 of the county police restrained Messrs. Fielden's mob from any act of violence.

The church-party had no choice but to send

> chaises, carts, waggons, and other vehicles . . . in all directions; public-houses were opened in all parts of the parish where free drink and refreshments of various kinds were liberally distributed to all who would promise to vote for the rates.

There was direct bribery and the manufacture of votes;

> . . . for one hovel of sods, in which wheelbarrows are kept on the Manchester and Leeds Railway, twenty-two labourers were constituted rate-payers; and all of these men, it is needless to say, voted for the rates. It is said that upwards of a hundred

of such votes were constituted for sod-huts etc, for the benefit
of the Church-rate party.

At the appointed close, finding his party trailing by seven votes,
the vicar again extended the poll, claiming that the radicals were
obstructing the arrival of the voters, as on the previous Wednes-
day, when, ' as two waggons filled with voters for the rate were
entering the town, a quantity of Bright's men stoned them, and
one poor woman had her head severely cut '. The poll was staggering—a victory for the rate by 6,594 to 6,481—and so were the
celebrations. The church-party rang the bells, and held a tea
drinking at the Flying Horse, followed by music and dancing;
the anti-rate party laid on tea for eleven to twelve thousand persons
at the public houses, with music and dancing all night.[18]

Expenditure on this scale had no relation to a halfpenny rate,
and the local tory press professed no doubt that the money and
organising effort in Rochdale had come from the national enemies
of the Church establishment.

> . . . the secret of all the hostility to the Church at Rochdale is
> not confined to the bosoms of the Fieldens, the Brights, and
> Bartons of the place; . . . Dr. Molesworth is a marked man
> among the political dissenters of the whole kingdom; and
> although the Rochdale schismatics may have had some share
> in hatching the scheme, the maw-worms of the Central Dis-
> senters' Committee, in London, have been the principal parties
> to the incubation.

A branch of the Religious Freedom Society (with John Bright in
the chair) had indeed been formed in Rochdale as the contest of
1840 began, but this tory counterpart of the conspiratorial vision
of the disestablishers was rash, how rash the sequel was to show. For
no church rate was ever granted by a vestry again, and the wardens
of Rochdale, like those of Manchester, never again appealed to a
poll. It proved fruitless to summon the church-rate defaulters of
1840 before the magistrates, the majority of whom were Liberal
and disclaimed jurisdiction. The Queen's Bench was sympathetic,
but afforded no practical means of collecting small arrears. Moreover the tory ranks in the parish were being riven both by politics,
and by personal reactions to the vicar's stiffness. Rochdale Wesleyans had put immense personal acrimony into prosecuting church
rates against their Warrenite enemies, but they were turned against

the Church by Graham's Factory Education Bill in 1843. The property settlement arranged in connexion with the marriage of Molesworth's nephew with Miss Entwisle, led to one quarrel with the tory clans, another caused the vicar's exclusion from the magistrate's bench. When Thomas Livesey secured another poll for churchwardens in 1843, not a single tory leader supported the vicar at the voting, and the radical list was carried by a huge majority. The new wardens would not enforce a legal rate; the vicar would neither preach for, nor subscribe to, a voluntary rate, so with nonconformist support the Chartists did both. Molesworth and his son produced their own vitriolic sheet, *Common Sense,* which John Bright and the leading Warrenites opposed with the *Vicar's Lantern.* Billingsgate met Billingsgate. If the vicar contrasted the ' men who have risen from penury and been bloated into their sudden affluence by accumulating capital and scraping it off the wages of the working men ', with the common interest enjoyed by gentry, clergy, and operatives, the *Vicar's Lantern* could acidly inquire whether ' when trade is declining and commercial embarrassment stares you in the face on every side, and the cruel Income Tax is the boon of a clerico-landlord parliament . . . [you] will yet submit to the local taxations of the State Church.' The vicar's high-minded obstinacy was ruinous if not supported by the tory caucus. When the bishop came for a confirmation in 1845, the bells did not ring, the ringers having ' struck work sometime ago for wages, as they have not received any for some years back '. The church became filthy, and in October 1848 even some of the anti-rate wardens were prepared to move for an exiguous rate. But nothing could be collected, and that winter the ultimate humiliation was inflicted. The rural dean required repairs to be undertaken. The wardens scraped funds from various sources, including the hire of three parish hearses. But there was now no money to license the hearses, and they were seized and sold for £16 14s. 2d. Thus, concluded the tory *Courier,* an ' almost indispensable means of conveying the remains of their deceased relatives and friends to the parish graveyard is denied to the people of Rochdale by the patriotic haters of the church at whose head is Mr. Bright '. Brierley's Bible had been almost matched. After a stormy meeting for the election of churchwardens in 1849 only the vicar's warden swore in : both the voluntary and the compulsory system as lately understood were at an end.[19]

The Church as a whole, like Rochdale parish, was being driven
back upon its endowments by the gradual failure of other methods
of public support, and the effort to exploit the endowments commercially may partly explain the collapse of the Rochdale church
party in the 'forties. In 1763 the parishes of Manchester, Bury
and Rochdale had obtained acts allowing them to lease out the
glebe (certain reserved portions excepted) for periods up to 99
years, and thus encourage building and industrial improvement.
Through these leases an important part of Rochdale had been built
on the glebe. In November 1844, the *Guardian* reported that the
vicar was applying to parliament for a new bill to regulate the
glebe leases, and that there was panic among the lessees who had

> obtained grants of land upon leases, for farming or agricultural
> purposes, and let it as building land for thirty or forty times
> more than they paid for it as grazing land. The difference be-
> tween these two prices the vicar claims on behalf of the church.
> . . . It so happens that those who have had such a nice slice of
> church property are its thick and thin defenders, who are ever-
> lastingly calling out ' the church is in danger'. Report says
> that several have already complied with the reasonable de-
> mands of the vicar, and obtained terms more favourable than
> they expected.

The lessees found that the vicar rebutted their contention that he
must renew leases on request, and conjured up visions of property
being taken in hand to the value of £22,000 p.a. The interests of
the railway and canal, both built on the glebe, were involved, not
to mention those of the Rochdale Improvement Commissioners and
the mills which took river water for their engines, and were now
threatened with a charge from the vicar as riparian owner on both
banks. It was the more provoking as the Rector of Bury, under
his act, renewed leases simply on the basis of the improved value
of the land, without any claim to the buildings. The lessees failed
to obtain a hearing from the Lords, but the Commons amended
Molesworth's bill in the direction of compromise, as perhaps he
had always intended. The rights of the Rochdale Commissioners
were reserved, and sharp limits put on the vicar's ability to dis-
possess lessees. There was to be no social revolution engineered by
the Church, but the living was raised from £1,600 to over £5,000,
a result attributed by the Ecclesiastical Commissioners to ' the busi-

ness abilities of the present vicar ', who had so tartly abused the commercial aptitudes of the Rochdale radical leaders.[20]

The object of the Primate (who held the advowson) in forcing up the value of the living, had been to augment the chapelries in the parish, but this consummation was delayed until Molesworth's death in 1866. After the vicar's act the tory press launched into protracted criticism of the progress of the Church.

The last Anglican chapel to be built in Rochdale was St James's in 1818, and all the pews were appropriated; since then the population of the town had doubled, and eight of the twelve meeting houses and the Romish Chapel had been built. 89 nonconformist preachers, lay and ministerial, kept up 66 services a week, while the ' sacred liturgy of the Church is performed only six times weekly in the three churches of the town by the five clergy there '. Nor would the Church regain the ground it had lost in the Sunday schools. Archdeacon Rushton reckoned that the places in the new Manchester diocese most in need of churches were Dukinfield and Rochdale, and even Molesworth admitted that though 'the founder of Christianity never intended to propagate his doctrines by the voluntary principle, . . . he would not deny that the voluntary principle was not useful and necessary on many occasions'. Bright and his friends might feel they had made their point; and having taken the arch-disestablisher Edward Miall to be their MP in 1852, they laid the gunpowder trail which eventually blew up the church establishment in Ireland. Yet not all the omens were favourable to them. Like the Manchester radicals they had failed to defeat a rate though they prevented its being levied. And the huge effort they had made depended more on secular forces than religious loyalties. The rising of the fringes of the parish against the centre, which we have noted as often important to religious revival, was crucial to the Rochdale church-rate issue. In the last contest of 1840 it was noted that ' the votes for the rate consisted chiefly of Rochdale men '. The battle was between Rochdale and its parish. Todmorden, especially, the furthest outpost of the parish (apart from Saddleworth which was virtually independent), had had a long-standing feud with Rochdale, and though it had never won the parochial status recommended by the Parliamentary Commissioners of 1650, it had celebrated its own marriages since 1669, Hardwicke's Marriage Act notwith-

standing. From 1800 Todmorden maintained its own poor, revived the claim to parochial status, and resisted both church
and chapel rates. In 1833 Todmorden was solid against the rate
and carried the opposition home. In 1834 and 1835 it was a
similar story. The votes in 1840 were not separately recorded,
but there were reports of the Fieldens' mill hands arriving by
the squad by train and waggon, and when it was known that
there was to be a second poll, James Fielden boasted that ' on
the last occasion 800 votes against the rate had come from Todmorden, but this time they shall poll 1,400 ', far more, of course,
than he could produce himself. Here was the red light for the
disestablishers. They were operating with secular forces beyond
their control, and if the centrifugal movement of those forces was
reversed before their objects were secured, sharp limitations on
their power would be revealed.[21]

If anyone in Manchester or Rochdale had supposed that the
church-rates question was not intimately connected with that of
disestablishment, events in Leicester would have disabused him.
In that Rochdale of the Midlands there was resistance to the
church-rate, and in 1840 there were great protest meetings about
the imprisonment of one recusant, William Baines. Baines was
a friend of the Rev. Edward Miall, one of the two chief Independent pastors in the town, who was at that moment laying the
foundations of the celebrated *Nonconformist*. Miall's anxiety
about Baines, and the melodramatic implications he perceived
in a typical local squabble, confirmed him in inveterate enmity
to the entire establishment. ' Get Thomas Carlyle's *Lectures on
Heroes* and read ', he wrote to Baines in gaol, ' especially those
on Luther and Cromwell—it will brace your mind like spring
water '. The church-rate struggle not only threw up great anti-
church politicians like Miall and Bright, it embodied the same
ambivalent relation between central and local politics as the
disestablishment agitation. One of the objects of the great church-
rate contests of the mid-'thirties had been to drive the government
to a settlement by Act of Parliament, and one of the things which
had checked the snowball was the evident impossibility of legislation by Melbourne's weak government after 1835. But it was
then arguably all the more important ' to make the Church anxious
for a settlement ', either by campaigns against the militants as in
Rochdale, or by litigation as at Braintree, the lessons of which

were expounded to the general public by Miall's Liberation Society in a tract entitled, *Practical direction to the opponents of church rates.*[22]

Disestablishment could not possibly be achieved without parliamentary action, and the problem of tactics was even more painful. The whig government had scarcely time to show its determination to head the dissenting left into any cause other than this, when it began to founder upon internal disagreements. The elections of 1835 and 1837 returned the whigs to office, but first greatly reduced, and then virtually annihilated their majority, altogether frustrating any possibility of their fighting a slogging-match with the Lords. In 1837 no one knew that this palsied condition was to become normal for English governments under the reformed system. Two exceptional crises, the reform crisis of 1830-32, and the dreadful recession of 1837-42, led to the election of governments with power to act, in the latter case that of Peel, who offered no joy to disestablishers. After Peel, the usual condition was a stalemate which arose from rigidities in the electoral structure. One election result was much like another, with the tories the largest party, but the whigs usually in office by virtue of their ability to secure support from the splinter groups, Peelite, Irish or radical, at the price of abdicating policy. Along with all the other extra-parliamentary pressure groups, the dissenters suffered the frustration of being unable to do anything but injure the only government from which they had anything to hope. If they went it alone, they generally got nowhere; if they were absorbed into a whig coalition, their support produced scant return. Dissenters, radicals and Irish could not avoid this dilemma, and each shifted from one unpleasant horn to the other several times in the course of the century. In the later 'thirties the dissenters divided for the first time on this insoluble problem of tactics, the conservative seeking to salvage something for a failing government, the radical turning for inspiration to a regional cause.

Robert Vaughan, one of the intellectual leaders of English Congregationalism, professor of ancient and modern history at University College, London, now produced *Thoughts on the past and present state of religious parties in England* which appeared to the *Wesleyan Methodist Magazine* a deliberate olive branch to the Church, and relegated disestablishment to the Greek Calends.

*While the social system of England shall be what it is, and
while the prevalent feeling in favour of an established Church
shall be what it is, there ought, as I conceive, to be such a
church* . . . And if there are Dissenters who having looked
to the monarchy and to the court of England, and to the
prepossessions on this subject of the persons who constitute the
upper and even the lower House of Parliament, and have expected to see these parties concur in anything approaching
towards an extinction of the State Church, *such expectation
must surely have been indulged in some of those delusive
moments when the passions do not allow the understanding to
perform its proper office.*

Dissenters might constitute half the nation, but were not strong
enough to compel ' the other half, with all its preponderance of
rank and wealth ' to forgo the principle of an Established
Church.[23]

To the provincial zealots this compromising spirit was an-
athema, and in any case unrealistic. For at the crucial moment
a shot in the arm came from Scotland, where establishment had
been as profoundly affected by the reform crisis as in England.
That crisis opened the door to evangelical power in the General
Assembly, much as evangelical parties had already secured power
in the United Secession Synod, in the Ulster Synod, and in the
Congregational and Baptist denominations in England. The evangelicals understood that the establishment must approve itself as
useful to the state, and must find security in the affections of the
people against the violent assaults of the Scottish voluntaryists.
In the first Assembly dominated by the evangelicals, a campaign
of church extension was launched which in four years had raised
£200,000, built 200 churches, and imparted a bracing sense of
achievement of a kind that always eluded the English establishment. At the same time the Assembly adopted the Veto Act which
provided that, when the majority of male heads of families,
being communicants, dissented without reasons from the nomination of a minister presented by the patron, the nomination was
null and void, and the presentee was rejected without any trial
of his qualifications by the courts of the church. As Dr McCrie
of the ' Auld Licht ' anti-Burghers, who, in their distaste for the
new evangelicalism, had withdrawn from their own General

Associate Synod, put it candidly, 'there is nothing that the Voluntaries dread so much as the abolition of patronage'. But in the Scottish Church, as everywhere else, the heroic and doctrinaire solutions of the 1830s speedily led to trouble. No one had contended harder than Chalmers for the principle of establishment, and the notion that endowment was the poor man's seat-rent. The Scots evangelicals never understood how English ministries were embarrassed by approaches for the endowment of new parishes, either in a political viewpoint, or in that of an open-ended commitment upon a flagging budget; but they did understand that they could not wait for ever. The Church therefore assumed the power to annex parochial charges to unendowed chapels, the crucial Assembly of 1834 admitting at one sweep all ministers of chapels. The new turn was denominationally useful in that it enabled the Assembly to receive ministers of the Associate Synod of Seceders, the ' Auld Licht ' anti-Burghers, in 1839. Nevertheless, when in 1838 the results of private effort in the Church seemed to justify a fresh approach to the state, the Scots dissenters were lashed into fury by the sense that the establishment was trying to have its cake and eat it. The Kirk was voluntaryist when it came to absorbing the ranks of dissent, established when it came to tapping the pocket of the state. They insisted that church extension was designed not so much to remedy spiritual destitution as to kill dissent by competitive building, a charge which received some support from Anglican and tory commentators. They carried the warfare down to London and the North-west of England, where they were welcomed by radical dissenters, and to the south Midlands where they helped to push Edward Miall into renewing the disestablishment agitation.[24]

The English radicals were in a receptive mood. Their alliance with the whigs had broken up, they had suffered disproportionate losses in the elections of 1835 and 1837, and must find some new impulse, preferably one that would resist the centrifugal tendencies of radical politics. The ballot, suffrage reform, reform of currency or tariff, the Charter, the abolition of church-rates or the Corn Laws—all were canvassed, all might provide a living for professional agitators now falling on hard times, all, in different degrees, were better adapted to the interests of particular regions than to providing a general rallying cry. Scottish disestablishment was another sectional cause on which a more general movement

might be built. The wilder men amongst the dissenters were as
disenchanted with the whigs as the radicals generally. By 1838
the Church was visibly recovering in political strength and self-
confidence, while the dissenters had obtained nothing more than
the state registration of births, marriages and deaths, and the
possibility of licensing their own chapels for the solemnisation
of marriages. Even this seemed to many a monstrous conspiracy
to rivet clericalism upon dissent, while others chafed as the
operation of the Marriage and Registration Acts was suspended
for months until unions were created under the Poor Law Amendment Act, through which they were to be administered.[25]

The disestablishment cause offered more than an outlet for
chagrin at the failure of the ' moderate' platform of dissenting
grievances; it might enable the strong men of the provinces to
seize control of the dissenting political organisations from the
nerveless hands of the London shop-window, and it led at once
to the establishment of Miall in London with his own paper.
Moreover it embodied a certain kind of political realism. It was
already clear that to move the reformed parliament by outside
pressure was harder than had been originally supposed. Resistance
to the claims of the Scottish church might in the short run provide
a basis for cooperation among Scots, Irish and English radicals
(as the disestablishment of the Irish Church did in the later
'sixties), while in the long run disestablishment might provide
the best insurance for men of the left who must bide their time.
The ominous feature of 1830 had been the way urban discontent
had been reinforced by a rural jacquerie. When things again
became unbearable, the farm labourers would again turn against
the Church as their most obvious oppressor; again the Establishment would be menaced by direct action; this time, so the radical
argument went, dissent must be ready for the opportunity, and
must not forswear it in the interests of unprofitable parliamentary
associations with the whigs. Miall was not in tactics the most
consistent of politicians, but at intervals he took this view. In
1847, addressing the Anti-State Church Conference, he maintained
that :

the feeling of the people was with them, gathering in strength
every day. The peasantry hated the State Church. It stood
constantly in their way and it had kept them where they were,

and as they were for many a long year . . . they knew the
Church had oppressed them, that in every step to improvement
they had been checked by the clergyman, and when the moment
came that it would be safe for them to show their feelings, the
public would be electrified by finding that those districts which
were most under the clergy would evince the most decided
feeling against the State Church. The Establishment, as such, was
doomed . . . (Great applause).

William Ferguson, an Independent pastor at Bicester, who knew
the plight of the south Midland farm labourers at first hand, the
same ' evil which at present threatens to convert Ireland into a
heap of graves ', agreed. For this evil the Church did not bear
the entire responsibility, but there was no denying its constant
petty oppression, its loss of the labourers' affections, its association
with the rural ruling classes, ' who hold the people in chains
that they may beat them to pieces at their pleasure '. That these
expectations were signally disappointed does not detract from their
intrinsic reasonableness. The aggravated subsistence crisis which
underlay the revolutions of 1848 on the continent had been paral-
leled in England in the past, but after the recession which ended
in 1842 British industry developed a rhythm of its own, its short-
term movements no longer dependent on the movements of the
agricultural sector of the economy. For the future the low peaks of
industrial and agricultural recession diverged, and the terrors of
the town mob were never again magnified by simultaneous
scattered disorders in the countryside, whether English or Irish.
By 1850, though no one knew it, one of the great bogies of English
public life had been laid.[26]

While the radical dissenters drew fresh courage from contemplating an armageddon which never in fact arrived, the Scots
Church raised the question of establishment to the level of political
theory for the first time since Coleridge. In the spring of 1838
Thomas Chalmers gave a course of lectures in London on the
principles of national establishments, a course which turned into
a great public demonstration, attended by the Duke of Cambridge,
members of both Houses of Parliament, the bench of bishops and
high society. Chalmers boldly claimed for the Church not only
state support, but complete spiritual independence. ' In things
ecclesiastical we decide all '. The Protestant Dissenting Deputies

brought down Dr Wardlaw, the distinguished Glasgow congregationalist, to answer this challenge. They noted contentedly that
his lectures were a publishing as well as a platform success, and
that

> the friends of . . . high Church doctrines at Oxford and of
> the low state doctrines now promulgated by the non-intrusionists
> of Scotland are alike loosening the connexion between the
> Civil and Ecclesiastical powers. Nor can the adherents of either
> establishment make any progress or attempt any alteration with-
> out feeling that their defences against Dissenters operate as a
> restraint on their own freedom.

The controversy was not easily stilled. The young Gladstone
contributed his celebrated tract on the *State in its relations with
the Church* (1838; 4th edition 1841), the great reviews joined
in, and by 1840 that most wooden and most Orange of evangelicals, Hugh McNeile, was lecturing in London, justifying
establishment as inevitable, as right, and as the only bulwark
against Popery.

> Our creed is fixed not by the state but by the Bible. There
> we find it, and present it in intelligible formulas to the civil
> ruler. . . . As to the charge that we cannot change an article
> of our creed, it is our glory that our creed is unchangeable. It
> is the one, the ancient, the true, the divine creed, which no
> man can change. . . . The dissenter, therefore, who rejects
> the primitive formulary, and the papist who adds to it, tradition
> written and *unwritten* (unwritten! there is an open door) stand
> equally excluded from safe union with the state. . . .[27]

The Deputies might think this more brittle than any position of
Chalmers.

Yet the second disestablishment movement was to fail, injured
by some of the circumstances which gave it an initial impulse.
In 1837 the economy began its descent into that dreadful recession
which continued without much relief until 1842, which reached
its worst over the winter of 1841-2, and left as deep a mark
on general opinion as that which culminated in the clash at
Peterloo. Ingrained fears seemed to be fulfilled that the economy
suffered from a structural weakness whereby efficiency generated
investment surpluses which, when ploughed back into efficiency,

must steadily reduce the rate of interest to the point where capital earned no return at all. In this generation recession always produced hard and doctrinaire attitudes, an atmosphere good for disestablishment; but the harrowing severity of these years, the structural changes they forced in the concentration of industry in the technologically advanced areas of the North and Midlands, the Chartist upheaval, and the emotional outburst of business interests against aristocracy entrenched in the political order—all this hardly suggested that a state Church was the root of all evil. On the other hand, Cobden and the Anti-Corn Law League produced a policy apt for both the immediate and the long-term problem.

In its early days when recession was the great spur to agitation, the League could argue that a reduction in food prices offered the best hope of restoring elasticity to the market; in the later stages when the cry for cheap food had been overlaid by fears of permanent dearth in the West, free trade seemed essential to the development of new sources of supply from the Black Sea steppes and even America. Free trade, in short, was attractive to a wider public than most radical causes, attractive even to disestablishers. Free trade, it was reckoned, would cut corn prices by 10–25 per cent, and as the tithe had been commuted in 1836 for a cash equivalent, based on seven-year averages of grain prices, it would be gradually reduced by free trade in the same proportion. No other measure of disendowment so substantial was in prospect. More generally free trade would damage the whole nexus of privileged institutions, whose selfish interests (it was held) cramped the development of the country. Certainly the League took in organisers from the Voluntary Church Societies, and the cash, enthusiasm, and political skill which it attracted were in a measure so much lost to the campaign for disestablishment.

The organisers of the League, moreover, knew how to dress up their campaign in simple moral terms, and were almost invited to exploit the potentialities of dissent by the unholy zeal of Anglican evangelicals to establish the economics of protection from the Old Testament. After the liberals' disastrous failure at the election of 1841, George Thompson, the former anti-slavery agitator, and J. W. Massie, a turbulent Manchester Congregationalist minister, were laid on to organise a great synod of ministers, mostly dissenting, in Manchester, to pronounce on the

o

question of the day. It followed immediately upon the Wesleyan
conference which had been ' sitting in great dignity in this town ',
and was designed to show, *inter alia*, that although official Methodist politics were triumphant, the connexion would be worsted yet.
The conference indeed revealed how the direct political action
of dissent was inhibited by denominational exclusiveness. Robert
Halley, one of the chief Manchester Congregationalist dignitaries,
who was only drawn in through League pressure skilfully applied
through leading members of his congregation, complained incessantly that he was ' rather jealous for the *honour of our own
body, and did not quite like the multitude of sects with which
they were mingled, and the persons of all sorts who called themselves preachers* ', and insisted on the impropriety even of repeat-
ing the Lord's prayer in a mixed gathering. James Scholefield,
the Bible Christian of Peterloo fame, was now a Chartist actively
opposed to the League, and was not there; nor in the main were
the Wesleyans. William Bunting, the son of Jabez, publicly
declined an invitation in terms which came oddly from so Orange
a politician, and from a member of a connexion smarting at
Tractarian exclusiveness.

> I am not able to bring within the range of those purely
> Christian politics, with which it is the peculiar duty of Christian
> ministers to interfere, a much disputed fiscal question, on which
> Holy Scripture vouchsafed no one principle, that I am aware,
> for our guidance in determining it. . . . I have a secondary
> objection in being associated in an assembly professedly and ex-
> clusively ' ministerial ', with certain gentlemen, whom, however
> much I might respect their personal . . . qualities, it is im-
> possible for me to recognise as evangelical ' pastors and
> teachers '.

The conference was carefully contrived, predictably anathema-
tised the Corn Laws as ' opposed to the law of God . . . anti-
scriptural and anti-religious ', terms which had lately been reserved
for the state church, and was a success. Halley was impressed with
the efficiency of the stage-management, and the enthusiasm generated. Baptist Associations which had kept out of secular politics,
and which were to keep out again until the age of Gladstone,
discovered that the Corn Laws ' concerned the interests of the
Redeemer's kingdom '. Again the efforts of the League's new

apologists detracted from the cause of disestablishment.[28]

The working-class response to recession was also damaging to the prospect of radical class cooperation on which hopes of disestablishment rested. As the demand for the remodelling of the political order reached its peak, it was clear enough that the churches were mostly on one side; Chartism, even more than free trade, made the contest among the churches irrelevant. The distance between the churches and the independent enterprises of the working class also became apparent. In England as in France much of the confusion which surrounded the political and religious loyalties of the working class was being dispelled. In both countries Jesus Christ was something of a hero in working-class propaganda, and His religion held to be the great guarantor, in France of fraternity, in England of democracy. For a time in both countries, combinations of a tory radical kind appeared viable, though a sense of working-class unity was continually developing, one element of which was large-scale non-participation in official religious institutions. The truth came out in the summer of 1839, when the Chartists took to organising processions to services at the parish church, especially in the North-west. This exercise of an unimpeachable right of public assembly might display their numbers; they might claim a place in the national church; and put the clergy on trial by asking them to preach on such texts as James v. 1-2, ' Go to now ye rich men, weep and howl for your miseries that are coming upon you. Your riches are corrupted, and your garments are moth-eaten.' The visits to church began in July 1839 at Stockport, and spread to numerous places, especially in the cotton-textile area. The striking feature of these demonstrations is that there seem always to have been more people in the streets to watch the fun than would ever turn out to church, even for a political demonstration. In Manchester they could not be brought out at all, and the only place where the regular congregation could be crowded out was Bolton. Here the churchwardens and police ' invited them forward, and solicited the *honour* of their attendance regularly ', but the next Sunday less than six hundred could be mustered, a large proportion of whom were boys. In the evening, Richard Carlile exhorted the Bolton Chartists to keep up their attendances, and put their own preacher in the pulpit if the clergyman did not suit them; he then gave a broad hint by preaching on a text the curate had used on the previous Sunday. There is, however, no record of any subsequent action. The Establishment and the Chartist working-men now lived in separate worlds, and could not easily be brought together for either conflict or cooperation.[29]

In many places in the North Chartists put up anti-church rate candidates in elections of churchwardens, and fetched up with a policy of complete disestablishment and disendowment; but this implied no happier relations with dissenting, than with tory, radicals. For the Chartists could neither maintain their stance without organising churches of their own in which democracy should be preached and practised, nor could they make a success of them. Christian Chartism began, significantly, in Scotland, where the churches had much deeper popular roots than in England, and although in 1839 Chartists claimed to have ' planted their humble places of worship in almost every corner of the land ', they did so on a very small scale and for a very short time. The Birmingham Chartist Church, for example, resolved in 1846, with only one dissentient vote, to join the Baptists, from whom most of them had originally come. There was nothing like the rash of Independent Methodist congregations (some of them alive today) formed at the time of Peterloo, still less the tide of Methodism and evangelical dissent which rolled across the country-side in the 1790s. Urban Chartists were not much hurt by the thunderbolts of Church or Conference, and felt relatively little need for a religious bulwark against them.[30]

If the disestablishment cause, revived by Scots pressure, was blunted by parliamentary stalemate, diverted into agitation against the Corn Laws, and side-tracked by social discontent, it was also undermined by the new viciousness of divisions among the dis-senters. Only yesterday evangelical Congregationalists had been at the core of the movement for ' catholic Christianity '; now a party of them coupled their efforts to bring down the Church establishment with a final drive to disendow the empty shell of the old dissenting establishment, the ex-Presbyterian Unitarian meetings. To the *Patriot* the two campaigns were part of a single struggle against the misappropriation of public funds.

. . . the major part of the old Presbyterian endowments are held and managed by parties who are no more Presbyterian than they are Lutherans or Wesleyan Methodists: and they are employed chiefly to prop up a cause incapable of maintaining itself, to keep alive a *paralytic heresy* which still performs its frigid rites in the sepulchres of departed orthodoxy.

The contest took its name from the hilarious polemic in which George Hadfield had fired the first salvo in 1825, *The Manchester Socinian Controversy*. At a farewell gathering for one of their ministers, the Cross Street congregation was treated to a lively after-dinner speech by the Rev. G. Harris of Bolton, in which he pointedly contrasted the generous and liberal spirit of Unitarianism with the mean and slavish spirit of orthodoxy. This brought a tart response from Hadfield upon the liberality by which Unitarianism survived upon the endowments of orthodox dissenters of the past. Of the 223 Unitarian chapels in England, Wales and Scotland, 178 were originally orthodox, and Lady Hewley's important charity founded in 1704 and 1707 for the assistance of poor godly preachers and their widows, was now in the hands of Unitarian trustees.[31]

Four years later the Lancashire Congregational Union got Hadfield to prepare a report on Lady Hewley's charity, and although only one-fourth of the income was applied to Unitarian objects, litigation was begun. The weakness of the Unitarian case in law was that when the endowment was made, Unitarianism was an illegal doctrine, and the testator could not have made her bequest to its present uses. The Unitarians had to resort to the entirely fictitious doctrine of the Open Trust, alleging that those meeting-houses which were not strictly tied to the Westminster Confession or some similar standard, were intended to be left open, and that Presbyterian meeting-houses were mostly of this type. But when the Hewley case came for decision in Chancery in 1836 the decision went against the Unitarians, who had to derive what satisfaction they could from the skilful manoeuvres by which the orthodox Presbyterians of the North-east put the Congregationalists in a tiny minority on the reconstructed trust. The Unitarians had no option but to appeal to the Lords, for under the logic applied in the court of Chancery, they could be dispossessed not only of Lady Hewley's bounty, but also of most of their meeting-houses; that these properties had been used by the same families for generations was not to the legal point.[32]

Immediate disaster now threatened the Unitarians. Hadfield

fought and won a number of cases, litigation began in Ireland, Risley chapel in south Lancashire was secured for the Scots Kirk by Anglican suits at law, and the Wesleyans conspired to gain possession of another chapel at Partington. In 1842 the Lord Chancellor declared against the Unitarians again, adding that 'two or three hundred suits are already talked of as likely to be initiated' for the purpose of ousting the present possessors. The last resort now was an appeal to the government for legislative protection. The Unitarians, impeccably whig, formed a joint Anglo-Irish Committee with authority to negotiate with Peel's conservative government. The Dissenters' Chapels Act, passed in 1844 with government support, provided that where no particular religious doctrines or mode of worship were prescribed in the trust, there should be protection to congregations able to prove twenty-five years of continuous possession. No history of the savage in-fighting which took place in this case after 1836 has ever been written, though abundant materials for it exist. The Unitarians found themselves supported by Roman Catholics who had held considerable school and chapel property before the Catholic Relief Act, and wished no questions to be asked. On the other side Anglicans were not prominent, though 'the *evangelical* clergy and their adherents were the most alert, relentless and persevering'. Quakers took no part, and Baptists were generally adverse 'although far less united and untiring in their attacks than Congregational nonconformists' who were the real driving force. The surprise came with the ferocious campaign waged by the Wesleyans, who might be supposed to have no standing in this case, and who complained incessantly about outside interference in their own affairs. But their hatred of Unitarianism had grown no less, and when what Bunting called 'this vile "Trusts Bill"' came on in 1844, the Wesleyans threw all their force against it, publicly and privately, in England and in Ireland. They said privately that in its original shape the bill would make it impossible to recover property from schismatic Methodists, as they had recovered it from the Kilhamites, and amendments were made to meet their objections. But the whole episode was a cheerless curtain-raiser to the great battle over Maynooth.[33]

These venomous disputes did no good at all to dissenting co-operation in the north, and as late as 1847 when Bright was a candidate for the Manchester seat in Parliament, vain efforts were made to bring him to repudiate his votes for the bill; but by then the radicals could not do without him, and he became ' the pet candidate of Mr. George Hadfield and the Manchester Independents '. In London the political consequences were more serious. When William Smith, the famous Unitarian chairman of the Protestant Dissenting Deputies, retired in 1832, he was already afraid: ' some of our brethren seemed to think differences of opinion on controverted points of theology sufficient grounds of separation even as to the common intercourse of life in civil affairs .' By the time of Lyndhurst's judgment in Chancery in 1836 the Unitarians found it impossible to stand their ground among the Deputies or among the body of the ministers of the Three Denominations, and seceded. Disputes over funds followed, and the Deputies suddenly found that Lord Holland would not present their petitions; his connexions had always been with the Unitarian shop-window of dissent. The Deputies were the core of the opposition to the Dissenters' Chapels Bill, and South Place, Finsbury, the one Unitarian congregation still represented amongst them, was not again summoned to their ranks. A completely unpredictable line-up of forces had saved the remnant of the old dissenting establishment from destruction by a powerful evangelical coalition; despite the bishops' folly in voting against the government-sponsored bill, the Church establishment might breathe more easily. Dispersion of authority was still the order of the day.[34]

The final reason for the failure of the disestablishment campaign lay in the inability of an intense denominational spirit to accomplish its minimum end of holding the flock together. No grand confrontation could be staged when one religious community after another became distracted by internal disorder. Immense zeal, courage and violence seemed merely to plough the sand, and no crux proposed by the enthusiasts would neatly polarise the hysterical public opinion of the 'thirties and 'forties. No religious body was harder to bring to the point of decision than the Church, for here dispersion of authority was at its greatest. Other bodies, more responsive to policy, were more difficult to hold together. These two themes form the subject of the final chapters.

8 The Dénouement II: The Limitations of Policy in the Church

The Church has not often had a leader as brimful of policy as Charles James Blomfield, Bishop of London, 1828-57, or one whose achievements have been so well charted by historians. His aim was to make it worth while for the state to support the Church, by pressing a valuable programme of church- and school-building. The wider hopes of this programme were disappointed, for although the state enabled the Church to redeploy her own resources, and poured money into education on terms which enabled the Church to claim the lion's share, it was inhibited by the religious and political situation from direct subsidies. And within a few years of Blomfield's death the state began to contract out of the traditional obligations of its union with the Church. But the organisation and logistics of the late Victorian Church were much what Blomfield made them.

At another level the tory radicals failed still more conclusively to find the Church a social role and social backing. In the Church of England, as in the religious establishments of France and Germany, the emergence of an unpalatable new society evoked a conservative analysis of the social problem. The times, it was plain, were out of joint. Society ought to be stable, peaceful and organically integrated, the lower orders looking to the higher for protection, guidance and betterment, the upper orders conscientiously providing it. In this scheme the Church played a key role of reconciliation and inspiration; nothing less than Christianity could persuade the lower orders to accept their lot, nothing less could keep the upper classes to a strenuous programme of regulation and welfare, the very notion of which they had abdicated generations before. The towns were the great affront to this paternalistic and rural perspective; they were dynamic and materialistic, and were thought to be irreligious and devoid of community spirit. Mills and millowners were another bogy; mill-owners got rich quickly, they were often dissenters or disciples of political economy, they enforced factory discipline and recruited child labour. Hatred and compassion, political tactics and religious policy, ensured that there would be conservative support for popular resistance to the new Poor Law, and to the regulation of factory work by the free play of the market. Lord Ashley entered the factory movement from the narrowest animosity towards a group of entrepreneurs whom he regarded as highly dangerous,[1] and the tory victory at the polls in 1841 brought into Parliament a group of squires of similar views, with roots deep in the industrial areas, and reasonable expectations of influence. For the Church much was at stake, yet nothing turned out as planned, and it proved impossible to turn the factory movement into a crusade of the Church against dissent.

For none of the parties would fulfil the role allotted to it in the conservative ideology. Ashley, though commencing as a political bigot, developed steadily into one of the great and good oddities of the nineteenth century, expanding his interests into the whole field of wage-labour, and ultimately of poverty. And although J. R. Stephens of Ashton, and West Riding Anglican clergy might feel deep moral revulsion at the new Poor Law, most of the southern gentry wanted both lower poor rates and protection by the Corn Laws, neither of which held any cheer for the pro-gramme of Christian and tory social harmony. Nor was official Conservatism more hopeful. The tory government of 1841 was headed by Peel and Graham, two devotees of political economy. It had no room for Ashley, set him down as a dangerous dema-gogue, and effected the ruin of the tory radical programme.

The Church too failed to meet the case. Ashley was always complaining that the clergy did not pull their weight, and only three bishops (one of whom was the whig Stanley) helped his Mines Act through committee. More important, Church sup-port for Ten Hours legislation did not reach its peak until the bill was on the threshold of success in 1847; by that date short-time working was so widespread that millowners themselves were accepting the bill, and the tory radical group in Parliament had ceased to function. The core of clerical support was in the West Riding, and in Lancashire (which was much less overrun by evangelical dissent) the Anglican clergy performed much less

impressively or adopted other ways of tackling the problem.
Lancashire clergy often gave the Ten Hours movement their
patronage, but often made it clear that they wanted the young
out of the factories in order to get them into church schools;
and they often failed to honour undertakings to take the chair
at meetings. In Lancashire, moreover, dissenters were far more
prominent in the movement than in Yorkshire; the great lay
leaders Fielden, Hindley and Brotherton were a Unitarian, a
Moravian and a Bible Christian (Swedenborgian) respectively; in
the second rank were dissenting laymen, like Edmund Grundy,
the Bury Unitarian, and ministers of all kinds, Baptist, Congregationalist, Warrenite, even Wesleyan, though Conference discipline and the itinerant life generally inhibited Wesleyan
preachers from putting down roots into movements of local
protest. Catholic priests also played a minor but notable part.[2]

There were two special difficulties for Anglicans. The tory
radical outlook did not encourage the independent participation of
the lower orders in politics, but the passionate outbursts of these
years were assertions of dignity and status as well as protests
against hardship. In December 1837, for example, the Rector
of Wigan moved a public meeting to establish a soup committee
for the relief of distressed hand-loom weavers, but when the
Catholic priest insisted on saying a word against the Corn Laws,
' the rector, the other clergy, and the tories generally left the
room in great chagrin '. The second difficulty was that too few of
the clergy of any kind could speak with knowledge about conditions in the mills, still less the economic circumstances which
influenced them. Press reports give the impression that both
Anglican and dissenting ministers were more prominent in a
movement which gained less notoriety, the Early Closing Movement; shops were on their beat in a way that mills were not.
Moreover the clergy had no tools with which to match the political
economists; evangelicals like McNeile and Stowell talked un-
certainly about excessive issues of paper money, and ' over-trading '
or ' over-speculation ', while the Manchester chapter made itself
ridiculous by supporting the Ten Hours Bill in the name of spreading employment more evenly over the year; variable as it was, the
cotton trade was not as seasonal as agriculture. Of course, their
eyes were fixed on the past. In a pamphlet on the condition of
the labouring poor, which the *Manchester Courier* thought worth

serialising, Richard Parkinson, one of the Manchester canons, lamented that

> there is far less *personal* communication between the master cotton-spinner and his workmen, between the calico-printer and his blue-handed boys, between the master tailor and his apprentices, than there is between the Duke of Wellington and the humblest labourer on his estate, or than there *was* between good old George the Third, and the meanest errand boy about his palace.[3]

Manchester society would never be an aristocratic idyll.

When pressing the claims of the Ten Hours Bill upon the Manchester preachers in 1833, Parson Bull asked why it was ' that in this dense population, among whom perhaps nearly 70 ministers reside, only two have appeared as public advocates of this humane and righteous cause ', though many were prominent on evangelical platforms. The answer was in part that the Lancashire evangelicals were pursuing an alternative method of bridging the gap between the upper and lower orders, that of Orange politics. Confessional conflict in Ireland was, as it has remained, powerful enough to prevent the emergence of the politics of class; perhaps it might succeed on Merseyside too. The first English Orange lodges were founded in English militia units serving in Ireland in 1798, and brought home to Manchester and most of the industrial towns of the region. They began to act as friendly societies and to recruit civilian members, some of them doubtless among the Protestant Irish immigrants, who seem to have had no organisation of their own until the Irish General Assembly provided preaching in the Manchester Corn Exchange, and ultimately a minister and church, for them in the mid-'forties. The Manchester tradition was that in 1807 Irish Catholics had created a serious riot by attacking a peaceful Orange parade, and provoking the Orangemen to reorganise and expand their movement. The English lodges always found gentry leadership hard to come by, but they posed as a significant counter-revolutionary force and source of patronage. In the Lancashire troubles which followed the Napoleonic wars

> the Orange system was rather encouraged, because it was found useful in aid of the magistracy. . . . The great manufacturers felt that their men being embodied in the Orange society, they

were ready at all times to come forward in the suppression of disturbances.[4]

Certainly one Orange magistrate and other lodge members were present at Peterloo.

The passage of Catholic emancipation in 1829 marked the failure of one main purpose of the Orange movement, but the crisis brought in the Duke of Cumberland and a number of British peers, who in the early 'thirties toyed with the notion of using the lodges as a sheet anchor in a revolutionary situation, and as the nucleus of an ultra-tory party. It was now that the worst troubles in Manchester began. On 12 July 1834 an Orange procession was badly harassed by the Catholics; the Orangemen, not to be denied, walked again later in the day, and serious disturbances began which continued for some days. The following year the deputy constable tried to talk the Orangemen out of their procession, but all they would give up was their insignia, and a series of skirmishes around the Protestant public houses followed. The radicals were now making the lodges an issue in Parliament; they got a select committee appointed which produced four huge volumes of damaging evidence; the king promised to take measures against Orangeism, and thereupon the Duke of Cumberland dissolved the lodges. Manchester no. 3 lodge devoted its funds to the formation of the Princess Victoria Sick and Burial Society, while the *Guardian* called for the auctioning of the lodge paraphernalia as an earnest of good faith.[5]

The Irish invasion of Merseyside intensified the struggle for daily existence and introduced an alien population which had immense difficulty in adjusting to town life. As that tolerant body the Stockport Sunday School reported in 1824,

the demand for additional labor has brought an influx of population that forms a striking contrast to the native inhabitants; the uncivilised manners and squalid appearance of their persons and of their children are only exceeded by the filth and disorder of their habitations. They are evidently come from those darker regions of moral degradation where society is only a remove from the level of brutish ignorance.

The Stockport school was for taking the new Irish under its undenominational wing, but to many of the vulnerable in the town population, Irish squalor seemed likely to be the ultimate fate of them all. After Emancipation the Irish could only be kept as second-class citizens by street violence, political blackmail and the manipulation of patronage. In this atmosphere the Orange lodges revived, and when they were dissolved it was simply a question through what alternative channels their spirit would flow. In 1835 a great conservative party drive for the foundation of Operative Societies began, especially in the North, and in Manchester it was always unclear how far those societies were Orange lodges in disguise, excluding dissenters and Roman Catholics; explicitly Protestant Operative Societies were soon functioning in the same milieu. Everyone knew that many clergy of the establishment had been involved in the Orange lodges, and the new Operative Societies showed a touching readiness to subscribe for distressed Irish clergy.[6]

One way of relieving necessitous ministers of the Irish Church was to appoint them to curacies in Lancashire. Bishop Sumner found that they provided the only means of filling the complement of unbeneficed staff in unpleasant industrial parishes, and in 1837 he was wildly accused of importing no less than 200. No one denied that the Irish were often gifted with extraordinary eloquence, they gradually worked their way into benefices, and some made a good thing out of what had been very derelict livings indeed. Sections of the Manchester public became chronically addicted to the torrential oratory of Irish clergy resident in their midst, men like J. H. McGuire, H. W. McGrath, and best of all, P. J. O'Leary, a converted popish priest. Everyone knew that

> the Irish are an irascible race, and they often mistake human passion for Christian zeal; they are furious against the Papists, and think opposition to Popery to be the only element of Christianity. . . . This fierce polemical spirit, where encouraged, becomes intolerant, overbearing and persecuting.

Yet when Hugh McNeile, the celebrated Ulsterman of Liverpool, and Hugh Stowell, the evangelical Manxman, for whom Christ Church, Salford, had been created under a special act in 1831, came to reconstitute the Protestant army after the dissolution of the Orange lodges, the émigré Irish clergy formed invaluable lieutenants.[7]

In 1836 McNeile was presented with a first-class issue by the

determination of the newly elected liberal council of Liverpool to
introduce undenominational education, based on the Irish national
system, into the corporation schools, and he and Stowell made
unscrupulous claims that this involved the exclusion of the Bible.
This subject has been studied at full length,[8] and need not be
rehearsed here. In Manchester, Stowell and his coadjutors put
their effort partly into the Operative Societies, partly into a revival
of the Reformation Society, which by 1838 had made the Protestant question the heart of popular conservatism. Under this banner
great demonstrations were put on in Manchester in 1839 and 1840,
in which Stowell barely disguised his intention of using force on
the streets.

> What has the Protestant Society accomplished in Manchester?
> [he asked]. It has tended to foster and shelter the combination
> of, I believe, from 700 to 800 decided, honest-hearted, right-
> minded protestant working men, in an unbroken phalanx against
> the incursions of popery: it has had a powerful effect in settling
> and over-matching the spirit which popery was assuming in
> Manchester. We have to a great extent got up in Manchester
> again that wholesome horror and antipathy of popery that, I
> am sorry to say, was fast sinking in the public mind. I say
> wholesome horror of popery, because though in many minds it
> is little better than a prejudice, yet a prejudice founded on truth
> is the next best thing to a principle.

This programme of street-fighting, by men of no particular religious conviction, had one ideological triumph: it secured the
public backing of Wesleyan connexional management. On the
platform with Stowell were two of Bunting's three sons (William,
the preacher, and Percy, the solicitor) and his life-long friend,
James Wood, who seconded the resolution. Bunting with his
usual acuteness had divined that Peel was going to win the next
election. The Reformation Society offered a way of climbing on
the band-waggon which could be justified within the Wesleyan
connexion as religion rather than politics; and Bunting's family
and friends were now habitually on its platforms. ' With merely
secular politics ', it was officially held, ' Methodism in its corporate capacity, has no concern ', yet on great moral issues, the arche-
types of which were the anti-slavery cause, Sabbath observance, the
defence of religious liberties, or the attempt ' to force upon a

nation a system of education generally believed to be essentially injurious to our common Christianity' (or as it was more tersely put, 'treating Protestantism and Popery on the same ground' in education), the united action of the connexion was indispensable.[9]

The more lurid Methodist views were exemplified by James Dixon, a stout conservative, furious protestant propagandist, and father of R. W. Dixon, the author of the massive *History of the Church of England from the abolition of the Roman Jurisdiction*. He maintained in 1838 that

> the whigs have set an example of political profligacy, and have done more to corrupt the morals of society in their short reign than any other party has done since the days of Sir Robt. Walpole. Can anyone now deny that they have *bought* the Papists and are in the constant habit of throwing sops to the Radicals? That in fact their whole system of government is one *grand* intrigue, carried out by the most disgraceful tricks of crooked policy.

At the time of Emancipation Bunting had strenuously opposed preachers 'speaking at Brunswick Clubs, or taking any public part in political discussions'; now they plunged uninhibitedly into public controversy on the Protestant issue. A particular noise was got up in Sheffield by James Dixon, S. D. Waddy and John McLean. McLean, who regarded himself as, in a peculiar sense, a protégé of Bunting, and had lived in his household as a probationer, made no bones that the object was to produce a parliamentary effect, and that the agitation was not so much an expression of outraged Protestantism as a cynical attempt to work up a panic.

> I . . . trust the Lord will furnish you with many opportunities of securing the cause of Protestantism. We have contributed our mite here, which I hope will be far more than its intrinsic value in St. Stephens. Nobody refused to sign, for indeed we have been working on their fears for months on the subject of popery, but we have scarcely one, unless it be amongst our poorer members, who possesses much individual zeal on the subject.

Correspondence of this kind helps to explain why Methodist

liberals felt that the 'No politics' rule was being rigged against
them.[10]

The connexional management, however, were in cleft stick. Old
Thomas Allan told the Committee of Privileges the only way to
keep the government from 'disposg. of the funds of the country
in support of popery or the declared enemies of the authsd.
version', was to keep them out of education altogether. But then
Daniel O'Connell raised the spectre of Wesley's role in the Protestant Association which had launched the Gordon riots in 1780,
and declared bluntly that if Wesleyans objected to paying for
false and injurious systems of religion they should oppose church
rates. Here was the rub. Wesleyan support for the establishment in
the 'thirties disqualified them from resistance to national education on voluntaryist grounds. Only the Protestant platform was
left. John McLean, at least, was delighted. 'We have drawn the
sword and our only honourable and successful course is to throw
away the scabbard.'[11]

Yet the Protestant line by which McNeile and Stowell hooked
official Wesleyanism to their demagogy was a policy which could
not be fully implemented at any of the levels at which it must
succeed. The original Orangeism of the Armagh peasantry had
been an undenominational defence for which gentry leadership
could be sought. The leaders of English Orangeism, Anglican or
Wesleyan, were last-ditch denominationalists, with no permanent
basis of cooperation, while working men, even those of Manchester
confronted with 'Little Ireland' by the Medlock, were more
interested in class conflict than in soliciting the patronage of the
upper orders. Orangeism was at its strongest in Liverpool where
it succeeded in creating a role for the Church, but it is not clear
that even there toryism recovered faster than in the country as a
whole. Nor could the Catholics quite fill the role allotted to them
in Orange propaganda, for, as the Chartist movement showed,
Catholic working men had a curious propensity to play the political
game according to English rather than Irish rules.

At the same time the English Church was hardly what the
Orangemen needed. Christ Church, Salford, had been built for
Stowell under a special act precisely because there was no other
way to take the patronage out of the hands of the Manchester col-
legiate church, who would never have exercised it in his favour.
The old high-church party in South Lancashire had defended

establishment and public order through thick and thin, and could teach Stowell a lesson about both the use and the limitations of mob force. They were indeed over-genteel when it came to patronage; there is not much doubt that it was the Manchester College which took the bishop to task in the *Manchester Courier* for preferring unlettered Irish over learned English clergy, when H. W. McGrath was appointed to St Anne's, Manchester, in 1837. But their hostility was rooted in an intellectual defence of the Anglican position. They claimed that basing a religion position upon the Bible alone had by a logical necessity led the English Presbyterians into Socinianism; nothing therefore could be more damaging than the crude fundamentalism of Stowell and the Irish. In 1839 in carrying a favourable account of Stowell's greatest Protestan meeting, the *Manchester Courier* again echoed the Manchester chapter in a comprehensive rebuke.

> Let him not mistake his position. He is a man of great natural talent, but he is by no means a learned or well-read man. In most of the requirements of an orator, nature has been bountiful to him; we have seen him quivering with artfully wrought excitement, until his voice has been strung up to a perfect scream, and his frame convulsed through every muscle; but he is not a John Knox, or even a Rowland Hill. In nervous diction, well-turned periods, and sketchy metaphor he has few superiors; but he is not a profound thinker. In the human heart, he is no doubt well versed; but it is a question whether he has ever examined the reach of man's understanding, or endeavoured to penetrate beyond the ordinary bounds of thought.

The inwardness of all this was revealed the following week in an exposition of the XXXIX Articles from the Hulsean lectures of one of the fellows of the collegiate church, Richard Parkinson. As we shall see, Stowell's revenge upon Parkinson was not long delayed; but as long as the high-church party was entrenched in the higher preferment, and held the views it then held, the Church would not respond with enthusiasm to the characteristic hatreds and hopes of the Orangemen.[12]

Thirdly and finally, there was no adequate basis for the Protestant line in general tory politics. For years Stowell had hammered away at the small grant made to the Irish Catholic seminary at Maynooth and also at Catholic emancipation. Neither of these

causes would endear him to Peel. On the eve of the election of
1841 the *Manchester Guardian* noted that ' the ultra-protestant
zealots . . . are found inconvenient, not to say dangerous, auxiliaries ', and with the election won, tory backing was cut off, and
Wesleyan top brass disappeared from the platforms overnight.
By 1844 McNeile and Stowell were admitting defeat. ' In some
localities protestant associations had been dissolved and the protestant flag for the moment furled. Why had it been so? Because
we had a protestant government.' But Peel's increased grant to
Maynooth proved that there was not even a Protestant government in Stowell's sense of the word, and the best issue which the
Orangemen ever had, demonstrated the fragility of their cause.[13]

The proposal to increase the grant to Maynooth in 1845, though
only an aspect of Peel's policy for pacifying Ireland, evoked one
of the most passionate storms of the century and had important
political consequences, hardly any of which were palatable to
the contestants. Dedicated voluntaryists could not accept this new
state endowment of religion—and Congregationalists and Baptists
were again toying with disestablishment. Evangelical nonconformity
generally was in an unusually restive state, its great triumph in
defeating the education clauses of Graham's Factory Bill in 1843,
having been followed by a dismal failure to block the Dissenters'
Chapels Bill in 1844. With old landmarks crumbling, Maynooth
offered an opportunity to reassert their power. The Wesleyans
had dropped the Orangemen and since 1843 had been acting with
the nonconformists; but they were under too much pressure from
Ireland to resile at this point. Then there were strains to be
exploited in the tory party, the back-benchers' suspicious isolation
from the leader, the protectionists' alarm at free trade budgets,
the discomfiture of the tory radicals. Maynooth was proof to
Ashley of Peel's treachery. Ordinary Manchester clergy talked of
combining to force the government to raise their stipends, since
public funds were evidently available for Irish Catholics.[14]

The violence of the campaign may be gauged by the tone of the
Wesleyans who had stepped prudently for so long. James Heald,
MP for Stockport, told a public meeting that ' he was a conservative, and as such anxious to preserve everything that was worth
preserving and to give up all besides; but whatever was the fate
of the Conservative government, he would hold his conservative
principles in abeyance to scripture '. The preachers played with an

address to the Queen to dissolve Parliament, though they could not get enough signatures to save their credit. But to the last, and in language extraordinary for one who had blocked action against Catholic emancipation, Bunting insisted that ' *protest* against the abandonment of what is left of our National Protestantism should be as *marked* and *extensive* as possible. This will make the sin in some sense, perhaps, *rather less national* '. Never had the burial of old differences in hatred of Rome been nearer, nor was any dream more completely exploded. The bill passed by an enormous majority, Members being notably reluctant to pledge their votes. Still worse, Protestant desperation ensured that there would never be a viable Protestant government again. Sir James Graham knew that ' a large body of our supporters is mortally offended, and in their anger are ready to do anything to defeat the bill or to revenge themselves upon us '. Within a few months the embittered Protestant and protectionist rump had broken Peel's party irreparably over the Corn Laws, but were themselves almost incapable of obtaining office.[15]

The consequences were equally far-reaching amongst the nonconformists. No semblance of union could be maintained between the voluntaryist and the Protestant opponents of Maynooth. The voluntaryists broke away from a conference called by the Anti-Maynooth committee, because of its ' no-popery ' character, and passed an address of sympathy to the Irish Catholics upon their grievance against the Anglican establishment, while John Blackburn, one of the Secretaries of the Congregational Union, went over to Dublin pledging himself to defend the Irish establishment against the dissenters.[16]

Miall and his friends were right in concluding that the Irish Catholics could contribute far more to disestablishment than the Protestant coalition. Twenty years later the alliance now adumbrated brought to an end not merely the Irish establishment, but the Regium Donum (a grant made by William III to poor Presbyterian ministers of Ulster) and the Maynooth grant as well. Meanwhile, the support of the whigs and radicals of secular mind for the Maynooth grant galled the disestablishers, as Peel had wounded the evangelical churchmen. They began therefore to prepare for a separate campaign in the election of 1847, Miall's Anti-State Church Association, formed in 1844, being machinery to hand. The Maynooth bill opened the door to Miall's association in Yorkshire, and the impress was deepened by the furore over Russell's education proposals of 1846-7. When the election came a Dissenters' Parliamentary Committee was set up in London, followed by an Anti-State Church Conference; Congregationalists in Scotland set up their own committee, and a new periodical, the *Nonconformist Elector,* was established. Voluntaryist candidates were to be run where there was hope of a creditable showing, and where not nonconformist electors were advised not to vote. War was declared upon members who had voted for the Maynooth bill or the education measures. Conservatively inclined Unitarians urged that the voluntaryists could not hope for success on this plaform in more than a dozen boroughs, whereas abstentions might cost the liberals fifty seats. And in fact Miall, Sturge and others were defeated by whig-Peelite coalitions, and not all the two dozen members who, they claimed, had been returned pledged to disestablishment, owed their success to the Anti-State Church Association. Moreover the pledge to exclude the State from education, to which the voluntaryists had committed themselves, was an incubus they had finally to drop if disestablishment or even a friendly government were ever to be had.

Maynooth gave an impulse not only to voluntaryism, but also to formal cooperation in the Protestant front which offered the last hope to the Orange cause. For some years individuals had been stirring to salvage some evangelical unity from the bitterness of denominational rancour. Sir Culling Eardley Smith had given a prize for essays on the theme in 1837, and Congregationalists of the old ' Catholic Christianity' school, like John Angell James and Leifchild, began in 1843 to hold meetings of mixed denominational character for prayer and Christian unity. The disruption in Scotland swelled the stream, the Free Church being anxious for outside sympathy and support. What the movement lacked was a tangible objective, and this was supplied by the anti-Maynooth agitation, which also brought in Anglican evangelicals and official Methodist support. The Anti-Maynooth Conference resolved to form ' a great Protestant Confederation, to embrace this Country, the Continent and the World ', and what was referred to in the Wesleyan Conference as ' a great evangelical anti-Popery meeting to be held in Liverpool ', gave birth to the Evangelical Alliance in 1845. The Protestant platform was not erected without difficulty. The more extreme voluntaryists knew there could be no place for them, and John Campbell added to his troubles with the Congregational Union by making no secret of the fact. Official Wesleyanism backed the Alliance strongly, but many Wesleyans had their doubts. Alfred Barrett wanted members of the Alliance to fulfil the canons of Wesleyan pietism; others a declaration against Antinomianism; others again feared that the Alliance would compete for the charitable offerings of the flock; and when the Wesleyan reform secessions began in 1849 there were not lacking accusations that the Alliance politicians were fishing irresponsibly in troubled waters. There were similar doubts among the Baptists, and unexpected American hazards surrounding the condemnation of slavery. Nevertheless the machine was launched, by 1851 it claimed to have developed a policy, and it commissioned ' scientific ' papers on the cause of divisions in the Church, Sabbath desecration, the aggressions of popery in the British Empire, and so forth.[17]

The Alliance could not turn the great agitation against the Papal Aggression to any permanent advantage, but it cruelly exposed the failure of the professional Orangemen. Stowell and McNeile had seen their Reformation Societies flagging at the very time the anti-Maynooth furore was at its height, and understood as clearly as the voluntaryists that there was no room for their kind of exclusiveness in the Evangelical Alliance. In 1846 Stowell headed a protest of Manchester clergy against the Alliance, claiming that it regarded schism as unimportant, and assumed that it would continue; when the Alliance held a meeting in Manchester in September, 1846, none of the Anglican clergy took part. Stowell and McNeile were thorough-paced establishment men, and as Stowell became preoccupied with the education question in the later 'forties, he needed the support of established clergy of other views, not least his high-church bugbears in the Manchester chapter, whose principal service to the town lay in developing a system of church schools. Moreover the Protestant issue, despite the Papal aggression and heavy working in the elections of 1847 and 1852, was really played out. In 1852 there were riots in Stockport in which immense violence was let loose by the incautious utterances of a Derby government supported by Stowell, and no reasonable man wanted any more. The Protestant platform of the mid-'fifties— demands for the withdrawal of Catholic emancipation and for the inspection of nunneries—was prurience rather than politics.

No one had sought more furiously to unify the in-group by anathematising the out-groups than the Orangemen; it was fitting that
none had failed more dismally. And after 1870 the Manchester
evangelicals kept Church schools afloat by a combination with the
Catholics on the School Board, and captured the Salford parliamentary seats for the Conservatives by arrangements which caused
traditional liberal Catholic voters to shudder at the prospect of
' the sad spectacle of his Lordship [of Salford] being marched to
the poll between the two champions of Orangism and Toryism,
Cawley and Charley '.[18]

Stowell's abiding legacy to the Church was not his public politics
but the model organisation of his parish, in which a great burden
of pastoral oversight was so divided among lay helpers that an
immense work could be accomplished, and time still found
for other things.

> With the aid of two curates, five services were held every
> Sunday in the parish; three in the Church and two elsewhere;
> Mr. Stowell himself always preaching morning and evening,
> and once a month publicly catechising in the church in the
> afternoon. On Wednesday evenings there was a service, fol-
> lowed by an expository lecture; each of the Gospels and Epistles
> being in turn plainly and practically explained. Schoolroom and
> cottage lectures were frequent during the week. On the Satur-
> day evening, previous to the monthly celebration of the Lord's
> Supper, there was a preparatory service in the church. Lent and
> Passion Week also brought their special services. The poor were
> sought out in their own houses by a large staff of volunteer
> district visitors, each with their special mission. The schools,
> Day and Sunday, were on a very large scale, and in a high state
> of efficiency. A striking feature in the latter was the number of
> grown-up persons, often married men and women, who regu-
> larly took their place among the scholars. There was an adult
> Sunday School, in which some of the pupils were past the three
> score years and ten; Ragged schools, and a refuge for the fallen.
> The teachers of these schools, and the district visitors, met their
> pastor once a month for counsel and advice; while every Satur-
> day evening, Rector and Curates met for prayer and reading
> the Word. There were libraries too, and a mutual improvement
> society, and clothing clubs, and other minor institutions of a

like sort; and all these required and received his continual supervision. The preparation of young persons as candidates for confirmation was a work upon which Mr. Stowell bestowed much time and pains, meeting them in classes weekly for many months previously and afterwards having a private interview with each of the candidates, often numbering nearly two hundred. Amply however was he repaid. . . .[19]

It is important, therefore, to observe the acrimony generated by the efforts of Stowell and his friends to improve the pastoral oversight of Manchester parish as a whole. 'The Manchester Church question' (as it became known) was in its own way as much a parable of the Church at large as the troubles at Rochdale.

Some of the organisational difficulties of the Manchester parish have appeared already. The old parish church, which in 1850 served a population of about 500,000, was a collegiate body, and the bulk of the pastoral service fell upon two chaplains and a clerk in orders who maintained regular daily services throughout the year, and got through a record number of baptisms and marriages. The indecorum and registrarial difficulties to which these led, were not the only source of irritation. When in the later 'thirties weddings could be held in district churches, double fees had to be charged (as for baptisms) in order to compensate the chaplains; but the latter, whose stipend was only £17 10s. 0d., had no inducement to forgo their rights. Moreover there was a striking contrast between the generous endowment of the parish church and the penury of the district chapels; in 1850 only Trinity Chapel, Salford, and Birch Chapel, Rusholme, had endowments exceeding £150 p.a., most had much less, a few had nothing, and the great majority had no residence. The wealth of the chapter formed the first and most serious source of criticism.

The chapter first got into the toils through the inquiries into capitular revenues which led up to the Ecclesiastical Duties and Revenues Act of 1840. The chapter declared the modest net income of £4,025, to the absolute incredulity of many, including Joseph Brotherton, the radical MP for Salford, and the *Manchester Guardian*. In 1854, Prince Lee, the first Bishop of Manchester, rebuked the chapter for lying in written replies to the Cathedrals Commission, and the veracity of the chapter was always suspect, particularly on financial matters. But if the chapter told the truth,

they must surely be guilty of gross mismanagement of their property. The price the chapter obtained for disposing of a strip
of land at Newton to the Manchester & Leeds railway in 1837,
suggested that it must accept much too low a yield on its property
as a whole. If the chapter was letting out property for a 99-year
term under its act of 1763 on beneficial leases instead of commercial rents, an investigation was required; and when, in 1838,
the chapter through the tory press denied any such transactions,
one of its tithe agents assured a parliamentary committee that he
had himself received a lease of chapter property for a small rent,
on payment of a fine of £100. In the Lords the Bishop of Salisbury
maintained that the Ecclesiastical Commissioners knew that the
Warden and four fellows had been receiving £2,500 and £1,250
respectively, and that this was why the Act of 1840 which constituted them the chapter of the cathedral of the future diocese of
Manchester reduced their incomes to £2,000 and £1,000. It was no
wonder that the clergy savoured anecdotes about Canon Wray.

> One day I heard him tell the Dean that he thought four thous-
> and a year a most desirable income, with which anyone might
> be content. ' You have enough ', he said, ' for your necessities
> and a few luxuries. No man need wish for more.' I thought
> so too; so did the Dean.

By 1840 both critics and friends of the Church were sure
that there were under-used resources in Manchester, which made
it impossible to ask fresh state support. The chapter revenues must
increase substantially when the original 99-year leases fell in, and
it could hardly be right to charge the whole expense of the chapter of the new diocese to a single parish, sadly short of pastoral
oversight.[20]
After the opening shots between 1837 and 1840, the Manchester Church question rumbled for six years, until a conjunction of three events produced a sharp clash between the chapter
and virtually all the other interested parties, and led to the
regulation of the parish by a special act which is still in force.
In 1836 Manchester churchmen, not to be outdone by Chalmers
in Glasgow, established the Manchester and Eccles Church Building Society, the first body of its kind in the country. The evangelical Bishop of Chester, J. B. Sumner, had recently organised the
first diocesan church building society, but the Manchester chapter

refused to support it, on the grounds that a local society would attract funds which would never go to the diocese. They could hardly avoid coming into the Manchester and Eccles Society, even though the evangelicals had already tied it to erecting churches under the act of 1 & 2 Wm. IV (under which Stowell had been established in Christ Church, Salford), selling its own title of patron to subscribers of £500, and vesting the patronage of the churches it built in trustees to be elected in the first instance from among the Society's patrons. This unwilling partnership could not last, and after five years, the evangelicals, finding funds exhausted, hived off into a Ten Churches Association of their own. After a year's hectic competition the Manchester and Eccles Society virtually collapsed, and the Association raised £25,000 with which they built five churches, the fifth of which, St Philip's, Bradford Road, hung fire for three years before its consecration in 1850, owing to the exhaustion of the Society's funds. A decade had taken Anglican voluntaryism to the limit, and the results were not impressive; down to 1849 only 837 persons in the two parishes had subscribed to either fund. The evangelical conclusion was that voluntary effort could build churches but not endow them, and that subscriptions were withheld on the grounds that there were under-used resources in the hands of the chapter.[21]

The second event which brought the Manchester Church question to a head came in September, 1846, when the Manchester churchwardens entered a resolution in the parish journal regretting that Canon Parkinson had accepted the additional preferment of the presidency of St Bees and the cure of its parish; ' the large parish of Manchester ', they maintained, ' requires an increase rather than a diminution of clerical superintendence '. That Parkinson was entitled in law to accept the preferment was not in question; but when he and the Dean paid no heed to the memorial the churchwardens called a meeting to express the discouragement of the laity, and from that moment the yield of the voluntary church rate dropped sharply. The chapter disclaimed pastoral responsibility, but it could be held that they were incumbents, and that in creating them a chapter, Parliament would not have left the parish without pastoral oversight.[22] The urgency of the whole question was increased by the long-awaited arrival of a bill in Parliament to create a Manchester bishopric; it now became indispensable to clarify the relations between the new diocese and the parish. Lord John Russell declared in the House that as the revenues of the chapter came almost exclusively from the parish, provision should be made for better pastoral oversight to be charged against them. A few days afterwards a motion was put in the terms of the Manchester churchwardens that the whole of the chapter revenues be applied to this purpose. The chapter could be in no doubt as to the purport of all this; the idea which Hook made fashionable at Leeds, that unmanageable parishes should be divided into smaller independent parishes endowed with a portion of the old living, had been anticipated in south Lancashire. The rectory of Winwick was divided in 1841, and the evangelical incumbent of Oldham had divided and endowed his ancient parochial chapelry. Prestwich parish was about to be divided, and the old Stand chapel, augmented by a gift of its tithe, to become a parish church.[23]

The crux of the matter was whether the chapter had cure of souls in the parish. They stoutly maintained that, like most chapters, they had not; they had always been an appropriate rectory, and the cure of souls was exercised by the hard-pressed chaplains. The nominal fines paid by the chapter upon non-residence were nominal because they were a simple alternative to residence. To these views the chapter won important converts in J. B. Sumner, Bishop of Chester, and Prince Lee when he became Bishop of Manchester. But the chapter's best ploys went sour on them in this contest; when Hibbert Ware edited their charter, Prince Lee concluded not merely that the chapter were wrong, but that they had faked their public defence by omitting the crucial words of the charter. The present chapter was nevertheless the first in which pluralities and non-residence had not been general, and they viewed the agitation as a personal vendetta. The public meeting got up to receive the Dean's reply to the wardens' memorial was attended by only six persons, four of whom were prominent Manchester evangelicals. Richard Birley, president of the Manchester Church Reform Association now set up to threaten the chapter, belonged to a well-known tory family which often acted with the evangelicals; Richard Gardiner, a merchant who gave generously to church building, a pillar of Christ Church, Salford, was vice-president and the most important figure in the Church Reform Association; Malcolm Ross was an immigrant Scots merchant who conformed to the English establishment, and joined the evangelicals; and Thomas Clegg, a trustee of St Philip's, Bradford Road, the financial straits of which helped to precipitate the issue. Nor is there any doubt that the Manchester Church Reform Association was a lay evangelical front, anxious to requite the ideological assault which Parkinson had made upon Hugh Stowell, to repay the obstructiveness and superior airs of the chapter, and to repair evangelical fund-raising failures from the cathedral endowments. Stowell himself kept dark until the final enquiry of the parliamentary committee on the Rectory Division Bill in 1850, when he made the best of his grievance against the chapter for resisting the building of his church.[24]

The Church Reform Association harried the churchwardens of the old church and out-townships, petitioned Lords, Commons and Ministers, and generally whipped the local dispute into a general issue. This agitation brought the chapter to the point of concession for the first time. They agreed that any revenue surplus to the incomes appointed by the act of 1840 should go to the relief of the spiritual necessities of the parish. The dean would reside for eight months of the year, the canons for nine months as incumbents of town churches. The minor canons or chaplains would reside as having cure of souls in the collegiate church district. The proceeds of one of their estates best suited for building would be devoted to the gradual extinction of the fees due from the district churches to the mother church, and then to the endowment of the poorer livings in the chapter gift. This proposal was acceptable to the wardens but not to the Church Reform Association. They pointed out that the act of 1840 diverted surplus revenues not to the parish but to the Common Fund of the Ecclesiastical Commissioners. Moreover the chapter were trying to turn an attempt to enforce their pastoral responsibility into arrangements which would enlarge their incomes by the addition of town livings. The augmentation of town livings enjoyed the lowest priority of their proposals, and the chapter livings were not those most in need.[25]

During 1848 general political excitement checked the progress of the Church Reform Association. Lord Ashley could not get their petition before the House, and the Mayor and Stipendiary Magistrate persuaded them not to contest the elections for churchwardens; as it was, the Chartists made a scene in the vestry. But the Association strengthened its propaganda position by producing a translation of the Manchester college charter, and a series of commentaries by Thomas Turner, a London lawyer, and trustee of St Philip's, Bradford Road. By contrast, the persistent obduracy of the chapter put them wrong when opinion moved rapidly the next year. On 13 December 1848, a meeting of incumbents of district churches was held at Stone, Staffordshire, condemning the present relations of district churches to their parishes, calling for legislation ' completely separating all districts of every kind into distinct parishes, as regards church rates, surplice fees, and the appointment of officers, and all other ecclesiastical and parochial purposes ', and proposing concerted action with clergy elsewhere. The Manchester Association called on its clergy to ' endeavour either with or without the cooperation of the rectors to obtain the complete division of the parish '. A meeting in London called on subscribers to boycott the Church Pastoral Aid Society and the Curates Aid Society, and drive incumbents by overwork to divide their parishes and endowments. In Yorkshire a bill was produced for the immediate sub-division of large parishes without respect to the rights of present incumbents, and on 18 January a re- markable gathering, purporting to be a meeting of the clergy of the Archdeaconry of Manchester, was held at Accrington. It was in fact called by five curates of Blackburn, to secure the division of the parish and overthrow the authority of its for- midable vicar, Dr Whittaker; and it included a powerful delega- tion from the Manchester Association, who claimed that their Manchester scheme went much further than the Yorkshire bill. The curates inveighed against the church building acts, ' all of which showed manifest symptoms of what, in the political world, was called class legislation (Hear, hear). . . . The mother church had cast off the daughter churches to support themselves as best they might '. Whittaker, an able and forceful man, now reaped a sour reward for having built 13 churches in his parish; having tried for over an hour to browbeat the curates into submission, he withdrew with his party, declaring that ' it was not to be ex- pected that he should go on building churches, for the purpose of having them taken out of his hands, by men of his own creation. . . . He would build no more churches if this measure passed into execution '. It slipped out that the Blackburn curates had been planning ' a clerical association in Lancashire, for the purpose of advancing reform in the church, especially as regarded the temporalities, the improvement of Church land, and also with a view of enlightening the Ecclesiastical Commissioners by views from the north ', when the Staffordshire balloon went up. Church extension had created a clerical proletariat, who now saw their income restricted, their usefulness circumscribed, their new churches already decaying, because of their subordinate status, lack of endowment and the double fee system; in hard times they would keep quiet no longer. The Church had not merely failed to clamp together a divided society, it could not keep the peace among its clergy.[26]

A fortnight later the clergy of the Whalley district had a more orderly meeting at Burnley, but passed a long series of unanimous, detailed, and important resolutions, that

> there ought to be a sub-division of large parishes, and that double fees ought to be abolished as speedily as possible, . . . that in the case of larger and more opulent livings, ecclesiastical superiors should exert their influence with the view of inducing the incumbents to give up the fees at once without the necessity of a voidance intervening: . . . that all new districts should be parishes, and that Easter offerings, if collected at all, should be collected by the clergyman belonging to the district.

It was a strange pass when the lower clergy threatened to expropriate their betters, but were they not following their betters' example? The churchwardens of Ashton-under-Lyne complained that their celebrated aristocratic non-resident rector had ' disposed of the whole of the coal under his glebe land, and the amount received by him would, if put out at common interest, realise not less than £500 a year, and in our opinion considerably more '. Meanwhile he drew from the parish £1,500 p.a., returning to his curates £220 p.a., and the use of the rectory. The Manchester clergy also came out in favour of parish division, the tory press crowning accusations that only evangelicals were summoned to the meeting, with offensive personal recriminations against Stowell and McGrath. Meanwhile Ashley had taken the lead in a Commons debate on the division of large parishes, and royal commissions were appointed to consider the management of episcopal and capitular estates and the division of large parishes.[27]

The general attack upon chapters which was a feature of the early 'fifties was now fairly building up, and the job of the Church

Reform Association was to keep events moving, while maintaining the special claims of Manchester in the general scramble for parochial resources. They established public support by carrying a list of churchwardens in 1849 against the list proposed by the retiring wardens. There was again a scene with the Chartists in the vestry, who claimed that what was wrong (apart from Sturges Bourne's Act) was the spirit of meanness which came in with the steam engine; the laity would no longer endow the poor, and would rifle cathedral funds rather than endow the clergy. The Association got a legal opinion that the chapter had cure of souls in the parish, and that the chaplains were in effect their curates, they primed both the royal commissions with their evidence, and canvassed parliamentary opinion. In November 1849 the churchwardens gave notice of a bill for the division of the Manchester parish and the scene was set for the final battle.[28]

In this there were three distinct engagements, the effort to win opinion, the struggle for the churchwardenships, and the in-fighting in Parliament itself. The wardens published their bill in New Year 1850, and began to talk radically of putting chapter property under representative lay management, and ensuring that there would be some surplus for parochial purposes, by cutting the stipends of Dean and Canons to £1,000 and £500 respectively (no surplus having been paid over to the Ecclesiastical Commissioners since 1840). The final propaganda battle now began; at a big meeting called by the wardens, and disturbed as always by the Chartists, the case against the bill was put by Canon Clifton and R. S. Sowler, whose *Courier* had been the mouthpiece of the chapter for a generation, and each side stated its case in pamphlets. The case of the chapter was still that the appropriation of the rectory severed the chapter from the cure of souls (to which the lie direct was returned), and also that chapters needed regulation as a whole and not piecemeal; to this the answer came that chapters were of various origins and no other derived its whole revenues within a parish of which it had the oversight. Clifton made conciliatory references to the chapter proposals of 1847, but there was no mistaking the asperity of his conclusion that the Association scheme raised ' a reasonable suspicion that the real and professed objects of the bill are not coincident '. Or as Sowler put it in his tory sheet, the whole affair is a mere job, devised by a self-constituted committee of laymen, some of whom were in former days dissenters from the very Church they seek to despoil, who represent the opinions of a small minority only of their fellow townsmen, and that embracing neither the most intelligent, nor the most influential portion of the community.

The Association rejoined that ' Clifton betrayed a crudeness and carelessness of research utterly inconsistent with the profession of the writer . . .' to state the real position of the college. The honours ultimately were even. The Association had the support of the bishop and 13,000 signatures to a petition for its bill (including 31 clergymen of the parish); a counter-petition displayed at the *Courier* office was headed by the churchwardens of 1846-7 who had first approached Parliament.[29]

In March 1850 the bill went into Parliament, and the Church Reform Association, led by the churchwardens in possession, had to get them re-elected at the Easter vestry to convince Parliament of their hold on opinion. In liberal eyes the chapter now sank to the ultimate in infamy, refusing to provide a chairman, their having done so in the past being treated as evidence that they had cure of souls. The church was packed with the usual agitators against Sturges Bourne's Act, now denominated Chartists, who, on a show of hands, carried one of their number, William Willis, to the chair. Willis, like many of his supporters had no title to be there, having paid no rates.

When the two opposing lists of churchwardens were put to the vote, he refused to divide the meeting, but declared the list containing his own name to be carried; and when a poll was demanded he refused to adjourn the meeting to the Town Hall for the purpose of taking a poll, or to preside at such a poll, or to appoint anyone as a substitute.

Willis's contumacy forced the retiring wardens to appeal to the Queen's Bench for a mandamus to hold a regular election, brought on them the ridicule of the *Courier* for being ' beaten hollow on a show of hands ', and deprived the parish of fully accredited wardens for two crucial months while the Manchester Rectory Division Bill was in Parliament. The election held under the mandamus at the end of May was even more lively. Willis drummed up his friends ' to fight the battle of " bricks against brains" and of " God against the devil " ', but an attempt to force him to the chair was defeated by a squad of police. A dreadful scene followed in which Willis' coat was slit down the back; the retiring wardens shouted him down, and adjourned the meeting to the Town Hall for a nominal poll in which they were reelected. Conspiracy between the chapter and the Chartists, and especially T. P. Heywood (who was reported to have been put out of the chair at a Chartist meeting for being drunk) had been suspected at the Easter vestry. Now

> Canons Wray and Parkinson, and Minor Canon Wilson [were seen] holding a conference in the churchyard with T. P. Heywood while his brother demagogues were desecrating the church with their uproarious declamations. After this conference Heywood returned to the church by the vestry or chapter-house door, which was at once opened to him, and on other parishioners presenting themselves for admittance at the same moment, they were coolly told the orders were to admit none by that entrance. Heywood, on returning to the church, rejoined his fellows, and the disgraceful proceedings originated by himself and his party, were continued an hour and a half longer.

As the Dean had lately said kind things to Oastler on a Ten Hours platform, the worst inferences seemed possible.[30]

In the third contest, in Parliament, the churchwardens had to fight with one arm tied behind their back. In committee counsel for the chapter made the best of their complaints of persecution and their opposition to upsetting general settlements for local purposes. The bill was completely rewritten and the chapter were plainly scheming to get it rejected in the Lords. The churchwardens carried the clause halving chapter salaries by one vote, one committee member being absent, and all the local members (being whig or radical) voting for. In consequence the promoters of the bill accepted the substance of all but three of the chapter amendments, and before the final election of churchwardens had taken place, the bill was guaranteed an easy passage through the upper house. It was a question who had triumphed in the haggling. The *Courier* claimed that the chapter had in fact written the bill, and they had undeniably retained their patronage, won most of the points affecting their status, and secured explicit provision against any future disappropriation of the rectory or dissolution of the chapter. On the other hand, a particularly obnoxious clause (promoted by the chapter at the very time they were inciting ' the masses ' forcibly to defend popular rights in the vestry) to confine the rights of the parishioners in the cathedral to the Derby chapel was lost: not two, but all four, canons were to hold livings in the town, and the chapter was to suffer a substantial cut in income. The chapter would hardly have made these concessions except under public pressure. But the promoters of the bill secured neither a lay committee of management for chapter property, nor a fund for local church repairs raised from the chapter revenues, nor the right to appropriate portions of the chapter property to endow district parishes. And worst of all, while the act bound the Ecclesiastical Commissioners to use the surplus of the chapter revenues for parish purposes, it enabled them to charge their present augmentations of the district livings (almost £1,500 p.a.) to the chapter surplus. In any case the expected surplus refused to materialise. In 1853 it was £101, in 1855 £97. These disappointments underlay the bitter allegations of the bishop and the churchwardens, that the chapter had undervalued their glebe by 90 per cent in their evidence to the Cathedral Commission in 1853. The Manchester livings would almost certainly have done better as a simple charge upon the Ecclesiastical Commissioners' Common Fund, and feelings rankled. Even in the 'eighties, when the chapter were contributing £15,000 p.a. to the parish, they were successfully taken to court by rectors in the town, to cut back the cathedral choir to the four singing men and four boys stipulated by the charter of Charles I, anything more being in excess of such ' necessary and proper expenditure as may lawfully devolve upon ' them under the Rectory Division Act.[31]

Like so many efforts either to overthrow, reform or unify the Church, the Manchester Church question ended with a curious inconclusiveness. The evangelical faction which had done so much (and often so deviously) to salvage the establishment in Manchester, had cut through the undergrowth of the Church Building Acts, and divided the town into parishes, an administrative unit understood by the flock; but they had not humiliated the chapter, still less made off with their endowments. They had committed the chapter to serve in town parishes without establishing that chapters, as such, had duties to perform. The Cathedrals Com-

Q

mission of 1853 brought home that according to the statutes there were two different types of cathedral. Cathedrals of the old foundation had been originally centred on the bishop, surrounded by his missionary priests, who had been *sine cura animarum* in order to be free for evangelism. Cathedrals of the new foundation, and those which were formerly monastic institutions, had been originally dedicated to study or perpetual worship, and in their statutes the bishop often played a very minor role indeed. Centres of evangelism or of religious studies (the glory of the learned deans of the 'fifties was secular scholarship—classics, mathematics or geology) would have been invaluable to the nineteenth-century Church, but by the time the Cathedrals Commission taught its lesson in 1854-5, a Parliamentary stalemate had developed which frustrated legislative action. Chapters continued, down to and since the Cathedrals measure of 1963, sinecure bodies in both senses of the word. In Manchester work was found for them in an urban parish system, ill-suited to the pastoral problem of the town. The ancient parish of Manchester, huge as it was, embraced the urban community and its satellites. It might have made an excellent missionary diocese or archdeaconry. The possibility of any concerted effort to tackle its problems was deferred indefinitely by the triumph of Anglican parish mythology in the Manchester Rectory Division Act. The best that can be said for the evangelicals is that there was no better hope in the collegial traditions and pretensions of the chapter.

The evangelicals are bound to loom large in a study of this kind because they were strong in policy at various levels. Stout establishment men, they were determined to extract the utmost from privileged status; they were active pastorally and politically at the grass-roots; and they supplemented the inherited mechanisms of the Church not only by private channels of instruction and devotion, but also by that formidable battery of propagandist, missionary, philanthropic and medical societies, which constituted the most powerful machine in the Church. After the middle of the century they turned to methods of evangelism which broke through the parish system and required fresh legislation. How it was that evangelical pressure on Church and society tended to run into the sands, we have already seen; it must be added that the party itself was suspect. Street-corner violence was not possible without wild men, and Alexander Haldane saved the *Record* from

ruin by tapping a market for sensation and scandal. Even if the
protests of the party respectability, Venn, Archbishop Sumner
and the *Christian Observer*, are discounted, no commentary on the
party could have been more cruel than Shaftesbury's disclaimer
of the leadership in 1856.

> This is a position too perilous, too uncertain, too useless for
> anyone to accept. No one can be an effective leader unless those
> who follow him are prepared to repose confidence in his judg-
> ment and guidance. . . . No one in these days has such a
> sentiment. All confidence has ceased; and people from a variety
> of causes take up their opinions or let them fall entirely in
> reference to themselves or their particular sections. . . . I
> think several of them vary far from charity or justice. Let them
> catch me tripping (and who can always walk upright?) and
> there would be as much real spite (though veiled under regret)
> and pleasure, as among the editors of newspapers or the con-
> gregation of Puseyism.[32]

The party in short was not able to bear the weight put upon it,
and, within a few years, sections of it at least were seeking renewed
inspiration at the deeper springs of Perfection and Holiness.

The Tractarians suffered a similar fate by different routes. They
play a small part in this study, for at this stage they had little to
offer the church in terms of policy, at either a political or popular
level. The core of the party were drawn together in support of
Sir Robert Inglis and the Protestant Constitution in the Oxford
by-election of 1829; this turned them against Peel, and threw up
the slogans about the march-of-mind, which they put to yeoman
service in academic and general politics in the 'thirties. The
movement reached its apogee in 1836 in the condemnation of
Hampden, the Regius Professor of Divinity, by the Oxford Convocation, in whose verdicts the Tractarians professed to recognise
the conscience of the Church. But the university's tory Chancellor,
the Duke of Wellington, knew, and Convocation knew, that reform was necessary, and, as long as they could, the Tractarians
resisted every reform into the last ditch. Ultimately the Tractarians
concluded that the very university constitution which they had
defended so strenuously was being twisted against them, and was
indeed illegal. Ths conviction drove them to common action with
liberals and the march-of-mind men, which produced the most

extraordinary convolutions in their later history. Not merely
locally, but in the Church generally, the basis for their leadership
crumbled in the later 'thirties. As a ginger group in a clerical
coalition reacting violently, but somewhat helplessly, to the
hammer-blows of social discontent, and of whiggery, popery and
dissent in politics, the Tractarians had been a power. But, as we
have seen, in the later 'thirties, the threat to the Church ebbed,
and with it ebbed the fortunes of the Tractarians. Moreover, the
more the Church refused to conform to the Tractarian image, the
harder it was for Tractarians to maintain their confidence in
her.

For confidence was a key issue to them. The Tractarians needed
the Apostolic Succession as a device for unchurching dissenters,
and for providing the Church with some authority less precarious
than establishment, but could never be content with it as a device.
Their grievance against the high-and-dry churchmen was that they
had made a device of what should have been a principle of
religious life.

> Experience has shown the inefficacy of the mere injunctions
> of church order, however scripturally enforced, in restraining
> from sin the awakened and anxious sinner. . . . Methodism
> and Popery are in different ways the refuge of those whom the
> Church stints of the gifts of grace; they are the foster-mothers
> of abandoned children.[33]

Young Tractarians reacted to the emotional pressure of the age,
valuing ' heart-work ' as much as the Ranter, and prizing dogma
and tradition and ministry as means by which men could enter
into the richness of the Christian heritage. To these enthusiasts
a blow to confidence was crucial, and it was shrewdly delivered
by Peel's government of 1841 and the Oxford University administration which followed in its wake. They had no use for Tractarian demagogues, and required conservative Churchmen to decide
who the friends of the Church were. Gladstone protested at the
pressure they applied, and spoke up for the Tractarians in public;
but the clergy mostly moved the other way. Moreover to W. F.
Hook, who, as Vicar of Leeds, was more in touch with urban
realities than any Tractarian, it was clear the doctrinaire anti-
Erastianism of the Oxford men was a mistake, and that the Church
could not fulfil her pastoral and educational mission without seek-

ing state help on the most reasonable terms that could be obtained.

There were also difficulites of a religious nature. What were the relations of faith and reason? Faith had no doubt a moral basis, the great safeguard of which was a right state of heart. But how much did this imply? In later life Newman proved receptive to much modern thought in the conviction that, unlike a scientific theory, faith as an act of will was not vulnerable to any predictable accumulation of awkward evidence; by contrast Pusey rejected liberal biblical criticism, on the grounds that it could only be the work of corrupt motives. The importance of the right state of heart led necessarily to a demand by both believers and pastors for the revival of the confessional. Here the Tractarians were following paths not open to the Church as a whole. When Keble protested that he could not know what was happening in the minds of his parishioners at Hursley without holding confessions, his friend and patron Sir William Heathcote perforce replied that if he did not know a parish of 400 souls without confessions he would not know it at all. *A fortiori* there never would be enough clergy to confess the English nation. Tractarian intellect and spirituality converted awkwardly into policy. The revival of corporate religious life in the Church of England owed much to them; but the Park Village community for women which was intended to reinforce the parish by visiting the poor and nursing the sick, was a failure. It was only when the religious life had taken root for its own sake that the Church acquired new weapons for its pastoral armoury. Moreover the intense pressure upon the Tractarians to realise their ideals quickly was from the beginning more than many of them could stand. As J. D. Dalgairns cried in 1844, somewhat on this side of ultimate despair, ' Rome, Rome, Rome, will be the only shelter for weary feet '.[34] The Tractarians were not, however, alone amongst good men in feeling compulsive pressures to break inherited bonds of religious communion, and we must now inquire how those pressures operated.

9 The Dénouement III: Schism

Though the Anglican doctrinaires hammered furiously at each other, the clergy were not readily detached from their status and endowments, and their spectacular and rapid losses of popular support were already over by the 'forties. The most striking episodes now occurred among churches closer to the lines of social cleavage, and the most striking of all, in two not unconnected cases of churches with powerful central machinery, the English Wesleyan Connexion and the Scots Kirk.

In the later 'thirties Wesleyanism had been the exemplar of triumphant denominationalism. The Warrenite revolt might be considered a salutary blood-letting. Agitators had left the old body, and were now quarrelling amongst themselves; places which suffered heavily in 1835 were not afflicted again. Bunting completed his denominational organisation. Laymen were admitted to the committees which managed the public funds of the Connexion, and the fruit of their support and enterprise was reaped in 1839, when an appeal to mark the centenary of the first society class raised an astonishing sum exceeding £220,000. The ministry itself was underpinned both institutionally and doctrinally. Ordination by laying-on of hands became the standard practice from 1836. The Centenary Fund enabled residential seminaries to be established at Richmond and Didsbury, which proved their value in the time of troubles which began in 1849. The agitators then were not young college-trained men, but veterans fighting old battles. At the same time the doctrine of the Pastoral Office was made a datum of revelation, the premise of the Church itself. ' The pastoral office as defined in holy Scripture plainly involves the whole care and oversight of the entire flock. Here the position of the minister differs essentially from that of every other member of the church, whether private or official.'

Its functions were the ministry of the word and of the sacraments, and ' *thirdly, admission into and expulsion from the communion of the church* '. The distinction between the local and the travelling preachers, so obscure to the man in the pew, was now so clear to the connexional apologists, that they damned Presbyterian authorities as ' opaque, confused and self-contradictory to a hopeless degree' on the status of the ruling elder, apparently ordained but certainly a layman.[1]

If a ruling elder did not occupy the Pastoral Office, a local preacher must on no account rule. Bunting declared ' in Conference, You have fought & won your battle with Kilham. Your next great battle will be with the local preachers '. Certainly preachers began to consider themselves beleaguered, ' surrounded . . . with a majority of hostile local preachers ', and to call for ' a full and fair Quarterly Meeting, purified from the jealous and invidious influence of local preachers'. They printed their names as ' ministers ' on circuit plans separately from the local brethren, sometimes driving the issue to the point where the usual social props of ministry began to give way. At Maidstone in 1848, W. M. Harvard

> was suddenly ' brought up ', as the phrase is, by our *most* managing and influential man (himself a political conservative) who assured me that if I persisted in introducing the term ' *minister* ' in opposition to the local preachers, on whose list he stands at the head, he and his family would withdraw from us altogether, and that other influential parties had made up their minds to do the same.

In this tussle there was wounded status on both sides. There had been hopes that the Centenary Fund which so lavishly supported ministerial training, would also support the relief of needy local preachers; but nothing was forthcoming. When, after half a century of repeated frustration, local preachers made their own provision by forming the Local Preachers Mutual Aid in 1849, they met with persistent hostility and obstruction from the connexional leadership. The great secessions which began that year put both sides in a difficult position. The LPMA, refusing to deny their charity to expelled local preachers in need, declared that ' the claims of our afflicted brethren are paramount to those of a disputable policy '; they were accused in return of directly and intentionally countenancing the assault on Methodism, and when they held their Aggregate meeting in Sheffield in 1851 the preachers closed all the chapels to them².

Moreover, it was still official doctrine that the Pastoral Office must act as a social regulator, sometimes impartially, sometimes less so. As Charles Welch saw it,

> Lay delegation may be sought by two very opposite classes of men in the Wesleyan Connexion and for very opposite purposes. Some of the wealthier men of our large towns would no doubt be glad to be liberated from the restrictions which the vast incorporation of Methodism necessarily imposes, and which obstruct precipitate and hazardous assimilation to other churches. . . . And will not the plebeian section, the cottagers and artisans of the societies, be the first to charge the Conference with venality or intimidation, in having pandered to the lay aristocracy, seated on the legislative bench to the detriment of the popular mass.

If the Wesleyan ministry was to bridge this social gulf it would need all its prerogatives; but perhaps the truth was let out by Alfred Barrett, who held that ' strictness of spiritual examination ' and ' a subordination of one to another ' were required ' especially among the industrial classes '. Barrett, a man of ' particularly chaste and elegant ' mind, and a successful minister at the Oxford-Road chapel ' attended by most of the élite of the Methodist body in Manchester ', expounded the doctrine of the Pastoral Office in its highest form, in a series of books which became standard pabulum for probationary preachers. To Barrett the undisputed and undivided authority of the Pastor was not merely a datum of revelation, it was essential to the constitution of the Church. A man whose ministry was attested by the flock and graced by the Holy Spirit

> became not a mere constituted authority but a necessary one. . . . He is a spiritual father; souls are begotten to Christ through his ministry, who look up to his wisdom for guidance and nurture; and by the same wisdom subordinate fellow-labourers are guided in their work, and all the members of the household sustained and enriched by the treasury of truth which he provides and keeps open. Where all hearts are right the

> rule of such persons is felt to be no other than a benefit. . . .
> All this shows the utter unsoundness and opposition to the
> Bible of a democratic theory of church government,

which could be supported by no analogy of nature or the Gospel.[3]

Barrett was here simply spelling out what the high Wesleyans had been saying for a generation; his special contribution was to give the Wesleyan polity symbolic status comparable with that of Rome, Geneva or the High-church. Wesleyan connexionalism had once been justified as a useful device for the pursuit of neglected purposes, unobjectionable to common sense or scripture. But to Barrett there was a ' necessary connexion between a definite form of doctrine, and a suitable, as well as definite, church regimen, in which to conserve it and teach it to all around. These two must and will always go together'. Wesleyanism taught the need to attest justification by a spotless life, and the hazard of losing the heavenly treasure by slothfulness and sin. This state of spiritual *angst* necessitated ' a mutual watchfulness amongst the ministry' and a jealous oversight, ' especially among the industrial classes'. Once the door had been so firmly closed to any empirical assessment of the minister's function in the community; once ministerial status had become the outward symbol of the inner faith, there could be no compromise. Preachers began to revere ' Wesleyan Methodism . . . as scriptural Christianity—a system of doctrine & discipline adapted to all times and nations', and in 1851 (as in 1835) to cry ' Can the laws of 1797 be swept away or so modified as to amount to something like that?' Even so consummate a folly as return to a primitive Wesleyanism which had never existed, might have to be faced if the regulations of 1797 obscured the symbol of God's truth.[4]

The immediate embarrassment was that the Pastoral Office was not an apt symbol for the recent developments in the ministry. As the Wesleyan community grew larger and more complex, ministerial authority had been extended to the Sunday schools, to appointments under the Missionary Society, to enlarging the scope of Minor District meetings. The growth point of the preachers' labours was organisation rather than pastoral care. John Peters, who joined the Warrenites in 1836, noted in his diary:

> February 5th and 6th [1836] Spent also in visiting. The people
> are greatly pleased in getting a visit from their Preacher. They

say it is the good old times of Methodism come back again. Some of them have assevered that they have been fifteen years members of the Society and never yet had a visit from the Preachers.

Everyone knew about the declining pastoral superintendence in the villages, but at the 1848 Conference, Bunting's loyal pupil, F. A. West, admitted that the towns had been no gainers. The low peak of recession in the winter of 1841-2 took its usual toll.

> We are . . . much in a crisis respecting our own home-work . . . in numbers finances & spiritual state . . . The spirit of the times, our commercial depression, & our notorious neglect of pastoral work (I [F. A. West] say it of myself & the bulk of our preachers) & alienating the minds of our people just so much as to make them ready to be querulous and offensive.

At the 1843 Conference Bunting himself admitted ' the declining attendance of poor people at our services ', and found ' the main cause of their estrangement from us . . . [in] radicalism, in-fidelity and socialism '. More adequate pastoral oversight was indisputably needed, and Conference was deluged with plans for better house-to-house visiting, and the extension of membership to adherents not meeting in class. The diminishing impetus of the Connexion also drew attention to the enormous leakage of the children of members. In 1844 it was reckoned that 30,000 children of members reached the age of Society membership annually, but the net increase in membership from all sources over a decade had been only 45,000. Again sterner pastoral oversight was called for—but so sane a man as George Osborn held that it was not possible to add to the present burdens of the ministry.[5]

With the Wesleyan ministry feeling the weight of its own claims, a number of its public policies began to go wrong, and increase the restiveness in the Methodist community. Evangelical Protestantism had seemed to be one way of joining, as well as propelling, the tory bandwaggon to victory in 1841, but the profits seemed to accrue to rational dissent (in the Dissenters' Chapels Bill) and to the Roman Catholics at Maynooth. Support for Church establishment had been another favourite cause and this led to acute embarrassments both in Scotland and England.

In Scotland the evangelical party had run the democratic rapids by adopting the Veto Act, and began an ambitious programme of Church extension for which no state endowment had been forthcoming. These policies had raised the establishment question to a new pitch of bitterness, and were, moreover, of doubtful legality. But the evangelicals were no more likely to obtain legislation than endowments from a whig government in alliance with the voluntaryists, and must bid quickly for popular support in the denominational contest. The gamble they made led to a clash with the secular courts which jeopardised the entire policy of the 'thirties. In the Auchterarder case the Court of Session, later upheld by the House of Lords, held that it was illegal for the Presbytery to reject the presentee without trial of his qualifications, on the simple grounds that he was vetoed by the people. In the Marnoch case, the Court of Session declared that the Presbytery was bound to make trial of the qualifications of a presentee vetoed by the people; the majority of the Presbytery, entering a declaration to this effect in their minutes, were then suspended by the Commission of the Assembly, and the Commission resolved to send deputies to preach in their parishes. The majority of the Presbytery then applied to the Court of Session for protection, and the Assembly's deputies were forbidden to use the church, churchyard or school house. If democratic sentiment could not be appeased by the Assembly's new legislation, it must be rallied against the secular courts. The Veto Act which had been intended to perpetuate patronage, was presented as an attack on it, and the Church's right to curtail patronage by those means was held to involve the Crown rights of the Redeemer. Dr Candlish, in particular, excelled in presenting Lord and people as common victims of state aggression, and the support of a large minority of ministers and people was ensured him in January 1843 by the Stewarton case. Here the Court of Session brought evangelical policy to complete ruin, by deciding that the Church courts had no power to made *quoad sacra* parishes. The acts by which the General Assembly had annexed ecclesiastical parishes to unendowed chapels were thus found invalid. In May 1843 the great Disruption of the Scots Kirk followed as a consequence.

The Disruption added directly to the tensions within the Wesleyan body. For some years they had taken advantage of Scots eloquence in the missionary cause, and when in 1838 Chalmers was brought to London to lecture on behalf of the establishment principle, Bunting was all respectful attention. From this time forward the inner circle of the Methodist management attached increasing importance to the views of the Scots evangelicals in clarifying their own position *vis-à-vis* the English establishment, the Roman Catholics, and the forces of Methodist democracy. As the crisis in the Scots church came to a head, the two parties took intimate counsel together, and in the 1841 preface to his semi-official *Compendium of the Laws and regulations of Wesleyan Methodism*, Edmund Grindrod declared that ' in our form of government we are a Scripture presbytery, resembling, to a great degree, the Established Church of Scotland, the model of which was taken from the platform laid down by the Genevan Reformer '. Thus the Wesleyans were claiming the ecclesiological ground to which the Scots evangelicals aspired; they believed they were the first to put the Scots church question prominently before the British public; and purred when warm notices about Methodism appeared in the Scottish press, and when efforts were made to get Bunting into the General Assembly of 1842 and into Dr Candlish's Edinburgh pulpit.[6]

As the crisis came to a head early in 1843, Bunting and John Beecham, his fellow secretary to the Missionary Society, signed a select petition, headed by the Duke of Argyle, to bring Chalmers back to London for a public discussion of the question ' how far the dependence of National Churches upon the state for temporal provision is compatible with their independence in spiritual things '. When the crash came in Scotland, the Methodist leadership were so free with sympathy and financial assistance for the evangelicals, as to be accused in the *Record* of fostering schism. It was not just, as one preacher put it, that ' the free Church of Scotland very much resembles the Wesleyan body now; & Dr. Chalmers and Dr. Hannah [President of Conference, 1842-3] hold . . . very similar offices '; it was that the predicament of the Scots, caught between their own unpalatable concessions to democracy and an establishment principle which had gone sour, bore only too agonising a resemblance to that of the Methodist leadership. As William Vevers wrote to Bunting:

I greatly admire your petition on Scotch affairs—and think with you that a very heavy blow will be struck at the Establish-

ment in this country [England]. The time has arrived when. we
as a body must distinguish between the Church and the Clergy.
I am sorry to say that though in towns a few of the clergy are
tolerant, yet in the country places they are our bitterest foes.
They are certainly the greatest enemies of their own Establishment.

Methodism's much-vaunted special relationship with the Church
had proved a one-sided affair in the end. Bunting bitterly admitted
in Conference that ' I once hoped that such a thing was possible
as an Established Church without state interference. But I now see
it to be impossible. I wish two thousand clergymen would leave
the English church in the same way '. He overbore Dr Dixon who
held that the Scots evangelicals would have done better to stay
in the General Assembly, and in the Conference Pastoral Address
pressed a strongly-phrased declaration of the right of every church
to unfettered liberty in matters ' spiritual and ecclesiastical, and
especially in relation to the sacred functions belonging to the
admission, appointment, supervision and deposition of ministers '.[7]

This paragraph, drafted by George Osborn, a stout defender
of establishment, implied a more critical attitude towards the
English Church than any official act of Conference for over half
a century, and it hazarded domestic difficulties as well. As Dixon
warned, ' Scotsmen are very headstrong in public meetings;
positions have been taken up by them in which we cannot agree '.
The rub in Scotland came not with admission or ordination of
ministers, but with local appointment, a matter which Conference
had no intention of yielding to the people. If the Free Church
' turn into a democracy it will not prove a blessing '. Dixon's fears
were fulfilled before the decade was out. Warm relations between
the two parties continued, and, hard-pressed as it was, the Free
Church opened its pulpits to the fund-raisers of the Methodist
Missionary Society in Scotland. But when serious trouble with
Methodist democracy began in 1849, the Free Church proved a
broken reed. ' The entire press of Scotland ', it was reported, ' is
against us ', and although the Free Church leaders were fed with
the conference view of the *Flysheets*, the best that could be said of
them was that ' they entertain more favourable views of Methodism than they think it right to express '. Half a dozen years later,

Bunting's protégé, John McLean, actually maintained that a regulated power of vetoing a minister . . . might . . . be safely and advantageously committed to [Methodist] congregations in Scotland '. Desertion by the Free Church leaders, and infiltration by Free Church principles, seemed a poor return for zealous Conference support. In Scotland two pillars of Conference policy had crumbled in turn, Protestant establishment and its voluntaryist successor.[8]

Methodist embarrassment with the English establishment and with its own domestic relations, was intensified by the emergence of the education issue, an issue to which Irish experience was again crucial. In 1831, under the superintendence of Archbishop Whately, the whigs had introduced a National Education scheme in which Irish children of various faiths were to receive a common education, with undenominational religious instruction given by the teacher from a text-book of scripture extracts approved by the leaders of the churches, and with the last hour of the school day made available to the clergy for denominational teaching to their own flock. This scheme was applied to its own schools by the new liberal corporation of Liverpool, and was urged on Lord John Russell as a means by which the state might equitably assist education in a denominationally fragmented society. In 1838 the Church showed signs of greatly extending its educational programme, and on the rebound Russell established the Committee of the Privy Council on Education, with James Kay-Shuttleworth as secretary. He had plans for a normal school and there was a general belief that the Government intended to defeat the Church's claims to ' a purely ecclesiastical scheme of education '. Hence Russell's modest proposals of 1839 were widely suspected of being the thin end of the Irish national education wedge. Like the Church, the Wesleyan Conference of 1838 had shown signs of making a forward move, passing a resolution in favour of general i.e. national, education and establishing local machinery to promote it. But the connexion was always under pressure from the Irish Conference against the Irish scheme, and from the beginning Bunting opposed it and fiercely put down men of the stature of Thomas Jackson and Richard Watson in a Conference controversy it aroused. His fears had grown no less; such a pillar of the old Methodist Protestant interest as Thomas Allan waxed hysterical that ' the united college of all the Jesuits could not have devised a better or more effective plan for making England again an appendage to the See of Rome '. In fact the general support which the connexion had been giving to the Establishment, its flirtations with the Orangemen who were committed to the fiction that the Irish scheme excluded the Bible from the schools, its hopes of tory revival, now all pointed in the same direction. The London preachers passed resolutions strongly condemning ' the introduction, in certain cases, of Romish versions of the Scriptures into schools supported by the public money ', and wound up with a wild motion by Bunting himself that mixed education was impracticable, ' and even if practicable by any conceivable compromise of conscientious principles and preferences, could only lead to perpetual collision and inconvenience, and would . . . produce among the children so incongruously mingled together, a dangerous spirit of scepticism and unbelief '. Without waiting for the government to expound its scheme, the Education Committee required hostile petitions to be got up from every circuit in the country. In Manchester the walls were placarded with bills announcing that sermons on the subject would be preached in every Methodist Chapel, and at Oldham Street John Rigg outdid even the Orangemen : ' If there were fifty Jewish children in the school, there must be a Jewish rabbi introduced, who, *of course, must* teach their (the Methodists') children that *Christianity was a lie, and that Jesus Christ was an impostor.'* If Protestant and Catholic Bibles were allowed in the same school, the children must conclude that both were false. In this furious agitation (which not unnaturally attracted the heavy artillery of Daniel O'Connell) the links with the Anglican politicians were publicly renewed, and Lord Ashley marshalled a joint force which put paid to the government's wider hopes, and opened the way to special advantages for the Church.[9]

Once again Bunting seemed to have backed the winner, at the price of committing the connexion to developing a system of day schools, a hope perpetually deferred over the next four years by the tepid enthusiasm of the Methodist people, the crippling effects of the business recession, and the rival claims of the Centenary Fund.[10] But in two respects future troubles raised their heads. Bunting hoped to turn the controversy to connexional profit, and for this reason grafted a powerful plea for denominationalism upon the mainly Orange line of the Wesleyan spokesmen. His complaint against the British and Foreign Society was that it did not permit Methodists to introduce their catechism into the schools. As he put it in a speech warmly reported by the tory press, ' the Church may introduce its catechism, and yet have public aid—why may not we introduce ours?' There was no simple consistency between this position and Bunting's Orangeism. Edward Baines, spokesman for the voluntaryists and editor of the *Leeds Mercury*, explained patiently to Bunting's son:

> It clearly implies that the Wesleyans, in as much as they ' pay ' to the support of the School Societies assisted by Government, have as much right as the Church to have their catechism used in those schools. Now we turned this position against your father . . . by showing that it was just as cogent for Roman Catholics as for Wesleyans; and yet he maintained that the former ought to receive no ' public aid ' whatever.[11]

Thomas Allan had the grace to recognise that the position they had taken up really committed the connexion to voluntaryism, but Bunting's aspiration to have his cake and eat it created further complications over the Maynooth issue and the educational proposals of the 'forties.

The second embarrassment also arose in Leeds, where Thomas Galland, the wealthiest and most whiggish of Methodist preachers, was superintendent of the West Circuit. Receiving from the President of Conference one Thursday a batch of petitions against the education proposals to be signed by the congregations the following Sunday, Galland took exception to both the object of the petition and its statement that the petitioners ' had given much and serious attention to the subject '. He nevertheless circulated the petitions without signing himself, and, when his conduct was impeached in the local press, wrote a long letter to the *Leeds Mercury*, explaining his position and making a complaint which was heard with increasing frequency:

> It being intimated that the whole proceedings were dictated by considerations purely religious, and in which politics had no share, I allowed that such might . . . be the case; but that this sort of agitation, so opportunely got up within the generally peaceful pale of Methodism, was mightily well calculated to serve political ends, whether it was so designed or not. . . . I

am sure that many persons will find it difficult to believe that politics had nothing to do with the so promptly calling forth into action all the potent machinery of our connection, especially when they find from the records of parliament, that the piles of petitions thus produced are hailed with such raptures of joy by a numerous and powerful party in the state, and the matter to which they refer made the occasion of a call of the house of commons . . .[12]

For this outspoken statement, Galland's character was impeached in Conference by one of his circuit colleagues, Robert Newton. The celebrated scene which followed was terminated by Galland's declining to contest the matter further; future critics would not always be so magnanimous.

The check to government in 1839 was to open to Wesleyans the prospect of grants to schools outside the National and British Societies, and apparently to close to Roman Catholics even the meagre prospect of school-building grants they had hitherto enjoyed.[13] But the great gainer was the Church of England, which secured not only that the Primate must approve inspectors appointed to church schools, but also more than four-fifths of the building grants of the next decade. Church advance was also the keynote of the next major measure, Graham's Factory Education Bill of 1843. Under this bill factory children's working hours were to be limited, and they were to attend school for three hours daily. Control of each school was to be vested in seven trustees, including a local Anglican priest as chairman, two churchwardens, two factory owners, and two others chosen annually by the magistrates. Anglican religious teaching was to be provided in addition to daily undenominational Bible lessons. Children would be taken to church on Sunday, though not required to attend. Graham persuaded himself that this scheme represented a combination of the National and British methods of teaching, but was able to persuade hardly anyone else.

For Graham's bill offended not only the whole of the dissenting interest, but the great northern Sunday schools as well, which saw their flock being diverted by an act of state to a Church establishment which had no means of coping with them. An immense outcry was raised against the bill, and by mid-May, when Graham's church policy in Scotland was foundering upon the

R

Disruption, it was already guessed that his church policy in England was facing shipwreck, and that his bill would be withdrawn. At this juncture the tactics of the Wesleyan leadership were devious. They came out fiercely against the bill, incurring the wrath of the conservatives of their own connexion (not to mention their erstwhile Orange allies) for ' aiding Popery, and schisms of every kind against the truly Christian Church of England '. When the connexional Committee of Privileges met early in May, the preachers found that the lay members ' were hotly disposed to urge us to declare against any combined system of education, and in favour of grants to Educational Societies, as the only practicable means of instructing the people '. This had been sufficiently orthodox Buntingism since 1839, but the preachers set out to muzzle the lay lions, and kept the committee in session over the crisis in the hope that the government would propose an accommodation. Peel, however, was not a man to buy off opposition, and the committee had finally to adjourn. ' I do not think that any favour will be proposed to be conferred on us by Sir James Graham ', concluded Joseph Fowler, ' or that if it were so, that ye project would succeed.'[14]

When the bill was dropped, connexional propaganda began to inflame the anti-Anglican animosities of so many of the flock, and pin the charge of popery upon the Church.

> . . . the leaders of the Church have declared war against the whole body of non-Episcopalians. The Church of England is the only true *Protestant* Church in the land; other ministers are intruders; other communities schismatic; nonconformists and wanderers from the true fold, whom clergymen are to seek to reclaim. . . .
>
> A preference for Papists over their brethren of the Reformation is in some cases openly avowed.

To plug the gap left by Graham's withdrawal, the connexion resolved to raise £200,000 over a period of seven years for day-school education. It was quite clear to those with their finger on the provincial pulse that this programme was unlikely to succeed. Apart from the havoc wrought in Methodist capacity to give by the ' recent pressure of commercial difficulty ', it was reported that ' our people generally (but especially in the districts where education is most needed) are *not alive to their responsi-*

bilities on *this subject*'. To attempt a subscription on the scale undertaken by the National Society would ' only show the want of correspondence between the *number* of our petitions and of our *subscribers*'. To form a Methodist Education Society like the British Society with its normal school would encounter ' the indisposition of our people, *at present,* to multiply institutions which shall abstract any more of our ministers from the itinerant work '. Certainly to Bunting's chagrin it proved impossible, particularly in Wales, for Wesleyans to go it alone in founding denominational schools, and there was no choice but to join in with the British or other combined systems.[15]

It was, nevertheless, politics rather than finance which created the next embarrassment. The appointment of Kay-Shuttleworth as Secretary to the Committee of Council had created a driving force within the government itself, and in the big towns there was at least one high-churchman in W. F. Hook, Vicar of Leeds, and one Congregationalist in Robert Vaughan, now Principal of the Lancashire Independent College in Manchester, who could see that urban educational deficiency could not be made up except by state action, and were prepared to seek it on politically reasonable terms. Kay-Shuttleworth conspired with Hook to fly a kite for a version of the Irish system, and in December 1846 Privy Council minutes were published for extending the training of teachers and the school inspectorate. The government was clearly moving from the creation to the maintenance of schools, and the development of educational policy. This fact alone was sufficient to set Edward Baines of the *Leeds Mercury* upon violent action against the Minutes, and upon reviving the coalition which put paid to Graham's bill four years before. In this conjuncture the attitude of the Wesleyans was a matter of the first importance. The dissenting press, the *Leeds Mercury*, the *Patriot* and the *Nonconformist,* reckoned them confidently in the ranks of opposition to government, while even the church *Guardian* reported that Samuel Jackson had been elected the next President entirely because of his ' opposition to the Government education scheme from the beginning '. Any scheme piloted by Lord John Russell, with whom the connexion had clashed personally and politically, was bound to be suspect, though some preachers held that the connexion could not afford to do without the money the government might offer. The united Committees on Education and

Privileges met in London, and if a leak to the *Leeds Mercury* may be believed, only the oldest, most conservative and pro-Anglican ministers were in favour of the Minutes of Council. The united committee was adjourned to Manchester in conditions of the strictest secrecy, while the great political interests tried to exert pressure upon it. Edward Baines insisted passionately to Bunting that an ' educational dictatorship ' and ' the State endowment of all religions ' were in prospect, and things seemed to be going his way; the committee resolved to make a statement of ' the great scriptural and protestant principles already avowed ' in 1839 and 1843, and on which alone they could agree to state-supported education. But while this implicitly hostile statement was being discussed, a message arrived from Lord Ashley, who was chairman of a committee supporting the Minutes, urging the Wesleyans to put their apprehensions before the Privy Council.

' Allow me again ', he added three days later, ' to impress on you the importance of putting your inquiries in the most friendly manner; of assuming, as it were, that your difficulties will receive a cordial attention & satisfactory explanation. I urge this the more earnestly because I am assured that such will be the case; and it would have been the case with the rejoinder to the Anti-Maynooth Committee, but they have thought fit . . . to write so imperious a letter that the Government will decline to give any additional explanations.[16]

Ashley's prescience was rewarded. On every point raised by the committee the government gave satisfactory assurances. The Wesleyan Education Committee would be recognised as a vehicle for state grants, so that the connexion could escape from the British Society. No inspector of Wesleyan schools would be appointed without the Education Committee's assent, nor would he have power to interfere in religious instruction. There had been much talk in the Church of reviving the diaconate to create an order of ordained school masters for church schools; the government put an end to any suggestion of recruiting established clergy at the public expense by undertaking to disqualify ' persons holding ecclesiastical titles or exercising ecclesiastical functions . . . as pupil teachers '. They could not stop National Schools requiring dissenters to accept instruction in the Anglican catechism, but would try to help children of Wesleyans in difficulty. The core of the ' scriptural and Protestant principles ', however, was the Authorised Version, for on it hung the prospect of grants to Roman Catholics and perhaps Unitarians. The Unitarian press was whipped to fury by the answer the Wesleyans received; Russell held that from December 1839 when the Minutes of Council ceased to mention the Douai version, it had been understood that only the Authorised Version might be used in schools, and that this principle had been followed consistently except in one case which did not affect the general issue. The Minutes had never specified the version of the scriptures to be used in state-supported schools, and Unitarians could barely credit Russell's statement. But the assurance did its work. ' Such use of the Sacred Volume these Committees [of Education and Privileges] regarded as offering one of the best securities which the state can require against Romanism and other forms of dangerous error [i.e. Unitarianism].' The government maintained its right to do something for Roman Catholics in future, and the connexional leadership reserved their right to oppose; but for the moment they gave their almost unanimous support to the minutes, and left the dissenters to a violent and only modestly rewarding effort to make voluntaryism in education a shibboleth in the general election which followed.[17]

The higgling of the market into which Graham and Peel had refused to enter in 1843, had been triumphantly managed by Bunting and his friends in 1847. This time there was no mistaking what they had done. They had deserted a nonconformist coalition which had lately rebuffed a strong government, and had done so for a price. James Everett, the carping critic of Dr Bunting and all his works, predictably reported that his *bête noire* ' having pronounced the Government measure bad-bad altogether —" irretrievably bad " . . . in consequence of a little attention from Lord Ashley . . . was smoothed down to cordial acquiescence '. In the depths of turbulent Suffolk, a preacher reported tremors, ' & Dissenters prophesy that there will be a division in our body. But they are not inspired by the true spirit of Prophecy —as I imagine '. Unhappily they were, and among the factors which contributed to the disastrous secession two years later was distaste for a leadership which seemed not merely to rule the connexion with a rod of iron, but to bargain unscrupulously with its political influence. Indeed, the high-water mark of Buntingism had come with the tory victory at the polls in 1841, which seemed to have completely vindicated the great man's foresight, and crowned a set of policies which might be supposed to have secured Methodism a considerable treasury of merit with both Church and government. The same principles were dominant in the connexional administration. Old George Marsden wrote to Bunting before the Conference of 1838,

> . . . I hear that either Mr. T. Jackson or Mr. Stanley is mentioned as our next President. I am as fully persuaded as ever, that Conservative principles are not only the principles proper for our body, but that they are founded on the Bible. And I would have all our constituted authorities keep close to Scripture principles, but if it be true (which I hear) that Mr. Stanley has changed his views, and that he is now what may be called a Conservative as to ecclesiastical affairs, I have no personal objection to his election.

Stanley was not elected. Indeed one of the sources of Conference malaise in the 'forties was the sense of injustice felt by preachers of liberal views before the tory strong-arm men.

> Dr. Beaumont: . . . Methodism ought to have no political line, whig or tory. Our mission is chiefly to the poor. As to politics, no minister must interfere with, or be interfered with, by any of his brethren . . . Every step we take towards politics reduces our character for high spirituality: thereby some are alienated from us by our political tone.
> Mr. Reece: Many of our people, wishing to do right in political matters, are wanting *direction;* and to whom should they look but to the President and to the men in London, who are wiser than we.

The claustrophobia exhibited by Beaumont in this exchange was exacerbated in the 'forties by the knowledge that the official line was alien to many of the flock, by the ultimate failure of its policies, and by resentment at the dominance of a Bunting now in his declining years.[18] Each of these factors is worth discussion.

Press reporting about the Methodist vote was largely influenced by hope of swaying it, but the radical *Manchester Times* assessment of Methodist behaviour in the general election of 1837 had the ring of truth:

It is satisfactory to mark the position which the Wesleyan Methodists have taken in recent borough elections, notwithstanding the influence exercised over them by several of the preachers. In Salford the baits of tory ingenuity had no charms, and three-fourths of the members of that religious body recorded their votes in favour of Mr. Brotherton. Mr. Garnett's professions as a churchman, and the support which he received from zealous but deluded members of the establishment, served to gull no conscientious Methodist. . . . We believe the preachers in this circuit prudently abstained from interfering with the political opinions of their flocks . . . but ' means and appliances ' had been officiously used, happily in vain, by some of the leading preachers in the connexion, in favour of the ' passive obedience and non-resistance ' theory, the liberal meaning of which is ' vote for the Conservative : or meddle not with those given to change '.

At Sheffield and Leeds the same disregard of ministerial dictation or advice was decidedly manifested, and the members of the societies there voted for the liberal candidates. At Sheffield, we understand, two of the preachers, Mr. Waddy and Mr. M'Lean, imprudently attempted to warp the minds of their hearers in support of a favourite candidate (Mr. Thornely) and consequently against Mr. Ward, the liberal candidate, a gentleman of sound and enlightened opinions. Those unpopular efforts failed and the result was as might have been anticipated, diminished regard for the political meddlers. . . . It is proper to add that Mr. Ibbotson, a class leader, seconded Mr. Ward's nomination.

At Leeds where Conference is now being held, and where the sacred ' Hundred ' might have been expected to exert some power, the ultra-reformer, Sir Wm. Molesworth, was elected instead of the tory bantling, Sir John Beckett, and to add to the horrors of such of the Methodist preachers as are coquetting . . . with the church, Alderman Musgrave (a Wesleyan of high character) actually proposed the radical baronet, and discanted on his political principles and integrity.

The potentialities and limitations of the official line were revealed most clearly in Manchester, where it was perhaps pressed harder than anywhere else. In 1832 the Manchester Wesleyans

voted overwhelmingly on the whig side, but in the great contest
of 1839 they came out almost solid for the defeated tory candidate Sir George Murray. This astonishing *volte-face* owed something to the steady growth of conservative sentiment in the
country generally in the 'thirties, and perhaps more to the Warrenite blood-letting of 1835; the Warrenites were liberals almost
to a man, their secession greatly weakened the liberal force in the
Methodist camp, and their agitation helped to identify liberal
political opinions with disloyal churchmanship in the connexion.
Still, the effect of official pressure and the Orange campaigns is
very striking, and in the general election of 1841 it was reinforced
by the education issue. There could therefore be no more poignant
comment on Bunting's tactics than a confidential letter despatched
to him by Lord Ashley in the middle of the election: ' Notwithstanding Mr. [Milner] Gibson's [whig] speeches & principles,
he will be returned to Parliament, I fear, by the votes of Wesleyans. . . . It is a terrible affair. I know full well, & appreciate
your difficulties. Pray let me have the letter back again.' Milner
Gibson was returned (but not the letter), and the tory unanimity
of 1839 had already perished.[19]

The harrowing year 1841 intensified the obstinacy of the
doctrinaires in Wesleyanism as in society generally. At Conference
time old Joseph Entwisle trembled ' lest unity peace and con-
cord should be lost in our Connexion. The gown, teetotallism,
politics, etc. each seems to supply its quota of material for creating
disunion. Be merciful unto us, O Lord!' The gown question
showed unmistakably how a triviality might become serious in
that atmosphere. In 1793 when pro-Church Methodists had
been demonstrating that preachers were not ministers, it had been
forbidden to wear the gown. But as ministerial pretensions rose,
and Bunting appeared to favour the Presidential gown, preachers,
including Bunting's son William, began to sport the new dress.
The issue was brought on in the Waltham Street Circuit at Hull in
1841 by S. D. Waddy, a bright young man of ' resolute &
bold temperament ', who wore gown and bands in defiance of
the instructions of his superintendent, William Smith. Smith
brought Waddy before a District Meeting presided over by the
superintendent of the next circuit, only to find that he

lonely & solitarily, had to contend against five preachers, all committed to the gown question, acting so much in concert, as could leave no doubt that the peculiar plan of operation was previously conceived & arranged by them, each knowing beforehand the part he should act. The trial of Waddy was the trial of them all.

Defeated in the District Meeting, Smith appealed to Conference, and it speedily transpired that he and Waddy would never again be able to travel in the same circuit. The Chairman of the District ' intimated that *one* of the preachers must be removed, & Mr. Waddy & his friends . . . made no secret of their intention of shoveling poor Smith out of the road & retain[ing] possession of the ground '. Not merely ministerial discipline, but the symbolism of the gown, were now at hazard, for

[Waddy] most distinctly avowed that the assumption of the gown by himself & others, ' was *but one of several important or organic changes*' which must shortly take place in our connexion, and which were necessary to our completeness or perfection as a christian community . . . [and that the] opposition to the mode of his introducing the clerical costume among us was ' *nothing less than a dead set at the ministerial character & office*'.

One of Waddy's ministerial allies in the next circuit reckoned that the preachers' ' feeling and those of at least nineteen-twentieths of the society and congregation have been sacrificed ' to the clamours of half a dozen troublesome individuals, a complete misjudgment of the strength of an opposition which braced itself against ' a plan having the very essence or stamina of Wesleyan Puseyism involved in it '. In Conference Bunting had the statesmanship not to fight the battle of the Pastoral Office on so narrow an issue, and declared bluntly that ' the tattle about organic changes originates with the devil '. A Conference committee forbade the wearing of the gown without the express sanction of Conference, and removed the entire staff of Hull West. Bunting had saved the day, though ructions in Hull continued, and the gown question was not forgotten when the wider divisions it portended began in 1849.[20]

In the 'forties Bunting seemed to lose the power to act with the tact he had shown in the gown case, and his personal future became a problem. Moreover the Methodist treasury of merit with the Church seemed curiously bare. There is no mistaking the changing tone of Methodist references to the Establishment as the Church revival gathered momentum. 'The Ch[urch] competition [is] such as I never before encountered': 'High Churchism on the one hand & <Rant>erism on the other, are ready to pounce upon the prey': and, a little later, 'the antagonism is from Popery, Puseyism, drunkenness etc'; these are typical preachers' comments on their circuit experience. That the Wesleyans had broken up the Manchester system of undenominational Sunday schools to enforce their own catechism, did not make the language of the curate of St Michael's to the German Street Sunday School in 1843 easier to bear:

> I beg to assure you that I am no *bigot,* nor ever was; but it is my solemn opinion that those persons who have received any part of their education through the instrumentality of the established Church, and join any class of dissenters, commit *no light sin;* that *dissenters* and *Wesleyan Methodists* in building *chapels* and *schools,* and striving to induce persons to attend them, are, in fact, promoting *infidelity* and *socialism,* by spreading schism in the church; . . . and children who attend dissenting and Methodist Sunday Schools were never taught the *Lord's prayer,* and were ignorant of the most common events narrated in the *Scriptures.*

The menace of clerical bigotry now was that it was so often a portent of legislation, Graham's Factory Education Bill in this instance, or a Burials Bill which might injure the revenues of urban chapel trusts to the profit of the parish church. Wesleyans had refused to license their chapels for marriages in 1836; by 1845 preachers were arguing that if marriage was to be a religious ceremony at all it should

> be performed by ministers of the parties, and not by ministers by whose labours they receive no spiritual profit, whom they do not regard with affection, and whose teaching they believe to be in many cases unscriptural . . . Because 4. Of the opposition of the clergy to our Connexion. To say nothing of annoyances they refuse to bury children baptised by Wesleyan Ministers, in opposition to the rubrics of their own Church, as

explained and enforced by their own Ecclesiastical Courts. It may
be thought right to yield to their professions of conscience on
this matter; but this will leave marriage as the only rite which
they have the opportunity of performing for our people: we
baptise them, counsel and instruct them, and administer to them
the Lord's supper; and the Clergy refuse to bury. . . . Why
then should they be selected to marry if marriage can be as well
performed by ourselves?

By this argument Bunting was convinced. Church schools
caused endless friction, especially when children were required
upon entrance to break ties with Methodist chapels or Sunday
schools. Again, secessions of preachers and people to the Church
had always taken place, but bore a new menace when the evangelistic appeal of the connexion began to weaken in the 'forties.

Wesleyan Methodism was becoming subject to many sorrows
and trials, both from the state of external society and from the
unfaithfulness of some of its own children . . . many young
men, sons of Wesleyan parents, coolly walked away from the
church of their fathers to some other religious communion,
where their tranquil dignity would be less severely tested. Some
of these were sons of preachers, and some young preachers
themselves who were seeking Episcopal ordination, men who
were laid under special obligation, one would think, to repay
the Church which nurtured them.

Bunting himself, nettled at ' all that has passed of late years in
reference to young men from the [Theological] Institution desert-
ing us, & going into the Church' spoke plainly to the candidates received into full connexion in 1844: ' We Wesleyans have
suffered much in our *forbearance*: never so much as now from the
Established Church . . . the time has come when young Wesleyan
ministers should be put on their guard in this direction.'[21]

Wesleyan embarrassment with the Church appeared to have
one source only, the growth of Catholic views among the clergy,
and this aggravated the case. For it was doubly mortifying that
the pro-Establishment and the Protestant line should fall to the
same error of judgment. In 1836 the *Watchman* reported that
' the intolerant spirit . . . occasionally met with among both high
and low church men . . . prevails, we believe, chiefly in a certain

class of evangelical churchmen ', but it was with them that the
connexion joined in the Orange cause. Tractarians who at first
seemed a welcome antidote to the hydra-headed monster of liberalism, were soon perceived as hell-bent for Rome, and an un-
mitigated political menace.

> . . . they change the very nature and substance of Christianity;
> and they affect the dearest rights of British subjects, undermin-
> ing the foundations of civil and religious liberty. These men
> deny the right of private judgment, and claim, for what they
> call ' the Church', a power to coerce the consciences of men. . . .

By 1841 the Wesleyan intellectuals were planning their own
Tracts for the Times, and were in head-on collision with the Tractarians and the high-church press. One innocent victim of the
swing in Wesleyan opinion was W. F. Hook, Vicar of Leeds,
that decaying Methodist Eden of the North, who was regarded
by Wesleyans as the leader of the Tractarian party. On Hook's
appointment to Leeds in 1837, William Vevers attacked him in
a pamphlet, and found himself in trouble in Conference; but from
1841 onwards Hook could be assailed with impunity in Conference or out.[22]

That Hook's critics included the most conservative and pro-
Anglican of Wesleyans was a measure of the failure of Bunting's
policies; perhaps Bunting was failing too. The victory which Dr
Warren never knew he won was to undermine the ox-like vigour
of his enemy. Working day and night to quell rebellion in the
ranks, Bunting had been oppressed by the evident willingness of
preachers to let him fight their battles for them, at a time when
he was sick of soul at the loss of a much-loved wife. The one
complaint of his vast correspondence escaped him at this moment
—' every heart knows its own bitterness; and many preachers
in the [Manchester] neighbourhood, who are in little local
difficulties, & want advice, insist on seeing me '. It was this
insistence which brought Bunting's authority in Conference to
its peak—' at the Leeds Conference of 1837 Dr Bunting's
absence for a single session brought business to a standstill '. But
it was significant that his preaching powers began to fail,
for, in the pulpit as in Conference, his method was that of the
sledge-hammer. By January 1842 Bunting was confessing to his
intimate John Beecham, ' I am no longer fit for public life. I

must retire as soon as possible, or irretrievably lose the frail &
little health I have left ', and the Mission House staff were bully-
ing him to take a rest. His attempt to get Conference to let him
retire in 1846 was sincere enough.[23]

The difficulty was that a particular line of policy was so closely
identified with Bunting personally that the preachers had turned
to him in every crisis, in 1820, 1828 and 1836; that not to re-elect
him as early as professional ethics permitted, i.e. in 1844, would
look like surrender; that any weakening simply increased the
difficulties which an ageing Bunting must face. As the Conference
of 1844 approached, Bunting received impassioned appeals to
soldier on.

> . . . your re-election just now . . . would act as a breakwater to
> the rapid flow of what are called liberal principles, but which
> I think savor very much of a levelling of those distinctions
> which to my mind appear manifestly to have their origin with
> God himself. . . . We have had the character hitherto of being
> conservative in our ecclesiastical, &, as far as we have at any
> time meddled, in our civil politicks also; but I think we are
> in some danger of forfeiting this honour. If you submit to
> become our President, which I do devoutly hope & pray may be
> the case, the object sought by those remarks will be greatly
> served.
>   . . . we are not prepared to fix upon any other fit person. If
> you don't come then we shall be split into numerous parties.
> . . . O, I pray you, dont jeopardise the Connexion.

Bunting again stepped into the breach, but the tide had turned.
Measures were carried against him, and at one point he was
betrayed into leaving the Presidential chair and threatening to
dissolve the Conference before the most important business was
done. Preachers began to act as if Bunting's days were past, and,
as forecast, to break into parties. Early in 1845, Bunting's protégé,
McLean, could scarcely believe that Jacob Stanley who had wrecked
his chances in the 'thirties by failing to toe the line on the education question, was in train for the succession.

> Is it indeed true that Jacob Stanley is to be our next President?
> Has the Bookroom [the connexional publishing house which
> acted as an unofficial cabinet] really so decreed it? Alas! alas!

I hope you will not be too good-natured in your old days. If that party had generously stood aloof at the last Conference one might have felt inclined to deal kindly with old Jacob. But instead of that they mustered their entire strength, and there seemed to me to be more of the animus of the Stephenite struggle in London than I have seen at any conference since. If you admit his party, stronger at present than they have been for a long time, you will be taking the Trojan horse into the city.

Stanley and the Trojan horse were nevertheless taken into the camp in the next year, by a larger vote than Bunting had received; in 1847 Samuel Jackson was carried against the Bunting faction, and old Robert Melson, 44 years a preacher, addressed a passionate letter to Conference, demanding reform, free speech, a return to primitive simplicity, and a complete change in the Mission House staff, of whom Bunting was chief. The letter was not read, but by 1848, free speech seemed to Bunting's friend John Rigg to be the ruin of the connexion.

I am greatly distressed with what has taken place, & indeed is daily taking place in our now divided Connexion. If the present state of things is to continue we must decline, & Methodism will soon be mingled with the ' wreck of things that were ' . . . Can nothing be done to prevent Methodist ministers from publishing in the *Wesleyan,* that ' execrable sum of all villainy ' such letters as have lately appeared? Is it not enough that during the sittings of the Conference we are at liberty to propose anything which does not threaten to overturn the foundations of our Connexion? But must we, in addition to this freedom of speech be allowed the ruinous licence of agitating the whole kingdom . . .? You, Sir, have been our pilot in many a storm & most fervently do thousands crave your help at this time.

At the 1849 Conference a contest was in prospect. On the ministerial left, William Griffith was exultant.

Great changes are about to take place. The tory party in Conference are, in my opinion, on their last legs. As soon as Dr. Bunting dies, they will prove a rope of sand. There is an undercurrent that will find vent as soon as he is removed. Liberalism

is spreading . . . We are now in the midst of a strong struggle.
The tories are desperate. Dr. Bunting is their life. Liberalism
will be the result.

It was in fact a close call. 'Strong and apparently nearly balanced
efforts are made to promote to [the Presidency] . . . the Rev.
Thomas Jackson, who is supposed to represent the conservative
and church party, and the Rev. Joseph Fowler who is supposed
to represent the liberal and dissenting party.' Thomas Jackson
carried the day, and George Osborn, a good tory, pressed that
all ministers should sign a declaration of loyal behaviour, asking
'What is the point at issue? It is: whether Methodism can exist
*if the Conference be divided into two parties—a Government and
an Opposition party.* If Methodism be divided into two parties,
it must come to an end.' Osborn's declaration was adopted with a
high degree of unanimity, but his alarm was not factitious. Wesleyan reform could not succeed without ministerial leadership.
The divisions and personal animosities among the preachers, to
which Bunting's decline had given rise, almost guaranteed that
there would be preachers to lead any restive movement among the
flock; *per contra,* a fight to the finish amongst the preachers would
commit the minority to exploiting tension in the flock. In 1849
personal acrimony among the preachers and discontent in the
congregations reached a head together, and something must be
said of each.[24]

As the Conference of 1849 approached, the malaise in the
ministry was distressing. Some were pained at the way Conference discipline was being turned against individuals. Others were
upset that when the old officialdom had seemed to be giving way,
old Robert Newton, no longer in the active work, had been summoned back for his fourth term as President in 1848. 'O that
something could occur to call us back to unity, and heal our
wounds!' cried another. 'I thank God that I am in Cornwall,
out of the way of it all.' More generally the preachers were feeling the tide turning against the churches, and could not have been
unprepared for the reproaches of their critics in 1851, who
showed that the decennial increase of membership per travelling
preacher, which had been falling since the 'twenties, had dropped
by almost half between 1839 and 1849. In Leeds, for example,
despite the growth of the town and endless chapel-building, peak

membership was passed in 1840, and continuous decline set in which by 1863 had taken the membership back to the level of the mid-'twenties. The financial implications of this decay were not peculiar to Leeds. At Conference in 1849, James Heald moved that for two years there should be no new building, except where the entire expense could be met in advance. The huge secessions which followed argued even more compellingly for restraint.[25]

Worst of all were the *Flysheets*, anonymous and fugitive leaflets, four of which were printed between 1846 and 1848 and despatched privately to the Wesleyan preachers. Their fire was directed against ' location, centralisation and secularisation ' in the connexion, arising from the ' exclusiveness, favouritism, and selfishness ' of ' Dr Bunting's whole system of government '. The newer developments in the connexional machinery were all assailed. ' Location ' meant the settlement of Bunting and others to run the new bureaucracy of the connexion, which was mostly centralised in London, away from the great centres of Methodist strength. Secularisation was the process of releasing ministers from the itinerancy to do the administrative work of the Mission House, the Theological Institution and the rest. The bulk of these charges were trivial. General talk about secularisation did not go to the real incongruity of the preachers' advancing their administrative claims by elaborating the doctrine of the Pastoral Office. The *Flysheets* were naïve to suppose the Wesleyanism of the 1840s could regain its primitive virtue by returning to its primitive lack of organisation. But the first page of the *Flysheets* hit hard with a characteristic excerpt from the Grindrod's *Compendium* :

> our [recent] legislation bears intrinsic evidence of being the production of one superior mind . . . it is obvious that one master hand, for the last generation, has framed the majority of the acts of our Conference. Besides many minor regulations . . . the invaluable system of finance, particularly in the department of the Contingent Fund; the entire constitution of the Missionary Society, of the Theological Institution, and of our Sunday-schools, were framed by the same honoured minister [the Rev. Jabez Bunting].

If all was not well with Methodism, there was no question where responsibility must lie. And the *Flysheets* hurt by their virulent attribution of corrupt motives, by their flagrant breach of the conventions of mutual confidence among the preachers, and by their evident intention to embitter divisions among them.

No pains were spared to identify the author. No one had any real doubt that the writer was James Everett (indeed the man who claimed to have printed the *Flysheets* was reported to have admitted that he printed them for Everett), but there was never conclusive proof. A young minister in the York circuit, William Radcliffe, claimed to have seen a MS on the study desk of his Superintendent, Daniel Walton, which contained a passage he had seen in the *Flysheets*. Months later he disclosed this to Bunting's son Percy, and Walton was brought before Minor District and District Meetings, and condemned to be admonished from the chair at Conference, and deprived for the time being of the superintendent's office. This whole proceeding inflamed the anxiety amongst the preachers.

We are not satisfied with the complexion of Walton's case. After all the special pleading we have read, the conviction remains strong with us that Radcliffe's conduct was excessively dishonourable, and that of his confidential friend far more inexcusable; and we entertain the hope that something may arise to save so admirable a man as Mr. Walton from the consequences of this treachery. I have often heard and used such an expression as this, in intercourse with brethren, ' Well, you are not Radcliffe, so you may come into my study '.

Perhaps the only relief from the insecurity bred by such proceedings, would be to call on the preachers in full Conference to declare that they had nothing to do with the *Flysheets*. George Osborn moved this at the Conference of 1848, and nearly half the Conference objected: but the litigation and propaganda warfare of the next year convinced many besides Thomas Jackson, the incoming President, that something decisive must be done. At the next Conference Everett, Dunn, Griffiths and Burdsall were asked directly from the chair whether they had anything to do with the *Flysheets,* and refused to answer. For this rebuttal of fraternal discipline, the first three were expelled with great unanimity, and the last, in consideration of his great age, was admonished.[26]

S

The ' three expelled ' were undistinguished specimens of the ministerial race. Everett had acted equivocally in the events which led up to the Warrenite secessions, himself drawing back at the last moment. He had never been willing to accept the fatigue of the itinerant ministry, though, while permitted to sit down as a supernumerary, he had revealed an astonishing capacity for special engagements of all kinds, especially Sunday school anniversaries. A self-assured autodidact, he nevertheless suffered the discomfort commonly occasioned to men of literary pretensions by the hostility of ordinary Methodist preachers, and generated a personal venom peculiar to himself. Everett, who had spent much of his ministry as a supernumerary, was the last man justly to reproach Bunting with ' location ', or indeed with tyranny; as the Conference of 1849 George Osborn's knockabout reply to the *Flysheets* told.

> . . . these irresponsible tyrants want all the liberty to themselves; they will give nobody else any liberty. They wont let me, or Mr. Heald, drink a glass of wine (laughter), [or] ride in a first-class carriage, as they say Dr. Alder does. They say Dr. Newton rides in a fourth-class (a laugh). To that I reply, Dr. Newton, I suppose, pleases himself: that is what I mean to do. . . . I wont be dealt with as a baby or an idiot (cheers). I wont be prescribed to, as to what I should eat or drink or wear.

So much for primitive simplicity. Everett's chief merit was that for a quarter of a century he had been consistently hostile to the person and policies of Jabez Bunting, which had lately become more generally irksome. Dunn had distinguished himself in the Camborne circuit, 1838-41, in strenuous efforts to impose standard Buntingite circuit administration upon the refractory Cornish. But his authoritarianism proved his undoing in his next appointment as Superintendent at Dudley in 1841. In his first year his District Meeting convicted him of

> (1) an arbitrary mode of conducting the Quarterly Meeting, and introducing questions which did not belong to it. (2) Of applying novel and unauthorised tests to the lay officials of the Circuit (3) Packing the Quarterly Meeting in order to carry his policy (4) Of arbitrarily dissolving the Quarterly Meeting when he found that he could not carry it.

Dunn proved very reluctant to meet Conference or its Committee on this case, and, concluding that he had been inequitably dealt with, refused to attend Conference for a number of years. He now discovered that the committee structure of the connexion was being manned by a very narrow circle, and early in Bunting's last Presidential year, in September 1844, appealed to him personally ' to maintain the true Wesleyan parity to the prevention of a dangerous oligarchy '. Dunn continued to nurse personal grievances, and though he disclaimed connexion with the *Flysheets,* he began a paper of his own, *The Wesley Banner and Revival Record,* dedicated to the principle that reform and revival were alike obstructed by the institutional rigidities of the new Methodism. Griffiths was an unstable character who had been in a number of scrapes early in his ministry, and during the 'forties turned against the official line of the connexion on educational and teetotal issues. In 1849 he found the people of his Glastonbury circuit ' all dead and stupid together ', and proposed after another move to retire in discouragement, ' unseen and forgotten by most '. In fact, he refused to answer the President's questions about his connexion with the *Flysheets,* and went out with a bang, never to be forgotten in the annals of Methodist Reform.[27]

Few in numbers and modest in personal stature, the expelled were also short in policy. They expounded their grievances up and down the country, but were undecided whether to advise their sympathisers to stay put and press for reform, or to move out and create a reform connexion of their own. In fact the impatience of the flock and hostility to the preachers' discipline combined to cost the Wesleyans 100,000 members, almost one third of the membership. Neither the causes nor the nature of this catastrophe have ever been properly explained. The London District Meeting of May 1851, noting the loss of a quarter of its membership in a year, reported that

Many of the persons who have separated from us have been long hostile to our discipline, and have therefore been hindrances to the progress of the work of God, so that their separation is rather a benefit than otherwise, that many well-meaning persons have been misled by the agitators, that the Brethren generally have maintained our discipline with great fidelity & kindness, that while we mourn over the people who have been drawn away from our Societies, we rejoice that our discipline is upheld, and is now with few exceptions in efficient operation.

This self-congratulary attitude was a sad mistake, for although the connexion eventually repaired its losses, it never regained its old expansiveness and never again sustained a rate of growth faster than that of the population. The official view continued to be that ' the whole of these distressing circumstances are to be attributed to the unprincipled efforts of certain parties to spread disaffection and strife among our Societies', the measure of their iniquity being that the bulk of the seceders were lost to the world, only 40,000 being gathered into the Free Methodist churches. There are, however, suggestions in the correspondence which cannot be checked statistically, that while many were doubtless lost to the world, the Church or the Independents, the number of seceders was actually about 50,000, most of whom were picked up by the reform movement, and that the remaining net loss arose from the connexion's failure to recruit normally during the years when its morale was lowest, and the internal conflict was at its peak. Certainly the membership losses were out of all proportion to the resources of the agitators.[28]

In truth the agitators exercised practically no influence on the form of the agitation, the same structural weaknesses being revealed as in 1835, the motive power of conflict deriving from the social animosities of the decade. The newest feature of the secessions of the early 'fifties, serious conflict in the countryside, and especially in East Anglia, though fought in terms of the Wesleyan constitution, essentially resembled the great rural losses suffered by the Catholic diocese of Orleans in the aftermath of the revolution of 1848. The Kent District Meeting in May 1851 reported that ' through the spirit of discord in some circuits and agricultural distress in others, a larger decrease has taken place than was feared'; in East Anglia and Lincolnshire the flock, which for a decade had been perfecting techniques of preacher-baiting through the teetotal movement, now gave the ministry a worse time than they had given the established clergy in the 1790s or 1830.

The dreadful effects of reform or deform ', wrote the minister at Swaffham, ' is severely seen and felt in this what used to be a good circuit, but when we came almost destroyed & wrecked.

Once near 1000 members, we found little more than 200 . . .,
47 on trial, they [the reformers] have 35 local preachers, we
have 19. They have got hold of half the places that used to
be on our plan. They are as bitter as ever, and would like to
starve us out, and would have done so had it not been for the
Connect[iona]l funds.

At Norwich the preachers were in equally desperate financial
straits, but the worst thing was

the perilous position of our unhappy people. A spirit, dark,
suspicious, fierce, has come over many of them, withering to
the root their meekness, gentleness, faith, charity. For the Superintendent of a circuit to be assailed in a class meeting with cries
of ' Shame, Shame ', in another with ' death or victory ', in a
third with ' that is a deliberate falsehood ', in a fourth with
' you are the agent of the devil ', in a fifth with ' the acts of the
Conference are tyrannical and iniquitous, but it will wink at
drunkenness, Bastardy, etc '. . . .

was a thing unparalleled.[29] As so often before, the farm labourers
made their protest by repudiating pastoral oversight, often with
such force and acrimony as to frustrate altogether the exercise
of discipline in the ordinary church courts.

Elsewhere the pattern was much as before. As before, the
preachers saw the issue so much in terms of class conflict that,
where the facts fitted the case awkwardly, they were hard put to
for alternative explanations. The standard comments were:

The respectable & really influential & useful members of our
body in this place [Derby] are all right & steadfast in their
attachment to the Conference.

A declaration has just been issued in the *Wesleyan Times*
signed by 36 officers of the Derby Circuit 22 of whom are local
preachers determining to do their utmost to obtain abrogation
of the law by which Mr. Everett was expelled. These I may
say are the tail of the Circuit. All our influential friends are
most steadfast.

Our [reform] legislators are men of but little moral worth,
no weight of character, and no respectability, and there are
none much above the other in influence, or property. They are

nearly all upon a level. All our respectable and influential men
. . . are firm in their attachment to Wesleyan Methodism . . .

Occasionally, as in the West Riding, the poor had to be glossed
to include the new rich.

Several of our circuits in these parts are very wrong. . . . Politics
has *prepared* the minds of some for their bad work, and Barker-
ism [the secession from the New Connexion] has prejudiced
the mass against the ministry. . . . All our leading friends or
nearly so, are sound. I fear politics, railway speculation, self-
importance, etc., have predisposed many of our respectable
people, not remarkable for spiritual religion, to enter into the
movement at Huddersfield, Wakefield and Halifax.

Taking this view of the matter, the preachers stopped their ears
to the reformers' carping attacks on the power of the rich in the
connexion, and as in 1835, turned to the men of property, openly
and repeatedly, for financial sustenance and advice as to the
minimum constitutional adjustment that would meet the case.[30]

The class-consciousness of the preachers was justified by a
repetition of the Warrenite troubles in old city-centre churches,
from which the prosperous classes had moved out. In Manchester
the ' inner belt ' itself could be seen moving outwards. In 1835
Oldham Street and Oldham Road were wrecked by the effects of
the removal of the affluent to Grosvenor Street, a church which
raised half as much again for the Centenary Fund as any other.
But Grosvenor Street was now losing its respectability to Oxford
Road, and the crisis cost it a third of its pew rents and about
three-sevenths of its membership. The Leeds circuits which had
been sagging throughout the 'forties, suffered again, losing over
2,000 members, almost one-third of the strength. Other old
Methodist urban strongholds were also ravaged. In the one year
1850 the membership of Bristol North fell from 2,491 to 950,
Bristol South from 1,358 to 645, Newcastle upon Tyne from
1,696 to 829, North Shields from 835 to 360, Sunderland from
1,700 to 940.[31]

Smaller industrial towns also suffered severely. Membership in
the Kingswood circuit declined in 1850 from 1,246 to 270. The
great majority of the Longton Quarterly Meeting in the Potteries
were radicals, who had the inspiration of suspending the new

Conference rule on the trial of members for a year, as they were
entitled to do. In the West Riding tempers rose to the pitch of
Peterloo. The preacher at Bramley

> had a terrible year with the radicalism of this distracted place.
> Abused, calumniated, involved in the midst of violent mobs,
> and denounced as being too bad even for hanging, [I have
> been] reduced in allowances to the lowest pitch, and now de-
> prived even of that, and seem to have no likelyhood of getting
> it, unless you can help us from the special funds.

At Pudsey there was 'a fearful outbreak' in 1850, 'when
(save 10) the whole society of 300 members were expelled and
scenes of mob violence shown'. Nine years later the preacher
reported continued 'antagonism . . . from a low radical democratic
feeling of great heatedness wh. shows itself alike about political
and religious matters, and is especially strong about the doctrine
of a "hired ministry".' Yeadon, where revival had succeeded
revival every seven years for a generation, is hardly recognisable
in the preachers' reports; the people knew that pastoral authority
had contributed little to the peculiar ethos of the place, and
resolved to stop the supplies. The preacher refused contumacious
leaders their class-tickets, and the people returned theirs wholesale.
At Ilkeston in East Derbyshire things were even worse.

> . . . at the last quarterly visitation of the classes, such is the
> state of anarchy and disruption in which we found the circuit,
> we have not been able to take any account of who are members
> and who are not, so that for the last quarter the Schedule Book
> is a *blank*. With the exception of *one* or *two* only of the con-
> gregations, all the congregations in the circuit are the most
> disorderly riotous assemblies of wild beasts: and the *pulpits*
> regularly the spit of contention between the *authorised* local
> preachers, and those patronised by the mob. I have instructed
> the Brethren on the Plan to retire quietly from the ungodly
> contest when they have claimed their places. . . . I have to do
> the same myself. . . . I do not think it right to be any further
> a party to the desecration of all that is sacred on God's day, by
> contending with infuriated men, some of whom have, again
> and again, squared their fists in my face in regular pugilistic
> style, and all but struck me in the performance of this necessary
> duty.[32]

In such circumstances the preachers' temper ran short and phrases like, ' We are resolved, the Lord being our helper, to have a clearance by Decr. 31st 1850 ', occur too frequently in the correspondence. Moreover, the preachers were not free agents. At the Conference Stationing Committee in 1850, they were called in to ' declare whether they would not uphold the discipline of the body by visiting delinquent Radicals with due punishment ', before being given their appointments. At a gathering immediately after the Conference, a group of preachers undertook to enforce discipline if conciliation did not succeed quickly. By 30 September, the message from the President was: ' Decisive measures against those who commit themselves by overt acts, as Leaders in the movement, ought now to be adopted.' Inevitably, preachers who tried to be conciliatory became unpopular with their fellows; inevitably, there were complaints among loyal laymen that superintendents were acting arbitrarily under the new legislation of 1835; inevitably, there were wild men among the preachers who wanted the repeal of even those safeguards to the people granted in 1797.[33]

The machinery for the discipline of members was of course useless against the non-members entrenched in the Sunday schools, and throughout the 'forties restiveness in the schools portended restiveness in the wider public associated with the churches. The recession of 1837 to 1842 intensified the strains. The Gainsborough circuit was reported in 1845 to have lost three Sunday schools in the previous six years, and the Chartists, like the radicals of Peterloo, laid claim to their own Sunday schools. At Bollington one of the objects of the chapel building scheme launched in 1837 was to provide accommodation for the children of the (undenominational) Sunday school. But in the 'forties, as earlier, there was friction over the teaching of writing in the school, which led in 1846 to the building of a specifically Wesleyan Day and Sunday School. The undenominational school continued as strong and independent as ever; they separated themselves from the Wesleyan library and established their own; in March 1849 they invited James Everett to preach their sermon; in 1850 all the teachers signed a protest ' against the language made use of by the Rev N. Curnock in Bollington Chapel to the teachers of this school '. Not surprisingly when the school got its own premises in the 'sixties, it gave shelter to all the protest movements against the Wesleyan establishment in the village, the Primitives, the New Connexion, the Apostolics, the National Reform Union, trade unions in the pits and mills, and after the Wesleyan superintendent had tried to put down the Sunday school procession, they resolved not to send their children to the chapel any more. Denominational warfare also caused its embarrassments. A generation before, the Wesleyans had ex-communicated the undenominational school at Macclesfield for the same reasons as the Stockport school, but in 1844 the preacher, learning that ' great efforts have been made of late years to make this institution entirely a church school and . . . that the Bishop has given leave to clergymen to lecture there', began gingerly to cast a wing over it, to the accompaniment of warnings from Bunting ' to concede nothing wh[ich] the public c[oul]d fairly construe into a sanction of the plan of that school. Refer par-ticularly to the absence of all responsible connexion with any branch of the Church, and to Sunday writing and arithmetic.' It was delicate also at Upper Mill near Delph, where the Sunday school was not settled on the Conference plan, and the committee was habitually summoned when the preacher was away. In 1845 they invited a Warrenite to preach their sermon, and the preacher, John Hannah, refusing to ' allow a person from *that* denomina-tion to preach in any chapel under my care ', found himself faced with a rupture in his congregation.[34]

From 1848 onwards these nightmares became daily realities. Even ' that nurse of Radicalism, the Stockport Sunday School ', which in 1841 had continued placidly in spite of tory charges of turning ' out from her walls many of the Socialists who are now polluting our town with the damnable doctrines they inculcate ', was in 1848 suffering from an ' opposition party' among the ' young teachers " standing up for their rights " on real Chartist principles '. In the Wesleyan world the hazard to ministerial authority created still more tension. In the general wreck at Ilkeston, the whole Sunday school system withdrew from the connexion, repudiated ministerial rights and took legal advice which confirmed it in possession of all the trust premises, including the chapel. There were horror-stories from Yeadon.

Their Sunday school is in as bad condition as their Soc[iet]y. They have about 400 teachers, several are infidels [presumably

radicals or socialists], and a large number of them never attend
public worship. They have all sorts of books in their S[unday]
S[chool] Library, amongst the number the " Fly-Sheets ". They
are wise in their own conceit and obstinate beyond con-
cep[tio]n . . .

At Milnrow in the parish of Rochdale,

in consequence of the expulsion of fifteen members from the
Wesleyan Methodist Society . . . considerable excitement . . .
prevailed in the village; and the trustees of the Sunday school,
rather than allow the expelled members to continue in the office
of teachers, have broken up the school and are forming it afresh
upon different principles . . . the expelled members are also
commencing a new Sunday school.

At Great Harwood a strange compromise ended in blows.

. . . a conference teacher in Great Harwood Methodist chapel,
charged Henry Hindle, a ' reform ' teacher, with having on
the previous Sunday assaulted him without provocation. It
appeared that the two religious parties occupy different sides of
the chapel, and that, on the day in question, the complainant
left his own party and insisted on teaching a class belonging
to the other. A quarrel ensued, and each endeavoured to throw
the other over the pew in which the class assembled. Mr. W.
Eccles, the magistrate, ordered each of the parties to enter
into his own recognisance to keep the peace.

In 1851 the Leeds District Meeting professed itself

more than ever convinced of the necessity . . . of the pastoral
oversight of our Sunday and other schools by frequent visits to
them for the purpose of addressing the children and by attending and presiding over the committee meetings and of a
regular and systematic course of pastoral visitation.

Only too often, this was shutting the stable door after the horse
had bolted. At the very same time, the Norwich and Lynn District
were reporting the loss of two-fifths of their members and no
less than 28 Sunday schools.[35]

As the steam went out of English social tension in the 'fifties,
peace came back again to the schools, but one final incident may

show how the contest between denominational and undenominational religion continued to rumble. At Middleton Junction the
old Hillock School for all denominations was by 1861 over-
crowded, and the Wesleyan superintendent prepared to raise
£500 for a larger building. This should serve as a day and Sunday
school, and should of course be Wesleyan. To this the undenominational men objected, and the upshot was that the new
school was not opened till 1873, by which time the scholars had
fallen away, the teaching staff declined from 26 to four, and
' there was some chafing under the restraints enjoined and practised by the new superintendents '. Nor could the deeds of the
school be found, though it transpired that the father of a local
landowner, J. L. Becker of Foxdenton Hall, had given the property to trustees now all dead. The old school was therefore returned to Becker, and the Wesleyans were left in full charge
of a cause that had to be worked up from scratch. By 1891 they
had succeeded to the point of adding a church to the school, only
to find in 1907 that they were no longer in quite full command
as they supposed. From the opening of the church the premises
had been used weekly by the Pleasant Sunday Afternoon Society,
which succeeded the Sunday school as a pillar of the undenominational principle. In 1907 the trustees determined that
the PSA was having an adverse effect upon attendance at public
worship and upon the finances of the church, and egregiously
resolved ' that the PSA friends be requested to change their name
from the Middleton Junction PSA Society to the Middleton Junction Wesleyan PSA Society '; a month later they ' decided unanimously to remind members of the PSA that permission to use the
Church had only been granted on the understanding that it would
be a distinctively Wesleyan Methodist organisation '. An ultima-
tum was presented, but like the Sunday school before them, the
PSA protested with their feet and got out.[36]

The other churches enjoyed no exemption from the troubles
which came so spectacularly upon the Wesleyans, least of all the
reformed Methodist bodies. The recruiting power of the New
Connexion like that of the old had sagged in the 'twenties, and
revived spectacularly in the 'thirties. But the recession at the end
of the decade brought on a crisis like that which hit Wesleyans
ten years later. At least one New Connexion preacher seems to
have been expelled for adopting Chartist opinions, and the

discomforts below found a powerful, if tetchy and unstable, spokesman in Joseph Barker. He

> found in the Connexion a complete division between the rich members and the poor members. The rich were a class, or caste to themselves, and the poor were another class or caste. The rich along with the travelling preachers, formed one world, the poor, left all alone, formed another world; and between the two there seemed to be a great gulf fixed. . . . The rich met at each others' houses; they had their regular parties, many of which were very extravagant and expensive: while the poor were completely lost sight of, as though they belonged to another race of beings.

Barker's complaints were in common form with those of the Wesleyan radicals; the singularity of the New Connexion situation was that his hostility to the lay patricians was shared by other preachers on professional grounds. Independent observers reported that trustee power in the New Connexion had a peculiarly paralysing effect on ministerial zeal, and in September 1840 one of the preachers, Samuel Hulme, published an Address complaining of the spirit which

> betrayed itself in withholding from ministers that respect to which their character and office scripturally entitle them. The authority of a pastor, as the ruler of the church, has been reduced to a mere name; he has often been left to struggle alone; or thwarted and dispirited, he has sunk into indifference.

When the New Connexion Conference assembled in June 1841, Barker was reported to be

> Flogging the Conference a good deal . . . and is likely to shake them to the foundation whether turned out or not. Their nos. fall off again. It is said that this Conf[erence] is a crisis with them, whether they will continue a Connexion any longer. They seem to be almost eaten up with internal cancers.

The old connexion had complained often (and with reason) of the New Connexion's interference with their internal embarrassments, and now improved their rivals' confusion by bringing out George Turner's *Constitution and Discipline of Wesleyan Methodism* as the New Connexion Conference assembled, inviting them in slashing style to ascribe all their woes to their having sold the pass of the Pastoral Office at the beginning. In the event Barker was expelled, taking with him about a third of the membership, complaining bitterly that ' their feelings had been lacerated by the recent cruelty and intolerance of the Methodist New Connexion '. Among the ministerial rump of the Kilhamites, this cataclysm led to a new feeling of fraternity towards the Wesleyans. Even William Cooke, who became identified with the policy of allying the New Connexion with other branches of free Methodism, fawned upon Bunting, congratulating him upon his ' enlightened judgment and candour ', his ' christian courtesy and kindness of heart', upon ' the exalted talents and extensive influence which the Great Head of the Church ' had given him. ' I have been informed ', he added, ' that you, though often calumniated and traduced as a tyrant, have done more to infuse lay-influence into the proceedings of the Wesleyan denomination, than any other minister, and I believe it.'[37]

The Warrenites, the Wesleyan Methodist Associaation, understood the inwardness of this, but were in the same vortex as Bunting and the New Connexion. Through the 'forties their numbers declined by about a third, and ' as many of the wealthier members ceased to attend ', the financial position became precarious. The secessions of the reformers from the old connexion offered them some hope, but by now they were engaged in savage in-fighting of their own, with their chief figure, Robert Eckett, a former hell-raiser from London, now figuring as a Warrenite Bunting, and using his power in Conference to smite down his opponents. Even in Rochdale, the Association, which had been in so great a measure a Sunday school revolt, itself suffered a Sunday school revolt in 1851, as a result of which George Ashworth of the Sunny Bank Mills founded the Holland-street Church and Sunday school. Patently the Warrenites were overdue for the infusion they received by union with the Reformers in 1856.[38]

If social tension made life difficult for the connexional churches in the 'forties, its effects were equally felt among the Independents. The Baptists had long provided ' dippers ' with a choice of theologies, polities and politics too. As far back as Peterloo there had been a notable increase in expulsions of members, and resolutions were taken to keep the churches out of corporate political activity. But Baptists like William Gadsby of Manchester con-

tinued politically active on the left. Joseph Harrison, a Baptist
New Connexion schoolmaster and preacher at Stockport, who became their first pastor in the town in 1840, was the local radical
organiser, rode in the coach with Hunt to Peterloo, and in 1820
was imprisoned for three and a half years for his political speeches
and preaching. The ambivalence between pietist abstention and
radical activism continued into the 'forties. A small group was
prepared to back radical middle-class causes, secular and religious,
arguing that at the bottom all political questions were religious.
Most of the pastors in this group served in large urban Association churches. A much larger group abstained from political
activity, and sought to condemn those who did not. The remainder
oscillated nervously between the two, unwilling to commit themselves to any political cause, least of all the causes championed by
labour radicals, but unwilling also to abstain from politics entirely. As it was possible to be a Baptist on a variety of terms, and
as secession to form a new congregation was relatively economical,
it is difficult to be sure what was happening in the Baptist community as a whole. The evidence nevertheless suggests that, like
the Methodists, the Baptists suffered set-backs in the recession of
1837 to 1842, and serious losses in the late 'forties. Radical as
were their traditions, many of the Stockport General Baptists were
' scattered abroad ' in this period. The Baptist congregation at
Stalybridge reported a ' severe shock ' in 1838, through ' intense
political excitement '; a quarter of the 98 members were excluded,
and there were other withdrawals later in the 'forties. Heywood
reported ' unhappy differences of opinion ' in 1847, leading to
secessions, and there was the same experience at Ashton and
Stockport. All the General Baptist Churches in the Lancashire
towns suffered great secessions in the 'forties, and the finanical
difficulties entailed by the recession had a generally inhibiting
effect, especially on working-class congregations. The judgment
of the most recent historian of the North-western Baptists is
that after 1844 they suffered a decade of stagnation, depression
and disappointment. Their progress slowed down or went into
reverse about the mid-century, and no real advance was made
until the revival decade of the 'sixties. The hopeful feature of their
history was that they went on making members at about their old
rate, but between 1845 and 1854 the rate of membership losses
doubled. A similar experience befell many of the churches of the

Midland Baptist Association. The church at Dudley had 258 members in 1844, 67 in 1855. That at Bettell Lane had 65 members in 1845, 37 in 1855. The Darkhouse, Coseley, had 206 members in 1844, 170 in 1855. Netherton had 92 members in 1848, 58 in 1855. Wednesbury had 53 members in 1848, six in 1855. And so the roll goes on. The impression is created that if Baptist numbers could be plotted against the whole population, as Dr Currie has plotted the Methodist membership, the curve would drop sharply in the years immediately following the social upheaval of 1848, and show a declining impulse thereafter.[39]

With the Congregationalists things were probably worse, despite their spectacular emergence as a political force. Their condition is vividly suggested by a review of Edward Miall's book, *The British Churches in relation to the British people* (1849), by the Unitarian, E. H. Higginson.

> Perhaps no denomination has (as a whole) undergone more rapid change during the last thirty years than the Independent; the change has been entirely (as we think) for the better, whether in its modified theology or its lowered *tone* of orthodoxy, or in its liberalised social spirit, or (which is the explanation of the whole process) in the higher general education of its ministers. Mr. Miall represents this process.

Yet Miall's book was a prolonged jeremiad against the separation of the churches (including his own) from the working class, and the ' pride of station, exclusiveness of spirit and contempt of the poor ' which were as strong in the churches as in society at large. The Congregational Union had anxiously discussed the matter in 1848, and A. E. Wells put his finger on the psychology of the situation.

> We cannot establish a day school, or join a sick or clothing society, but must turn the opportunity to religious account. This is plainly discerned by the working class, but it is not justly appreciated. It is not attributed to honest and loving fervour. It is ascribed to sectarianism, not to benevolence. We are thought to work for a party, not for their souls. They think we would get them to chapel, not that we would conduct them to heaven. Our good is evil thought of. What ought to attract, in fact, repels. Further the working of our church system casts

itself too much in the aristocratic mould to present a pleasing aspect to the working classes.

Here the working-class sense of being an outsider looking in, its class conformity in non-participation in religious worship, are vividly depicted. The Congregational Union could only suggest courses of lectures adapted to working-class hearers, upon the intellectualist assumption that working men were the victims of false ideas.[40]

Congregationalists, moreover, were anxious not so much about their limited penetration of the working class, as about the speed with which they had lost such following among working men as they recently had had. It was calculated that in 1830 Manchester Congregationalists had attracted congregations of 4,000, morning and evening, most of whom were adults and 1,400 of whom were communicants. By 1850 they had spent £65-70,000 in building, and two and a half or three times that amount in pastoral or evangelistic labour, yet the census gave them a morning congregation of 8,535 (some 6,600 of whom were Sunday scholars and their teachers) and an evening congregation of 4,150. Small wonder that Thomas Binney was already announcing that ' our mission is to the middle classes '. It was a similar story in Yorkshire, where the county union was told of at least one large town where the population had trebled in fifty years, and Congregationalist attendances had dwindled to one-third. Nor was there any disagreement as to the sector of the social spectrum in which the losses occurred; indeed many of the town churches had followed the remnant of their more prosperous pew-holders into the suburbs. And at a level below church membership, the Warrington dissenters had to reckon in 1846 that they now had unfilled Sunday school accommodation for no less than 1,000 scholars.[41]

Social tension did not make general religious communion (any more than other forms of social cooperation) impossible in England, but made it far more difficult to sustain than ever before. And whereas in 1790 the state could not solve the problem of public order without the aid of organised religion, by 1850 the churches had become unable to solve their problems without the aid of the state and other external forces.

Epilogue

Both in the long and in the short run the changes in the relations between the churches and the people modified their relations with each other, their internal dispositions and their relations with the state. The great contest between the Church and dissent had been joined on two main fronts, disestablishment and education, and had ended in a drawn battle. Despite some damaging losses, Establishment survived, and, even on the most promising terrain, the dissenters showed a curious inability to strike a really telling blow. On the education front, the defeat of Graham's Factory Education Bill destroyed whatever hopes the Establishment had retained of being the sole vehicle for the education of the people, and although Methodist support had enabled the Church to confine the state's educational assistance to religious, and almost exclusively to Protestant, bodies, the future was already casting its shadow before. For the heady enthusiasm which went into voluntary educational effort after the defeat of Graham's Factory Education Bill, and which, at least in the Church and in Wesleyan Methodism, received a new impetus from the Education Minutes of 1846 and 1847, barely survived the trial of the next four or five years. Indeed in the most progressive parts of the country, it was acknowledged to have reached its limit.

In those hard years the one unmistakable success of state-stimulated educational voluntaryism was made a reproach by its friends. For in school- as in church-building, the denominations provided far more accommodation than a free public would ever use, especially in recession times. The declining attendance of working-class children during a period of bad trade and high food prices was noted in Manchester in 1847, and little more than a year later Hugh Stowell was saying in public that

T

the Church of England (taking Manchester as a fair specimen) had twice as much school accommodation in readiness as the people would avail themselves of, at this moment. He had long felt that there ought to be some wholesome constraint on ignorant and heedless persons, to oblige them to do their duty to their children, by sending their children to our schools.[1]

Whether it was that church-based education was too expensive, or too unpalatable for parents, to save the system by so Draconian an alteration in the terms of the public contract was a desperate resort indeed. And whatever the success of the system in providing a surplus of accommodation, everyone knew by the later 'forties that it worked worst in the areas least able to help themselves, areas which, if one was to believe the correlations confidently made between educational deprivation and high incidence of crime, most needed the schools. The failure was confessed the more readily, because it suited the polemics of church Establishment against pure voluntaryism.

By 1850 the system was known to operate very unevenly in time as well as space. Money could generally be raised for school-building; the problem had always been to maintain subscriptions for recurrent expenses. The Manchester Chapter candidly confessed the woes of the two National Schools which had been enthusiastically established in the town in 1811. £7,000 was raised for building and £550 p.a. for maintenance, which for a decade enabled about 1,000 children to be educated. But as the original subscribers died or removed, it proved impossible to replace them, and the system flagged. British schools suffered a similar fate; too often the master had to take over the school on a commercial basis. Moreover the achievements of private effort owed much to state stimulus, and most of all to the threat of large-scale state intervention in Graham's Factory Education Bill; the cold douche came when the recession in 1848 followed so closely upon the aid provided by Russell. The great effort of the mid-'forties could not only not be repeated, but the viability of the new system, even with increased state aid, came in question. The Manchester Church Education Society had been organised in 1844 by Dean Herbert, and had represented the chapter's principal service to the town. In May 1848 the Secretary, the Rev. Charles Richson, had to report such a ' decrease of subscriptions in consequence of the pressure of the times,' that but for the credit provided privately by the treasurer, ' the operation of the society must have been brought to a sudden and injurious close.' The Society dismissed its school inspector, gave up their artisan schools, and discontinued their grant to the Bennett Street schools. But most of the district schools would close without the society's grant, and they had felt compelled to gamble with their treasurer's credit, to get over a crisis which proved not yet to have reached its worst. Even the bishop had no idea of the seriousness of the situation until he received the report just before the annual meeting. The bishop and Canon Richson were not surprisingly among the early advocates of obtaining public funds on whatever terms they could be got.[2]

Moreover it became a question whether churches whose cohesion was failing as that of the British churches was failing in the 'forties, could conceivably maintain the cohesion of society by social engineering in the schools. Cobden went on record that there was

> looming in no very remote distance a schism in the Church of England itself—that there were two parties—one the stronger probably in number, but the other far more strong in intellect and logic, which were going to divide that Church . . . He saw the Wesleyan body torn asunder by schism, which he thought the most sanguine could hardly hope to see healed; and he did not think that several other religious bodies were perfectly tranquil in their organisation. . . . With these prospects before us, was it desirable, even if practicable—which he believed it was not, that our national system of education should be one knot, as it were, to be bound up with the religious organisations, when the schisms that prevailed amongst them must necessarily be transferred with even increased violence to the schools . . . bear in mind what we now saw prevailing in Scotland where there was an irreconcilable difference with regard to the appointment of masters to the parochial schools, between the members of the old kirk and the free church . . .

Or as one of Her Majesty's Inspectors put it soon afterwards in a report on Manchester schools, the future stability of all those religious denominations on which we are urged to rely is always questionable '.[3] Indeed the social strains which upset the continental monarchies, in England divided the churches. Church order was unable any longer to bear the weight put upon it.

If the dire ecclesiastical break-up which in 1851 might not unreasonably be expected never quite arrived, there was no mistaking the change in temper in the education controversy of which Manchester was now the pacemaker. Those who minimised the role of public authorities in education, whether from the side of high-church doctrines or from the side of low-state doctrines of the voluntaryists, cut little ice. Baines and the Congregational Education Board came into the town, pleading for free trade in education and

> deprecated the application of the principle of communism to the education of the country, and argued that the carrying out of this principle would require the adoption of legislative enactments and local assessments for feeding and clothing, and giving employment to the local people, as well as for educating them; and that intemperance and improvident marriages, and in short every social evil should be checked by force of law.

But they could do no more than keep the Congregationalists in line; the schools promised by the voluntaryists did not materialise. It was the same story on the high-church side. The views advocated by Archdeacon Denison, that ' all education in any proper sense of the term is based upon the doctrine of regeneration in Holy Baptism ', that it was part of the parochial charge controlled by the parson, subject to appeal to the bishop, could never be widely held in Manchester where the location of the cure of souls was uncertain, and the relations of the leading clergy with their bishop were bad. The *Guardian* might well ask why the Church's responsibility was undischarged. ' The Church, if rightly represented by this gentleman, is a jealous impotent tyrant. Unable from weakness, or unwilling from indolence, to perform its duties, it would rather they should be left undone than taken off its senseless hands.' Fortunately Denison proved unable to carry the National Society in his opposition to the standard management and conscience clauses by which the state sought to do some justice to the religious pluralism of the national life, and the gulf which separated him from the clergy in touch with the working world was vividly illustrated in 1851 in his vicious attack on the bill which the Manchester clergy had promoted.[4]

The troubles of the late 'forties had evoked two schemes in Manchester, each of which went well beyond the Education Minutes of 1846 and 1847. The first was the work of the Lancashire Public School Association, one of the successor organisations to the Anti-Corn-Law League. The LPSA originated in 1847 in a meeting in Lloyd Street United Secession Chapel, which supplied six of the original seven members. Looking for a promising new cause, the radicals investigated European and American educational systems, and found them superior to those at home. But the European systems were too centralised to be politically feasible here, and the chief interest was aroused by the public system of Massachusetts. Their proposal was to establish county boards (in Lancashire in the first instance) which should raise an education rate, control the local schools, train teachers in a Normal School, and provide undenominational religious education by selections from the scriptures. There should be a hierarchy of administrative committees, one for each parish and township, another for each hundred, and finally a county board chosen by indirect election. Within a couple of years the Association had pressed far beyond Lancashire, and metamorphosed into the National Public School Association.[5]

It was predictable that this scheme would be abused as Irish, godless and anti-scriptural, and almost encouraging that that ferocious abetter of lost causes, Joseph Rayner Stephens, came out of political retirement to denounce it as a plan to enable a self-elected board of twelve to levy taxes and make a new Bible. (He returned to politics just twice more, first to support the South in the American Civil War, and then to scourge the licensing legislation of the 'seventies.) When in March 1849 a town's meeting was called in Manchester to petition Parliament in favour of the scheme, Stowell and the Wesleyans attended in force, and by the narrowest of margins defeated the motion. The following year, however, although Stowell was again supported by the Wesleyans, and used his Protestant mob to try to occupy the hall before the supporters of the motion could arrive, and then to break up the meeting after it had begun ('a regular fight appeared to take place in the body of the hall, most of the people rising from their seats') he was this time soundly thrashed.[6]

More important, Manchester clergy were already producing schemes for involving the state more closely in the educational system, without violence to parents' conscience. In the earliest days of the LPSA, the *Manchester Courier* carried a plan probably drawn up by Canon Richson, under which education commissioners were to be appointed for every area, and to provide up to two-thirds of free places in the schools, ' provided only that no child shall be sent into any school in which the religious principles inculcated shall be such as his parent disapproves '. This scheme was developed to embrace parliamentary boroughs, in which the commissioners were to create school places for all who were too poor to pay for their education. None of these provisions was to interfere with any of the arrangements made by individuals or societies under the recent Privy Council minutes. The political strength of the Church case throughout was that it started from what actually existed, and sought to supplement it, rather than to make a new system *ab initio*. By 1851 the thinking had crystallised into a draft bill, for the boroughs of Manchester and Salford, promising free education for every child, paid for by local rates managed by committees selected from their own number by the municipal councils. There was to be an effective conscience clause, and Privy Council consent was to be obtained before new schools were erected. This scheme provided an alternative approach to the local problem to that of the NPSA, equally national in its implications, and won support from the Chapter and from Canon Stowell, from Wesleyans and Independents, from Unitarians, Roman Catholics, and Sir James Kay-Shuttleworth,

> the nearest approximation to the millennium that our imperfect nature has yet witnessed. . . . We say it almost with fear and trembling, but we cannot refrain from thinking that a royal salute may be fired in honour of the greatest discovery of a common ground on which the education of the people may at last commence.[7]

There is no space here to discuss the legislation promoted by the two parties—in 1855 there were no fewer than five bills before the Commons at once—nor the difficulties they encountered with the Aberdeen coalition and the most ungovernable parliament of the generation, nor yet the mountain of pamphlet controversy they generated. The important fact was that two schemes which had had a family resemblance from the beginning, grew closer as the two sides consulted together, and perceived the political and administrative advantages of each other's position. By 1855 the Manchester men had come virtually to the point reached nationally in Forster's Education Act in 1870, when decisive parliamentary action became possible again. An undenominational public system was to make good the inadequacies of Church enterprise, which continued as the premise of the system, embodying conscience clauses. Schools of both kinds were to be rate-supported, and subject to a mixture of central and local policy. The Manchester compromise was a fitting conclusion to a period of rapid political and religious movement, and belated recognition by all sides of social realities. The radicals were not going to dislodge the churches from the work they had accomplished, but the churches were not strong enough to maintain the wilder positions they had taken in the 'forties. The Establishment was not going to educate the nation, nor prevent the state from acknowledging pluralism in society. The Wesleyans must retreat from their hopeless attempt to keep the state Protestant. The voluntaryists could not have national education without state intervention, whatever the hazard to private enterprise.[8]

The drawn battle in the political system was poignantly illuminated by the religious census of 1851. Though the census was incomplete, suspect in detail, and somewhat biased against the Church in its assumptions, there has never been much doubt about the rough justice it embodied. Horace Mann, who organised the census, reckoned that if everyone who was free to attend church took his place, accommodation would be needed for 58 per cent of the population (a figure within the range of those arrived at by the church building societies at the time). 10,398,013 persons might have gone to church on census Sunday; how many individuals actually did so could not be precisely established from the gross attendance figures, but it appeared to Horace Mann probable that 5,288,294 persons, able to attend religious worship at least once, neglected to do so, and that those who did attend were divided almost equally between the Church and the rest. As on other occasions, the distorting mirror of the reformed political structure had produced an image not unrecognisably distorted after all. The indecisiveness of the battles over disestablishment, church rates and education, had its roots in a real balance of power in society at large; and although the census offered no basis for computing the size of the population severed from all religious influence, it emphasised the lesson of the education contests, that the churches could no longer cope with major tasks of social engineering. The Wesleyan George Osborn had attacked the LPSA on the ground that it ' had committed an egregious fallacy in attempting to distinguish between the nation and the [religious] bodies which, taken together, constituted the nation. The nation was nothing but the different sects in their public and corporate capacities.'[9] Everyone now knew that this at least was not true. In the 'sixties Parliament began to withdraw from its obligations to the Church, while dissenters began to abandon their voluntaryism in favour of state-supported elementary education. The revolution in government must provide what two generations of desperate activity by the churches had failed to supply.

The religious census was taken at an opportune moment, for the era of rapid displacements in English religious life was ending, and a pattern taking shape which was subject in future to erosion rather than upheaval. The forces which took the steam out of English social conflict are not easily delineated. It was partly that twenty years of almost continuous prosperity took the edge from one form of discontent, and that gently rising prices made social adjustments easier; partly that the forces of discipline in society grew stronger, that new safety valves became available, and that individuals and the nation corporately learned how to cope better with the new social order. It was partly that the rigidities of the electoral structure inhibited contests from coming to a head, and partly that the system showed a capacity for concession which gave the lie to its sterner critics. It was not easy to present a system which repealed the Corn Laws as a simple front for aristocratic rule, nor that which yielded the Ten Hours Act as a simple front for capitalist manipulation. It was equally unlikely after the religious census to behave simply as a front for ecclesiastical Establishment, as Miall liked to imagine, or as a device for latitudinarian, Roman or dissenting persecution of the Church catholic, as, in their less lucid intervals, the Tractarians had conceived. The Church itself bore witness to the lowered temperature. The general strains of society, the gradual collapse of the unreformed constitution, continuous opposition in the Church (and especially the Irish Church) had preoccupied a certain sort of evangelical with the Last Things, and had given a peculiar urgency to the signs of the Second Coming. If present forms of church life were hastening to judgment, now might be the moment for the faithful remnant to withdraw. More than a hundred books and journals were devoted to this theme in the first forty years of the century, and in 1839 so unevangelical a character as Thomas Arnold could

> watch with the most intense interest the result of the harvest, believing that the consequences of a bad crop may be most serious and having also a belief that there are many symptoms about of one of those great periods of judgement which are called Comings of Our Lord.

When Arnold talked in this vein, a degree of emotional pressure was being exerted which would make agreement about the Last Things impossible; too much in the way of practical consequences hung upon it. Yet in 1854 Samuel Waldegrave's Bampton Lectures, moving back the Second Coming to the end of the world, really wound up the question for the evangelical party in the Church of England. They devoted themselves to supplementing the parish ministry with non-parochial enterprises of all kinds, much as Arnold's pupils gave themselves up to tutoring, examining, university reform, and public school development. Neither side expected cataclysm; each was concerned to improve and perpetuate this present age.

Popular religion also exemplified the signs of the times in at least two major respects. Revival, the showers of blessings shed by free grace, had not only created new forms of religious allegiance across much of the countryside, but had given rise to a tenacious understanding of the whole history of the church in revival terms. But the technology of revivalism developed in the United States by men like C. G. Finney and Calvin Colton had never quite become naturalised, though of course American practitioners had always worked here, and had a respectful hearing in some quarters. The 'forties and 'fifties marked the watershed between revival and revivalism. The disputes which gathered round James Caughey, the Irishman who intruded into English Methodism from America, derived their edge from the knowledge that the native springs of spontaneous revival were drying up. Whether the proper answer to the drought was the organised oversight of the Pastoral Office, or an organised assault upon the

hard ground which now resisted the gospel seed, informed by that
analysis of the laws of the spiritual world developed in America
by Finney and others, was a serious question; but both sides perceived that the protective shell with which men covered their inner
emotions was no longer being broken open by the strains of ordinary existence, as in the recent past. The great revival of 1859 and
1860 showed that the old order was not yet dead, but it owed
much to American example, and American practitioners were
prominent in it. Henceforward only the American names, Moody
and Sankey, Torrey and Alexander, Billy Graham, were to count
at all. And the shocking thing about the religious census of 1851
was that it showed how uneven a process revival had been. Great
triumphs in Cornwall and Wales, the south Midlands and the
Eastern counties were matched by torpor elsewhere, and especially
in London and the South-East. This unevenness was accentuated
in the revival of 1859 and 1860. Abnormal psychological manifestations were common in Ulster and Scotland, virtually unknown
in England; and there was reason to think that the moral and
spiritual power of the revival was in direct proportion to its
ability to produce abnormal manifestations. For the premise of the
revivalists was that at the bottom of every heart there were frag-
ments of faith and conscience still unblunted, capable of being
revived and made effective, if only it were possible to break up
the overlaying crust of habit, indifference and sin. In 1859 the
Presbyterian minister at Ballymena in Antrim noted precisely this:

> First the extraordinary conviction of sin which made the
> burden of sin loathsome and intolerable. The intense fear was
> in some cases accompanied by extreme physical weakness or col-
> lapse, which lasted minutes, hours or even days. In the mental
> realm memory was revived inconceivably, past sins being re-
> membered vividly as well as long-forgotten passages of
> Scripture learned in childhood.[10]

If, particularly in urban England, the protective crust, the ' hard
ground ', were not only getting thicker and harder, but the residual religious faith beneath were disappearing, there were difficult days to come, though Moody and Sankey's hymns provided
a remarkably successful culture for that undenominational
tradition which had always been the core of popular evangelicalism.

The second sign of the times was the new mood in the teetotal movement. Teetotalism, as distinct from temperance, had originated as a piece of working-class self-help, a moral or religious programme from below, and as such it was opposed by the churches generally (though not by the ministry universally). Those communions which had a powerful stake in working-class religion and especially the Roman Catholics and the Primitive Methodists, soon responded to the astonishing pressure which built up, but even here the first impression was unfavourable. In the minutes of the Stalybridge Primitive Methodist circuit it was resolved

> September 1840. 'That the sacrament be not administered with Bread and water in any place. That Bro. Marriott be censured for his preaching politics and teetotallism at Hyde.'
> June 1845. 'That Bro. Compton . . . must not deliver Teetotal lectures when he should preach the gospel.'

The resistance of official Wesleyanism to the teetotal cause, and their efforts to close the chapels to its advocates are a famous story; less famous is the doctrinaire way the teetotal cause was pressed. The private correspondence leaves the impression that part of the attractiveness of teetotalism for the labourers of East Anglia, for example, was that it was a good way to create trouble for the Wesleyan preacher, and the preachers replied in kind.

> 'The writer of this,' commented a preacher on a letter to Jabez Bunting, 'is a most depraved person, notorious for his subtlety, falsehood and indeed for almost every evil work except that of drunkenness. Nothing higher can be said of his character than that he is a teetotaller, and as such has no special regard for the character of a Wesleyan minister.[11]

The teetotallers worked like the revivalists, seeking out the drunkards in their stews, and, with the pledge, bringing on a crisis like conversion or believer's baptism. Moreover they understood the need to provide an alternative set of social institutions in which the reclaimed might escape the cross-pressures of ordinary social life.

By 1850 huge numbers had been brought to the light by these methods, yet the strategy of the movement began to change, and so did its relations with the churches. For the successes of the teetotal movement seemed to bring the end of the liquor problem little nearer. The verdict of the American Temperance Union that 'moral suasion has well-nigh done its work'[12] was equally true of England (and also of the movements of religious propaganda which the teetotallers emulated). The teetotal movement therefore turned its energies to two new channels. It undertook a programme of mass education in the Sunday schools, with a view to creating anti-liquor sentiment before the drinking habit began; this had the incidental effect of changing the status of the pledge, which now became a normal incident in an alcohol-free upbringing, much as infant baptism was a normal incident in Christian upbringing. They also attempted to reinforce the individual appeal by manipulating social arrangements, forming the United Kingdom Alliance in 1853, to secure total prohibition or some variety of the Maine Law. This was a most important moment for the whole milieu in which teetotallism had sprung up, for in most respects its prejudices were against state action. It was also an important moment for the question, beloved of American and entirely neglected by English historians, whether evangelicalism was capable of generating social policy. Certainly the thin end of the teetotal wedge could lead to demands for other forms of social regulation, even for socialism.

The movement of the teetotallers towards social engineering might have been expected to inflame their difficult relations with ecclesiastical statesmen. In fact exactly the opposite happened, and by the 'seventies all the main churches had more or less official temperance programmes and organisations, all, that is, except the Primitive Methodists, who took it for granted that every preacher and member was a total abstainer, and left the propaganda to the Band of Hope. One of the reasons for the churches' change of front was the recognition that, in so far as the teetotal movement put its members on the path to respectability, it put them in the way of church membership, and hence offered the churches an impulse they could not afford to neglect. In the hottest days of Wesleyan opposition to total abstinence, Bunting was informed that the new movement was growing fast in York.

. . . Wherever these Societies have made any progress, there has been a proportionate accession to the Church of God, from the ranks of Teetotalers. But I have also noticed with regret, that in consequence of the zealous and almost general advocacy of Teetotalism by the *ministers of the Wesleyan Methodist Association, they* are securing the majority of those new converts, who, along with religious instruction, are learning notions very prejudicial to our own body. I am convinced the ' Association ' is thus gaining much strength, and the new converts are sincere, bold and zealous men, who bid fair to make Methodists of the right sort. I feel sorry that we who have so much influence, and such superior accommodation for converts, should lose such men, but it is quite natural for the Teetotalers to flock to those places on the Sabbath where their advocates preach, and to those societies who lend their chapels and schoolrooms.

When Hugh Bourne ascribed in his journal the doubling of the membership of the Durham circuit in one quarter of 1843 to the fact that all the preachers were teetotallers, he was doubtless thinking not merely of their zeal, but of their foothold in another movement which was adding its power to the church.[13]

The teetotal impulse was never powerful enough to solve the problems, for example, of the Methodist reformers, and the new policies of the churches were not merely the baptism of a new ally into the fold; they were also an acknowledgement of the very difficulties which had transformed the teetotal movement itself. The declining value of the direct approach suggested that social engineering might be an assistance. The Nonconformist Conscience was not exclusively nonconformist, and was a platform rather than a conscience, a platform of causes like the temperance cause, which could only be secured through liberal political action. And in its turn, common action through this secular vehicle was another confession of the failure of the high-powered denominationalism of the middle of the century. It needed only the tide of liberal theology which early in the present century forced its way in everywhere, and, in the less institutionalised communities like the Congregationalists and Primitives, swept all before it, to obliterate the old denominational landmarks almost altogether.

But the churches were mostly dependent on the limited efficiency of their pastoral machines in dealing with a society stratified by class, but no longer in a state of vigorous class conflict. How difficult common worship and the sharing of common values were was admitted even by those who thought them possible.

> An association, consisting of the gentry, trades people, and other competent persons, having for its object the care and improvement of children on the Sunday, might be fraught with the greatest benefit, and soften the asperities of competition; nor would it be necessary for such an association to be so intimate as to be alike unpleasant to all parties of dissimilar habits and pursuits. A union of this description could not exist; but one having regard to the feelings and conduct originating in long-established custom would be sufficient for all practical purposes, and gradually lead to a closer approximation.

Where a movement was fluid enough to offer an alternative to class stratification, it might make rapid progress, as the teetotal movement did in its early days. ' In our society we pay no deference to rank or station; all our members are equal, and we have no privates, no drones; all must labour. All are kings and priests unto God.' In developing communities, not yet congealed into an established order of rank and station, the old methods might still flourish. A Methodist analysis of the mid-'sixties, making no bones about the decline of the movement, relative or absolute, in old areas of strength, found that

> in a number of rising towns, and of newly occupied and largely peopled manufacturing neighbourhoods, Methodism has within the last twenty years developed more rapidly, more generously, and in better and happier proportions than has perhaps been known in its history. Such instances have occurred especially in Lancashire, some parts of Yorkshire and Staffordshire, in Durham and in South Wales.[14]

Difficulties were to be expected when the mobility went out of the new towns in another generation, and in due course they made themselves felt. When secular forces generated a great new wave of social mobility in the mid-twentieth century, they were too late to benefit the churches.

References

Introduction (pages 1-6)

1 R. Huish. *The private and political life of Henry Hunt Esq., M.P.* (London, 1836) i 16.

2 T. P. Bunting, *The Life of Jabez Bunting* (London, 1859-87) i. 22-5: J. Macdonald, *Memoirs of Joseph Benson* (London, 1822) p. 99: *Some annals of Great Bridgwater Street Chapel, Manchester* (Manchester, 1888) p. 7: W. Jones, *Memoirs of the life, ministry and writings of the Rev. Rowland Hill* (London, 1834) pp. 38, 143: E. Sidney, *The life of Sir Richard Hill* (London, 1839) pp. 455-6: R. W. Dale, *History of English Congregationalism* (2nd. ed. London, 1907) p. 591.

3 *The autobiography of the Rev. William Jay* ed. G. Redford & J. A. James (London, 1854) pp. 300-327 (For a more sophisticated controversy on the same theme, see Ford K. Brown, *Fathers of the Victorians* (Cambridge, 1961) ch. 12, and David Newsome, ' Fathers and sons ', *Historical Journal* vi. 295-310): C. Smyth, *Simeon and Church order* (Cambridge, 1940) pp. 249, 255, 281, 300, 310: Macdonald, *Benson*, p. 299.

Chapter 1 (pages 7-20)

1 S. Greatheed, *General union recommended to real Christians* (London, 1798) pp. 75-6.

2 *Conversations between the Church of England and the Methodist Church: an interim statement* (London, 1958) p. 19: P. F. Rudge, *Ministry and management* (London, 1968).

3 For a fuller development of this theme see my paper on ' The tithe question in England in the early nineteenth century ', *Journal of Ecclesiastical History*, xvi. 67-81.

4 *Reports of the society for bettering the condition and increasing the comforts of the poor* (4th ed. London, 1805-8) i. 164: ii. 5.

5 R. A. Ingram, *The causes of the increase of Methodism and dissenssion* (London, 1807) p. 87: Thomas Taylor, *A defence of the Methodists who do not attend the national church* (reprinted, Newry, 1814) p. 11 (Cf. M.C.A. MSS. George Baldwin to Joseph Benson, 22 February 1793: Tyerman MSS. i. fo. 122): M.C.A. MSS. Joseph Cownley to Joseph Benson, 5 July 1791: S. Drew, *The Life of Thomas Coke* (London, 1817) pp. 289, 293: ' The Parish ' is partly and inaccurately published in J. W. Tibble, *The poems of John Clare*

(London, 1935) i. 542 seq.: *The Letters of John Clare* ed. J. W. and Anne Tibble (London, 1951) p. 161.

6 B. Gregory, *Sidelights on the conflicts of Methodism, 1827-52* (London, 1899) pp. 179, 247.

7 *Evangelical Magazine* v. 279: *Report from the clergy of a district of the diocese of Lincoln* (London, 1800) pp. 9, 11-12; *Methodist Magazine* xxiv. 249.

8 J. Bogue and J. Bennett, *History of the dissenters* (London, 1808-12) iv. 389-90: [James Bean], *Zeal without innovation: or the present state of religion and morals considered* (London, 1808) p. 3. The same roving tendency affected urban Sunday Schools, *Sunday School Repository ii.* (1815) p. 174: *Publications of the late Rev. Joseph Bealey . . .* (Manchester, 1814) p. 24: C. A. Bolton, *Salford diocese and its Catholic past* (Salford, 1950) p. 91: John Rippon, *Baptist Annual Register* (London, 1793-1802) iii. 21.

9 C. Bayley, *An address to the public on Sunday schools* (Manchester, 1784) pp. 4-5: *Manchester Mercury*, 3 November, 10 November, 1789: J. Bennett, *The advantages of Sunday schools* (Manchester, 1785) pp. 4, 11, 13, Chetham's Library, Manchester. MS. Minute books of the Manchester Sunday school committee, 7 March 1785. (Hundreds of copies of Watts's *Divine songs for children* were circulated as school prizes. *Ibid.* 4 April 1785): C. W. Bardsley, *Memorials of St. Ann's Church* (Manchester, 1877) p. 120n.

10 W. Turner, *Sunday schools recommended . . .* (Newcastle, 1786) p. 40: J. Toulmin, *The rise, progress and effects of Sunday schools* (Taunton, 1789) p. 15: *A report on the present state of the Stockport Sunday School . . .* (Stockport, 1806): Benjamin Smith, *Methodism in Macclesfield* (London, 1875) p. 223: John Earles, *Streets and houses of old Macclesfield* (Macclesfield, 1915) pp. 83-4: W. H. Oliver Lake, *A centenary history of the Wesleyan Methodist Church of Bollington in the Macclesfield circuit* (London, 1908), p. 29: E. Orme, *A brief centenary history of the Hurdsfield Sunday school, Macclesfield* (Macclesfield, 1908) p. 11: H. F. Mathews, *Methodism and the education of the people, 1791-1851* (London, 1949) p. 44: Stockport Sunday School MSS. Notes by Ben Hadfield on the *Annual report of Thornsett Sunday school,* 1797: H. F. Burder, *Memoir of Rev. George Burder* (London, 1833) p. 133: *Hill Top Methodist Church centenary: Burslem Sunday school ter-jubilee, 1787-1937* (n.pl.or d. [1937]) p. 3: *Victoria County History of Staffordshire* viii. 278: C. Hulbert, *Memoirs of seventy years of an eventful life* (2nd ed. Shrewsbury, 1852): Hulbert's obituary, *Shrewsbury Chronicle,* 6 November 1857.

11 R. O. Ball, *One more light. A history of Middleton Junction Methodist Church, 1800-1951* (Middleton, 1951) p. 8: H. Howarth, *A brief account of Baillie St. Sunday school, Rochdale . . .* (Rochdale, 1883) p. 14: H. Fishwick, *History of the Parish of Rochdale* (Rochdale, 1889) p. 259: W. H. Mowat, *Rochdale parish church reunion souvenir, 1903* (Rochdale, 1903) pp. 3-5: *The Methodist Church, Baillie Street, Rochdale. A centenary history, 1837-1937* (Rochdale, 1937) p. 14: G. A. Weston, ' The Baptists of Northwestern England, 1750-1850 ' (Unpublished Sheffield Ph.D. thesis, 1969) pp. 97, 491: E. Hudson, *History of Delph Methodism from 1750 to 1850* (Oldham, 1902) p. 20: C. A. O'Neil, *An account of the origin of Sunday schools in Oldham and its vicinity* (Oldham, 1848) pp. 7, 15: *Cowhill School, 1849-1949* (Oldham, 1949) p. 6: Chetham's Library. Phelps collection. Cuttings on Sunday schools, letter from Thomas Barnes, November 7, 1793 to the *European Magazine* (December 1793) reprinted in *Manchester City News,* 24 November

1900. Cf. J. Mayer, *A defence of Sunday schools attempted* (Stockport, 1798) p. 52: *Arminian Magazine* xi. 489-90, J. K. Meir, 'The origin and development of the Sunday school movement in England from 1780 to 1880 in relation to the state provision of education' (Unpublished Edinburgh Ph.D. thesis, 1954) p. 93: M.C.A. MSS. Thomas Preston to James Everett, 1 September, 1826.

12 *United Methodist Free Church Magazine* 1863 p. 82. Cf C. Bayley, *Address to public on Sunday schools* pp. 4-6: *Journal of John Wesley* ed. N. Curnock (London, 1938) vii. 3: *Wheeler's Manchester Chronicle*, 12 November 1791: R. Roberts, *History of Methodism in Almondbury* (London, 1864) p. 28: Mathews, *Methodism and the education of the people* p. 40: W. Sessions, *York and its associations with the early history of the Sunday school movement* (York, 1882) pp. 4, 10: J. Salt, 'Early Sheffield Sunday schools', *Transactions of Hunter Archaeological Society* 1967, p. 180: J. J. Graham, *History of Wesleyan Methodism in Sheffield Park* (Sheffield, 1914) pp. 16-18: M.C.A. MS. Scrapbook of James Everett fo. 411.

13 Meir, 'Origin and development of Sunday school movement' p. 80 [Colchester]: W. Brewers and F. H. Owers, *The story of a hundred years, 1808-1908. Being an account of the rise and progress of the Chelmsford London Road Congregational Sunday school* (Chelmsford, 1908) p. 14: J. Liddon, *The general religious instruction of the poor, the surest means of promoting universal national happiness* (London, 1792) [Hemel Hempstead]: J. Ivimey, *History of the English Baptists* (London, 1811-1830) iv. 72-3: A. C. Underwood, *History of the English Baptists* pp. 180-81 (Fox also launched one of the undenominational monthlies, *The Protestant Dissenter's Magazine* in 1794): W. H. Watson, *History of the Sunday School Union* (London, 1853) pp. 10-13. The Wesleyans set up a corresponding committee in London to support their own work, but exclusiveness had not yet come upon them; in 1805 one of the earliest Sunday School Union sermons was powerfully preached by Jabez Bunting who was shortly to boycott even Methodist schools for laxity. *Methodist Magazine* xxv. 389: S. Warren & J. Stephens, *Chronicles of Wesleyan Methodism* (London, 1827) i. 395-6: W. H. Groser, *A hundred years' work for the children* (London, 1903) p. 10: T. Pole, *History of the origin and progress of adult Schools* . . . (Bristol, 2nd ed. 1816): *Sunday School Repository* (1815) ii. 25, 27-9, 230-32: *Evangelical Magazine* v. 381: Rippon, *Baptist Annual Register* i. 430: J. Sibree and M. Caston, *Independency in Warwickshire* (London, 1855) p. 252: C. I. Foster, *An errand of mercy: the evangelical united front, 1790-1837* (Chapel Hill, N.C., 1960).

14 R. B. McDowell, *Irish public opinion, 1750-1850* (London, 1944) pp. 72-3: J. Corrie, *Sketch of the character of the late Rev. Wm. Hawkes of Manchester* (Manchester, 1820) pp. 4, 5, 8.

15 Sidney, *Sir Richard Hill* p. 185.

16 Bogue and Bennett, *History of dissenters* iv. 237: *Evangelical Magazine* ii. 458: J. H. Newman, *Apologia Pro Vita Sua* (ed. London, 1900) pp. 9-10: A. W. Brown, *Recollections of the conversation parties of the Rev. Charles Simeon* (London, 1862) p. 269 (Cf. Smyth, *Simeon* p. xii.: M. M. Preston, *Memoranda of the Rev. Charles Simeon* (London, 1840) pp. 24-6): Wm. Jay, *Autobiography* pp. 167-8.

17 *The works of the late Wm. Gadsby, Manchester,* ed. J. Gadsby (London, 1851) p. 55: Sidney, *Sir Richard Hill* p. 176: John Eyre, *Union and friendly intercourse recommended among such of the various denominations of Calvinists*

U

and the members of the late Mr. Wesley's Societies as agree in the \essential *truths of the Gospel* (London, 1798) pp. 25, 31-2: T. Taylor, *The Reconciler* . . . (Liverpool, 1806) pp. v-vi (Cf .A. Strachan, *Recollections of the life and times of Rev. George Lowe* (London, 1848) p. 130): Rippon, *Baptist Annual Register* i. 17-25, 274: *Baptist Magazine* iv. 434: Strachan, *George Lowe* p. 197: *The Works of Robert Hall* ed. O. Gregory (London, 1832) ii. 14, 162. (Even in 1780 the New Road Baptist Church, Oxford, had been founded on a covenant granting membership and full communion to paedo-baptists): E. Parsons, *Civil, ecclesiastical, literary, commercial history of Leeds and the manufacturing district of Yorkshire* (Leeds, 1834) ii. 18: Walter Wilson, *History and antiquities of dissenting churches and meeting-houses in London, Westminster and Southwark* (London, 1808-14) iv. 545-6: C. Hulbert, *A concise and impartial statement of the religious opinions which divide the British Christian Church* (Shrewsbury, 1809) pp. 49-50: Macdonald, *Benson* p. 362.

Chapter 2 (pages 21-53)

1 U. Henriques, *Religious toleration in England, 1787-1833* (London, 1961) pp. 59-63: *Manchester Mercury* 15 December, 1789: 23 February, 1790.

2 H. F. Burder, *George Burder* pp. 145-6: *Manchester Mercury* 9 March, 2 March 1790: B. L. Manning, *The Protestant Dissenting Deputies* (Cambridge, 1952) p. 218: Bogue and Bennett, *History of the dissenters* (1833 ed.) ii. 478.

3 R. B. Rose, ' The Priestley riots of 1791 ', *Past and Present* no. 18 pp. 68-88: Macdonald, *Benson*, p. 223: [Samuel Heywood] *High Church politics* (London, 1792) p. 59: Bogue & Bennett, *History of dissenters* (1833 ed.) ii. 485.

4 A Prentice, *Historical Sketches and personal recollections of Manchester* (2nd ed. London, 1851) pp. 7, 9: J. Pope, *Two sermons preached to a congregation of Protestant dissenters at Blackley* (London, 1792) p. 41: *Manchester Mercury* 11 November 1794: 27 January, 3 February, 10 February 1795: H. T. Crofton, *History of Newton Chapelry* Vol. II pt. ii. Chetham Soc. series LIV (Manchester, 1905) p. 197: W. Entwisle, *Memoir of Rev. Joseph Entwisle* (8th ed. London, 1862) p. 133.

5 On this see I. Sellars, ' Liverpool Nonconformity, 1786-1914 ' (Unpublished Keele Ph.D. thesis, 1969) pp. 271-5.

6 H. S. Skeats and C. S. Miall, *History of the Free Churches of England, 1688-1891* (London, 1891) pp. 403-4: J. Bull, *Memorials of the Rev. William Bull of Newport Pagnell* (London, 1864) pp. 218-19, 221: [Samuel Heywood] *High Church politics* pp. 54-6: W. Stokes, *The history of the Midland Association of the Baptist Churches from . . . 1655 to 1855* (London, 1855) p. 55: A. Brockett, *Nonconformity in Exeter* (Manchester, 1962) pp. 142-5: W. Wilson, *Meeting-houses in London, Westminster and Southwark* iv. 549: G. A. Williams, *Artisans and sansculottes* (London, 1968) pp. 13, 65-6. Sellars, ' Liverpool Nonconformity ' p. 275.

7 L. Radzinowicz, *History of criminal law* (London, 1948-68) iii. 238-46, 513-20.

8 J. R. Western, ' The Volunteer movement as an anti-revolutionary force, 1793-1801 ', *English Historical Review* 1956, pp. 603-14.

9 J. P. Dodd, ' South Lancashire, a study of the crop returns for 1795-1801 ,' *Transactions of the Historic Society of Lancashire and Cheshire* cxvii. 98, 102, 106.

10 Radzinowicz, *History of criminal law*, iii. 310-11.

11 M. C. A. Tyerman MSS. i. fo. 122: ii. fo. 32: M.C.A. MSS. Thomas Coke to Joseph Benson, 15 July 1791.

12 George Smith, *History of Wesleyan Methodism* (London, 1857-61) ii. 32: M.C.A. MSS. Thomas Coke to Joseph Benson, 15 July 1791: S. Bradburn to R. Rodda, 19 April 1792: Tyerman MSS. iii. fos. 203-5: Entwisle, *Memoir of Joseph Entwisle* p. 88. The Conference decision of 1791 was said to be a prudential resolution inspired by fears created by the Birmingham riots. [J. Blackwell], *Life of Alexander Kilham* (London, 1838) pp. 147-8.

13 M.C.A. MSS. Adam Clarke to H. Sandwith, June 16, 1829 (a copy appended to H. Sandwith to T. Jackson, October, 1832): Tyerman MSS i. fos. 122; 134-6; iii. fos. 194-6 (Partly printed in *Wesleyan Methodist Magazine* lxviii. 214), 222-4: Harman collection of MS. Letters of Methodist Presidents I. fo. 11, S. Bradburn to R. Rodda, 27 December 1791 (copy in MS. Scrapbook of James Everett fo. 437): M.C.A. MSS. S. Bradburn to R. Rodda, 23 June, 19 April 1792.

14 M.C.A. Tyerman MSS. i. fos. 130-1, 134-5: M.C.A. MSS. S. Bradburn to R. Rodda, 23 June 1792; 7 December 1791.

15 Smith, *History of Wesleyan Methodism* ii. 698: Entwisle, *Memoir of Joseph Entwisle* pp. 98-9. Cf. M.C.A. Tyerman MSS. iii. fos. 254-5: M.C.A. MSS. Samuel Frost to J. Benson, 12 September 1794: T. Jones to J. Benson, 31 January 1795: Macdonald, *Benson* p. 239.

16 Smith, *History of Wesleyan Methodism* ii. 26-8, 104: *Wesleyan Methodist Magazine* lxviii. 319: xxi. 401 seq. (This episode was prudently omitted from Macdonald's *Benson* pp. 271-2): M.C.A. MSS. Folder entitled ' Benson, Joseph. Re. Portland Place dispute'. James Creighton to J. Benson, 8 October 1794: Printed Minutes 16 September 1794 in Thos. Coke's MS. corr.: J. Moon to J. Benson, 17 October 1794: Z. Yewdall to J. Benson, 14 October 1794: MS. Memorandum ' Bristol Conf. dispute '94: To charge of laying train to blow up Methm.': R. Rodda to J. Benson, 1 September 1794: T. Jones to J. Benson, 15 October, 6 December 1794: Peter Mill to J. Benson, 26 October 1794: Wm. Myles to J. Benson, 4 October 1794: M. Longridge to J. Benson, 9 October, 1794: E. Lewty to J. Benson, 29 December 1794: Wm. Pine to J. Benson, 24 October 1796: D. Barraclough to T. Crowther, 27 August 1798: Adam Clarke to George Marsden, 8 January 1795: Samuel Frost to J. Benson, 12 September 1794: M.C.A. Tyerman MSS. iii fos. 250-2: J. Kendall, *Miscellaneous and free structures on the practical position of the Wesleyan connexion towards the Church of England* . . . (London, 1836) p. 20.

17. M.C.A. MSS. Letters of Presidents of the Wesleyan Conference collected by J. E. Wright, J. Benson to   ?   ?   . 26 April 1800: T. Allin *et al.*, *The jubilee of the Methodist New Connexion* (London, 1848) p. 82: M.C.A. MSS. T. Coke to J. Benson, 21 December 1795: T. Coke to Messrs. Bogie, Cummins and Eversfield, 19 September 1794: J. Creighton to J. Benson, 8 October 1794: T. Jones to J. Benson, 15 October, 27 November, 6 December 1794: 31 January 1795: E. Lewty to J. Benson, 29 December 1794: Samuel Frost to J. Benson, 12 September 1794: T. Hanby to J. Entwisle, 1 November 1794: Mrs. S. Crosby to J. Benson, 2 October, 28 October, 5 December 1794: 11 March 1795: Tyerman MSS. i. fo. 27: iii fos. 250-2, 254-5, 263-5: J. Everett, *Adam Clarke portrayed* (London, 1843-9) i. 329: Macdonald, *Benson* p. 275: Entwisle, *Memoir of Entwisle* pp. 126, 129: *Wesleyan Methodist Magazine* lxviii. 325-6: Smith, *History of Wesleyan Methodism* ii. 43 (The

Plan of Pacification is printed as Appendix D to Smith, *op cit.* ii. 699-700).

18 M.C.A. MSS. Adam Clarke to George Marsden, 8 January 1795: *Wesleyan Methodist Magazine* lxviii. 314 (Reprinted in Smith, *History of Wesleyan Methodism* ii. 97-8. Jonathan Crowther put it thus: ' It is not and never was from a mere admiration of the *hierarchy*, but on the ground of its usefulness, that the Methodists have continued and still continue in the Church'. J. Crowther, *The crisis of Methodism* (Bristol 1795) p. 6): Smith, *History of Wesleyan Methodism* ii. 124, 703: M.C.A. MS Letters of Presidents of Wesleyan Methodist Conference Vol. I 1744-1838 fo. 113. George Marsden's notes on the Lichfield meeting: M.C.A. MSS. S. Bradburn to T. Coke, 17 April 1794: Wm. Thompson to J. Benson, 8 May 1794: Wm. Thompson to R. Rodda, 19 May 1794.

19 T. Allin, *Jubilee of Methodist New Connexion* pp. 85-6: [John Blackwell], *Life of Alexander Kilham* p. 211: M.C.A. MS. Bradburn Papers, S. Bradburn to Mr. Reynolds, 12 April 1796: S. Bradburn to J. Benson, 5 February 1800.

20 M.C.A. MSS. T. Coke to J. Benson, 21 December 1795: T. Coke & J. Pawson to J. Benson, n.d. [endorsed: December 1795]: T. Coke to J. Benson, 6 February, 1796: MS. Bradburn Papers, S. Bradburn to Mr. Reynolds, 12 April 1796: M.C.A. MSS. F. Wrigley to J. Benson, [27] February 1796: W. Thompson to J. Benson, 2 February 1796: W. Thompson to F. Wrigley, 27 February 1796.

21 Macdonald, *Benson* p. 301: Entwisle, *Memoir of Entwisle* p. 141: [R. B. Aspland] *The rise, progress and present influence of Wesleyan Methodism* (London, 1831) p. 38.

22 Hartley Victoria College, Manchester. MS. Kilham Papers, T. Welch to A. Kilham, 8 August 1797: A Kilham to J. Harrop, 19 September 1796: M. Longridge to J. Harrop, 11 March 1796: Robert Hall to A. Kilham, 4 May 1798: M.C.A. Tyerman MSS. iii fo. 191: Macdonald, *Benson* pp. 310-11: Printed broadsheet, ' To members and friends of the Methodist Society ', signed, Henry Longden and Edward Miller, M.C.A. MSS. G. Highfield to J. Benson, 23 June 1797: R. E. Leader, *Sheffield in the eighteenth century* (Sheffield, 1901) pp. 336-7: J. Salt, ' Early Sheffield Sunday schools ', *Transactions of Hunter Archaeological Society* 1967 p. 80: Entwisle, *Memoir of Entwisle* pp. 147-8: E. A. Rose, *Methodism in Ashton-under-Lyne* (Ashton, 1967-9) i. 32-41.

23 Hartley Victoria College, Manchester. MS. Kilham Papers. D. Alexander to A. Kilham, June 1797: M.C.A. MSS. R. Emmet to J. Benson, 13 March 1797: Tyerman MSS. iii fo. 320: J. Crowther, *The Methodist manual* (Halifax, 1810) p. 31: M.C.A. MS. Letters of Presidents of Wesleyan Methodist Conference I (1744-1838) J. Pawson to G. Marsden, 3 September 1800.

24 *Manchester Mercury* 15 November 1796: 24 April 1798: 20 August 1799: 29 June, 13 July, 10 August 1802: 8 May 1804: R. I. & S. Wilberforce, *The life of Wilberforce* (London, 1838) ii. 163: Chester C.R.O. MS. Episcopal Visitation of Chester Diocese, April 1804. Return for Manchester Collegiate Church.

25 In Chester the Methodists collected funds from the town generally until the mid-nineties. J. K. Meir, ' Origin and development of the Sunday school movement ', p. 86: M.C.A. Tyerman MSS. ii fo. 201: Stockport Sunday School MSS. Ben Hadfield's lecture on ' The Methodist Sunday School, Stockport, 1793-1805 ': Mathews, *Methodism and education* pp. 43-60: Burder, *Memoir*

of *Burder* p. 133: J. Bennett, *Advantages of Sunday Schools* p. 5: Joseph Aston, *A picture of Manchester* (Manchester, n.d. [1816]) p. 139: Bradburn's diary, 30 Sept. 1799, printed in both E. W. Bradburn, *Memoirs of the late Rev. Samuel Bradburn* (London, 1816) pp. 128-9, and T. W. Blanshard, *Life of Samuel Bradburn, the Methodist Demosthenes* (2nd. ed. London, 1871) pp. 174-5: C. Bayley, *Questions for children on the ministerial office* (Manchester, 1795).

26 See the *Annual Reports* of the Methodist Sunday School in Stockport for those years.

27 J. Mayer, *A defence of Sunday schools attempted in a series of letters to the Rev. M. Olerenshaw* (Stockport, 1798) pp. 52, 79-80, 83: Stockport Sunday School MSS. Ben Hadfield's papers. MS. copies of letters of W. Radcliffe to T. Whitaker, 25 September 1798: A. Bowden to same, 8 December 1798. Also *Annual report of the Thornsett Sunday School*. 10 January 1797: M. Olerenshaw, *Sermon on the religious education of children and the usefulness of Sunday schools* (Manchester, 1798): T. Whitaker, *Four letters to Mr. J. Mayer of Stockport on his defence of Sunday schools* (Manchester, 1798) (For Olerenshaw and Whitaker, C. Hulbert, *Memoirs of seventy years* p. 36: Thomas Wade, *The character of a good man* (Bury, 1819)): E. P. Thompson, *The making of the English working class* (London, 1963) p. 378: *Anti-Jacobin* iii. 321: S. Horsley, *Charge to the clergy of his diocese, 1800* in his *Charges* (Dundee, 1813) pp. 145-6.

28 Chetham's Library, Manchester. MS. Minute Books of Manchester Sunday School Committee, *passim*: C. W. Bardsley, *Memorials of St. Ann's Church* pp. 122, 124-7: E. Farrow and C. J. Wallworth, *A souvenir of Great Bridgwater street Wesleyan Chapel and Sunday School, Manchester* (Manchester 1898) pp. 19-20, 35-6, 38-9: J. Benson, *A vindication of the people called Methodists* (London, 1800) p. 24: M.C.A. MSS. M. Longridge to J. Benson, 26 May 1798: *A statement of the original and present condition of the Sunday schools for all denominations in Manchester* (Manchester, 1836).

29 *A report on the state of Sunday schools in Stockport, 1797-8* (One copy in Stockport Sunday School MSS., Ben Hadfield's papers): *Annual report of the Stockport Sunday School, 1810* (Stockport, 1810) p. 5.

30. H. Howarth, *Baillie St. Sunday School* p. 9: W. H. Mowat, *Rochdale Parish Church Sunday School Souvenir* pp. 5-9: *United Methodist Free Church Magazine* 1863 p. 82: Leeds Central Library John [should be Thomas] Wray's MS. History of Methodism in Leeds viii. fo. 135 M.C.A. MS. History of Methodism in Leeds ii fo. 87: John Ward, *Historical sketches of the rise and progress of Methodism in Bingley* (Bingley, 1863) p. 55: Richard Roberts, *History of Methodism in Almondbury* pp. 28-9.

31 Robert Hall, *Works* vii. 334.

32 M. Horne, *Letters on missions addressed to the British churches* (Bristol, 1794) pp. 20-1: R. Lovett, *History of London Missionary Society, 1795-1895* (London, 1899) i. 51, 75-7: J. Eyre, *Union and friendly intercourse recommended* pp. 5-6: Bunting, *Life of Bunting* i. 214: Jay, *Autobiography* pp. 160-73: Macdonald, *Benson*, pp. 361, 465: *Evangelical Magazine* i. 3; x. 38; xi. 38: Entwisle, *Memoir of Entwisle* p. 31: A. S. Ruston, *Wesleyan home missions in Chatteris* (Printed for private circulation, 1864) p. 16: *Baptist Magazine* i. 157.

33 *Evangelical Magazine* v. pp. ii-iii, 276-9: *The life of Thomas Taylor,*

chiefly written by himself in *The lives of early Methodist preachers* ed. T. Jackson (London, 1838) iii. 343: J. Rippon, *Baptist Annual Register* ii. 459-64: R. A. Ingram, *Causes of the increase of Methodism* pp. 84-6: Bogue and Bennett, *History of dissenters* iv. 204-5: Wilson, *Dissenting churches of London, Westminster & Southwark* iv. 545-6.

34 Richard Treffry, *Remarks on revivals of religion with brief notices of the recent prosperity of the work of God in Hull* (London, 1827) p. 7: *Report from the clergy of the diocese of Lincoln* (London, 1800). Cf. D. Davies, *The case of the labourers in husbandry* (London, 1795) p. 94.

35 Josiah Bull, *Memorials of Rev. Wm. Bull of Newport Pagnell* (London, 1864) pp. 102-3, 257: *Evangelical Magazine* v. 276-9.

36 S. Greatheed, *General union recommended to real Christians* (London, 1798) pp. xiv, 72, 75: *Evangelical Magazine* vi. 30, 256-7; ix. 253: J. Sibree & M. Caston, *Independency in Warwickshire* (London, 1855) pp. 393-8.

37 *Evangelical Magazine* iii. 257: v. 253, 255, 383-4, 424, 472-3: vi. 424, 426, 511: vii. 557: viii. 217: x. 290: Rippon, *Baptist Annual Register* iii. 424-5: D. Douglas, *History of the Baptist churches in the North of England* (London, 1846) pp. 241-2.

38 Rippon, *Baptist Annual Register* ii. 405, 465, 484: iii. 184, 339: John Browne, *History of Congregationalism . . . in Norfolk and Suffolk* (London, 1877) pp. 203-4: *Evangelical Magazine* iv. 206: v. 298-300, 381: vi. 1, 425: vii. 128: J. Waddington, *Congregational History* (London, 1869-80) iv. iii, 218, 253: R. Slate, *Brief history of the rise and progress of Lancashire Congregational Union . . .* (London, 1840) pp. 5-6: G. A. Weston, ' Baptists of North-western England ' p. 76: W. T. Whiteley, *Baptists of North-west England, 1649-1913* p. 169: G. Burder, *Village Sermons* 7 vols. (London, 1797-1816). (Apart from a Welsh edition, and editions in America, these sermons reached a 14th edition in England in 1849. Burder was a literary hack only less productive than John Wesley. Cf. *Evangelical Magazine* vii. 33, 74): J. Bennett, *History of the dissenters 1808-1838* (London, 1839) p. 136: J. Ivimey, *History of the English Baptists* iv. 72-3: *Baptist Magazine* v. 279: Jay, *Autobiography* p. 129.

39 Horsley, *Charges* p. 145: Wilberforce, *Life of Wilberforce* ii. 361: Wm. Kingsbury, *An apology for village preachers* (Southampton, 1798) pp. 35-6: J. Petty, *History of the Primitive Methodist Connexion . . .* (ed. London, 1864) p. 13.

40 Robert Young, *Showers of blessing, or sketches of revivals of religion in the Wesleyan Methodist Connexion* (London, 1844) p. 415: *Methodist Magazine* xxi. 240 seq.: xxiv. 114n: Joseph Nightingale, *Portraiture of Methodism . . .* (London, 1807) pp. 166-8: M.C.A. Tyerman MSS. ii. fos. 258, 269: Thos. Wray's MS. History of Methodism in Leeds v. fos. 39-49: Bogue and Bennett, *History of dissenters* (1833 ed.) ii. 559. For Leeds: Leeds Central Library. John [should be Thomas] Wray's MS. History of Methodism in Leeds xi. fos. 131-9. For Manchester M.C.A. Tyerman MSS. ii. fo. 255; *Arminian Magazine* xviii. 76. In the late 'nineties, the young Jabez Bunting was involved in this work: J. H. Huddleston, *History of Grosvenor Street Wesleyan Chapel, Manchester, 1820-1920* (Manchester, 1920) p. 3.

41 *Report from clergy of diocese of Lincoln* p. 12.

42 Bull, *Memorials of William Bull* p. 246: M.C.A. MSS. Adam Clarke to George Marsden, April 8, 1800: *Evangelical Magazine* v. 279: vii. 413 *Anti-*

Jacobin ii. 218, 447: iii. 319-22: iv. 34: T. E. Owen, *Methodism unmasked, or the progress of puritanism from the sixteenth to the nineteenth century* (London, 1802) p. v.: J. Benson, *Vindication of the people called Methodists* p. 4: *A letter to the Lord Bishop of Lincoln* (London, 1800) pp. 8-10: Macdonald, *Benson* pp. 317, 319.

43 The report circulated not in Lincolnshire but in official circles in London. M.C.A. MS. Letters of Presidents of Wesleyan Conference collected by J. E. Wright, J. Benson to ? ? , 26 April 1800: Wm. Kingsbury, *An apology for village preachers*: Brian Monckhouse, *A letter to Wm. Kingsbury in answer to his apology for village preachers* (Salisbury, 1798): John Malham, *A broom for the conventicles* (Salisbury, 1798): *Anti-Jacobin* ii. 97-100, 215-19, 446-8: iii. 84-7, 319-22, 359: iv. 345-9, 352-63: v. 190. Bogue and Bennett, *History of dissenters* iv. 353: M.C.A. MSS. Sir R. Hill to [Jonathan Crowther?], 29 November 1798: For the hostility of evangelicals to Methodists: *Evangelical Magazine* xiii. 503: A. Pollard, ' Evangelical Parish Clergy, 1820-40 ', *Church Quarterly Review* 1958 p. 392. Cf. Bull, *Memoirs of Wm Bull* p. 221: Macdonald, *Benson* p. 392.

44 Hist. MSS. Comm. Fortescue MSS. vi. 5-21, 84, 86-9, 160, 181, 197: Wilberforce, *Life of Wilberforce* ii. 335-6, 361-5: Robert Hall, *Works* v. 421-2: *A Letter to the bishop of Lincoln*: G. Pretyman [-Tomline], *A charge delivered to the clergy of the diocese of Lincoln . . . in June and July, 1800* (London, 1800). On M. A. Taylor: *The contest: being a complete collection of the controversial papers, including poems and songs, published during the late contested election for the City of Durham, in March 1800* (Durham, 1800) pp. 5, 6, 23: *The addresses, poems, songs &c relative to the elections of the county and city of Durham* (Durham, 1802) pp. 44-5, 50, 52-3. Reprinted in *The representation of the county and city of Durham* (Durham, 1802): James Everett, *The village blacksmith, or, piety and usefulness exemplified in a memoir of . . . Sammy Hick* (5th ed. London, 1834) pp. 140-4, 232: Macdonald, *Benson* pp. 357-8: M.C.A. Tyerman MSS. iii. fos. 75-9. The heads of Taylor's bill were published in *Monthly Repository* 1814 p. 165.

45 M.C.A. Tyerman MSS. iii. fo. 79: Bunting, *Life of Bunting* i. 230.

Chapter 3 (pages 54-69)

1 [James Bean] *Zeal without innovation* pp. 1-4, 19-20: Hist. MSS. Comm. Fortescue MSS. vi. 21.

2 M.C.A. Tyerman MSS. iii. fo. 320: Lambeth Palace MSS. Archbishop Manners-Sutton's Visitation, 1806. SR/41 Lenham. Cf. SR/40 Barfrestone: G. F. Nott's Bampton Lectures, 1802, *Religious Enthusiasm* reviewed in *Methodist Magazine* xxx. 115 seq: A. Peel, *These Hundred Years* (London, 1931) p. 36: *Manchester Mercury* 26 July 1803 *et passim*: 25 December 1804: M.C.A. MSS. John Hughes to Joseph Benson, 10 June 1813: Robert Newton to Jabez Bunting, 1 December 1809.

3 G. Pellew, *Life and correspondence of the first viscount Sidmouth* (London, 1847) iii. 38-49: R. F. Wearmouth, *Methodism and the working-class movements of England, 1800-1851* (London, 1947) pp. 42-3: John Vickers, *Thomas Coke. Apostle of Methodism* (London, 1969) pp. 220-1: M.C.A. MSS. Joseph Entwisle to Jabez Bunting, 10 June, 29 June 1808: Jabez Bunting to [Richard Reece], 17 March 1809: Adam Clarke to George Marsden, 8 April 1800: 14 March 1810: 29 April, 6 May, 13 May 1811.

4 *Monthly Repository* 1811 pp. 299-308, 332-6, 358, 425-31, 490-5, 502-4: *Evangelical Magazine* xvii. 366-73: B. L. Manning, *Protestant Dissenting Deputies* pp. 132-8.

5 M.C.A. MSS. Joseph Butterworth to Thos. Allan 26 October: Thos. Allan to Jabez Bunting, 28 July 1810: *Wesleyan Methodist Magazine* cviii. 530-1n. Allan's MS. correspondence remains in the Methodist Church Archives, the bulk of it in boxes bearing his name, but a proportion scattered right through the general archive.

6 W. Wilson, *Dissenting meeting houses in London, Westminster and Southwark* iv. 541-2: *Evangelical Magazine* xvii. 376: xix. 304, 356: M.C.A. Thos. Allan MSS. ' Mr Gurney's Notes ': Lord Erskine to Thos. Allan, 17 May 1811: ' Sketch of business to be done agst. Lord Sidmouth's Bill ' (in Allan's hand).

7 T. Jackson, *Memoirs of the life and writings of the Rev. Richard Watson* (London, 1834) pp. 101-6: Bunting, *Life of Bunting* i. 371-4: M.C.A. MSS. Jabez Bunting to Theophilus Lessey, 31 May 1811.

8 M.C.A. Thos. Allan MSS. J[ohn] W[ard] to R. Middleton, Durham, 20 May 1811, enclosing Lord Holland to John Ward, 16 May 1811: *Wesleyan Methodist Magazine* lxviii. 538-9: Richard Reece, *A compendious martyrology, containing an account of the suffering and constancy of Christians in the different persecutions which have raged against them under pagan and popish governments* (London, 1812-15) p. iii. When tracts like this finally appeared they did double duty as anti-Catholic propaganda.

9 M.C.A. MS. petition originating in the Allan Library, entitled in a modern hand, ' Dr Coke's writing. Re Lord Sidmouth's Bill, 1811 ': Adam Clarke to George Marsden, 13 May 1811: Pellew, *Sidmouth* iii. 52-5: Many of the papers prepared for the Committee of Privileges are in M.C.A. Thos. Allan MSS., and the public proceedings were recorded in *Wesleyan Methodist Magazine* xxxiv. 530-60 and *Monthly Repository* 1811 pp. 491-5.

10 Wilberforce, *Life of Wilberforce* iii. 507-9: Pellew, *Sidmouth* iii. 59-60: Devon C.R.O. MS. Sidmouth Papers. ' Church ' to Sidmouth, 27 May 1811.

11 Pellew, *Sidmouth* iii. 62: M.C.A. Thos. Allan MSS. Sundius to Thos Allan, 22 May 1811. Thomas Allan's papers are full of warm letters of thanks to whig peers which consort oddly with the usual clichés about Wesleyan toryism. One of the iciest replies came from Liverpool himself, who expressed his assurance that the public would always prefer Anglicanism where church buildings and pious clergy were provided. M.C.A. Thos. Allan MSS. Lord Liverpool to Thomas Thompson, 27 May 1811. Sidmouth remained under high-church pressure to revive his bill, and Robert Southey was said to be investigating the domestic politics of the Methodist New Connexion with a view to pinning charges of radicalism on the whole Methodist body. Devon C.R.O. MS. Sidmouth Papers. T. Le Mesurier to Ld. Sidmouth, 3 June 1811: 17 October 1811: M.C.A. Thos. Allan MSS. J. Ward to Thos. Allan, 27 July 1811: Thomas Thompson to Thos. Allan, 25 January 1812.

12 M.C.A. MS. private notes in Thos. Allan MSS. Cf. *Evangelical Magazine* xx. 114-19, 194, 241-8.

13 *Wesleyan Methodist Magazine* xxxvi. 544-5: *Evangelical Magazine* xx. 243: M.C.A. Thos. Allan MSS. Draft letter, 1812 (The complaints of the Committee of Privileges were printed as a circular to superintendents of circuits, 31 July 1812, over the signatures of Adam Clarke and Joseph Butterworth, the

Methodist M.P. and famous law publisher): M.C.A. MSS. Walter Griffith to Jabez Bunting, 8 February 1812.

14 Pellew, *Sidmouth* iii. 61: Manning, *Protestant Dissenting Deputies* pp. 141-2: M.C.A. Thos. Allan MSS. Joseph Butterworth to Thos. Allan, transmitting resolution of the Committee of Privileges, 24 February 1812: 'Hints for conversation with Mr. Perceval': MS. Copy of a letter from Spencer Perceval, 10 April 1812: Allan's draft of the bill: pamphlet of documents relating to case later issued by the Committee of Privileges, entitled *Religious Toleration*.

15 There is an immense correspondence about all this in M.C.A. Thos. Allan MSS. May-August 1812: see also 'Notes of Observns to the Confce.', *ibid.*, and *Wesleyan Methodist Magazine* cviii. 530-1n.

16 *Baptist Magazine* v. 392-3.

17 *Monthly Repository* 1809 pp. 325, 608: 1810 pp. 60, 69: 1813 pp. 183, 185: 1817 pp. 88-9: 1818 p. 656: 1819 p. 673: 1823 pp. 341-6. Cf. J. H. Thom, *Letters embracing his life of John James Tayler* (London, 1872) i. 39: *Memorials of the late Rev. William M. Bunting* ed. G. Stringer Rowe (London, 1870) p. 35.

18 *Monthly Repository* 1809 p. 486: 1810 p. 65: 1813 p. 372: *Baptist Magazine* i. 70.

19 *Monthly Repository* 1809 p. 323, 487, 559: 1810 p. 64, 68, (Cf. J. Aston, *A picture of Manchester* pp. 96-7) 239, 490-4: 1812 pp. 51 seq, 120 seq: 1813 pp. 55 seq, 131 seq: 1815 pp. 261, 718 seq, 768 seq: 1816 pp. 680 seq: 1817 pp. 284-9, 717: 1818 pp. 57, 184, 273, 656: Joseph Nightingale, *Portraiture of Methodism* (Cf. [R. B. Aspland] *The rise, progress and present influence of Wesleyan Methodism*): S. Hulme, *Memoir of Rev. Thomas Allin* (London, 1881) pp. 51-2.

20 J. J. Tayler, *A retrospect of the religious life of England* (2nd ed. London, 1853) pp. 320, 323: J. J. Tayler, *The present position, prospects and duties of Unitarian christians* (London, 1839) p. 7.

21 *Monthly Repository* 1809 p. 486: 1810 p. 236: 1818 pp. 272, 303: 1823 pp. 392, 683: M. I. Thomis, *Politics and society in Nottingham, 1785-1835* (Oxford, 1969) pp. 130-5: J. J. Tayler, *Present position of unitarian christians* pp. 10-11.

22 Bogue & Bennett, *History of dissenters* (1833 ed.) ii. 548-9: *Monthly Repository* 1809 p. 560: 1810 p. 12: O. Chadwick, *The Victorian church* (London, 1966-70) i. 430: Durham C.R.O. MS. Pease Papers. Society of Friends, Reports to Meetings. Causes of disownment in North Warwickshire. For Darlington, *Ibid.* Letters Group 52 no. 38. J. F. Clapham to John Pease. My attention was kindly drawn to these documents by my pupil, Mr D. J. Hall, who has taken the whole matter further in 'Membership Statistics of the Society of Friends, 1800-1850', *Journal of the Friends' Historical Society* lii. 97-100.

23 Isaac Crewdson, *A beacon to the Society of Friends* (2nd ed. London, 1835) pp. v, 144: Isaac Crewdson, *Glad tidings for sinners. To which is prefaced a short memoir of his life.* (Printed but not published, Manchester, 1845) pp. 6-9, 12-13: Isaac Crewdson, *Water baptism an ordinance of Christ* (London, 1837): P.R.O. RG4/2694 (1837): Northern Baptist College, Manchester. MS. Union Chapel Church Book, 26 December 1842: *Encyclopaedia Britannica* (7th ed. 1842) xviii. 772.

Chapter 4 (pages 70-104)

1 *Methodist Magazine* xxxvii. 376.

2 *Monthly Repository* 1812 pp. 634-5: 1816 p. 413.

3 Rowland Hill, *A plea for union, and for the free propagation of the gospel* . . . (London, 1800) pp. 90-1: Wilson, *Dissenting meeting houses in London, Westminster and Southwark* iv. 550-2: W. Wilson, *Remarks upon the present state of the dissenting interest* . . . quoted in Waddington, *Congregational History* iv. 374.

4 e.g. J. Browne, *Congregationalism in Norfolk and Suffolk* pp. 203-4: F. Wrigley, *History of the Yorkshire Congregational Union* (London, 1923): R. Slate, *Lancashire Congregational Union* pp. 5-6: A. Peel, *These Hundred years* pp. 7-8.

5 *Evangelical Magazine* xviii. 468-71: xx. 518: xxi. 227: J. Sibree and M. Caston, *Independency in Warwickshire* pp. 245-6: Cf. *Baptist Magazine* v. 279: Weston, ' Baptists of Northwestern England ' p. 84.

6 A. Peel, *These hundred years* pp. 36-7.

7 R. W. Dale, *Congregationalism* pp. 587-92: *Evangelical Magazine* xxiii. 352 seq., 443 seq.: xxiv. 126.

8 How their minds worked is illustrated by Thomas Oxenham, *Fruits of the Bedfordshire Union. A letter to the Rev. R. Whittingham* (London, 1799) p. 7.

9 J. Gadsby, *A memoir of the late Wm. Gadsby* (London, 1870) pp. 32-5: *Circular letter of the Yorkshire and Lancashire Association* 1807, quoted in Weston, ' Baptists of Northwestern England ' p. 64.

10 W. T. Whitley, *Baptists of Northwest England 1649-1913* (London, 1913) pp. 148, 157: R. Ashton, *Manchester and the early Baptists* (Manchester, 1916) pp. 37-8: Gadsby's hymn book contained the verse:

> Lord, pity outcasts, vile and base,
> The poor dependents on Thy grace,
> Whom men disturbers call.

11 *Evangelical Magazine* xxiv. 138-9: Weston, ' Baptists of Northwestern England ', p. 207.

12 See the interesting discussion of this whole body of literature in the *Evangelical Magazine* for 1816, in instalments begining at xxiv. 52, 98, 138, 143, 177.

13 J. T. Wilkinson, *Hugh Bourne 1772-1852* (London, 1952) p. 38.

14 Margaret Batty, ' Contribution of local preachers to the life of the Wesleyan Methodist Church until 1932, and to the Methodist Church after 1932 ' (Unpublished Leeds M.A. thesis, 1969) pp. 39-40: M.C.A. MSS. J. Entwisle to J. Benson, 21 June 1802.

15 M.C.A. MSS. John Barber to George Marsden, 22 October 1814. In Liverpool he had reported: ' Last quarter we joined about 130, but the removals backsliders and deaths have been so many that we have little increase in point of numbers ', M.C.A. MSS. J. Barber to H. Moore, 14 April 1806. Cf. *Baptist Magazine* v. 321-4: *Methodist Magazine* xxxviii. 220-5.

16 *The Journals of William Clowes* (London, 1844) p. 59: Wilkinson, *Hugh Bourne* p. 42.

17 *Ibid.* p. 42: Hartley Victoria College, Manchester. MS. Journals of Hugh Bourne D. fo. 15: F. fo. 131, 2 June 1811. Cf. *Journals of William Clowes* pp. 90-1, 287.

18 Hartley Victoria College, Manchester. James Everett's MS. Memoranda Books i. fos. 219-20: C. Hulbert, *Memoirs of an eventful life* p. 170.

19 Hartley Victoria College, Manchester. MS. Journals of Hugh Bourne F. fo. 121: E. fo. 299: *Journals of William Clowes* pp. 43-4.

20 Bunting, *Life of Bunting* i. 115-16: C. Hulbert, *Memoirs of an eventful life* p. 154.

21 J. Nightingale, *Portraiture of Methodism* p. 489. Cf. p. 219.

22 *Ibid.* p. 266: M.C.A. MSS. Joseph Entwisle to George Marsden, 30 November 1802: Jabez Bunting to Richard Reece, 15 July 1803 (Copy). Cf. same to same, 11 June 18[03]: Jabez Bunting to George Marsden, 10 June 1803.

23 Leeds Central Library. John Wray's MS. History of Methodism in Leeds x. fos. 145-7: M.C.A. Thomas Wray's MS. History of Methodism in Leeds ii. fo. 86: M.C.A. Tyerman MSS. i. fos. 351, 374-5: M.C.A. MSS. Robert Lomas to Jabez Bunting, 2 July 1803: Jabez Bunting to Richard Reece, 15 July 1803. In 1807, the Screamers were taken back into Society. For Bourne's rather low opinion of Sigston, Hartley Victoria College. MS. Journals of Hugh Bourne C. fos. 3, 4, 22.

24 M.C.A. Tyerman MSS. iii. fos. 479, 489: MS. letter of J. Birchenall to L. Tyerman, 28 December 1870, enclosed in Tyerman MSS. iii. fo. 1: M.C.A. MSS. J. Barber to H. Moon, 14 April 1806: W. Jenkins to Jabez Bunting, 29 January 1806.

25 *Ibid.* (A version of this letter, silently omitting the more discreditable passages, was printed by T. P. Bunting, *Life of Bunting* i. 272-4): the pamphlet partly reprinted in Bunting, *Life of Bunting* i. 425-38: [James Everett], *Methodism as it is* (London, 1863-5) i. 88. The connection between separation and recession is assumed in M.C.A. Tyerman MSS. iii. fos. 81-3.

26 *Journals of Wm. Clowes* pp. 94-5: J. T. Wilkinson, *William Clowes 1780-1851* (London, 1951) pp. 39, 47-8: Robert Hindmarsh, *Rise and progress of the new Jerusalem Church in England and America and other parts* (London, 1861) pp. 396-7.

27 M.C.A. MSS. J. Barber to George Marsden, 7 February 1816: J. Braithwaite to B. Slater, 10 September 1816: Wm. Leach to Jabez Bunting, 20 January 1816: James Nichols to Jabez Bunting, 8 February 1816: R. Wood to Jabez Bunting, 9 March 1816. Cf. Samuel Broadbent to Joseph Agar, 17 October 1815: Hartley Victoria College. James Everett's MS. Memorandum Book i.fo.219.

28 M.C.A. MSS. Miles Martindale to Jabez Bunting, 9 July 1816.

29 K. P. Russell, *Memoirs of the Rev. John Pyer* (London, 1865) *passim;* George Pocock, *A statement of facts connected with the ejectment of certain ministers from the Society of Wesleyan Methodists in the City of Bristol* (Bristol, 1820): George Pocock, John Pyer and Samuel Smith, *Facts without a veil* (Bristol, 1820): S. Stocks jun., *A reply to the Rev. John Pyer's 'Few plain and indisputable testimonies' explanatory of the affairs of Canal Street Chapel* (Manchester, 1830): John Pyer, *Six letters to a trustee of Canal Street*

Chapel, Manchester (London, 1830). For the Anglican history of the church, as St Jude's, *Manchester Guardian* 4 July 1964 p. 3.

30 ' Our people in these parts live too near the Bishop of Exeter, and experience too much unfriendliness from his clergy to love, with such a love as the *Watchman* would have them love, the established Church '. M.C.A. MSS. J. Davis to Jabez Bunting, 3 March 1837.

31 M.C.A. Tyerman MSS. iii. fo. 355 (another account of the same events by the same writer was printed in the *Monthly Repository* 1814 pp. 377-8, from a flysheet published at York). Cf. M.C.A. MSS. Richard Roberts to Robert Pilter, 9 June 1814. Roberts was a Cornishman.

32 M.C.A. MSS. James Blackett to Jabez Bunting, 12 September 1828: W. Dale to Jabez Bunting, 15 July 1842: 12 July 1839.

33 M.C.A. MSS. John Mercer to Jabez Bunting, 14 March 1820.

34 M.C.A. MSS. W. Dale to Jabez Bunting, 12 July 1839: John Baker to Jabez Bunting, 16 June 1834.

35 M.C.A. MSS. W. Dale to Jabez Bunting, 15 July 1842: T. Shaw, *A history of Cornish Methodism* (Truro, 1967) p. 81.

36 M.C.A. Tyerman MSS. i. fos. 358-9, 362-3.

37 M.C.A. MSS. J. Entwisle to T. Stanley, 27 April 1812: T. Jackson, *Recollections of my own life and times* ed. B. Frankland (London 1873) pp. 136-7: Wearmouth, *Methodism and working class movements, 1800-50* pp. 44, 169.

38 This was the significance of the publication late in 1811 of a wild sermon against Jacobinism, preached by John Stephens in February 1810. *Methodist Magazine* xxxiv. 905.

39 M.C.A. Thos. Allan MSS. J. Stamp to Thos. Allan, [19 June 1813].

40 M.C.A. MSS. Jabez Bunting to George Marsden, 28 January 1813: *Methodist Magazine* xxxvii, 373 seq., 377, 462 seq., 541 seq.

41 M.C.A. MSS. John Ward to Jabez Bunting, 27 March 1809: MS. Copy of a circular sent by Mr Isaac to the Superintendents of Circuits, relative to the foregoing publication and the Minute of Conference concerning it. [This MS. was apparently printed as a pamphlet at Grantham, December 1816]. The trouble spread to the Newcastle and Sunderland circuits, M.C.A. MSS. T. Lessey snr to Jabez Bunting, 17 January 1811.

42 M.C.A. MSS. J. Everett to J. Stanley, 13 March 1813: T. Hutton to Jabez Bunting, 6 July 1811: J. Griffiths to Jabez Bunting, 24 November 1820: W. Bird to Jabez Bunting, 30 November 1820: Jabez Bunting to W. Bird, 12 December 1820.

43 M.C.A. MS. Letters of Presidents of the Wesleyan Conference, collected by J. E. Wright, letter of John Stephens, 28 June 1819: Jabez Bunting to George Marsden, 24 June 1815: *An exposition of the proceedings of the old Methodist Conference with reflections on the nature and the tendency of its system of government* (Manchester, 1815) pp. 13n, 14.

44 T. Jackson, *Recollections* pp. 171-9: M.C.A. MSS. J. Entwisle to J. Everett, 12 September 1820: J. Hebblewhite to J. Everett, 15 March 1820: J. Stephens, *The mutual relations, claims and duties of the rich and poor* (Manchester, 1819): *A letter to the Rev. John Stephens, occasioned by some recent transactions and occurrences in the Methodist Society in Manchester* (Manchester, 1820): *Manchester Observer* pp. 836, 894-5.

45 M.C.A. MSS. W. Leach to Jabez Bunting, 5 November 1817. For the conflicting information which appeared in the press, Thompson, *Making of the English working class* pp. 394, 667n. 5.

46 M.C.A. Thos. Allan MSS. Thos. Allan to Joseph Allan, 27 November 1819. Cf. Charles Atmore, *Serious advice from a father to his children, respecting their conduct in the world, civil, moral and religious* (Manchester, 1817) p. 12.

47 *Manchester Observer* pp. 100, 809: Jackson, *Recollections* p. 176: M.C.A. MSS. J. Hanwell to J. Everett, 15 October 1821: J. Edmondson to J. Crowther, 16 November 1819.

48 P.R.O. H.O. 42. 198 (1819) quoted in D. A. Gowland, ' Methodist secessions and social conflict in South Lancashire, 1830-57 ' (unpublished Manchester Ph.D. thesis, 1966) p. 14: Wearmouth, *Methodism and working class movements 1800-1850* pp. 145-6, 168: M.C.A. Thos. Allan MSS. Thos. Allan to John Elliot, to Rev. Mr. Collison, and to Lord Liverpool, all on 3 December 1819.

49 M.C.A. MSS. J. B. Holroyd to Jabez Bunting, 23 December 1819; 26 January 1820. A similar letter to the first reached the Home Office, Wearmouth, *Methodism and working class movement 1800-1850* pp. 146-7.

50 M.C.A. MSS. H. & S. Kellett to T. Ingham, 24 February 1820: J. Hebblewhite to J. Everett, 27 May 1820.

51 Waddington, *Congregational History* iv. 285-6.

52 J. Stephens, *Mutual relations of rich and poor* p. v.: Macdonald, *Benson* p. 311.

53 M.C.A. MSS. J. Stephens to Jabez Bunting, 1 February 1821. Cf. T. Jackson to Jabez Bunting, 26 March 1821.

54 M.C.A. Thomas Wray's MS. *History of Methodism in Leeds* v. fo. 55: *Manchester Observer* p. 1144.

55 M.C.A. MSS. John M'Owan to R. Nutter, 5 January 1828: R. Pilter to Jabez Bunting, 23 October, 5 November 1819: 5 July 1820: Bunting, *Life of Bunting* ii. 167: W. H. Stephenson, *The loyalty of Methodist preachers exemplified in the persecution of their brethren . . .* (Newcastle, 1819): Hugh Kelly, *The stone cut out of the mountain* (Newcastle, 1821): *A dialogue between a methodist preacher and a reformer* (Newcastle, 1819): *Manchester Observer* p. 1197.

56 M.C.A. MSS. J. Entwisle to J. Everett, 12 September 1820: W. France to T. Jackson, 22 December 1821: G. Douglas to Jabez Bunting, 26 October 1820.

57 James Everett, *Adam Clarke Portrayed* (London, 1843-9) iii. 251-2.

58 R. C. Swift, ' Methodist Sunday Schools in Nottingham ', *Proceedings of Wesley Historical Society* xxxiii. 36 seq.

59 This account is based on the MSS. of the Stockport Sunday School and M.C.A. MS. Conference diary of Charles Atmore (1809).

60 B. Smith, *Methodism in Macclesfield* p. 223: *A history of Macclesfield* ed. C. Stella Davies (Manchester, 1961) pp. 219-20: J. Earles, *Streets and houses of old Macclesfield* pp. 84-6.

61 Chetham's Library. MS. Minute books of Manchester Sunday School Committee, 24 September 1819.

62 *Manchester Observer* p. 782. These loyal proceedings were reported to the

Home Office. Wearmouth, *Methodism and working class movements, 1800-1850* p. 147.

63 *Manchester Observer* pp. 801, 809: C. Deane Little, *Our old Sunday school* (Wigan, 1933) p. 23.

64 *Annual report of the Stockport Sunday school* for each of the years 1817, 1818, 1819: Stockport Sunday School MSS. (Ben Hadfield), copy of an address presented to the magistrates, 12 August 1819.

65 *Remarks on the sermon preached by the Rev. John Stephens . . .* By the Rev. James Scholefield, reprinted in *Manchester Observer*, p. 944: *Ibid.* pp. 874, 895, 952: *Manchester Mercury* 9 November 1819. Cf. *An appeal to the public on the subject of Union Sunday schools* (Manchester, 1820): J. Scholefield, *Letters and tracts on religious subjects* (Manchester, 1827-41): *Manchester City News* 15 December 1883.

66 M.C.A. MS. Conference Journal 1820-21. Cf. the subsequent speech by G. Thompson. For Conference legislation: Samuel Warren and John Stephens, *Chronicles of Wesleyan Methodism* (London, 1827) i. 396-400.

67 M.C.A. MSS. Joseph Entwisle to George Marsden, 2 March 1816: R. Miller to R. Reece, 11 July 1816: W. Worth to Jabez Bunting, 23 January 1818: R. Miller to T. Blanchard, 13 March 1819: R. Miller to Jabez Bunting, 1 April 1819 (2 letters): Jabez Bunting to Samuel Taylor, 10 March 1814: Miles Martindale to Jabez Bunting, 9 July 1816. Eventually Conference fixed the number of children circuits should support in proportion to the membership and arranged for any surplus to be maintained by a connexional Children's Fund. M.C.A. MSS. James Akerman to Jabez Bunting, 31 July 1821.

68 Bunting, *Life of Bunting* ii. 162-3: M.C.A. MSS. J. Edmondson to J. Crowther, 16 November 1819: J. W. Cloake to Jabez Bunting, 29 March 1820: J. Sharp to Jabez Bunting, 20 April 1819.

69 M.C.A. MSS. W. Myles to Joseph Dutton, 3 June 1814.

70 *Minutes of the Wesleyan Methodist Conference* iv. 330-1: *The works of Adam Clarke* (London, 1836-7) xii. 336: M.C.A. MSS. T. Webb to J. Gaulter, 14 April 1818: T. Holdich to Jabez Bunting, 21 May 1818: J. Dutton to Walter Griffith, 14 January 1814: R. Miller to R. Reece, 11 July 1816: J. Edmondson to J. Crowther, 16 November 1819: Jabez Bunting to [George] M[orley?], 25 January 1815. Cf. Jabez Bunting to James Wood, 7 January 1815.

71 J. Crowther, *Thoughts upon finances* (London, 1817) pp. 24-5: M.C.A. MSS. C. Atmore to G. Marsden, 3 April 1818: *Monthly Repository* 1820 p. 168.

72 Bunting, *Life of Bunting* ii. 80: M.C.A. MSS. J. Barber to G. Marsden, 18 January 1813: W. Myles to Jabez Bunting, 5 June 1819: M. Martindale to Jabez Bunting, 9 July 1816: MS. Letters of Presidents of Wesleyan Methodist Conference I 1744-1838 fo. 58: J. Taylor to G. Marsden, 7 February 1811.

73 Alwyn D. Rees, *Life in a Welsh countryside* (Cardiff, 1968) pp. 102-6.

74 M.C.A. MSS. W. Worth to Jabez Bunting, 23 January 1818: Crowther, *Thoughts upon finances* pp. 11, 12.

75 *Ibid.* pp. 16, 29: M.C.A. MSS. W. Myles to R. Blunt, 1 November 1813: J. Entwisle to Jabez Bunting, n.d. [before 18 December 1812]: T. Lessey Jnr to Jabez Bunting, 6 May 1815.

76 M.C.A. MSS. Z. Taft to Jabez Bunting, [7] May, 1818: W. Myles to Jabez Bunting, 5 June 1819.

77 M.C.A. MSS. Jabez Bunting to I. Clayton, 14 July 1815.

78 Cf. E. Grindrod, *A compendium of the laws and regulations of Wesleyan Methodism* (ed. London, 1848) pp. 284-6.

79 M.C.A. MSS. Samuel Taylor to Jabez Bunting, 22 July 1819: E. Hare to Jabez Bunting, 12 June 1810: Z. Taft to Jabez Bunting, [7] May 1818: John Mercer to Jabez Bunting, 14 March 1820. Cf. W. Evans to Jabez Bunting, 2 August 1820.

80 M.C.A. MSS. J. Mercer to Jabez Bunting, 14 March 1820: J. W. Cloake to Jabez Bunting, 29 March 1820: Robert Lomas to Jabez Bunting, 5 July 1806: 16 February 1808.

81 M.C.A. MSS. J. Entwisle to J. Benson, 21 June 1802: Jabez Bunting to the Stewards and Leaders of Macclesfield, 11 August 1802. Bunting reckoned that in 1801 a married preacher with five children would have received £75. 18. 0. In 1806, Bunting then serving in Manchester with one child reckoned his income for income tax purposes at £83, not including any reckoning for the value of his furnished accommodation. Bunting, *Life of Bunting* i. 281-2.

82 Crowther, *Thoughts on finances* pp. 20-21: *Methodist Magazine* xxxviii. 779.

83 Smith, *History of Wesleyan Methodism* iii. 5.

84 *Ibid.* iii. 34: M.C.A. MSS. Henry Moore to J. Wood, 29 May 1818.

85 J. C. Bowmer, 'Church and ministry in Wesleyan Methodism from the death of John Wesley to the death of Jabez Bunting' (unpublished Leeds Ph.D. thesis, 1967) pp. 94, 229: M.C.A. MSS. Thomas Preston to Jabez Bunting, 11 March 1800: Jabez Bunting to George Marsden, 13 December 1803.

86 Smith, *History of Wesleyan Methodism* iii. 35: M.C.A. MS. Conference Journal 1820-1.

87 M.C.A. MSS. J. Edmondson to B. Slater, 11 November 1819: MS. Conference Journal 1820-1. Cf. Jabez Bunting to T. Lessey, 31 May 1811: J. Entwisle to Jabez Bunting, 8 June 1812: J. Riles to [Jabez Bunting], 17 July 1820: D. Stoner to J. Entwisle Snr., 24 October 1822.

88 *Minutes of Wesleyan Conference* xi. 697: Bowmer, 'Church and Ministry' pp. 304-7: Smith, *History of Wesleyan Methodism* iii. 34.

89 G. F. A. Best, *Temporal Pillars* (Cambridge, 1964) Ch. VI.

90 Crowther, *Thoughts upon finances* p. 18.

Chapter 5 (pages 105-134)

1 M. Cove, *An inquiry into the necessity, justice and policy of a commutation of tithes* (Hereford, 1800): *Parliamentary history* xxxvi. 483-5.

2 J. Wade, *Extraordinary Black Book* (London, 1831) pp. 54-5n.

3 W. Pitt, *A general view of the agriculture of the county of Worcester,* (London, 1810) p. 35: *Parliamentary history* xxxvi. 476: 57 Geo. III c.99 s.2 (They could farm more with the permission of the bishop, 1 & 2 Vict. c.106 ss.

29-30). For non-residence compare, e.g. P.P. H.C. 1808 ix: H.L. 1816 LXXIX pp. 42-3: H.C. 1833 XXVII.

4 C. Hodgson, *An account of the augmentation of small livings by the Governors of the Bounty of Queen Anne* . . . (2nd ed. London, 1845) p. 15: M. R. Austin, ' The church of England in the county of Derbyshire, 1772-1832 ', (unpublished London Ph.D. thesis, 1969) p. 170: P.P. H.C. 1836 XL Church patronage (England and Wales).

5 *The Church in Manchester. Report of the Bishop of Manchester's special commission, 1905-14* (Manchester, 1914) pp. 66-9: P.P. H.L. 1818 XCIII p. 215: *Manchester Rectory Division Bill. Report of the evidence given before the committee of the House of Commons.* (Printed for the Manchester Church-wardens, 1850) pp. 6, 109-12.

6 P.P. H.L. 1816 LXXIX. An account of the population and capacity of churches and chapels in all benefices . . . wherein the population consists of 2,000 upwards, and the churches and chapels will not contain half. Cf. P.P. H.L. 1818 XCIII. Abstract of number of benefices and population of each diocese: W. H. Egerton, *The pew system* (London, 1862).

7 W. R. Ward, ' The Cost of Establishment: some reflections on church building in Manchester ', *Studies in Church History* iii. 287.

8 *Manchester Guardian* 6 July 1822: 30 June 1821: 11 August 1821: 1 September 1821.

9 *Ibid.* 16 March, 4 May, 21 September, 7 December, 14 December, 1822: 10 May, 31 May 1821.

10 *Ibid.* 24 January, 27 March, 29 May, 24 July 1824: 4 June, 25 June 1825: 3 June 1826: *Manchester Courier* 2 July 1825.

11 *Manchester Courier* 15 September, 22 September 1827: *Manchester Guardian* 29 September 1827.

12 On this whole question see my paper on ' The tithe question in England in the early nineteenth century ', *Journal of Ecclesiastical History* xvi. 67-81.

13 *Anecdotes of the life of Richard Watson, Bishop of Llandaff, written by himself* . . . ed. R. Watson (London, 1817) pp. 306-9. A measure of this kind had been discussed between Pitt and the Primate as early as 1792. P.R.O. 30/8/161: Abp. Moore to W. Pitt, 19 January 1792.

14 *Monthly Repository* 1819 p. 427: 1823 p. 155.

15 J. Ivimey, *History of the English Baptists* iv. 163: *Monthly Repository* 1822. p. 159.

16 R. W. Davis, ' The strategy of " dissent " in the repeal campaign, 1820-28 ', *Journal of Modern History* 1966 pp. 374 seq.: W. R. Ward, *Victorian Oxford* (London, 1965) p. 69.

17 M.C.A. MSS. Gideon Ouseley to Joseph Butterworth, 26 March 1804: James Nichols to Jabez Bunting, 8 February 1816: Gideon Ouseley to John Thurston, 1 April 1829: John Murrow to Jabez Bunting, 22 November [1817].

18 M.C.A. Thos. Allan MSS. ' Hints for a conversation with Mr Perceval ': M.C.A. MSS. J. Noble to J. Kerr, 5 October 1814.

19 Wm. Stewart, *Letter addressed to the Methodist preachers of Ireland* (Dublin, 1814): M.C.A. MSS. John Murrow to Jabez Bunting, 22 November [1817]: J. Sutcliffe to Jabez Bunting, 31 October 1820: Adam Clarke, *To the*

Methodist preachers in Great Britain 21 October 1822.

20 *Ibid.*: M.C.A. MSS. Robert Huston to the Wesleyan Community, 17 September 1846: Robert G. Cather to ?, 26 December 1848.

21 M.C.A. Thos Allan MSS. Gideon Ouseley to [Thos. Allan?], 24 November 1812.

22 M.C.A. MSS. Gideon Ouseley to J. Butterworth, 26 March, 29 May, 1804: 10 July 1805: 14 May 1813: Thos. Allan MSS. J. Creighton to J. Butterworth, 5 April 1806; 16 December 1806: Thos. Allan to J. Butterworth, 3 December 1812: Peter Roe to J. Butterworth, 13 March 1813: S. Tucker to H. Deery, 4 May 1820, *et passim.* Cf. The Irish rebellion of 1798, Macdonald, *Benson* p. 319.

23 M.C.A. MSS. J. Barber, J. Benson *et al.* to Thomas Allan, 6 December 1811. Thos. Allan MSS. [Thos. Allan] to J. Blanshard, 3 December 1817: J. Barber to George Marsden, 18 January 1813.

24 M.C.A. Thos. Allan MSS. T. Allan to J. Butterworth, n.pl.or d.

25 M.C.A. MSS. J. Barber to George Marsden, 18 January 1813: Thos. Allan MSS. S. Tucker to H. Deery, 4 May 1820: M.C.A. MSS. Adam Clarke to Jabez Bunting, 27 June [1823]. Cf. Same to same, 4 July 1823: Gideon Ouseley to Zechariah Taft, 5 July 1823.

26 M.C.A. MSS. e.g. John Aikenhead to Jabez Bunting 21 February 1829: John Hodgson to Jabez Bunting 24 February 1829: W. Vevers to Jabez Bunting, 16 March 1829.

27 M.C.A. Thos. Allan MSS. Thos. Allan to Thomas R. Allan, 9 March 1829; 25 April 1829: 19 March 1829: M.C.A. Jabez Bunting to Matthew Tobias, 23 February 1829.

28 *Manchester Mercury, passim* e.g. 18 July 1797: 20 December 1808: *Brief memoirs of the Rev. Rowland Broomhead of Manchester* (Manchester, n.d. [1820?]: Joseph Curr, *A discourse delivered at St. Augustine's Chapel, Manchester. 18 October 1820, at the funeral of the Rev. Rowland Broomhead* (Manchester, 1820): Melville Horne, *The Congratulation* (Manchester, 1822) p. 3: Melville Horne, *Letter to the Rev. Joseph Curr occasioned by his letter to Sir Oswald Mosley* . . . (3rd. ed. Manchester, n.d. [1822?]) p. 34.

29 Melville Horne, *Anti-Curr: or the Protestant address to the public* (Manchester, n.d.) p. 41: J. Curr, *An address to the public occasioned by the recent letters of the Rev. Melville Horne and the Rev. Nathaniel Gilbert, on the subject of Bible Associations* (Manchester, 1821).

30 W. Roby, *Protestantism: or an address particularly to the labouring classes in defence of the Protestant principle* . . . (3 parts, Manchester, 1821-2): J. Curr, *A letter to Sir Oswald Mosley* . . . (Manchester, 1821): J. Curr, *Catholicism, or the old rule of faith vindicated from the attack of W. Roby* (Manchester, 1821): *Anti-Horne; or an address to the public* (Manchester, 1821): *A Catholic address to the inhabitants of Manchester* (Manchester, 1822): N. Gilbert, *A letter to Sir Oswald Mosley* . . . *occasioned by the letter of Rev. Joseph Curr* (2nd. ed. Manchester, n.d. [1821 or 2]: Melville Horne, *The Great Mass Idol* (Manchester, 1822): Melville Horne, *Purgatoria Phantasmagoria* (Manchester, 1822): B. Braidley, *An authentic account of circumstances connected with the case of Margaret R———N; containing remarks on the Rev. J. Curr's particulars of her conversion and subsequent apostasy* (Manchester, 1822): *The Catholic; or Christianity not Popery* (Manchester, 1821-2): *The*

Catholic phenix or Papal scourge (Manchester, 1822): *The anatomy of Popery* . . . (Manchester, 1821): *The poor man's claims to the Bible* . . . (Manchester, 1821).

31 M. Horne, *The Congratulation* p. 4: *The disturbed state of Ireland, with its causes and remedies* (Manchester, n.d. [1821]): W. E. Andrews, *A candid appeal to the common sense of the people of Manchester and its vicinity on the present controversy respecting Bible-reading, popery and priestcraft* (London, 1822).

32 J. Scholefield, *A reply to the ' Address to the labouring classes of Manchester and Salford ', together with remarks on the subject of the Auxiliary Bible Society* (Manchester, 1821) p. 13: *Manchester Guardian* 23 November 1822.

33 *Ibid.* 23 April, 30 April; 7 May, 14 May 1825. Cf. the tory account, *Manchester Courier* 30 April, 7 May 1825.

34 *Parliamentary debates* n.s. xxiv. 821-2. More fully printed in W. R. Ward, ' The tithe question ', *Journal of Ecclesiastical History* xvi. 79.

35 Horace Mann, who organised the census of religious worship in 1851, reckoned that not more than 58% of the community could attend church at a given time, and hence that there was no need to provide church accommodation for more than that proportion. *Census of Great Britain, 1851. Religious Worship Report* pp. cxix-cxxi The independent calculations of church-building societies in the same period also produced conclusions in the range of 50-60%.

36 E. A. Rose, *Methodism in Ashton-under-Lyne* ii. 40-1: *Manchester Guardian* 28 July, 4 August 1821: *Manchester Times* 2, 9, 16, 23, 30 November 1833: 7 December 1833: *Monthly Repository* 1822 p. 713: A. Prentice, *Historical sketches and personal recollections of Manchester* (2nd ed. Manchester, 1851) pp. 224-7.

37 *Christian Reformer* 1832 pp. 55, 58: 1833 p. 82.

38 P.P. H.C. 1830 IX: *Manchester Guardian* 29 August 1829: *Manchester Courier* 29 August 1829: *Manchester Times* 22 August 1829.

39 *Report of a committee of the Manchester Statistical Society on the state of education in the borough of Manchester in 1834* (2nd. ed. London, 1837): *Report of a committee of the Manchester Statistical Society on the condition of the working classes in an extensive manufacturing district, 1834-6* (London, 1838): *Manchester Courier* 6 November 1830: *Manchester Times* 14 June 1834.

40 G. A. Weston, ' The Baptists of North-western England ', pp. 144, 147: Whitley, *Baptists of North-west England*, pp. 179, 281.

41 *Monthly Repository* 1819 pp. 125, 174-9, 198, 357-62, 377-9: 1822 pp. 354-9, 486-8: 1828 pp. 73-9.

42 M.C.A. MSS. R. Watson to J. Anderson (postmarked) 16 September, 26 September 1831.

43 J. G. Miall, *Congregationalism in Yorkshire* (London, 1868) p. 171: A. Peel, *These hundred years* pp. 51, 58.

44 *Papers on the present condition of Congregationalism in Manchester and Salford* (Manchester, 1853): E. Parsons, *Civil, ecclesiastical, literary, commercial history* . . . *of Leeds and the manufacturing district of Yorkshire* ii. 18, 28 seq., 76 seq.

45 *Statistical report of the Scottish population of Manchester taken in 1837* (Manchester, 1838) pp. 10-11.

46 Waddington, *Congregational history* iv. 51. Cf. C. Leach, *Manchester Congregationalism: its rise and progress* (London, 1898) pp. 20, 31-3, 47.

47 J. M'Kerrow, *History of the Secession Church* (Glasgow, 1841) pp. 577, 919-20.

48 W. McKerrow, *Letters on church establishments in reply to the Rev. Hugh Stowell:* J. M. McKerrow, *Memoir of William McKerrow* (London, 1881) pp. 44-5.

49 Henry Duncan, *A sermon on the constitution of the Church of Scotland, and its effects on the moral and religious character of the people* (Manchester, 1828) pp. vii-viii.

50 *Patriot* 21 November 1839. I owe this reference to the kindness of my pupil, Dr. H. R. Martin.

51 *Manchester Times* 30 November 1833: *Manchester Courier* 24 December 1833: *Manchester Guardian* 7 December 1833: 8 March 1834.

52 *Ibid.* 15 February, 8 March, 29 March 1834. Similar meetings followed at Oldham, and elsewhere.

53 Waddington, *Congregational history* iv. 398-9.

54 J. H. Thom, *Letters embracing his life of John James Tayler* i. 102-3, 105-10.

55 *Manchester Guardian* 7 December 1833: 18 January, 1 February, 8 February, 22 March 1834: *Christian Reformer* 1834 pp. 161-3.

56 *Manchester Guardian* 8 March, 15 March, 10 May, 17 May, 24 May, 21 June 1834.

57 *Christian Reformer* 1834 p.423.

Chapter 6 (pages 135-176)

1 M.C.A. MSS. Joseph Sutcliffe to Jabez Bunting, 13 December 1836: MS. Scrapbook of James Everett fo. 421: *Methodist Magazine* xxxix. 704: George Jackson, *Wesleyan Methodism in the Darlington circuit* (Darlington, 1850) p. 45. Equally unpalatable was the sight of schools well entrenched in the affections of the community, and well supplied with funds which could not be tapped for society purposes without special taxation. M.C.A. MSS. Joseph Wood to Jabez Bunting, 16 May, 1829.

2 M.C.A. MSS. J. S. Stamp to Jabez Bunting, 13 March 1836.

3 M.C.A. MSS. Thomas Eastwood to Gervase Smith, 1 September 1853: J. W. Swan & J. Hampson, *Methodism at Fletcher Street* (Bolton, 1911) p. 5: *Methodist Magazine* xxxvii. 378, 466, 542-3; M.C.A. MSS. J. Riles to Jabez Bunting, 21 January 1824: C. Wawn to Z. Taft, 21 October 1816.

4 M.C.A. MS. Scrapbook of James Everett fo. 421.

5 J. Pearson, *Life of William Hey* (London, 1822) Pt. ii. 191, 307-14, 321-32: *Arminian Magazine* xi. 489-90: *Evangelical Magazine* vi. 57 seq: Stockport Sunday School MSS. Gilbert Wardlaw to J. Mayer, 24 December 1830: John Brown, *Discourse in St. Andrew's Church, Edinburgh* (Edinburgh, 1826): M. Olerenshaw, *Sermons on the religious education of children and the usefulness of Sunday schools* p. 12: T. Whitaker, *Four letters to J. Mayer of Stockport,* p. 12n.

6 M.C.A. MSS. 'Observations on the management of Sunday schools respectfully submitted to the Conference at Liverpool, By William Hey, Esq. of Leeds '. There is a printed version in Pearson, *Hey* Pt. ii. 307-14.

7 M.C.A. MSS. Jabez Bunting to [Richard Reece], 1 October 1808 [copy] (partly printed in Bunting, *Life of Bunting* i. 320-1): W. H. Groser, *A hundred years' work for the children* p. 10: M.C.A. MSS. Jabez Bunting to Mr. Marrott Junr., 20 December 1805: Bunting, *Life of Bunting* i. 321-3, 357: M.C.A. MSS. Jabez Bunting to Theophilus Lessey [sen.] 30 May 1809: MS. Conference diary of Charles Atmore, 1809: Theophilus Lessey to Jabez Bunting, 7 June 1809. Cf. H. Moore to Jabez Bunting, 7 March 1810 (printed in Bunting, *Life of Bunting* i. 353-5): C. Gloyne to Jabez Bunting, 30 March 1811.

8 M.C.A. MSS. J. Entwisle to Jabez Bunting, 20 May 1809: Robert Denholm House, Nutfield, Redhill. MS. Minute Book of the Sunday School Union Committee, 18 July 1810: W. H. Watson *History of the Sunday School Union* (London, 1853) pp. 15-16: *The important question discussed whether teaching the art of writing on the Lord's Day, be defensible on Christian principles* (Sheffield, 1824): Abraham Watmough, *Observations on teaching the art of writing in Sunday schools* (Rochdale, 1832): T. Pole, *A history of the origin and progress of Adult Schools* pp. 73-4.

9 Joseph Barker, *Teaching the children of the poor to write on the Sabbath day proved to be in perfect agreement with the Word of God* . . . (Manchester, 1837) pp. 1, 46, 49, 53: J. Mayer, *Defence of Sunday Schools* pp. 14, 68, 69, 80: B. Braidley, *Sunday School Memorials* (Manchester, 1831) p. x.

10 E.g. *Houghton Methodists (Two Trees Lane) 1810-1960* (n.pl.or d.) p. 7: R. Wilkinson, *Methodism at Mankinholes* (n.pl., 1964) pp. 9-10: W. J. Warner, *The Wesleyan movement in the Industrial Revolution* (London, 1930) p. 235: T. Shaw, *History of Cornish Methodism* p. 60.

11 M.C.A. MS. Scrapbook of James Everett fo. 421 (Bunting's own MS. notes for this speech survive at Duke University, Durham, N.C.): *A statement of the origin and present condition of the Sunday schools for children of all denominations in Manchester* p. 4: MS. Diary of Rev. John Peters, 7 March 1836: *15th Report of the Wesleyan Methodist Sunday Schools in the third or South Manchester Circuit* (Manchester, 1842).

12 Leeds City Archives. MS. Sunday school minute book, 1816-42: G. Smith, *History of Wesleyan Methodism* iii. 109-15, 123-4.

13 M.C.A. MSS. W. Myles to Jabez Bunting, July 13, 1825: MS Report of Conference committee on Liverpool disputes, 19 August 1825: W. Atherton to T. Slugg, 2 August 1825: I. Sellars, 'Liverpool Nonconformity' p. 158.

14 M.C.A. MSS. J. Riles to Jabez Bunting, 11 October, 3 December 1825.

15 Leeds Central Library: John [i.e. Thomas] Wray's MS. History of Methodism in Leeds x. fos. 85, 87: Leeds City Archives: MS. Sunday School Minutes Book, 1816-42: M.C.A. MSS. Jabez Bunting to Thomas Galland, n.d. [c.1827]: I. Turton to Jabez Bunting, 4 October 1827: T. Stanley to Jabez Bunting, 18 October 1827: W. Gilyard Scarth to Jabez Bunting, 30 September 1835. Correspondence between the two survivors from 1819 onwards.

16 Leeds City Archives: MS. Minute Book of Brunswick Chapel Trustees, 14 May 1827; 1 August 1827: MS. Records of the Methodist Society at Leeds, 1801-27: MS. Leeds District Minute Book 1800-29, 15 May 1827:

M.C.A. MS. Proceedings of the Conference commenced in London 30 July 1828 (Cited as MS. Conference proceedings, 1828) *passim* and p. 10: M.C.A. MSS. J. Barker to J. Entwisle, 24 November 1827: W. Dawson to R. Pilter, 10 December 1827.

17 M.C.A. MSS. Isaac Keeling to [Richard Watson] n.pl. or d. [1827]: Thomas Galland to Jabez Bunting [post-marked] 20 November 1827: W. Dawson to R. Pilter, 10 December 1827: Edmund Grindrod to [Jabez Bunting], 28 November 1827: Leeds City Archives. MS. Minute Book of Brunswick Chapel Trustees, 1 August 1827.

18 M.C.A. MSS. Jabez Bunting to Joseph Entwisle, 22 December 1827: Grindrod described the opposition as 'generally of the very poorest'. Jabez Bunting to E. Grindrod, 10 May 1828: There is a very full account of the commission's proceedings in Leeds City Archives: MS. Leeds District Minute Book 1800-29, Minutes of Special District Meetings, 5-11 December 1827.

19 M.C.A. MSS. Thomas Galland to Jabez Bunting, 4 January, 18 January 1828: Jabez Bunting to Edmund Grindrod, 10 May 1828: Edmund Grindrod to Jabez Bunting, 23 June 1828: Leeds City Archives. MS Sunday School Minute Book, 1816-42, 3 January 1828: MS. Leaders' Meeting Minute Book 1828-77, 17 March 1828.

20 *United Methodist Free Church Magazine* May 1863, p. 292: M.C.A. MSS. Thomas Raffles to J. Sigston, 17 May 1828: John Bowes to J. Sigston, 1 December 1828.

21 M.C.A. MSS. James Gill to Jabez Bunting, 21 September, 10 October, 30 October, 1829: J. Mason to Jabez Bunting, 30 October 1829: John Rigg to Jabez Bunting, 19 January 1830.

22 M.C.A. MS. Scrapbook of James Everett fo. 411, Joseph Comley, 'Rise and progress of Sunday Schools in Sheffield in answer to questions proposed by Mr. James Everett, 1822': MS. Resolutions of Sheffield Leaders' Meeting, 17 July 1809 [in Bunting's hand]: *Sheffield Iris* 23 May, 6 June, 1809: J. Holland and James Everett, *Memoirs of the life and writings of James Montgomery* (London, 1854-6) ii, 247-8.

23 M.C.A. MSS. David M'Nicholl to Jabez Bunting, 11 September 1809: Edward Hare to Jabez Bunting, 5 September, 12 September, 19 September, 20 November, 25 December 1809: W. Myles to Jabez Bunting, 26 September 1809: MS. Scrapbook of James Everett fo. 411: J. J. Graham, *Methodism in Sheffield Park* pp. 18, 47: *A retrospect of the origin, proceedings of the Sheffield Sunday School Union 1812-24* (Sheffield, 1824): *Sunday School Repository* 1815, ii. 32, 85, 292-4.

24 M.C.A. MSS. Samuel Jackson to Jabez Bunting, 21 March 1832, 26 November 1829: Wm. Henshaw to Jabez Bunting, 9 January, 15 September, 8 October 1828: 19 January 1829: J. Farrar to Samuel Smith, 27 October 1828: Jabez Bunting to Joseph Entwisle, 24 October 1828.

25 M.C.A. MSS. J. Scott to Jabez Bunting, 23 January 1829: 1 January 1830: John Beecham to Jabez Bunting, 30 March [1829]: 1 April, [1830]: David M'Nicholl to Thomas Jackson, 11 February 1832: B. Gregory, *Sidelights on the conflicts of Methodism* (London, 1899) p. 80.

26 J. Beecham, *An essay on the contitution of Wesleyan Methodism* (3rd ed. London, 1851). The first edition was published in 1829, the second and third in 1850 and 1851, when the Wesleyan reform secessions were in flood-tide, and Beecham was President.

27 *Ibid.* pp. 2-3.

28 *Ibid.* pp. 81 *seq.,* 107.

29 *Ibid.* p. 105.

30 M.C.A. MSS. J. Bicknell to Jabez Bunting, 2 March 1835: Cf. J. Entwisle to George Osborn, 9 December 1835.

31 M.C.A. MSS. Adam Clarke to ?   ?   ?, 2 April 1826: John Gaulter to Joseph Entwisle, 25 April 1819: Adam Clarke to Humphrey Sandwith, 16 June 1829. Copy appended to Humphrey Sandwith to Thomas Jackson. 1 October 1832.

32 M.C.A. MSS. F. Calder to Jabez Bunting, 5 March 1821: J. Saunders to Jabez Bunting, 13 May 1822: T. Preston to Jabez Bunting, 6 October 1826: T. Salt to Jabez Bunting, 20 July 1826.

33 *Monthly Repository* 1823, p. 536. Cf. *Manchester Guardian* 6 September, 1823: R. W. Dixon, *Life of Rev. James Dixon, Wesleyan Minister* (London, 1874) pp. 125-30: M.C.A. MSS. Jonathan Barker to Jabez Bunting, 15 September 1826: Thomas Galland to Jabez Bunting, 2 October 1826: Jabez Bunting to Edmund Grindrod, May 10, 1828.

34 M.C.A. MSS. Wm. Myles to John North, 5 October 1819: Robert Johnson, John Doncaster *et al.* to [Jabez Bunting] 19 February 1824: R. Johnson to Jabez Bunting, 4 December 1824: T. Galland to Jabez Bunting, 30 June 1825. See Mark Robinson's *Observations on the system of Wesleyan Methodism* (London, 1824).

35 J. Shepherd, T. Brigham, J. Harrison and G. C. Taylor, *An appeal to the Methodist Conference in a letter to the President, the Rev. Robert Newton, against an attempt on the part of the Methodist preachers to expel from their Society Mr. Mark Robinson* . . . (London, 1825) p. 5 n: Wilberforce, *Life of Wilberforce* v. 272-3: M.C.A. MSS. H. Sandwith to Jabez Bunting, 10 November 1824: 31 January, 5 March 1825: Thomas Galland to Jabez Bunting, 2 October 1826.

36 M.C.A. MSS. R. Miller to H. Moore, 27 March 1824: J. Bate to Jabez Bunting, 8 April 1825: Joseph Entwisle to Jabez Bunting, 17 January 1826: Jabez Bunting to Joseph Entwisle, 24 January 1826. The Wisbech programme was ' for a combination of L[ocal] Pr[eachers], Leaders &c. to *compel* the Conference to admit either Lay Delegates into the Conference, or *another house to sit at the same time, consisting of representatives of the people, wch.* shall act with the Conference &c., &c.', Joseph Entwisle to S. Woolmer, 18 January 1826. In view of what happened at Leeds the following year it is noteworthy that Bunting pushed Entwisle into making a Presidential intervention at Wisbech, and declined a pressing invitation to accompany him on another to Scotland. Jabez Bunting to Joseph Entwisle, 25 February 1826.

37 M.C.A. MSS. Thomas Galland to Jabez Bunting, 2 October 1826: 21 December 1827: 25 January 1828: T. Thompson to T. Jackson, 23 May 1828: Jabez Bunting to John Beecham, 16 November 1835: *Memoir of the Rev. Robert Wood* (privately printed, London, 1854) p. 80.

38 M.C.A. MSS. Jabez Bunting to H. Sandwith, 10 February 1825: H. Sandwith to Jabez Bunting, 5 March 1825; Jabez Bunting to James Kendall, 24 April 1834: *Wesleyan Methodist Magazine* 3s. xiv. 543.

39 M.C.A. MSS. Thomas Galland to Jabez Bunting, 30 June 1825: J. Hickling to George Osborn, 1 October 1834,

40 *Circular to Wesleyan Methodists* (Liverpool, 1830-3): M.C.A. MSS. J. R. Stephens to I. Holgate, n.d. (postmark appears to be 5 August 1833): Edmund Grindrod, to Jabez Bunting, 17 April 1834; Jabez Bunting to Edmund Grindrod, 14 March 1834: *Manchester Guardian* 5 January 1833: 8 March, 24 May, 1834.

41 Gregory, *Sidelights* p. 152: M.C.A. MSS. John Bowers to Jabez Bunting, 29 April 1834. On Bowers' part in the proceedings, [J. Everett], *Methodism as it is*, i. 134 n.

42 *Manchester Times* 5 April 1834: *Manchester Guardian* 24 May, 31 May 1834: *The Case of the Rev. J. R. Stephens* (n.pl.or d.): *Manchester Courier* 17 May 1834: M.C.A. MSS. Thomas Galland to Theophilus Lessey, 22 May 1834: Joseph Hargreaves to Jabez Bunting, 4 July 1834.

43 M.C.A. MSS. P. C. Turner to T. P. Bunting, 5 August 1834: Gregory, *Sidelights* pp. 155, 157: *Manchester Guardian* 16 August 1834.

44 Gregory, *Sidelights* pp. 155, 160-1: E. A. Rose, *Methodism in Ashton-under-Lyne* ii. pp. 33-8: *Manchester Guardian* 4 October, 11 October 1834: M.C.A. MSS. Thomas Dunn to Jabez Bunting, 29 July 1836: M. S. Edwards, *Joseph Rayner Stephens 1805-79* (Ashton, 1968).

45 R. Aitken, *An address to the preachers, office bearers and members of the Wesleyan Methodist Societies* (London, 1835) p. 6: Robert Young, *Showers of blessing or sketches of revivals of religion in the Wesleyan Methodist Connexion* pp. 455-7: *Wesleyan Reformer* 1851, p. 99: M.C.A. MSS. W. Leach to Jabez Bunting, 15 November 1834: J. Hull, *A short and plain answer to William Read's ' Candid Address'* (Manchester, 1834) pp. 9-10.

46 On the training and examination of preachers: M.C.A. Thos. Allan MSS. M. Longridge to Thos. Allan, 18 July 1807: Cf. M.C.A. MSS. Josiah Hill to Jabez Bunting, 24 July [1827]: MS. Conference Journal 1821: T. H. Horne to Joseph Benson, 20 May 1820: B. Slater to R. Rymer, 30 November 1829: W. Barton to Jabez Bunting, 16 May 1833: J. Taylor to Jabez Bunting *et al.*, 27 October 1834: P. C. Turner to T. P. Bunting, 22 November 1833: J. Beecham to Jabez Bunting, 1 July 1834; Jabez Bunting to John Beecham, 3 July 1834: n.d. [post-marked 5 July 1834]: Thomas Waugh to Jabez Bunting, 13 July 1834: [J. Beaumont and J. Everett] *Wesleyan Takings* (London, 1840) p. 133: Gregory, *Sidelights* p. 105.

47 Hartley Victoria College, Manchester. MS. Memoranda Book of James Everett, iii. 14 May 1834: S. Warren, *An account of the proceedings of the Special District Meeting held in Manchester* (London, 1834) p. 30.

48 S. Warren, *Remarks on the Wesleyan Theological Institution* (London, 1834) p. 23: M.C.A. MSS. Jabez Bunting to Edmund Grindrod, 27 September 1834: T. P. Bunting to Jabez Bunting, 23 October 1834: Jabez Bunting to [John Beecham], Friday Morng. [21 November 1834]: *Manchester Times* 18 October, 25 October, 1834.

49 *Captain Barlow's narrative of the blessed battle fought, and glorious victory gained at the Wesleyan Missionary Meeting* (Manchester, 1834): R. Gill, *Great Bridgwater Street Chapel, Manchester, 1801-98* [Bound cuttings from *Manchester Weekly Times* 1898]: *Manchester Times* 1, 8, 15, 22 November 1834: *Manchester Guardian* 1, 8, November 1834: M.C.A. MSS. C. Prest to Jabez Bunting, 30 October 1834.

50 *Manchester Guardian,* 1 November, 29 November 1834: *Manchester Times* 1, 15, November 1834: M.C.A. MSS. J. Taylor to Jabez Bunting, 27 October

1834: J. Dixon to Jabez Bunting, 14 March 1835: Jabez Bunting to T. P. Bunting, n.d. [post-marked 25 March 1835]: C. H. Kelly, *Memories* (London, 1910) p. 24

51 M.C.A. MSS. Wm. Leach to Jabez Bunting, 15 November 1834: John Beecham to Jabez Bunting, 15, 18, 22, 24, 26 November 1834: Joseph Taylor to T. Waugh, 29 December 1834: Jabez Bunting to T. P. Bunting, 4 November 1834: 18 June 1835.

52 M.C.A. MSS. John Budden to Isaac Rathbone, 19 August 1835: W. Bird to W. Smith, n.d. [post-marked 5 August 1835]: Elijah Hoole to George Cubitt, n.d. [August, 1835]: Jabez Bunting to T. P. Bunting, 9 July 1835: J. Bicknell to Jabez Bunting, 2 March 1835: *Manchester Times*, 18 July, 3 October, 10 October, 28 November 1835: *Manchester Courier* 8 October 1836: George Smith, *History of Wesleyan Methodism* iii. 315-16.

53 For a fuller account of the following, see the thesis of my former pupil, Dr. D. A. Gowland, ' Methodist secessions and social conflict in South Lancashire, 1830-1857' (unpublished Manchester Ph.D. thesis, 1966): also I. Sellars ' Liverpool Noncomformity', and ' The Wesleyan Methodist Association in Liverpool, 1834-5 ', *Proceedings of the Wesley Historical Society* xxxv. 142-8.

54 *Manchester Times* 27 June 1835.

55 *Ibid.* 25 July 1835: M. Baxter, *Memorials of the United Methodist Free Churches* (London, 1865) p. 237: *Chancery Lane Wesleyan Sunday School, Ardwick. Souvenir of 125th Anniversary* (Manchester, 1911) p. 8: J. H. Huddleston, *History of Grosvenor Street Wesleyan Chapel, Manchester, 1820-1920* (Manchester, 1920) pp. 31, 32: *Manchester Guardian* 10 November 1879: *A centenary memorial of the Wesleyan Sunday School, Grosvenor Street, Manchester* (Manchester, 1885) p. 21: *Origin and present condition of the Sunday Schools for children of all denominations in Manchester*: MS. Diary of Rev. John Peters, 7 March 1836.

56 M.C.A. MSS. Jabez Bunting to Edmund Grindrod, 2 March 1831: 3 March 1832: *A catechism for Wesleyan Methodists* (Liverpool, 1834) p. 27: I. Sellars, ' Liverpool Nonconformity', pp. 162, 166.

57 M.C.A. MSS. Peter McOwan to Jabez Bunting, 3 March 1850: Thomas Kaye to Jabez Bunting, 9 July 1834: Samuel Jackson to Samuel Smith, n.d. [post-marked 18 December 1834]: *Declaration of the Wesleyan Methodists in the Liverpool North Circuit* (Liverpool, 1834):

58 M.C.A. MSS. M. Ashton to Jabez Bunting, 3 January 1835.

59 *Illuminator* 1 April 1835.

60 M.C.A. MSS. B. Slater to J. Hall, 13 September 1826: J. Hargreaves to Jabez Bunting, 4 July 1834: MS. Journal of the transactions in the Rochdale Circuit (1813-34) quoted in Gowland, ' Methodist secessions and social conflict' pp. 213-14. The following narrative owes much to Dr. Gowland.

61 H. Howarth, *A brief account of Baillie Street Sunday School* p. 21: M.C.A. MSS. Jabez Bunting to John Beecham, 16 November 1835: *The Methodist Church, Baillie Street, Rochdale. A centenary history, 1837-1937* (Rochdale, 1937) pp. 14-15.

62 *Manchester Guardian* 27 September 1834.

63 T. Allin, *Letters to Rev. John Maclean* (Sheffield, 1834-5): *The life of Joseph Barker* ed. J. T. Barker (London, 1880) pp. 177-81: *Manchester Times*

22 October, 29 October 1836: 14 January, 4 February, 25 March 1837: *Manchester Guardian* 14 January, 18 January 1837: MS Diary of Rev. John Peters, 11 January, 12 January, 28 February, 21 March, 18 April 1837: *United Methodist Free Churches Magazine* 1863, pp 361-3: MS. Minute Book of Baillie Street Quarterly Meeting, 12 June 1837, quoted in Gowland, 'Methodist secessions and social conflict', p. 234.

64 M.C.A. MSS. T. Stanley to Jabez Bunting, 18 October 1827: R. Waddy to Jabez Bunting, 2 December 1834: T. Edwards to Jabez Bunting, 28 March, 31 March, 1835: Francis Heeley to Jabez Bunting, 31 March 1835: Robert Melson to Jabez Bunting, 10 July 1838: John H. Adams to Jabez Bunting, 15 October 1836: Gregory, *Sidelights* p. 207: T. Allin, *et al., The jubilee of the Methodist New Connexion* (London, 1848) p. 354.

65 *Manchester Times* 14 October 1837: 13 October, 20 October 1838: *Manchester Courier* 20 October 1838: M.C.A. MSS. Letters of Ministers I: F. A. West to George Osborn, 13 October 1837: S. Warren to Miss Tooth, 19 April 1855: Joseph Entwisle to Jonathan Edmundson, 13 November 1840: Kezzie Crawford, *The autobiography of a Methodist preacher's daughter* (London, n.d. [1850?]) p. 72: C. H. Kelly, *Memories*, p. 25.

66 MS. Diary of Rev. John Peters, February 5 and 6 [1836]: *Manchester Guardian* 23 January, 28 May 1836.

67 M.C.A. MSS. Thomas Preston to James Everett, 1 September 1826: J. R. Stephens to I. Holgate, 5 August 1833: *Centenary celebration of Sunday Schools, Bolton, 1880* (Bolton, 1880) p. 22: J. Musgrave, *Origins of Methodism in Bolton* (Bolton, 1865) p. 43.

68 M.C.A. MSS. Jonathan Barker to Jabez Bunting, 15 September 1826: Thomas Harris to Jabez Bunting, 13 February 1834: 22 January 1835: *Hill Top Methodist Church Centenary: Burslem Sunday School Ter-Jubilee, 1787-1937* (n.pl. or d.): *Victoria County History of Staffordshire* viii. 278.

69 M.C.A. MSS. Samuel Jackson to Jabez Bunting, 26 August 1831: J. J. Graham, *Wesleyan Methodism in Sheffield Park* p. 75.

70 M.C.A. MS. Scrapbook of James Everett, fos. 426, 428: Wm. Lord to John Beecham, 30 August 1850: *Watchman* 30 November 1836, p. 382.

71 John Ward, *The rise and progress of Wesleyan Methodism in Blackburn and the neighbourhood* (Blackburn, 1871) p. 70: R. Wilkinson, *Methodism at Mankinholes* p. 11.

72 T. Allin, *Letters to Rev. John Maclean* Letter 4 pp. 4-7.

Chapter 7 (pages 177-205)

1 *Manchester Guardian* 18 January 1845, p. 6: 13 May 1846, p. 7.

2 *Manchester Times* 14 May 1831, p. 576: 29 October 1831, p. 764: *Manchester Guardian* 2 June, 1832: *Manchester Courier* 2 June 1832.

3 *Manchester Guardian* 13 April, 20 April 1833: *Manchester Courier* 13 April 1833.

4 *Manchester Times* 18 May 1833: *Manchester Guardian* 25 May, 1 June 1833: *Manchester Courier* 18 May, 25 May 1833.

5 *Manchester Guardian* 3 August 1833: *Manchester Times* 1 June, 22 June, 10 August, 24 August, 28 September 1833.

6 *Manchester Guardian* 30 November 1833: 10 May, 23 August, 30 August 1834: *Manchester Courier* 23 August, 30 August 1834.

7 *Manchester Guardian* 6 September, 12 September 1834: *Manchester Courier* 6 September, 1834: *Christian Reformer* 1834, p. 727: *Manchester Times* 20 December 1834: 4 April, 18 April, 1835.

8 *Manchester Times* 30 May, 11 July, 1835: *Manchester Guardian* 11 July 1835: 24 January 1849, p. 6: *Manchester Courier* 11 July 1835: 11 March, 1837. There were occasional politically inspired rumours that a compulsory rate was to be revived: *Manchester Guardian* 6 August 1836: *Manchester Courier* 11 April 1840, p. 4: 15 November 1848, p. 735. When the yield of the voluntary rate fell off, the wardens of St. George's, Hulme, one of the 'government churches', repeatedly applied for a compulsory rate to be levied: *Manchester Guardian* 30 March 1853, pp. 4-5: 2 April 1853, p. 6.

9 *Manchester Courier* 11 March, 1 April, 15 April 1837: 18 April, 1849, p. 247: 21 April 1849, p. 252: *Manchester Guardian* 18 January 1837; 7 January 1843: 12 February, 19 February, 29 March 1845: 15 November 1848: 26 June, 12 October 1850: *Report of Select Committee on Church Rates* P.P. H.C. 1851 IX, pp. 97, 98, 327: P.P. H.C. 1856 XLVIII *Return of parishes in which church rates have been refused in the last 15 years*, p. 86.

10 *Ibid.* pp. 80-3. See entries for Didsbury, Heaton Mersey and Manchester. For the case of Keswick where the division of a parish led to a clash, *Westminster Review* n.s. xiv, 46-7.

11 The press only began to catch up with Rochdale church rates in the mid-thirties, and the following narrative owes much to an unpublished Durham undergraduate dissertation by my former pupil, Miss Eithne R. Nightingale based on the rich MS. resources of the Rochdale parish chest, and other archives.

12 MS. Rochdale Church Vestry Book, 20 May 1829, quoted in Eithne R. Nightingale, 'The Church in Rochdale, 1820-1870', p. 3.

13 *Manchester Courier* 15 June 1833: MS. correspondence cited in Nightingale, 'The Church in Rochdale', pp. 7-10: G. B. Smith, *Life and speeches of John Bright* (London, 1881) i. 46: H. Petrie, *Threads from the life of John Mills* (London, 1899) pp. 14-15: G. M. Trevelyan, *Life of John Bright* (London, 2nd ed., 1925) p. 36: *Manchester Guardian* 4 October, 11 October 1834: 23 May 1835: 11 February 1837.

14 *Manchester Times* 18 April, 2 May 1835: *Manchester Guardian* 22 August 1835: 22 July 1837.

15 *Manchester Guardian* 3 July, 13 July, 24 July 1839.

16 *Manchester Guardian* 28 December 1836: 13 February 1841: 19 February, 29 March 1845: *Manchester Courier* January 1840 *passim* (e.g. 4 January, 25 January 1840): 1 February, 29 February 1840: 15 May 1841: 11 September 1841.

17 *Manchester Guardian* 1 April, 8 April, 15 April, 25 April, 2 May, 6 May 1840.

18 *Manchester Courier* 18 July, 25 July, 8 August 1840: 21 March 1849, p. 180: *Manchester Guardian* 15 July, 29 July, 1 August, 8 August, 12 August, 22 August, 26 August, 5 September 1840.

19 *Manchester Courier* 15 August 1840: 23 January, 27 February, 22 May

1841: 7 October 1848: 12 May 1849: *Manchester Guardian* 1 August 1840: 20 January, 23 January, 27 January, 10 February 1841: 26 April, 29 April, 14 June, 15 July, 2 September 1843: 2 July 1845: 7 October, 9 December 1848: *Manchester Times* 11 May 1844, p. 6: Eithne R. Nightingale, ' The Church in Rochdale ', p. 26.

20 *Manchester Guardian* 27 November 1844: 15 February, 19 February, 21 May, 28 May 1845. For proceedings on the bill, *Ibid.* 19 March, 4 June, 11 June, 25 June, 2 July, 5 July, 12 July, 23 July, 26 July, 30 July, 6 August, 30 August, 3 September 1845. For an arbitration case, *Ibid.* 6 February 1847, p. 2: MS. correspondence between the Vicar and Primate quoted in Nightingale, ' The Church in Rochdale ', p. 51: Church Commissioners Office: MS. Benefice file: Parish of Rochdale.

21 *Manchester Courier* 18 July, 1 August 1840. For criticism of Church, *Manchester Courier* 1846, *passim,* especially 19 September, 10 October 1846 (this collection was reprinted as a pamphlet: *Letters of the Church in Rochdale* by Adam de Spotland (1846)): *Manchester Guardian* 25 April 1846, p. 8: Manchester Central Reference Library. Archdeacon Rushton's MS. Visitation Vol. 63: MS. Rochdale Church Vestry Book, quoted in Nightingale, ' The Church in Rochdale ', p. 41.

22 A. Miall, *Life of Edward Miall* (London, 1884) pp. 26-7, 49: *Christian Reformer* 1839, pp. 121-2.

23 *Wesleyan Methodist Magazine* 3s. xvii. 365-9 (1838): R. Vaughan, *Congregationalism, or the polity of Independent churches viewed in relation to the state and tendencies of modern society* (2nd ed. London, 1842) pp. 172-3.

24 The Manchester radicals first flirted with Irish disestablishment in 1836, *Manchester Guardian* 20 February, 27 February 1836: *Manchester Courier* 20 February 1836. On Scotland, *Ibid.* March 31, 1838: *Manchester Guardian* 28 March, 11 April, 25 April, 1838: *Manchester Times* 7 April 1838: Miall, *Life of Edward Miall* pp. 37-8.

25 *Manchester Guardian* 20 February, 6 August 1836: *Manchester Times* 9 April 1836 (cf. 20 February, 27 February 1836): 4 March, 1837: Peel, *These hundred years* p. 105. Conservative unitarians were well satisfied, and Cross Street was the first Manchester chapel to apply for a licence: *Manchester Guardian* 25 January 1837: *Manchester Times* 1 July, 1837.

26 E. Miall, *The nonconformist's sketch book* (London, 1845) p. 5: *Guardian* 27 October 1847, p. 644: E Miall, *The social influences of the state church* (London, 1867) pp. 42 *seq.*: W. Ferguson, *The impending dangers of our country, or hidden things brought to light* (London, 1848) pp. 97-8: W. Ferguson, *Our rural churches, their perils & the remedy* (London, 1849).

27 W. Hanna, *Memoirs of Thomas Chalmers* (ed. Edinburgh, 1854) ii. 413: B. L. Manning, *Protestant Dissenting Deputies* pp. 389-91: H. McNeile, *Lectures on the Church of England* (London, 1840) pp. 58-9. These lectures also went through several editions in the year.

28 *Manchester Guardian* 27 November, 7 December, 21 December 1839: 29 January, 7 March 1840: 19 June, 21 August, 24 August, 8 September, 13 October 1841: J. Guinness Rogers, *An autobiography* (London, 1903) p. 81: Waddington, *Congregational History* iv. 557-566: N. McCord, *The Anti-Corn Law League, 1838-1846* (London, 1958) p. 103: Whitley, *Baptists of North-West England* p. 281.

29 H. U. Faulkner, *Chartism and the Churches* (London, ed. 1970) ch. I, esp. pp. 35-41. Faulkner's dates and figures need correction by the local press, e.g. *Manchester Guardian* 27 July, 31 July, 7 August 1839: *Manchester Courier* 17 August 1839, p. 7.

30 On this topic generally, Faulkner, *Chartism and the Churches* pp. 42-6: *Manchester Guardian* 29 April 1846, p. 7. Prominent Chartists rebuffed Tory attempts to induce them to break up meetings of the Religious Freedom Society. *Ibid.*, 24 April 1841.

31 *Manchester Guardian* 20 February 1836: *The Manchester Socinian Controversy* (London, 1825) pp. xliv-xlvi, 11, 28, 194, 219.

32 Waddington, *Congregational History* v. 485: *Manchester Guardian* 18 January, 1837.

33 *Manchester Courier* 26 July, 27 October 1838: *Manchester Times* 28 February 1835: *Parliamentary debates on the Dissenters' Chapel Bill* (London, 1844) p. ix: *Christian Reformer* 1845, pp. 3-4: *Wesleyan Methodist Magazine* 3s xv, 235: xxiii. 415-17, 660-1: M.C.A. MSS. Jabez Bunting to [George Osborn?] 19 June 1844: John Beecham to Rt. Hon. Lord Worsley, M.P., 27 May 1844.

34 *Manchester Times* 5 March 1836: *Manchester Courier* 25 March 1837: *Christian Reformer* 1847, p. 62.

Chapter 8 (pages 206-235)

1 G.F.A. Best, *Shaftesbury* (London, 1964) pp. 81-3.

2 J. T. Ward, *The factory movement, 1830-1855* (London, 1962) pp. 217, 227: *Manchester Guardian* 13 April 1844, p. 4: 20 April 1844, pp. 5-7: 27 April, 1844, p. 6: 21 January 1846, p. 7: 25 April 1846, p. 8: 6 May 1846, p. 7.

3 *Manchester Guardian* 2 July 1842: 20 December 1854, p. 6: *Manchester Courier* 30 January 1841, p. 6.

4 J. C. Gill, *The Ten Hours parson. Christian social action in the eighteen-thirties* (London, 1959) p. 187: *Manchester Guardian* 11 July 1835: 30 November 1844, p. 4: H. Senior, *Orangeism in Ireland and Britain, 1795-1836* (London, 1966) pp. 152-3: *Report from Select Committee on Orange Institutions* P.P. H.C. 1834 xvii, p. 33.

5 *Manchester Guardian* 19 July 1834: 11 July, 18 July 1835: 19 March 1836: *Manchester Courier* 18 July 1835.

6 *Annual report of the Stockport Sunday School, 1824* (Stockport, 1824) p. 13: R. L. Hill, *Toryism and the people, 1832-46* (London, 1929) pp. 48-60: *Manchester Guardian* 12 September, 21 November 1835: 6 February 1836: 6 November 1839; 4 November 1840: *Manchester Courier* 8 August, 5 September, 7 November 1835: 2 January, 13 February, 12 March 1836: 21 September, 9 November 1839. By March 1836 conservative Operative Societies in south Lancashire and north Cheshire mustered over 3,000 members, *Manchester Courier* 5 March 1836. The *Courier* was full of appeals for the Irish clergy at this time, e.g. 21 November, 1835.

7 *Manchester Courier* 28 October, 4 November 1837: 3 August, 27 July 1839: *Manchester Guardian* 25 October, 1 November 1837: 24 August 1853, p. 7: 27 August, 1853, p. 9: J. Evans, *Lancashire authors and orators* (London, 1850) p. 170.

8 J. Murphy, *The religious problem in English education. The crucial experiment* (Liverpool, 1959).

9 *Manchester Guardian* 28 September 1839: 8 February, 26 February, 4 March 1840: 24 February 1841: *Manchester Courier* 21 September, 5 October, 1839: G. Turner, *The constitution and discipline of Wesleyan Methodism* (London, 1841) pp. 126-7: *Watchman* 1837, p. 251.

10 M.C.A. MSS. James Dixon to Thomas Galland, 27 March 1838: Jabez Bunting to Mathew Tobias, 23 February 1824: A. Clarke Wardlaw to Jabez Bunting, 30 May [1837?]: MS. Letters of Presidents of Wesleyan Conference collected by J. E. Wright, letter by Thomas Jackson, 1 April 1841: *The Christian Cabinet* 3 August, 1859, p. 61, (cutting in M.C.A. Presidents of Wesleyan Conference, MS. Letters): J. McLean to T. P. Bunting, 11 June 1839: *Manchester Guardian* 26 February, 4 March, 29 April 1840.

11 M.C.A. MSS. Thos. Allan to Jabez Bunting, 11 June 1839: John McLean to Jabez Bunting, 25 June 1839: D. O'Connell, *Letters to the ministers and office bearers of the Wesleyan Methodist Societies of Manchester* (2nd ed. Manchester, 1839). Cf. also his *Second letter* . . . One Wesleyan preacher of some distinction desperately plunged into research in the British Museum to minimise Wesley's connexion with the Protestant Association: M.C.A. MSS. George Cubitt to Jabez Bunting, 29 July 1839: 30 July 1839: 1 January 1840: G. Cubitt to John Bowers, 10 August 1839: 12 August 1839.

12 *Manchester Courier* 21 October, 28 October, 4 November 1837: 5 October 1839. *Manchester Guardian* 25 October, 1 November 1837. It was the worse because Stowell had no option but to be sensationalist in exposing the errors not only of catholic priests but of crypto-papists among his brother clergy, e.g. *Manchester Guardian* 20 May, 2 September, 9 September, 12 September, 19 September, 18 November 1840.

13 *Manchester Guardian* 1 January, 8 February, 27 June 1840: 6 March, 9 March 1844: 12 March 1845: *Manchester Courier* 23 March, 20 April 1839.

14 *Christian Witness* i. p.x. (This new journal dedicated to disestablishment was launched in 1844 under the auspices of the Congregational Union): M.C.A. MSS. W. Campbell to [Jabez Bunting], 1 May 1845: E. Hodder, *Life and work of the seventh earl of Shaftesbury* (London, 1887) ii. 100: *Manchester Courier* 19 April 1845.

15 *Manchester Courier* 19 April 1845: *Manchester Guardian* 30 April 1845 p. 6: M.C.A. MSS. Jacob Stanley to Jabez Bunting, 28 May 1845: Jabez Bunting to George Osborn, 28 May 1845: N. Gash, *Reaction and reconstruction in English politics, 1832-52* (Oxford, 1965) p. 152.

16 G. I. T. Machin, 'The Maynooth grant, the dissenters and disestablishment, 1845-7', *English Historical Review* lxxxii. 69-70: *Manchester Guardian* 14 May 1845, pp. 4, 6: *Christian Reformer* 1845, p. 523.

17 Machin, 'The Maynooth grant' p. 74: *Christian Reformer*, 1845, pp. 788-93. (In the copy consulted the article was annotated in MS. as being by Edward Higginson): 1846, p. 628: Peel, *These hundred years,* p. 147: M.C.A. MSS. Alfred Barrett to [Jabez Bunting], a major policy statement, undated, but clearly written after the Liverpool Conference, late in 1845: E. B. Underhill to W. Bevan, 4 December 1848: J. W. Thomas to Jabez Bunting, 20 August 1846: Joseph Lawton to Jabez Bunting, 26 October 1846: W. M. Bunting to [? F. J. Jobson] 8 January 1851: J. Beecham to Jabez Bunting, 4 October 1849: *Baptist Magazine* 1846, pp. 274-85: *Manchester*

Guardian 18 November 1846, p. 8: *Wesleyan Methodist Magazine* 4s. vii. pt.ii. 989 *seq.*

18 J. B. Marsden, *Memoirs of the life and labours of Hugh Stowell* (London, 1868) p. 166: *Manchester Guardian* 23 September 1846, p. 6: 24 January 1852, p. 8: 20 March 1852, p. 8: 22 May 1852, p. 8: 3 July 1852, pp. 6, 8: 23 October 1852, p. 8: H. McNeile, *The manifested oneness of the church of Christ: with some reasons for not joining the proposed Evangelical Alliance* (London, 1846). Stowell's suspicions of the Alliance were justified to the extent that one of the leading evangelical clergy to support it, Baptist Noel, went over to the Baptists in 1847, explaining that establishment was the great barrier to the triumph of evangelicalism in the Church. B. W. Noel, *Essay upon the union of church and state* (London, 2nd ed. 1849). Cf. *Manchester Guardian* 4 February 1874, p. 7: 5 February 1874, p. 8: 6 February 1874, p. 4.

19 Marsden, *Stowell* pp. 47-8.

20 I am indebted for references to the MS. Chapter Minute Book to an unpublished paper, written from a quite different viewpoint, by Archdeacon Hetley Price on ' The Manchester Church Question ', for the loan of which I am very grateful. See also: *Manchester Guardian* 15 April, 27 May, 31 May, 16 August, 2 September 1837: 11 April, 25 July, 1 August, 8 August, 11 August, 15 August 1838: 22 January 1840: 3 June 1843, p. 4: 21 June 1843, p. 4: *Manchester Courier* 4 August 1838: George Huntingdon, *Random recollections of some noted bishops, divines and worthies of the ' Old Church' at Manchester* (London, 1893) p. 286: J. McClure, *Some remarks on the state of the established church in Manchester* (2nd ed. Manchester, 1841).

21 *Manchester Courier* 6 February 1836: 27 February 1841, p. 3: 17 March 1849, p. 173: *Report of the Committee on the Manchester Rectory Division Bill* (printed for the Manchester Churchwardens, 1850) pp. 98-9, 101-2: *Manchester Guardian* 10 April 1839: 27 November 1844, p. 6: 16 October 1847, p. 6.

22 *Ibid.* 26 September 1846, p. 6: 24 October, 1846, p. 6: 28 October 1846, p. 3: 31 October 1846, p. 7: 4 November 1846, pp. 4, 8: 21 November 1846, p. 6: 14 April 1852, p. 6.

23 *Ibid.* 10 February 1844, p. 5: 23 March 1844, p. 6: 30 November 1844, p. 3: 14 July 1847, pp. 5, 7: 17 July 1847, p. 6: 21 July, 1847, p. 4: 24 July 1847, p. 7: 26 January 1848, p. 5: McClure, *Remarks on established church in Manchester* p. 28.

24 *Manchester Guardian* 13 March 1847, pp. 7, 8: 17 March 1847, pp. 4, 5: *A copy of the petition presented to the House of Commons by Lord Ashley on . . . 15th December 1847, and the observations of the chapter of Manchester thereon* (n.d., printed for private circulation): *Manchester Courier* 13 February 1847, pp. 100-1: 17 March 1847, pp. 172, 176: 7 April 1847, p. 220: 2 February 1850, p. 59: *Report of Committee on Manchester Rectory Division Bill,* pp. 99-100, 156-9, 224. (The Chapter's defence was that Stowell wanted to build his church 300 yards from one of the new government churches.): *The City Lantern* IV. 178 (Manchester, 1 March 1878).

25 *Manchester Guardian* 7 April 1847, p. 7: 22 May, 1847, pp. 6, 7: 16 June 1847, pp. 4, 5: 14 July 1847, p. 5: *First annual report of the [Manchester Church Reform Association]* (Manchester, 1848): *Reform in the ecclesiastical provision for the parish of Manchester* (Manchester, 1847): *Reply of the Association for promoting a reform in the ecclesiastical provision for the*

*parish of Manchester to an article . . . in the Manchester Courier of . . . 30th
June, 1847* (Manchester, 1847).

26 *First annual report of Manchester Church Reform Association: Second
Annual Report . . .* (Manchester, 1849). Thomas Turner, *First Appendix to Mr.
Turner's letter to the Bishop of Manchester . . .* (London and Manchester, 1850):
Manchester Guardian 5 January, 1848, p. 4: 8 January 1848, p. 9: 11 March
1848, p. 7: 18 March 1848, p. 7: 22 March 1848, p. 5: 25 March 1848, p. 7:
26 April 1848, pp. 4, 6: 6 May 1848, p. 10: 16 August 1848, p. 5: 3 January
1849, p. 6: 17 January 1849, p. 8: 20 January 1849, pp. 6, 9: 24 January
1849, p. 7: *Manchester Courier* 30 December 1848, p. 839: 3 January 1849,
p. 5: 6 January 1849, p. 12: 10 January 1849, p. 21: 17 January, 1849, p. 8:
20 January 1849, pp. 42, 43: 24 January, 1849, pp. 49, 50: 27 January 1849,
pp. 57, 59.

27 *Manchester Courier* 10 February 1849, p. 91: 3 March 1849, p. 139: 14
March 1849, p. 166: 17 March 1849, p. 173: *Manchester Guardian* 1 August
1849, p. 5.

28 *Manchester Guardian* 4 April 1849, p. 5: 11 April 1849, pp. 4, 6: 14
April 1849, pp. 6, 8: 4 August 1849, p. 6: 14 November 1849, p. 5: *Manchester Courier* 31 March 1849, p. 203: 7 April 1849, pp. 220-1; 11 April
1849, p. 228: 14 April 1849, p. 236: 9 June 1849, p. 366: 16 June 1849, p.
382: *Third Annual Report of [Manchester Church Reform Association]* (Manchester, 1850): *Church Reform Association. Case submitted to Mr. Badeley
relating to the Collegiate . . . Church . . .* (Manchester, 1850).

29 *Manchester Guardian* 5 January 1850, p. 6: 9 January 1850, p. 5: 12
January 1850, pp. 6, 8-9: 26 January 1850, p. 6: 9 March, 1850, p. 7: 16
March 1850, pp. 6, 8: *Manchester Courier* 5 January 1850, pp. 4, 6: 12
January 1850, p. 18: 19 January 1850, p. 30: 26 January 1850, p. 43:
9 March 1850, p. 115: 16 March 1850, p. 126. For the chapter: R. C.
Clifton, *The collegiate church of Manchester . . . with observations on
the proposed bill for the sub-division of the parish of Manchester* (Manchester, 1850): H. Gordon, *Observations on the Manchester Rectory Bill
. . .* (London, 1850): *Manchester Church question plainly stated* (London,
1850). Against the chapter: T. Turner, *A letter on the collegiate parish church
of Manchester . . .* (London, 1850): *Second appendix to Mr. Turner's Letter
to the Bishop of Manchester* (London, 1850): Richard Birley et al., *Scheme
for dividing the parish of Manchester . . .* (Manchester, 1850): *Third Annual
Report of Manchester Church Reform Association.*

30 *Manchester Guardian* 27 March 1850, p. 4: 3 April 1850, pp. 4, 5:
6 April 1850, p. 6: 29 May 1850, p. 4: 1 June 1850, pp. 6, 8, 10: 8 June
1850, p. 10: *Manchester Courier* 6 April 1850, p. 163: 11 May 1850, p. 222:
1 June 1850, p. 258: *Daily News* 7 June 1850.

31 *Manchester Rectory Division Bill. Report of the evidence given before the
committee of the House of Commons,* pp. 181-91: *Manchester Courier* 13
April 1850, p. 173: 20 July 1850, p. 6: 27 July 1850, p. 351: *Manchester
Guardian* 6 May 1850, p. 6: 8 May 1850, pp. 4-5: 15 May 1850, pp. 4, 6-7:
27 July 1850, p. 6: 31 July 1850, p. 4: 28 August 1850, p. 5: 4 December
1850, p. 4: 27 November 1852, p. 8: 13 April 1853, p. 4: 27 July 1855, p. 3.
(Cf. 25 June 1851, p. 6): 7 July 1864, p. 4: *First Report of Her Majesty's
Commissioners for inquiry into the condition of the cathedral churches in
England and Wales . . .* P.P. H.C. 1884-5 XXI, p. 3.

32 G. R. Balleine, *A history of the evangelical party in the Church of England* (ed. London, 1951) p. 163: E. Hodder, *Shaftesbury* iii. 3.

33 Advertisement to Vol. I of *Tracts for the times*, 1834.

34 Keble College MSS. J. D. Dalgairns to J. M. Gresley, 10 December 1844.

Chapter 9 (pages 236-278)

1 George Turner, *The constitution and discipline of Wesleyan Methodism* (London, 1841) pp. 64-8 (Cf. Charles Welch, *The Wesleyan crisis . . .* (London, 1835) p. 19): Gregory, *Sidelights,* p. 334.

2 M.C.A. MSS. J. Rigg to Jabez Bunting, 16 November 1849: J. Sutcliffe to Jabez Bunting, 11 July 1836: W. M. Harvard to Jabez Bunting, 26 January, 1 February, 15 February, 15 March 1848: M. Batty, 'Contribution of local preachers to . . . the Wesleyan Methodist Church' pp. 217-20.

3 C. Welch, *The claims of Wesleyan lay-delegation fully examined* (London, 1850) p. 43: John Evans, *Lancashire authors and orators* p. 30: A. Barrett, *The ministry and polity of the Christian Church* (London, 1854) p. 15.

4 *Ibid.* pp. 31-2: M.C.A. MSS. Oliver Henwood to Thomas Clulow, 23 April 1853: Wm. Binning to [Jabez Bunting], 10 July, [18]51.

5 M.C.A. MSS. J. Loutit to [? J. Beecham] 25 February 1850: F. A. West to George Osborn, 1 July 1842: R. Newstead to Jabez Bunting, 31 August 1844: 13 September 1844: Edward B. Pinder to Jabez Bunting, 2 November 1853: R. Hardy to J. Hannah, 16 March 1852: J. Mood to Luke Tyerman, 6 October 1848 (Cf. Thos. Allan MSS. Thomas Allan to Edmund Grindrod, 9 March 1840): J. Stephenson to Jabez Bunting, 27 November 1844: Gregory, *Sidelights* pp. 346-7, 399, 417, 427: MS. Diary of Rev. John Peters, 5 and 6 February 1836.

6 M.C.A. MSS. W. Vevers to Jabez Bunting, 27 September 1836: Jabez Bunting to T. P. Bunting, 26 April 1838: G. Cubitt to Jabez Bunting, 1 January, 6 January 1840: 21 July 1841: J. Kendall to Jabez Bunting, 14 November 1840: J. Beecham to Jabez Bunting, 22 March 1841: P. Duncan to Jabez Bunting, 25 March, 5 April 1842: E. Grindrod, *Compendium . . .* (3rd ed. London, 1848) p. ix.

7 *Wesleyan Methodist Magazine* 3s. xxiii. 117 *seq.*: M.C.A. MSS. John Beecham to Jabez Bunting, 12 January, 14 January, 1843: Bernard Slater to Jabez Bunting, 26 May 1843: W. Vevers to Jabez Bunting, 14 March 1843: Gregory, *Sidelights* pp. 348-50.

8 M.C.A. MSS. John McLean to [Jabez Bunting], 30 January, 6 February, 24 March, 30 October 1845: 18 August 1855: Jabez Bunting to Wm. Lindley, 2 April 1845: Robert Harrison to Jabez Bunting, 5 January 1849: W. Horton to Jabez Bunting, 13 September, 20 October, 27 October 1849.

9 Gregory, *Sidelights,* pp. 119-23, 259-61: *Manchester Guardian* 21 October 1837: 29 May, 1 June 1839: 18 March 1840: M.C.A. MSS. John S. Elliott to Jabez Bunting, 20 February 1839: Jabez Bunting to Thomas Binney, 5 April 1838: Edward Baines to Jabez Bunting Jnr., 19 June, 1839: Lord Ashley to Jabez Bunting, 7 June [1839]: Thos. Allan MSS. Thos Allan to Thomas Jackson. 6 August 1838: 17 May 1839: Thos Allan to W. Dealtry, 27 May 1839: *Proposed scheme of National Education* [Broadsheet, May,

1839] : W. Dealtry to Thos. Allan, 28 May 1839: *Wesleyan Methodist Magazine* 3s. xvii. pp. 69, 260: *Manchester Courier* June 1, 1839, p. 1: 25 May 1839, p. 4: D. O'Connell, *Letters to the ministers and office-bearers of the Wesleyan Methodist societies of Manchester* (Manchester, 1839).

10 M.C.A. MSS. J. W. Gabriel to Jabez Bunting, 25 June 1839: Robert Newstead to Jabez Bunting, 2 August 1839: 10 October, 5 November 1842: 10 February, 14 July 1843: R. M. MacBrair to Jabez Bunting, 7 March 1840.

11 *Manchester Courier* 15 June 1839, p. 7: M.C.A. MSS. Edward Baines to Jabez Bunting Jnr., 19 June 1839: Thomas Allan to Jabez Bunting, 11 June 1839.

12 Galland's letter to the *Leeds Mercury* was reprinted in *Manchester Guardian* 12 June 1839: Gregory, *Sidelights* pp. 268-275.

13 *Christian Reformer* 1847 pp. 373-4.

14 *Manchester Courier* 29 April 1843, p. 8: M.C.A. MSS. J. Scott to Jabez Bunting, 13 May, 1843: Joseph Fowler to   ?   ?   , 24 May 1843. Cf. Gregory, *Sidelights* pp. 511-13.

15 *Wesleyan Methodist Magazine* 3s. xxii. 615, 1026-30: M.C.A. MSS. Edward Corderoy to Jabez Bunting, 28 October 1843: Edward Morris to Jabez Bunting, 1 December 1843: Hugh Carter to Jabez Bunting, 15 October 1844: H. Hughes to Jabez Bunting, 18 November 1844.

16 *Guardian* 17 March 1847, p. 163: M.C.A. MSS. Wm. Vevers to Jabez Bunting, 25 February, 23 March, 29 March 1847: Thomas Cutting to Jabez Bunting, 13 March 1847: E. Baines to [Jabez Bunting] 23 March [1847]. (Partly printed in Bunting, *Life of Bunting* ii. 337-8): Lord Ashley to Jabez Bunting, 3 April 1847: Gregory, *Sidelights* p. 224. *Manchester Courier* 1 August 1835: *Wesleyan Methodist Magazine* 4s. iii, pt.i. p. 395.

17 *Wesleyan Methodist Magazine* 4s iii. pt.i. pp. 499 *seq.*, 505 *seq.*: Guardian 21 April, 1847, p. 246: *Christian Reformer* 1847, pp. 304-5.

18 [James Everett] *Methodism as it is* (London, 1863-5) i. 193: M.C.A. MSS. George Marsden to Jabez Bunting, 29 May 1838: Gregory, *Sidelights* p. 265.

19 *Manchester Times* 5 August 1837: D. A. Gowland, ' Methodist secessions and social conflict ', Appendices A and B: *Manchester Courier* 7 December 1839: *Manchester Guardian* 23 June, 28 June 1841: M.C.A. MSS. Lord Ashley to Jabez Bunting, 11 July [1841].

20 Entwisle, *Memoir of Joseph Entwisle* pp. 454-5: M.C.A. MSS. Wm. Smith to Jabez Bunting, 21 June 1841: C. Welch to M. Cousin, 21 June, 22 June, 23 June, 24 June, 25 June, 2 July 1841: P. Duncan to Jabez Bunting, 10 May 1841: H. Sandwith to [Jabez Bunting], 1 August 1842: Gregory, *Sidelights* pp. 304-5.

21 M.C.A. MSS. A. E. Farrar to Jabez Bunting, 6 June 1844: James C. Hindson to Jabez Bunting, 9 July 1845: H. Beeson to C. Prest, 5 December 1859: W. Barton to Jabez Bunting, 26 August 1842, 12 February 1845: W. Vevers to Jabez Bunting, 14 March 1843: J. Shipman to Lord Lansdowne: 14 April 1847: Jabez Bunting to [George Osborn] 14 December 1844: *Manchester Guardian* 22 March 1843, p. 7: Gregory, *Sidelights* pp. 358, 361, 390, 399: A. Barrett, *Consolator; or recollections of a departed friend, the Rev. John Pearson* (London, 1856) p. 69.

22 *Watchman* 20 January 1836, p. 20: *Wesleyan Methodist Magazine* 3s. xxi. 64, 661, 745, 841: xvi. 215: xviii. 234, 636: xx. 1003: M.C.A. MSS. J.

Beecham to Jabez Bunting, 13 January 1842: H. Christmas to Jabez Bunting, 5 January 1841: F. A. West to George Osborn, 12 April 1841: W. Vevers to Jabez Bunting, 26 January 1847: Gregory, *Sidelights* pp. 241, 346.

23 M.C.A. MSS. Jabez Bunting to John Beecham, 16 November 1835: 13 January 1842: T. Stead to [Jabez Bunting] 23 April 1839: R. Alder to Jabez Bunting, 17 January 1842: J. Hanwell to John E. Coulson, 6 August 1846: Gregory, *Sidelights* pp. 251, 281-2: R. A. West, *Sketches of Wesleyan Preachers* (London, 1849) pp. 17-18.

24 M.C.A. MSS. E. Walker to Jabez Bunting, 8 July 1844: B. Slater to Jabez Bunting, 15 July 1844: J. MacLean to [Jabez Bunting] 30 January 1845: Robert Melson to Conference, 2 August 1847: R. Melson to Jabez Bunting, 13 April 1850: John Rigg to Jabez Bunting, 16 October 1848: Gregory, *Sidelights*, pp. 375-8, 453: R. Chew, *William Griffiths, memorials and letters* (London, 1885) pp. 28, 38: *Manchester Guardian* 18 July 1849, p. 5.

25 M.C.A. MSS. F. A. West to George Osborn, 5 December 1848: John H. James to George Osborn, 17 May 1849: John Hanwell to J. E. Coulson, 1 August 1846: S. N. Christophers to B. Carvosso, 4 November 1847: *Wesleyan Reformer* 1851, p. 99: *United Methodist Free Church Magazine* 1863, p. 424: *Manchester Guardian* 28 July 1849, p. 8.

26 M.C.A. MSS. James Grose to Jabez Bunting, 21 August 1849: Frederick Jobson to [Jabez Bunting] 17 May 1849: John Kirk to T. P. Bunting [17 May 1849]: John H. James to George Osborn, 17 May 1849: John W. Thomas to [Jabez Bunting] 15 December 1848: Gregory, *Sidelights* p. 438: *Manchester Guardian* 28 July 1849, p. 8.

27 *Manchester Guardian*, 28 July 1849, p. 8: Gregory, *Sidelights* pp. 324, 384, 408, 429: M.C.A. MSS. Samuel Dunn to Jabez Bunting, 14 September 1844: W. Griffiths to [?], 12 July 1849.

28 M.C.A. MS. Minutes of London District Meetings 1850-51: MS. Minutes of Norwich & Lynn District Committee 20-23 May 1851: MS. Minutes of Halifax and Bradford District Meeting, 20-24 May 1851: D. Hay to Luke Tyerman, 12 June 1854: J. G. Miall *Congregationalism in Yorkshire* p. 208.

29 M.C.A. MS. Minutes of Kent District Meeting 20-23 May 1851: J. Mortimer to [?], Swaffham, 10 May 1852: J. J. Topham to F. J. Jobson, 16 December 1850: (For starving preachers out, cf. W. Baddeley to F. J. Jobson, 26 February, 19 March 1851): G. Birley to T. P. Bunting, 24 August, 1853: J. Cullen to John Beecham, 5 November 1850: W. Bacon to John Beecham, 25 September 1850.

30 M.C.A. MSS. R. Alder to Jabez Bunting, 29 August 1849: W. H. Clarkson to Jabez Bunting, 13 September 1849: Wm. Bacon to John Beecham, 25 September 1850: W. Lord to Jabez Bunting, 1 February 1850: W. H. Clarkson to Jabez Bunting, 27 March 1850: John Fernley to John Hannah, 15 March 1852: J. Wardle to J. Hannah, 15 March 1852: [James Everett] *Methodism as it is* i. 215-17: *Wesleyan Reformer* 1851, p. 128.

31 J. H. Huddleston, *History of Grosvenor Street Wesleyan Chapel, Manchester* (Manchester, 1920) p. 32: M.C.A. Minutes of Bristol District Meeting, 20 May 1851: Minutes of Newcastle District Meeting, 20-22 May 1851.

32 M.C.A. MSS. A. Watmough to Jabez Bunting, 11 October 1850: W. Binning to [Jabez Bunting], 10 July 1851 (Cf. W. Binning to John Beecham, 16 November 1850): Henry Beeson to C. Prest, 5 December 1859: William

Lord to John Beecham, 24 December 1850: Cf. same to same, 30 August, 6 December, 21 December 1850: Alexander Hume to John Beecham, 5 November 1850.

33 M.C.A. MSS. Isaac Denison to John Beecham, 26 November 1850: John H. Beech to [?] 16 August 1850: John Beecham to Wm. Bacon, 30 September 1850: R. M. MacBrair to [Jabez Bunting], 5 July 1850: R. Wilson to John Beecham, 10 September 1850: Robert Melson to Jabez Bunting, 26 April 1850: R. Insley to Jabez Bunting, 8 May 1851: George Heap to Jabez Bunting, 26 July 1851: James Loutit to Jabez Bunting, 17 December 1851: Wm. Binning to [Jabez Bunting] 10 July 1851.

34 M.C.A. MSS. James C. Hindson to Jabez Bunting, 9 July 1845: Thomas Harris to Jabez Bunting, 19 December 1844: J. Hannah to Robert Newton, 2 May 1845: H. U. Faulkner, *Chartism and the Churches,* p. 51: W. H. Oliver Lake, *Centenary History of the Wesleyan Methodist Church at Bollington,* p. 74: MS. Minute book for Bollington Sunday School 1833-60, 26 September 1847: 25 March 1849: 20 October [1850]: 6 October 6 1858: MS. Minute book 1860-1874, 27 May 1867: 12 July, 9 August 1869: 16 November 1869: 28 November 1872: MS. Minute book 1874-83, 22 January 1877: 20 October, 1879: 30 March 1880.

35 *Manchester Courier* 21 August 1841, p. 7: 4 September 1841, p. 7: Stockport Sunday School MSS. N. Armitage to J. Lomax, 9 September 1848: M.C.A. MSS. Alexander Hume to John Beecham, 5 November 1850: Wm. Lord to John Beecham, 30 August 1850: MS. Minutes of Leeds District Meeting 20-23 May 1851: MS. Minutes of Norwich and Lynn District Committee 20-23 May 1851: *Manchester Guardian* 1 February 1851, p. 10: 14 January 1852, p.7.

36 R. O. Ball, *One more light,* pp. 9-13, 21.

37 *Manchester Guardian* 1 May 1839: 2 July 1842: *The life of Joseph Barker ed.* John Thomas Barker, p. 109: A. Strachan, *Recollections . . . of Rev. George Lowe,* p. 210: George Turner, *The constitution and discipline of Wesleyan Methodism* p. v: M.C.A. MSS. F. & E. W[est] to ?, 3 June 1841: Wm. Cooke to Jabez Bunting, 2 February 1847.

38 *Manchester Guardian* 26 October 1853, p. 5: *Methodist Church Baillie Street, Rochdale. Centenary History* pp. 28-9.

39 G. A. Weston, 'Baptists of North-western England', pp. 597-618, 116, 160, 179, 181: Wm. Stokes, *History of the Midland Association of Baptist Churches from its rise in the year 1655 to 1855* (London, 1855), pp. 65-75 passim.

40 *Christian Reformer* 1850, p. 257: E. Miall, *The British churches in relation to the British people* (London, 1849) p. 218: *Congregational Year Book 1848,* pp. 82, 86, 97, 114.

41 *Papers on the present condition of Congregationalists in Manchester and Salford.* By a Christian Observer (Manchester, 1853): F. Wrigley, *The history of the Yorkshire Congregational Union 1873-1923* (London, 1923) p. 68.

Epilogue (pages 279-292)

1 *Manchester Guardian* 3 November 1847, p. 7: 31 March 1849, p. 6. Baines maintained that there was accommodation for 27,000 church scholars in Manchester, and that only 9,000 were in attendance. *Ibid.* 21 April 1849, p. 6.

2 *Ibid.* 10 April 1847, p. 5: 17 April 1847, p. 7: 24 May 1848, pp. 3, 6: *Manchester Courier* 24 May 1848, p. 334.

3 *Manchester Guardian* 25 January 1851, p. 5: 16 August 1851, p. 6.

4 *Ibid.* 21 April 1849, pp. 6, 8: 25 April 1849, p. 8: 28 September 1850, p. 10 (Methodist artisans became equally sceptical of unfulfilled assurances of what would be done by the rich men of Methodism, *Ibid.* 1 May 1850, p. 8): 2 August 1851, p. 7: 27 September 1851, p. 6: 8 October 1851, p. 7: H. J. Burgess, *Enterprise in education* ch. xi.

5 *Manchester Guardian* 15 January 1848, p. 10: 23 February 1848, p. 6: 21 October 1848, pp. 7, 10.

6 *Ibid.* 9 February 1848, p. 7: 16 February 1848, p. 6: 31 March 1849, p. 6: 3 April 1850, pp. 2-3.

7 *Manchester Courier* 29 January 1848, p. 66: 8 March 1848, p. 158: *Manchester Guardian* 4 January 1851, p. 6: 8 January 1851, p. 4: 11 January 1851, p. 6: 22 February 1851, pp. 6, 8. For objections from the other side, *Ibid.* 8 March 1851, p. 6.

8 *Ibid.* 30 August 1851, p. 6: 14 February 1852, p. 10: 18 February 1852, pp. 6, 7: 24 December 1853, p. 10: 30 April 1856, pp. 2, 3.

9 *Ibid.* 31 March 1849, p. 9.

10 J. E. Orr, *The second evangelical awakening in Britain* (London, 1953) p. 42.

11 E. A. Rose, *Methodism in Ashton-under-Lyne* ii. 43: M.C.A. MSS. T. Withington to Jabez Bunting, 3 August 1844. This passage was written before the appearance of Brian Harrison's excellent *Drink and the Victorians* (London, 1971) and has been left unchanged.

12 P. T. Winskill, *The temperance movement and its workers* (London, 1891-2) ii. 268.

13 M.C.A. MSS. T. Smith to Jabez Bunting, 20 February 1837: Hartley Victoria College, Manchester MS. Journals of Hugh Bourne N. fo. 10. 1 March, 5 March, 1843.

14 J. M. Morgan, *A brief account of the Stockport Sunday School, with thoughts on the extension and improvement of Sunday schools in general* . . . (London, 1838) p. 25: Winskill, *Temperance Movement* i. 102: J. H. Rigg. *The connexional economy of Wesleyan Methodism in its ecclesiastical and spiritual aspects* (London, n.d. [1879]) pp. 201-2. [This volume contains reprints of papers published earlier.]

Index